Sustainability Planning and Collaboration in Rural Canada

Sustainability Planning and Collaboration in Rural Canada

Taking the Next Steps

Lars K. Hallström, Mary A. Beckie, Glen T. Hvenegaard
and Karsten Mündel, *Editors*

The University
of Alberta Press

Published by

The University of Alberta Press
Ring House 2
Edmonton, Alberta, Canada T6G 2E1
www.uap.ualberta.ca

Library and Archives Canada Cataloguing in Publication

Sustainability planning and collaboration in rural Canada : taking the next steps / Lars K. Hallström, Mary A. Beckie, Glen T. Hvenegaard and Karsten Mündel, editors.

Includes bibliographical references and index.
Issued in print and electronic formats.
ISBN 978–1–77212–040–0 (paperback).—ISBN 978–1–77212–095–0 (epub). —
ISBN 978–1–77212–096–7 (mobi). —ISBN 978–1–77212–097–4 (pdf)

1. Sustainable development—Canada—Planning—Case studies.
2. Community development—Canada—Planning—Case studies.
3. Universities and colleges—Canada—Public services—Case studies.
4. Canada—Rural conditions—Case studies. I. Hallström, Lars K., 1973-, editor II. Beckie, Mary, 1954-, editor III. Hvenegaard, Glen Timothy, 1964–, editor IV. Mündel, Karsten, 1974–, editor

HC120.E5S88 2015 338.971 C2015–908142–4

First edition, first printing, 2016.
Printed and bound in Canada by Houghton Boston Printers, Saskatoon, Saskatchewan.
Copyediting and proofreading by Meaghan Craven.
Maps by Wendy Johnson.
Indexing by Stephen Ullstrom.

The University of Alberta Press gratefully acknowledges the support received for its publishing program from the Government of Canada, the Canada Council for the Arts, and the Government of Alberta through the Alberta Media Fund.

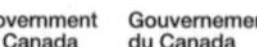

Contents

Acknowledgements

Many individuals have contributed to this book. Along with the numerous authors, investigators, and community partners whose time, energy, resources, and both conceptual as well as empirical work form the actual content found herein, we are extremely grateful to the numerous students, and workshop and conference attendees who helped form the original grist for this mill. In particular, a substantial amount of work has been provided by the research assistants and staff at the Alberta Centre for Sustainable Rural Communities, including Devin Keay, Erika Heiberg, Naomi Finseth, and Sara Deris. The editors are particularly thankful to David Douglas and Roger Epp, who in different ways have both inspired and contributed to the broader rural themes, questions, hope, and frustrations that have led to this book, and were kind enough to provide the foundational and concluding chapters.

We are similarly grateful to the editorial team at the University of Alberta Press, and particularly Peter Midgley, who have displayed great patience and support as the project came into being. We owe much to their professionalism and attention to detail. At the University of Alberta more broadly, support and encouragement from the Augustana Faculty and the Faculty of Extension has been important, as have the efforts of the Research Service Office in supporting the work that led to this book.

While the list of individuals to thank is much too great to list here, we would also like to explicitly acknowledge our gratitude to the communities and community partners who have contributed so much to this book, the projects on which this book is based, and their continuing engagement and involvement with the projects that continue to emerge and succeed in rural communities across the country. As the contributions to this volume show, such efforts can yield significant results. Similarly, the funding for this project, was provided by the Social Sciences and Humanities Research Council (SSHRC), and without that funding, the project could not have happened.

Finally, we are indebted to our families, and to their sympathy, support, and understanding, as this book moved along its unique journey to publication. Special thanks, then, to Erin Yulka, Logan, Freya, and Willow; to Alan Weninger and Noah; to Pam Hvenegaard, Carson, and Leif; and to Deena Hinshaw, Tobias, and Dieter.

Introduction

Lars K. Hallström

Concerns about the resilience, sustainability, and even the very survival of rural communities in Canada are far from new and are well documented. Subject to a combination of both internal dynamics (such as aging populations, the shifting scale of agriculture, urbanization, and declining infrastructure) and external influences (including global patterns of investment, resource dependency, and fiscal policy), rural communities are often the first indicators or casualties of economic downturns. At the same time, rural communities continue to be important to Canada's economy and are increasingly being acknowledged as having a key role to play in terms of environmental sustainability. They welcome immigrants and entrepreneurs from both within and outside Canada's borders, and they have also played a (if not the) key role in the socio-political development of the country and are seen by many as embodying the core values, ethics, and identities of what it means to be Canadian.

From the standpoint of public policy (which, generically, can include planning, public administration, public management, and governance), rural Canada presents a series of challenges, not the least of which being its substantial capacity for change, diversity, and connectivity.

While typically characterized (as was the case at the First Annual Rural Research Workshop held in Ottawa, May 2011) as problematic by nature of both distance (rural spaces, especially in Canada, can extend far beyond the scope or even imagination of many Canadians, especially when the North is included) and density (a large amount of space with very few people),[1] rural Canada is, above all, a combination of both physical and imaginary spaces that are extremely heterogeneous. This heterogeneity, which includes physical, economic, social, cultural, linguistic, ecological, and political characteristics, both reflects and compounds the reality of both making and analyzing public policy in and for rural Canada. Not only is there no "rural ministry" at the federal level that encompasses these many different domains but there is similarly no singular approach or "magic bullet" that has affected the sustainability, resilience, and flourishing of some rural communities, while so many others are in a spiral of economic decline, diminishing and aging populations, and reduced political and policy-making capacities. Rural Canada is, therefore, both a place/space and a cultural orientation.

The question or concern of "the rural" is far from unique to Canada, yet it is particularly pronounced in this country. Every province, from British Columbia to Newfoundland and Labrador, is home to a university-based or -affiliated research centre that is oriented toward the sustainability and life of rural and small communities (and, admittedly, some toward cities and their surrounds, too). Each year, along with publishing a dedicated academic journal *(The Journal of Rural and Community Development)*, the Rural Development Institute in Brandon, Manitoba, sees conferences, workshops, and research groups from across the country focused on multiple, different elements of rural life, often far beyond the conventional purview of agriculture and the importance of farming. Questions of culture, governance, food, investment, social capital, the social economy, and capacity building have all emerged from such initiatives, and not only from the academic and research communities.

Increasingly, rural communities themselves have taken the initiative, both alone and in collaboration with different partners, to address some of the challenges identified above and find ways to reimagine and reposition themselves as new hubs for innovation, targeting all pillars of sustainable development (economic, social, ecological, and possibly cultural and governance). While many of these activities have been undertaken with leadership and initiative from the third sector and civil society, in 2005 the federal government launched an initiative that has had significant impact on communities across the country.

In 2005, following a White Paper from the Prime Minister's Office (PMO), the federal government presented a strategy to promote integrated and sustainable planning and development in Canada's cities and communities, in order to "accelerate the shift in local planning and decision making toward a more *long-term, coherent and participatory approach to achieve sustainable communities*" (Prime Minister's Office [PMO], 2005, p. 4—emphasis in original). The intention was to move beyond land-use planning and development to consider and include the other dimensions of sustainability, and to do so in a way that both reflects and promotes the integration of these dimensions within planning, implementation and analyses of public policy and programming (PMO, 2005, p. 19). What was initially known as the New Deal for Cities and Communities (Finance Canada, 2005) saw agreements established between the federal government and each province or territory as a way to return a portion of fuel tax to local governments for much-needed infrastructure upgrading and replacement.[2] The New Deal and the federal Gas Tax Fund (GTF) made sustainability planning a key part of infrastructure development in communities across Canada, and are slated to invest approximately $13 billion in sustainable municipal infrastructure such as transit, waste management, water, and green energy by 2015, with an additional $10.4 billion invested by 2019. As part of the eligibility criteria for accessing these funds, communities were encouraged or required to develop an Integrated Community Sustainability Plan (ICSP), depending on the provincial/territorial agreement that was struck. The ICSP is defined as "a long-term plan, *developed in consultation with community members,* that provides direction for the community to realise sustainability objectives it has for the environmental, cultural, social and economic dimensions of its identity" (cited in PMO, 2005, p. 4). This integrated and long-term framework distinguishes the ICSP from other municipal plans. Rather than focus on a single dimension, such as land use or transportation, and a shorter, 5–10-year time frame, these plans (while created under wildly variable conditions) were generally intended to spark both citizen engagement and more integrative thinking across the pillars of sustainable development.

Many communities have now completed ICSPs (or a provincial variant) as part of a process of integrated problem solving and policy design. What has emerged is a wide range of approaches, tool kits, and strategies from across the country that differ along regional, population, economic, and political lines. As such, no singular model emerges for, or from, community sustainability planning; instead, the case studies presented in this volume suggest that successful practices include public engagement, dialogue, and deliberation during the planning and policy process, as necessary conditions for anticipated uptake and long-term success (Swanson & Bhadwal, 2009).

At the same time, two additional gaps in the sustainability planning and policy context have emerged. First, there is little known about how the context and complexity of rural environments impacts the operationalization, implementation, and assessment of these plans, even while rural communities now face the reality of attempting to convert often wide-ranging strategic goals and priorities into measurable, justifiable, and meaningful actions. Developing such plans is one important step in fostering a sustainability-based process that is meaningful, inclusive, and adaptive, yet a real challenge lies in the relationship between the rational ideal of how these plans can become action and the larger "social mess" of multiple and interrelated dynamics across social, cultural, economic, political, and ecological domains.

The second gap lies in the participatory intent of the sustainability planning and policy process. While it has been suggested that engagement, deliberation, and participation may be necessary conditions for both environmental sustainability and community development (Baber & Bartlett, 2005; Lafferty & Meadowcroft, 1996; Roseland, 2005), civic communication is also central to establishing the legitimacy, transparency and accountability of the sustainability and planning process (Cooper & Vargas, 2004). That said, the wide range of approaches, models, tools, and individuals involved in the development of these plans (including interprovincial variation in terms of conditions and requirements) has meant that there is far from a uniform approach to the content of plans, or to the tactics used to engage citizens before, during, or after the planning process.

There is no question that different models of engagement, collaboration, and participation have taken place, and in many cases these have included inputs from, and partnerships with, universities and the research community. Such partnerships are diverse and wide-ranging, and increasingly focus less upon the university and researcher as "experts" to provide knowledge and guidance in order to foster behavioural or cognitive change, but more upon the researcher and institution as "partners" in a collaborative process of research design, knowledge acquisition, interpretation, synthesis, exchange, and capacity building. This is particularly true for rural communities. While there is no paucity of examples of urban-researcher partnerships, the heterogeneity and challenges faced by rural communities have provided ample opportunity for community-based and participatory action research, and the shift toward sustainability planning, integration, and resilience-oriented policy-making and capacity building have reinforced these opportunities. At the same time, what is less prevalent are mechanisms for exchanging knowledge, not just between researcher and community, but at a higher level across the national scale. While academic conferences continue to draw researchers who present and discuss the results of their work, much less common are opportunities for both researchers and community partners to co-present, discuss, and share their findings, experiences, and perspectives with other researchers and other rural communities.

In light of the lack of opportunities, in 2010 the Alberta Centre for Sustainable Rural Communities at the University of Alberta hosted a national conference focused on sustainability planning, policy, and participation in rural communities. Created with the support of the Social Sciences and Humanities Research Council Environmental Outreach Program, the Taking the Next Steps conference was different from most rural research conferences in a number of ways. In addition to being held in Camrose, a rural city (population: 17,000) approximately one hundred kilometres from Edmonton, Alberta, a key requirement for attending and presenting at this conference was that participants include the formal research community as well as rural communities (broadly defined to include non-governmental organizations [NGOs], community groups, and municipalities, etc.). More specifically, when the call for submissions was issued, a condition of acceptance was that presentations come from dyads of researchers and communities.

Held in October of 2010, and with a follow-up event in January of 2012, over one hundred delegates from across the country shared their data and findings, and they also shared their experiences, perspectives, challenges, and success stories. Unfortunately, while participants from Manitoba attended the conference, they were unable to contribute to this volume. Additionally, Quebec (while home to significant rural research and community-based action) was not represented at this conference so could not contribute to this volume. Despite these absences, what emerged at the conference was consistent with rural Canada more generally—a heterogeneous collection of collaboration, research, and interventions that cover the gamut of sustainable communities questions and extend across the pillars of sustainable development. A selection of the presentations given at Taking the Next Steps forms the content of this volume.

Organization of the book

There are three key themes driving the organization of this text. The first, and perhaps implicit, theme is that sustainability is a critical element of public policy in rural communities. More specifically, rural municipalities and the organizations that work within them have both an opportunity and a challenge as they attempt to reconcile the opportunities and directions set by their sustainability plans with broader social, political, and infrastructural questions. As a result, increasing and sharing our knowledge of how rural communities and organizations have collaborated, and in many cases succeeded, is an important element of building capacity in rural communities (Kulig, Edge, & Joyce, 2008).

The second theme that runs through this text, and which is noted above, is the importance of engagement and collaboration. As part of a broader shift toward including post-secondary institutions in the design, delivery, and evaluation of public policy and programming, partnerships between communities and researchers are both increasingly common (and have been supported by Canadian Tri-Council research funding programs) and seen to have value for both research and non-academic communities. In rural communities this is particularly relevant, as such partnerships can yield significant gains in terms of increasing capacity, providing third-party and often expert input into programming and evaluation, and, of course, linking the administrative, research, and brokerage capacity of post-secondary institutions with non-academic communities.

The final theme guiding this book, which includes the two themes above, lies in the "policy process" and its application to both the content of this text and the general process within which community–research partnerships often work. When the New Deal for Cities and Communities was put forward, the importance of including monitoring and evaluation early in the process was flagged as a necessary condition for success, as was the early and accurate documentation of implementation and subsequent effects. In other words, there was an early assumption that plans would translate into policy and programming, and that sustainability could be achieved via a positivist assessment of cause and effect within and across multiple domains (DeLeon, 1998; Fischer, 1993, 1998; Fisher & Forester, 1993; Howlett & Ramesh, 1998).

While implementation and evaluation are acknowledged as critical elements of the policy process more generally (Fesler & Kettl, 1991; Hajer, 1995; Lasswell, 1956; Nachmias, 1979), and planning is historically anticipated to link to public policy and even politics (Pressman & Wildavsky, 1984), the ways this applies to sustainability planning presents a number of challenges. The gap between the ideal and reality of the policy and planning process has been well-documented (Lasswell, 1951; Lasswell, 1956; Pressman & Wildavsky, 1984), but this gap is in many ways even more pronounced for community sustainability due to the multiple sectors or pillars involved; the difficulties of assessing causation and consequences across multiple, related domains; and the heterogeneity of community priorities and characteristics noted above.

Specifically, while the performance-based approach to sustainability planning and implementation hinges on a rational, linear progression through the planning–policy process, this does not accurately reflect the nature or dynamics of the broader problems the GTF and ICSP initiatives were intended to address. In fact, the assumption and processes that anticipate a natural shift from plan to action tend to ignore both the highly political nature of public policy (Stone, 1997) as well as the variation, complexity, interconnection, and potential "unsolvability" and intractability of the dynamics that compose community sustainability. This is not, however, to imply that no action can or should be taken, but rather that (a) we must begin to move beyond a simple, linear, problem-solving approach to understanding these dynamics; and (b) we must acknowledge both the presence of "wicked problems" (Brown, Harris & Russell, 2010) and immense complexity as core elements of our approaches.

In keeping with this, work from policy scholars such as Hajer (2003) has pointed to not only the difficulties faced by contemporary political institutions when challenged by such complexity but also the potential benefits of more deliberative approaches. Specifically, Hajer and Wegenar (2003) note that contemporary responses to significant and potentially intractable policy problems can be better addressed by expanding the processes of both policy-making and policy analysis to be: (a) interpretive and contextually situated, (b) deliberative and participatory, and (c) oriented toward informing practice, and in turn, practicality.

While this book is not explicitly informed by deliberative public policy, there is no question that the partnerships and collaborative projects that form the content of this book are indicative of a similar approach to rural sustainability and development. Defined by the importance of leveraging different forms of capacity to support rural communities, the projects and interventions presented here are implicitly consistent with the criteria put forward by Hajer and Wegenar (2003), but also the broad patterns and phases through which public policies emerge, develop, are implemented and revised. This book is, therefore, structured in such a way that it mirrors the policy process, and an ideal, linear/rational-type progression from problem identification, to engagement, solutions, and evaluation. This structure (somewhat ironically) is really an imposition of what Lasswell (1951) identified long ago as an overly simplified model on a highly complex, socio-political process. However, as the longevity of the policy process demonstrates, there is a utility to such models, even if only to serve as an organizing heuristic.

In keeping with this, we have divided the book into four parts based on a simplified model of the policy process. We begin with a section entitled Contexts and Challenges for Rural Sustainability. In this section (which should be seen in the same light as the problem-solving or contextual phase of the public-policy process), four different chapters point to key factors in identifying and contextualizing sustainability in rural communities. Focused in particular on place, locality, and the importance of engagement, these chapters address the ways in which sustainability can, and has, moved onto the agendas of rural communities, and the different factors that influence uptake, resonance, and viability within different rural environments. Chapter One, by David J. A. Douglas, begins the section with a cautionary perspective on the larger sustainability imperative and its implications for rural communities in particular. Don Alexander and Bernie Jones then provide a chapter that emphasizes the importance of place and the applicability of a "lenses of place" to understanding community development and sustainability. The final two chapters in the section (by Glen T. Hvenegaard and Michael Barr; and Sean Connelly, Kelly Green, Sean Markey, and Mark Roseland, respectively) speak to different patterns of engagement and partnership in mobilizing community support and action in two rural contexts: Camrose, Alberta, and Craik, Saskatchewan.

The second section in this volume, Sustainability Planning, Capacity, and Collaboration, is devoted to questions and experiences of planning and policy-making. The section's four chapters speak to the critical or increasingly necessary conditions for successful initiation and progression in the sustainability-policy process. Each of these chapters emphasizes a different element in this developmental and strategically important phase in the policy process, such as engagement in the planning process (Moira J. Calder, Mary A. Beckie, and Shelly McMann), different mechanisms for bridging theory and practice to foster strategic and adaptive capacity (Melanie Irvine, Robert Keenan, and Kelly Vodden), and fostering partnerships between post-secondary institutions and rural communities in Ontario (Yolande E. Chan and Jeff A. Dixon) and northern British Columbia (Laura Ryser, Marc von der Gonna, and Greg Halseth). As a whole, these chapters provide significant insight into the intersection, and interaction, of community-based sustainability planning, community capacity (to both decide and to implement), the importance of sectors outside the conventional socio-economic paradigm, and the increasing viability and impact of well-designed partnerships between rural communities and post-secondary institutions.

The third section of this book focuses on the twinned concepts of implementation and action, and so is titled Implementation and Action: Lessons from the Front Lines. Drawing from the experiences of rural and Aboriginal communities in a number of regions, this section hinges on identifying both the challenges and opportunities presented to rural communities as they "take action." As might be expected, and building on the section before, questions of community capacity, leadership, and the models that drive or support community-sustainability action are of key importance here. Chapters in this section include an examination of the process of implementing the Official Plan for Pelee Island in southern Ontario (Jennifer Summer and Claire Sanders), First Nations perspectives from Nova Scotia and northwestern Ontario on sustainable tourism (Rhonda Koster and Kirstine Baccar) and social change (L. Jane McMillan, Kerry Prosper, Morgan E. Moffitt, and Anthony Davis), and a local food-mapping initiative in central British Columbia (Jon Corbett, Casey Hamilton, and Shayne Wright).

Section four is simply titled Assessment. Drawing from two, different, yet integrative, models, this section underlines the importance and complexities of understanding the effects of sustainability-oriented planning, action, and programming. Although evaluation has historically tended to emphasize the problem-solving and proximal relationships between policies and outcomes, these chapters point toward a broader set of options, including the importance of assessment across multiple domains, the difficulties and complexities of assessing both proximal and distal causation, and the ways in which assessment as a reflexive process can inform the capacity of a rural community. Specifically, Karen Morrison, Karen Houle, and Meredith Carver present an ecohealth-based framework and case study for evaluation, while Kelly Vodden, Ryan Lane, and Craig Pollett examine the municipal self-assessment process used in Newfoundland and Labrador.

The final chapter of this volume (by Roger Epp) provides an informative and valuable counterpoint to the chapter provided by David J. Douglas in his opening piece. While Douglas points to the challenges and potential inadequacies of rural sustainability planning, policy, and activism, Epp draws our attention to the positive and potential that lies in rural Canada. Writing in part as a response to the other contributors, and to provide a synthesis of the lessons learned, Epp points to the potentiality of both *beginning* and *innovation* for rural communities. He emphasizes the very real importance (beyond the symbolic) of rural communities as places and people that have (as this book demonstrates) begun to take action, to seek change, and to shift empowerment, particularly at the local level. As a result, not only are rural communities increasingly the place where the challenges of contemporary society are often first felt (consider peak oil, climate change, and demographic shifts) but they also represent a social and political space where knowledge, and how that knowledge is derived and applied, matters. As the contributions to this volume all demonstrate, the traditional (although not always deserved) role for universities in this context is changing, and the collaborative, cooperative, and innovative ways in which rural communities and universities are finding mutual paths forward also reflects a new beginning.

Conclusion

As the breadth and diversity of not just this volume but also the related work being conducted at rural research centres across the country demonstrates, rural communities have done more than just begin. In many parts of Canada, and indeed in other parts of the world, rural communities are finding ways to become empowered (often in the face of declining fiscal budgets and devolutionary policies), to build community engagement and capacity, and to identify the paths that lead not only to economic development but also to the cultural, social, environmental, and related institutional or governance pillars of sustainability. They do so in the face of pronounced social, political, economic, ideological, and even environmental challenges—not only are the economic and climatological challenges of agriculture as relevant as ever, but the increasingly dominant trends at both national and provincial levels toward declining budgets, shifting accountabilities, responsibilities, and risk to both individuals and communities, and declining revenue streams for local governments, point to no easy path ahead.

At the same time, as many point out, rural citizens are no strangers to hardship, bad weather, or economic challenges, and they are well aware of the broader trends of devolution and decreasing fiscal transfers. In fact, such challenges have formed part of the cultural character and personality of rural Canada. That said, while the trials of the past may inform how rural communities face the future, there is no question that innovation, creativity, and new methods of dealing with both old and new problems is a necessary part of the "new" rural Canada. As different regional and other intermunicipal and intercommunity partnerships emerge, the rural counter is one of innovation, creativity, collaboration, and resilience. As each of the chapters in this volume demonstrates, there are many examples of such innovation and creativity, and many communities that seek out new ways to build the capacity, and autonomy, necessary to survive and even flourish in the 21st century.

Notes

1. Some 80% of Canadians live in urban areas (Statistics Canada, 2011).
2. The "infrastructure deficit" experienced by Canadian municipalities and First Nations communities is the result of over two decades of downloading and offloading of responsibilities by the federal and provincial governments, without sufficient transfer payments (Mizra, 2007; Mirza & Haider, 2003).

References

Baber, W. F., & Bartlett, R. V. (Eds.). (2005). *Deliberative environmental politics: Democracy and ecological rationality.* Cambridge, MA: MIT Press.

Brown, V. A., Harris, J. A., and Russell, J. Y. (Eds.). (2010). *Tackling wicked problems through the transdisciplinary imagination.* New York: Earthscan.

Cooper, P. J., & Vargas, C. M. (2004). *Implementing sustainable development: From global policy to local action.* New York: Rowman & Littlefield.

DeLeon, P. (1998). Introduction: The evidentiary base for policy analysis: Empiricist versus postpositivist positions. *Policy Studies Journal, 26*(1), 109–113.

Fesler, J. W., & Kettl, D. F. (Eds.). (1991). *The politics of the administrative process.* New Jersey: Chatham House Publishers.

Finance Canada. 2005. *A new deal for Canada's communities.* Retrieved May 26, 2015, from http://www.fin.gc.ca/budget05/pamph/pacom-eng.asp.

Fischer, F. (1993). Response: Reconstructing policy analysis: A postpositivist perspective. *Policy Sciences, 25,* 333–339.

———. (1998). Beyond empiricism: Policy inquiry in postpositivist perspective. *Policy Studies Journal, 26*(1), 129–146.

Fisher, F., & Forester, J. (Eds.). (1993). *The argumentative turn in policy analysis and planning.* Durham & London: Duke University Press.

Hajer, M. (Ed.). (1995). *The politics of environmental discourse: Ecological modernization and the policy process.* Oxford: Clarendon Press.

Hajer, M. (2003). Policy without polity? Policy analysis and the institutional void. *Policy sciences, 36*(2), 175–195.

Hajer, M. A., & Wagenaar, H. (Eds.). (2003). *Deliberative policy analysis: Understanding governance in the network society.* Cambridge: Cambridge University Press.

Howlett, M., & Ramesh, M. (1998). Policy subsystem configurations and policy change: Operationalizing the postpositivist analysis of the politics of the policy process. *Policy Studies Journal, 26*(3), 466–481.

Kulig, J., Edge, D., & Joyce, B. (2008). Understanding community resiliency in rural communities through multi-method research. *Journal of Rural and Community Development, 3*, 77–94.

Lafferty, W.M., & Meadowcroft, J. (Eds.). (1996). *Democracy and the environment: Problems and prospects.* Cheltenham, UK: Edward Elgar.

Lasswell, H. (Ed.). (1956). *The decision process: Seven categories of functional analysis.* College Park, MD: University of Maryland, Bureau of Governmental Research.

Lasswell, H.D. (1951). The policy orientation. In D. Lerner and H. D. Lasswell (Eds.), *The policy sciences* (pp. 3–16). Stanford, CA: Stanford University Press.

Mirza, S. (2007). *Danger ahead: The coming collapse of Canada's municipal infrastructure.* Ottawa: Federation of Canadian Municipalities–McGill.

Mirza, M.S., & Haider, M. (2003). The state of infrastructure in Canada: Implications for infrastructure planning and policy. *Infrastructure Canada,* 29(1), 17–38.

Nachmias, C. (Ed.). (1979). *Public policy evaluation: Application and methods.* New York: St. Martin's Press.

Prime Minister's Office [PMO]. (2005). *Integrated community sustainability planning: A background paper.* Ottawa: Prime Minister's External Advisory on Cities and Communities.

Pressman, J.L., & Wildavsky, A.B. (Eds.). (1984). *Implementation: How great expectations in Washington are dashed in Oakland.* Berkeley: University of California Press.

Roseland, M. 2005. *Toward sustainable communities: Resources for citizens and their governments* Revised ed. Gabriola Island, BC: New Society.

Statistics Canada. (2011). Canada's rural population since 1851—Population and Dwelling Counts, 2011 Census. Retrieved May 26, 2015, from http://www12.statcan.gc.ca/census-recensement/2011/as-sa/98-310-x/98-310-x2011003_2-eng.cfm.

Stone, D. (Ed.). (1997). *Policy paradox: The art of political decision making.* New York: W.W. Norton.

Swanson, D., & Bhadwal, S. (Eds.). (2009). *Creating adaptive policies: A guide for policymaking in an uncertain world.* Ottawa: International Development Research Centre.

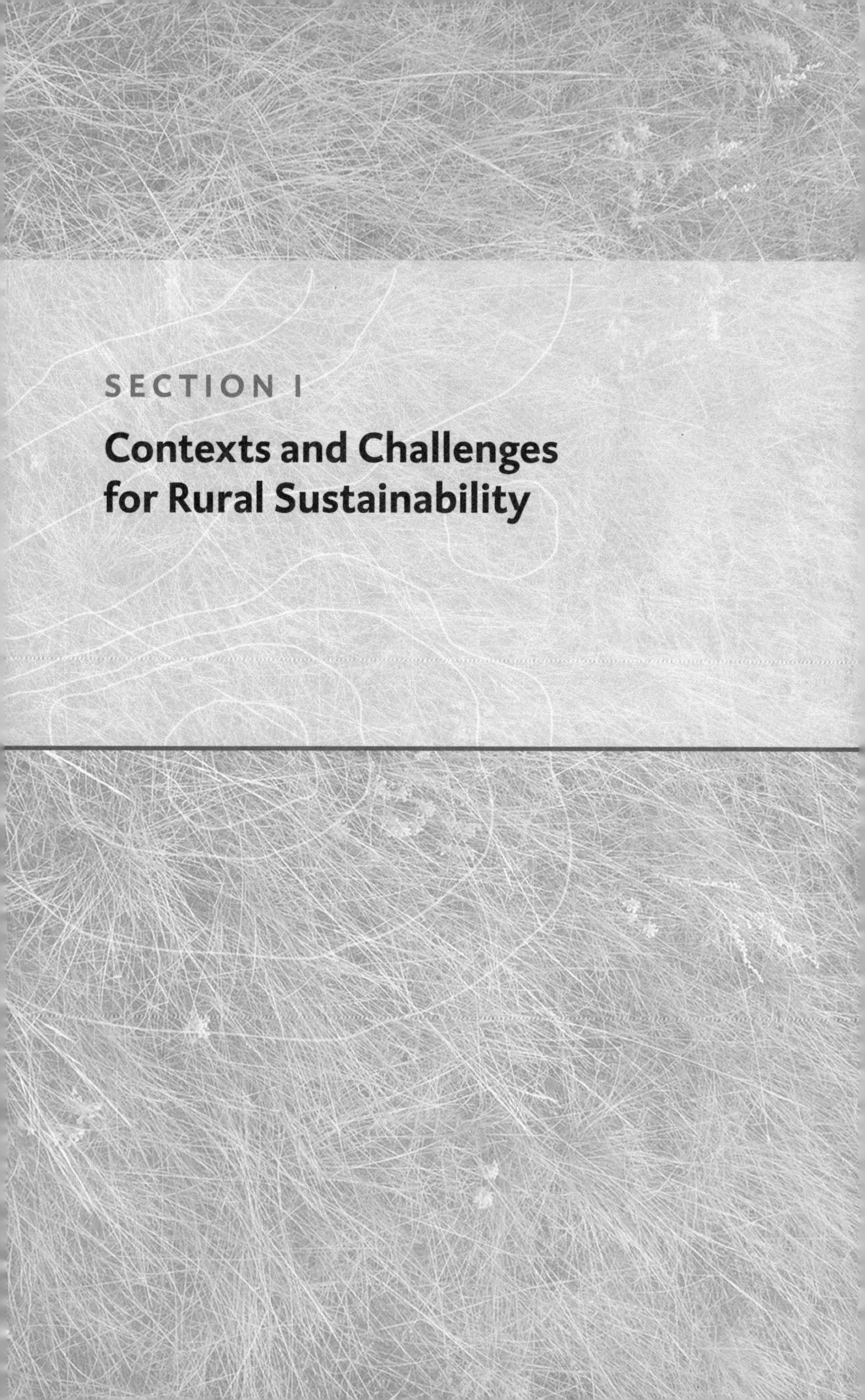

SECTION I

Contexts and Challenges for Rural Sustainability

ONE

Roots, Regions, and Radical Practice

Rural Communities in Societal Survival and Transformation

David J.A. Douglas

Introduction

Standing at the sustainability precipice, *time* is now of the essence, as never before. At the precipice, systemic societal change is non-negotiable, especially in the all-pervasive, global culture of mass consumerism. And these two colliding dimensions underpin the tenuous feasibility of sustainability and condition any and all attempts at survival.

In this chapter I will critically explore the shape and possible directions of a rural-development activism in Canada that attempts to respond to the urgencies of survival within a global context. I will address the theoretical underpinnings informing this activism, its relationships to the values and other inheritances of rural Canada, its ideological dimensions, and the organizational, spatial, and other characteristics of a transformative development-planning praxis in and from rural Canada.

Taking a position, albeit with considerable doubt, that we might be able to do something about our sustainability prospects, I will posit some likely strategies for rural-community survival. Associated with this, I will critique our inherited policy, practice, and conceptual perspectives and argue that many of these are actually part of the problem. From there I will set out what would be required of a transformative praxis for rural communities and regions in Canada, and set out a proposition for a radical development-planning practice.

The fundamental premise: The "exit scenario"

The rural-development planning scenario presented here is premised on a thesis that three interrelated and converging facts mean that humankind's tenure on Earth is likely coming to a close (Douglas, 2012). In summary, these facts are (a) our record of inattention to thousands of signals from a great diversity of sources over the last three-quarters of a century (e.g. Brundtland, 1987; Homer-Dixon, 2011; International Union for Conservation of Nature [IUCN], 1980; Leopold, 1949) that tell us we are living well beyond our ecological means; (b) the continuing and rapid growth of the world's population, especially a burgeoning, wealthy, and high-appetite middle class; and (c) a systemic, ingrained, deep-seated, and celebrated culture of consumerism that has gone as far as to confuse self-actualization with material accumulation. It has been argued that these and other facts are rapidly bringing us toward a situation where our tenure will no longer be feasible. The lynchpins in this imminent exit are humankind's clearly demonstrated inability and unwillingness to listen, hear, and, especially, change our behaviours, and the reality of time itself. And, as noted earlier, time, this go round, was never of such essence. What has been referred to as the dearth of "actor elasticity" in humanity means that the prospects of a successful and rapid U-turn are improbable. It is recognized that much of this has been said before, and that a host of counter-arguments are there, many involving another saving round of Promethean techno-fixes. However, our Western epistemologies and value systems, and their market-driven adoptions in most of the world, now suggest that our ways of being in this world have become untenable. They will bring about the "exit scenario."

Saying "yes" and rural communities getting to "how?": Toward a strategy for survival

Against this foundational prospect, I take it as axiomatic that we really want "to stay," and I assume for the purposes of the present chapter that, contrary to the above argument, somehow or other we will find the ways and means to do so. So as we approach the cathartic ends of our life-lines, a strategy for survival might be devised by rural Canadians.

Regardless of the degree to which the rest of Canadian society comes to grips with the realities of our unsustainable lifestyles, our incongruous worldviews, and our apparent unresponsiveness to the question of dangerously short timelines for radical change (Douglas, 2012), rural Canada will have to address the pivotal question of internalizing these realities.

Rural communities, individually or in various groupings, will have to internalize the realities articulated throughout this book and especially the question of time and the urgency for system-wide behavioural change. Solutions, remedial prescriptions, or even autocratic dictates are not in evidence from other legitimized sources, such as territorial, provincial, or federal governments. This is no mean task for rural society and indeed might be described as a designed paradigm shift, if not a revolution. It will involve what has been described as societal, double-loop learning (Argyris & Schön, 1974) where the very value foundations of rural society will have to be revisited and critically interrogated. Conventional course-correction responses (e.g., better wetlands management, increased residential densities, transit incentives) will not suffice. The requisite shift here lies in deep-structure values.

This purposeful shift, of course, cannot be divorced from those deep-structure values that inform and shape the course of Canadian society as a whole—consider such maxims as: growth is desirable, competition is healthy, and selective redistribution of public resources is appropriate. However, there will be selected value sets that might receive greater attention as being particularly, though not exclusively, rural (e.g., Sim, 1988). There might be selected inheritances relating to the conduct of daily life in rural, remote, and smaller community contexts that rural communities identify with and cherish as quintessentially "rural" (e.g., Reimer, 2006, 2009). What have the lived realities of smallness, scale, lower densities, distance, remoteness, the immediacy of natural systems, and the stories of variously living off the land and waters, engendered in terms of particular values? What have they engendered in terms of the intensity with which these values are held? What have the intimacy of life with family and neighbours, the practices of governing with modest fiscal and other resources, the folklore and traditions accumulated over generations, and all of the other elements of diverse, rural contexts meant in terms of ways of being in the world, and being in the world together (Reimer & Bollman, 2010)? What have the vastly different histories of regional settlement and rural peoples' songs and stories engendered? These values, held dear by rural communities, families, individuals, organizations, and others, will have to be revisited, re-articulated, and selectively drawn upon to underpin the new reality of consciously designing a strategy to "stay," that is, to survive.

This will be a pivotal process of conscientization within rural Canada, a dialogical process of collective introspection and critical self-assessment of the local rural condition, especially as it relates to the people's power and powerlessness, and the root causes of these conditions (Freire, 1984; Rahnema, 2003). This critical collective analysis of the objects of "power over" and the sources of "power over," and the institutionalized norms that have at once codified and reproduced the prevailing power relations will illuminate any degrees of difference between rural Canada and Canadian society as whole. At the centre of this collective consciousness will be the crafting of a "new normal" and, related to this, an internalizing of an understanding that the status quo has become (and has been for some time) a nonstarter. Rural Canada and urban Canada are not separate entities, have become increasingly integrated, and live in a complex web of diverse interdependencies (e.g., Greenwood & Vodden, 2011). However, part of the "getting to how" in a rural-survival strategy will involve a candid and critical reappraisal of the nature of these changing relationships, particularly concerning, whether in a conscious strategy for survival, especially in a time-compressed imperative, the interrelationships are benign or otherwise.

These relational considerations will range from food systems, watersheds, airsheds, and regional, land-use management arrangements to infrastructure networks, fiscal protocols, and a great variety of other formal and informal interrelationships. As an example, if there are differences between urban and rural Canada in terms of the degree of delinking from the societal and market mantras of competitive individualism, and if they are heightened within the complexities of the urban–rural dynamic, how will those differences be resolved? Further, if the social-learning outcomes that will accompany a move toward the dissemination of closed-loop systems in all facets of production and consumption are significantly different along an urban-to-rural continuum, how will this be resolved? If the distribution of costs and benefits clearly manifests significant disparities prejudicing rural welfare, how will this be resolved? If local food production and security of supply becomes a matter of life and death, far beyond today's fashionable dalliance with this concept, how will rural–urban relationships respond? If relative energy costs erode the logic of mass commuting in metro-adjacent regions, how will the urban–rural balance in locational competitiveness be resolved? How will the concomitant erosion of the urban fiscal base be balanced with the possible enhancement of neighbouring rural communities' fiscal positions? Rural Canada will likely continue to function within complex and shifting interrelationships with the country's urban systems and perhaps in an increasingly attenuated manner with other global urban systems. Its strategy for survival and sustainable development will have to reflect these, and more, changing and perhaps increasingly contested realities.

The process of "getting to how" will be macroscopic, systemic, structural, and at times cathartic in nature. This is not an incremental process of fine tuning, marginal adjustment, and discretionary periodic adaptation (Douglas, 2012). This process involves a rapid sea change in rural society's behavioural systems and practices, which have to be underpinned by a similarly massive resetting of values (or at least some) and the norms of society itself. At its root, "getting to how" requires a political critique, an incisive, collective, and rigorous inquiry into what rural Canada is, why it is as it is, where it appears to be going and why, and the principal factors influencing choice and change. At the centre of all of this will be the nature of power in and over rural Canada, and the configuration of power relations in the rural world (Friedmann, 1987, 1992). It will have to be inspired and fuelled by the urgency at hand and an increased commitment to take charge, secure control, direct the course of change, and, in effect, rescript the political, social, cultural, and other narratives that currently guide rural Canada.

Moving from concern and awareness into societal conscientization and from there to mobilization and activism will at once constitute the early stages and fuel continued processes of societal transformation in rural Canada.

The inherited technologies: Pernicious props

How are we equipped to come to terms with and respond to these rapidly emerging realities? I am not convinced that humankind does have the wherewithal to respond effectively in time. However, if we posit that there is some semblance of hope, that indeed there might be a last-minute realization of the urgency of the situation and that there might be a concerted, system-wide response, then it behooves us to look to our current political, cultural, institutional, organizational, and other technologies to assess their role and relevance in the designing of what would have to be a paradigm shift. I will only touch on a sample of these.

Do we have an inventory of rural-development policies or even a practice of rural-development policy formulation and implementation? My conclusion is that we do not. We have, of course, a great variety of policies that relate to many aspects of rural life, livelihoods, and environments from the federal, provincial, and territorial governments (e.g., Rural and Co-operatives Secretariat, 2010). There are some that are presented as a "plan" or "strategy," but they are very partial (e.g., focus on agricultural production, watershed management, value-added processing, rural roads) and extremely general in nature, and few, if any, could be considered as holistic and in any sense strategic. Quebec stands out as something of an exception here, but even there the dominance of economic and public-administration perspectives is evident (Gouvernement du Québec, 2006; Organisation for Economic Co-Operation and Development [OECD], 2010). Likewise, rural regions and communities come under a plethora of acts, programs, and regulations relating to education, health, taxation, environment, transportation, drainage, small-business development, justice, local government, the arts, immigration, and many other topics. There is no political commitment that has brought to the fore comprehensive legislation on rural-development planning and management. The technology here for a massive, rapid, and structural shift for all aspects of rural societies and environments, well beyond a conventional course correction, is not in place (Douglas, 1997, 2010; Greenwood, 2010)

One might have thought that land use and related physical-planning legislation and practices might offer some hope (e.g., Caldwell, 2010; Canadian Institute of Planners, 1990; Hodge & Gordon, 2008). But the highly focused nature of most legislation and regulations have created isolated silos and highly fragmented perspectives on rural planning and development. The record of planning in rural contexts is hardly inspiring and certainly not the stuff for systems transformation. It is generally conservative, deferential to the short-term logic of the market, highly responsive to private-property rights, and largely driven by objectives of public costs minimization, intervention as a last resort, and an approach to planning that is regulatory and rarely formative, and even more rarely strategic. Planning has not secured Canada's foodlands; indeed the system has transferred them to other uses as markets set the priorities (e.g., residential suburbs, transportation and energy corridors, commercial strips, industrial parks). The natural environment has been protected to varying degrees, but it remains a highly and at times an intensely contested arena. Regardless of the accumulation of environmentally related legislation (e.g., Environmental Assessment Acts, laws and regulations, conservation legislation), headwaters, wetlands, areas with rich biodiversity, landscapes with particular heritage and/or aesthetic values, shorelines, and many other parts of the rural environment are constantly under fire from market-driven interests (e.g., residential developers, aggregate operators, mining companies, bottled-water interests, property speculators). The record over the last century, while populated with many significant achievements (consider the Oak Ridges Moraine, Ontario, and the guiding intent of the original Agricultural Land Reserve, BC), is not one to suggest that we have the legislative and regulatory technology in place to underpin any significant systemic shift in the way rural communities and environments are planned and managed (e.g., Grant, 2008; Hodge & Gordon, 2008; Hodge & Robinson, 2001; Krueger, Sargent, de Vos, & Pearson, 1970; Perks & Robinson, 1979).

Canada's "rural" policy and related technologies have evolved over two centuries characterized by an active government, but one operating well within the confines of a privileged market economy. It has evolved from a dominantly staples economy (e.g., Innis, 1956; Savoie, 1986), set within imperial privilege, to today's mixed-market economy, characterized by increased integration with the global, especially the global economic systems and dominantly oligopolistic market structures. A strong staples dimension persists in the nation's economy, largely under the control of non-Canadian owners. Our policy technology and its paraphernalia (e.g., legislation, regulations, agencies, civil servants, institutional protocols) and practices are not only unlikely to be suitable for a rapid, systems-transforming intervention, as they are themselves very much "the system," but they are more likely to impede, resist, and otherwise blunt the transformative process itself. They are very likely to be, as the saying goes, part of the problem and not the solution. "It should by now be clear that the reason they have not happened [institutional change], or do not work, is because they are imagined, designed and implemented by the very people responsible for the dilemma" (Judt, 2010, p. 167).

Might the market itself provide the decision making, institutional, and other technologies to facilitate a rapid and transformative shift? Some might argue that if we really did get the "prices right" it could do so. If safe drinking water becomes scarce enough, we will not only pay a very high price for it but we will start treating it as if it really is scarce and to be highly valued, indeed to be rigorously managed as part of our life-lines. If foodlands continue to become scarce and if demands continue to rise, and indeed accelerate, then the price will escalate to a degree that we will substitute foodlands for many of the alternatives currently displacing them in the market (e.g., golf courses and low-density, rural estates). The problem with this neo-classical economic argument is that it pays no attention to the distributional dimension of the postulate. Those who can afford the escalating prices will outbid those who cannot, creating in times of increased ecological and social stress intolerable conflict, chaos, and very likely physical altercation. And there is the fundamental question of limits, part of the Achilles heel of conventional economics (e.g., Henderson, 1978). What can the market do when there is about to be none of the "commodity" left (e.g., Ekins, 1986; Ekins & Max-Neef, 1992)?

What of civil society, that amorphous overlapping portion of rural society not fully embedded in the market or in the formal structures of government? We have seen instances of reasonably rapid transformation in our times, including some rebalancing of our perspectives related to gender equity, attitudes toward smoking and human rights, attitudes toward driving and the consumption of alcohol, our expectations of parents and parenting, and others. The roots of these examples are diverse and long. However, it might be argued that the materially transformative episode has been quite rapid, some spanning little more than a few decades. This is at least partially plausible. We can change and sometimes quite rapidly.

The soft underbelly of the argument here relates to the modest breadth and extent of rapid change that society has accommodated under what we might call normal times. What we are addressing here is the possibility of society rapidly changing most facets of its normative and other structures in a relatively short time. These would include our ingrained attitudes toward consumption, including the material appetites that are fed but never sated by consuming, the competitive prowess that it responds to, and not the least important the self-esteem and misplaced self-actualization that has become associated with accumulation. The functioning of our society pivots around these interrelationships, which as has been argued (e.g., Daly, 1977; Rees, 1991) all involve consumption and never the logic of production. Our complex array of institutions, governing systems, market organizations, policing and other coercive systems, customs and informal practices, our tacit understandings of the way the world works and how we function within it, and even popular cultures, provide a dense scaffolding for this societal construct. To alter all of these toward a systems transformation in a very short span of time takes us well beyond the piecemeal and sequential changes that we have witnessed in the recent past. The breadth, depth, and pace of transformation is so different in degree, it becomes different in kind. We cannot assume that our recent acquisition and use of social-adjustment technologies will materially contribute to the time-compressed transformation imperative envisaged here (Douglas, 2012).

We conclude, therefore, that most of our inherited societal technologies that we might relate to change, adjustment, adaptation, and effective response are likely to prove inadequate, and for some they would more than likely prove to be as much part of the problem as part of any putative solution.

Toward a transformative praxis for a sustainable rural Canada

Given the sheer order of magnitude of the paradigmatic change that is posited here, given the rapidity with which this structural change is expected to happen, and given the inadequacy of our policy, legislative, institutional, and other technologies, the logical conclusion is that a "stay" option for rural Canada can only be attempted through a development practice that is radical, overtly political, in part at least insurgent and oppositional in nature, and systems transformative in its intent and effect.

The political critique

The first order of business here is a political critique of the condition of rural Canada or, more appropriately, the several "rurals" that exist across this country (Reimer & Bollman, 2010; Statistics Canada, various dates). This is a fundamental prerequisite because without a collective critical awareness of the evolved condition, a rural conscientization cannot be achieved, and as a consequence mobilization will be stunted and the agenda for survival dissipated or hijacked. I use the term *praxis* quite purposefully here because there will be a recursive relationship between all public action, reflection, learning, remembering, knowledge, and critical awareness (Arendt, 1958, 1968; Freire, 1984). This is especially the case as it relates to an understanding of the sources and centres of power, the modalities through which various powers are exercised, the relational map of power in rural contexts, and, most urgently, the processes through which power relations are systemically reproduced (Forester, 1989). Power relations will need to be critically interrogated across rural society, encompassing: the ownership, production, and distribution of food; the ownership of land; the ownership of and control over energy sources; and the control of physical infrastructure (e.g., water systems, telecommunications systems). The collective critique of power will also encompass the institutions and processes we associate with representative democracy and associated priorities setting and decision making (e.g., local government, energy and resource boards), the way rural communities, environments, and interests are selectively represented (e.g., politically, media), and many other facets of rural Canada.

This is very much the stuff of the extended, complex, and diverse rural-restructuring discourse (e.g., Cloke, Marsden, & Mooney, 2006; Douglas, 2005). However, in the context of the precipitous U-turn we are positing here, what has been amply accommodated in academic and political discourse over the last two decades must now be forcefully compressed and translated into action. Given this, the milieu depicted here will be one well-populated by the forces of anarchy, fear, autocracy, insurgency, and conflict.

Values and value systems

This political critique may create the ground conditions for a reassessment of the inherited value systems that underpin Canadian rural society. This challenge cannot be minimized or underestimated. It is daunting. Rural people do not live in a bubble isolated from the other 70–80% of

Canadian society, nor from our increasingly integrated global society. All of the messages relating to conspicuous consumption, to what has been called planned obsolescence, to augmenting one's self-esteem and position among one's peers through material consumption, to zero-sum competitiveness and individualism, and many others that prop up advanced market capitalism have arrived and had substantial effect across all rural communities in Canada, including Aboriginal communities. They are embedded in our life-worldview (Douglas, 1996). These constructed values would have to be vigorously addressed. They are part of the political and social critique. Without this interrogation, social mobilization would be stultified and the conditions for autocratic intervention and even widespread violence would be advanced.

Alongside these values, others will be brought forward for reassessment. These have been brought into and have grown in the cultural, political, and other streams of rural society in Canada over the centuries, and they have developed their own derivative values and norms, as well as revealed behaviours—personal and collective behaviours touching on honesty, attitudes to natural systems, social solidarity, gender relations, neighbourliness, and others. Clearly leaders, champions, and courageous and dedicated activists will be central to this process of critical reassessment. The trenchant questioning of deep-structure and now well-rooted values will be inevitably unsettling and contentious, at best. Part of this collective process of double-loop learning (i.e., learning that revisits the normative premise itself), informed by intensive episodes of social learning, will feed on the dynamic of critical reflection that goes with radical praxis. Time being of the essence, however, will serve to compress the nested cycles of learning by doing and doing from learning. A compressed, tension-taut spring, with all the latent energy for work (both positive and negative) is a useful metaphor here. This will not be Dewey's (1980) intergenerational process of trial and error and experiential learning. There will literally and figuratively be no or very little time for any measured recursive process. This lack of time inevitably will foster various tensions, some anomie, belated denial, polarization of positions, partisan reactions, reactive regrouping on the part of the centres of established power, internecine fractures, and concomitant tendencies toward counter-insurgency, strife and conflict, and perhaps violence.

Politics and political structures

The politics of this transformative praxis will have to seek out a precarious and challenging dynamic balance. This will be between, on the one hand, a tactical degree of closure of rural systems (e.g., social and economic activity systems, energy systems, nutrient systems) depending upon the prevailing social, economic, environmental, and political conditions in urban Canada and beyond, in these times of turmoil, and, on the other hand, acceptable degrees of internal division and closure. The degree to which urban Canada's survival and other priorities compromise rural Canada's life-line priorities for sustainability (e.g., access to clean water, basic foodstuffs) will determine the degree of interdependence that can be accommodated and therefore the degree of closure to be enforced. Remember the foundational objective here is survival. The degree to which common purpose and control must be forcefully exercised in conditions of urgency will determine the degree to which centralized decision-making processes are adopted, at least for some time. Related to this, the degree to which critical mass and solidarity become imperatives across the heterogeneity that makes up rural Canada will determine the degree to which more autocratic modes of governing are favoured, at least for a period of time.

In some contrast to this will be the need to radically reverse the longer-term trends toward open systems and global integration. Rural Canada will very likely be spatially and functionally reorganized in a polynuclear structure of relatively independent and closed regions and their constituent communities. Minimizing the consumption of energy and minimizing the now heightened risks of any external dependence (e.g., for food, water, electrical energy, health care, fossil fuels), rural regions will be planned to be increasingly self-reliant and, to a lesser extent, self-sufficient. The designed interdependence among a federation of rural regions will be such as to minimize energy consumption and other inefficiencies, terminate unnecessary and dangerous dependencies (including those with urban systems), and maximize the critical mass and solidarity across rural Canada itself. This strategic closure as a life-sustaining imperative would also be designed to maximize the synergies across the diversity of rural regions. The admixture of increased self-reliance and self-determination takes on a degree of appropriated devolution within the Canadian political system through the assertive critical mass of rural communities in a period of crisis.

Regional and community governance

Rural development planning at the regional level would likely emphasize radical governance as an appropriate process to maximize participatory process; shift the centre of gravity of established power structures and relations; counterbalance the tendencies toward autocratic decision making in times of fear, uncertainty, and transition; and maximize access to the regional communities' diverse pools of resources. The tenets of governance revolving around "shared power" process, pooled resources, networks, and fluid opportunistic and issue-oriented organizations would be activated (Rhodes, 1996; Stoker, 1998). Communities and regional networks of collaborating communities would move to shift the emphasis from "power over" toward the collective "power with" to attain the "power to" for effective agency (Douglas, 1996; Douglas & Annis, 2010). The appropriated devolution of power and authority now recentred in rural Canada would be mirrored internally in a highly decentralized network of rural regions with strong constituent community governments. Social capital, notably communal capital, would be at a premium to draw upon and foster trust, norms of reciprocity and common cause, and the most effective exploitation of diverse social, economic, and other networks (Reimer, 2006).

Some rural regions might reconfigure their territorial framework on the basis of identified bioregions (Carr, 2004). The negotiated spatial arrangements might be such as to maximize the social and cultural cohesion of the rural region, configure it as close as possible to its ecological life-support systems (e.g., watersheds, foodsheds), and make it a manageable unit for multi-community governance processes. Radical practice would address the long, contentious issues around the civil commons, such as secure access for all to food, safe water, public open space, community-based health care, child and elder care, shelter, personal security, and so on (e.g., Sumner, 2005, 2010). Sustenance, social justice, environmental rights, distributional equity, and closed-loop production and consumption systems would increasingly become the norm for political and social development priorities. Given the internal contradictions within our current advanced capitalism, our culture of mass, material consumption and the momentum of global demographic growth, radical praxis across rural Canada would be guided by the imperative of survival and the requisite systems transformation.

Then and now: Outcomes

Obviously this scenario, this rural-Canada praxis made feasible because of our desire to "stay," would be very different from the rural Canada we know today. It would also be radically different from the rural-Canada context we might normally anticipate as a likely future (e.g., Douglas et al., 2010). No less important, it would be very different from the rural Canada that our professional planners, local and other governments, and the market are planning for today.

Contrary to the growing interrelationships between urban and rural Canada that we now observe (Bruce, 2009; Greenwood & Vodden, 2011; Partridge, Ali, & Olfert, 2010; Statistics Canada, various dates), the imperatives of sustaining life, life systems, and local livelihoods in the catharsis of designed and necessarily rapid change will set in place a reconfiguration of strategically selective interrelationships. These will all be premised on the new agenda of systems transformation for survival. Some of this might involve the tactical decoupling of rural from urban. Thus, the now conventional, market-driven interrelationships (e.g., food and other commodity-supply chains, recreation services, retail markets, labour force and commuters) would very likely be critically reconfigured on the basis of the requirements for the survival and sustenance of individuals, families, and rural communities.

Development planning might transfer the ownership of foodlands to community food corporations to ensure a safe and reliable supply of nutrition for rural communities. Multi-community cooperatives might come into being to manage a secure source of water. Waste management in community-based, closed-loop systems would operate very differently from today's landfills, cross-boundary transfers, and the burgeoning markets for waste. Local and regional economies would minimize transport and transfer costs, be characterized by much higher proportions of live-work patterns, and place much greater emphasis on product stewardship and durability, adaptive re-use and recycling potentials. They would have much higher proportions of home-based businesses, a significantly greater number of community enterprises, an expanded cooperatives sector, and make even more intensive use of advanced telecommunications and of diverse, decentralized, and appropriate energy sources.

Rural communities might have fully integrated educational, health, social welfare, and local government systems and structures. Our current toying with alternative residential patterns, alternative design standards and building technologies would be quickly replaced by intensive, higher-density, mixed-use settlement forms, buildings that generate most of their own electrical requirements, with small, urban gardens and intensive food-production systems, and a very small fraction of community space and infrastructure devoted to the residual private automobiles, or their successors. With increased fibre production, distributed energy sources, expanded and diverse local-food systems and other developments, and these intensively nucleated settlement patterns, Canada's countryside and its varied landscapes would look very different than the rural world we know today.

Then and now: Process

The process of development planning would be significantly different than that which prevails today. The moving force would be the abandonment of market capitalism as the primary source for setting societal priorities, given its ruinous repercussions and its revealed inability to address vital elements of society that are beyond conventional market metrics (e.g., Daly & Cobb Jr., 1989). Private property would be renegotiated as a limited set of private rights counterbalanced by an extended array of social responsibilities, well beyond those embedded within our current laws and regulations. Collective rights and priorities, such as those relating to safe and secure food supplies, a healthy environment, secure energy supplies, shelter and education, and others, will dwarf those currently addressed or acknowledged in our laws, regulations, and planning practices. Survival and the needs of the community, and rural society as a whole, will dictate an approach to development planning that places participatory process in the front rather than as a parallel or reactive process, as it is placed today. Social-, economic-, and environmental-impact assessments will pivot on the precautionary principle, a radical reorientation from today's practice, where negative externalities or the potential welfare and other risks are summarily passed off to society as a whole, and to future generations.

Private benefit will only be accommodated within the longer-term security of the collective, the rural community. For some, this remaking of rural society will be redolent of Karl Polanyi's critique and thesis, where a structural inversion takes place and the social and cultural foundations of society are reinstated over market-based economic interests (Polanyi, 1957).

What we in North America commonly know as the public realm, where it is something of an afterthought, an historical leftover, or as an unusual and idiosyncratic bonus, would now take centre stage. In some respects Canadian rural society will take on some of the current characteristics of rural societies elsewhere around the world, notably in so-called "developing" contexts. Development and planning will perforce be integrated. The formal economy will be better understood as one, and only one, component of the whole economy. Physical development will be more directly tied to the anticipated social, economic, cultural, and other costs and benefits. In addition, the longer-term public good or interest will be the starting point for most development initiatives—land use, built form, economic, social provision, infrastructure, environmental, public administration, and others, not something to be addressed in a reactionary manner on the heels of private privilege, and what are held as assumed and unassailable rights.

Community-based governance, within extended networks of rural regional governance would be the prevailing modus operandi in this reformulated development-planning process. It is a radical praxis as its goes to the root of fundamental values of humankind, relating to actualization of the individual within the collective as a fundamental construct found throughout the natural world. It serves to turn on the Cartesian delinking and reconnect individuals with their own kind, including their environment, and respond to the welfare of the collective by a reinformed balancing of the needs of the societal group and the needs, wants, and rights of the individual. The balance among these will no longer be determined by capitalist market mechanisms. Rather it will be determined by negotiated human dialogue and choice involving a whole new array of criteria (e.g., survival, social justice, heritage value, ecological integrity) well beyond conventional market mechanisms, valuing first and foremost the longer-term security and welfare of the rural community as the priority, and the appetites and asset-based leverage of the individual as a secondary factor in choices and decision making.

It must be acknowledged, however, that this rationally instrumental process outcome, forged as it would be in the context of catharsis and conflict, is only one of a number of possibilities. Others could include brutal dictatorships, entrenched cabals defending their increasingly encircled privileges, neo-feudal tribal configurations, or rampant social anarchy and disintegration. In this scenario I am positing the successful, if stress-bound, installation of a new, community-centred, survivalist, rural-development planning process.

The region as a strategic spatial construct

As noted above, the region would be expected to be the spatial unit of choice here, to contain networks of collaborating rural communities. While the local community, in a fairly circumscribed territorial unit, would be expected to organize around its daily life-support systems (e.g., water, energy, food), the uneven distribution of some fuel, fibre, and food sources (e.g., forests, rivers) will still encourage degrees of specialization in processing and production, and limited intercommunity exchange. In addition, area-wide cooperatives will avail of appropriate scales of production by drawing upon a regional labour force. Basic infrastructure requirements (e.g., roads maintenance, drainage upkeep) would also provide a rationale for region-based collaboration. Specialized health services and facilities would also be expected to require multi-community arrangements that would manifest themselves at the regional level.

While much of the advanced capitalist market economy would be replaced by communal, cooperative, commonwealth, informal economy, social economy, and other practical arrangements, a limited amount of capitalist market activity would likely remain. This would reflect the asymmetric distribution of production and other skills among the rural labour force, the exchange opportunities provided by differences in natural endowments (e.g., soil types, water power) and other factors. Again, the regional settlement system would accommodate this limited array of market activity. The scarcity or absence of transportation fuel, the social priorities pre-empting the allocation of scarce fuels and other resources, the deterioration in interregional infrastructure (e.g., freeways, gas pipelines, electrical transmission corridors), and other factors will greatly attenuate traffic and transfers of all sorts beyond the confines of the region. Urban centres would be under particular stress with decreased access to a now relatively immobile labour force, extremely high costs for transporting foodstuffs and scarce energy supplies (e.g., liquid fuels), loss of some economies of scale, and decreases in municipal fiscal resources. Under these conditions, urban agriculture would be expected to expand rapidly.

This new spatial reconfiguration of rural Canada will respond to the practicalities and community-development opportunities that the regional scale affords (Douglas, 1999; Douglas & O'Keeffe, 2009), provide for opportunities in sustainable development (Cabaj, 2009), and allow for a bottom-up process for rural regional governance. This would accord with the prevailing social, cooperative ethos of the new rural society. The concept of negotiating the configuration and the spatial extent of the region would in itself be a significant development initiative (Douglas, 2006).

The centrality of praxis and radical development planning

The term *praxis,* in contrast with *practice,* has been the term of choice here. Arendt's concept of the historical erosion of politics (Arendt, 1958) combined with the possible assertion by the state of necessary hegemonic, if not totalitarian, powers under the conditions of crisis, scarcity, and impending collapse that I have suggested here, all point to the absolute necessity of what Freidmann and others have called a reappropriation of political community (Friedmann, 1987). Counteracting the rearguard response of an endangered, advanced capitalism, as the crisis sets in, and offsetting the possible response of the state as steward and sponsor of capitalist interests, will require direct action to secure the public interest. Meaning and identity are expressed through collective public action to secure personal, family, and community safety and sustenance as society approaches the precipice. Action as a mode of human togetherness and solidarity is a fundamental facet of this scenario.

The absence of critical reflection and associated collective action so central to praxis today has been succinctly summarized by Cabaj. Even among Canadian activists he has noted "how essentially conservative many of us remain when imagining our collective futures, even in times like these. We resist long term planning and rarely think in terms of socio-economic systems, never mind social-ecological ones" (Cabaj, 2009, p. 21).

A pivotal consideration in praxis is the notion of the intersubjective construction of the world. Providing alternative epistemologies is a radically important dimension of community and public concern here.

As Judt (2010) wrote, "We need to act upon our intuitions of impending catastrophe" (p. 166). It is especially so in the context of crisis, impending catharsis, and societal stress, when "expert" interpretations of the condition of society and the privileged sway of bureaucratized regulation and decision making could essentially disenfranchise rural society.

> All change is disruptive.... Men and women will be thrown back upon the resources of the state. They will look to their political leaders and representatives to protect them: open societies will once again be urged to close in upon themselves, sacrificing freedom for 'security'. The choice will no longer be between the state and the market, but between two sorts of state. It is thus incumbent upon us to re-conceive the role of government. If we do not, others will. (Judt, 2010, p. 9)

A counter-hegemonic process through political critique, mobilization, and praxis sets out to "take charge" both of the survival agenda and the now appropriated planning process. As noted, for sustainability the rural local state is community focused, regionally organized, and selectively, interregionally federated.

The rural-development planning practice here is radical, very distant from today's regulatory process that essentially maintains the system of advanced market capitalism, bureaucratic ascendancy, and the therapeutic myth that we are, through informed and judicious (i.e., allowable) incrementalism, planning our future in a sustainable manner. Because we have indeed run out of time, it is posited that the process is assertive, insurgent in tone and urgency, survivalist in its priorities, and atomistic in its appropriation of power at the local level. Systems transformation is the project at hand. The principle of subsidiarity that promotes decision making in close proximity to the problem and opportunities at hand, and so long wanting in conventional Canadian development planning (Sachs, 1984), is rediscovered and implemented with dispatch. Social activism and political engagement are intensely intertwined.

Conclusion

This chapter steps back from a posited cessation of human occupation on this planet (Douglas, 2012), posing our understandable wish to "stay." I address what would have to happen in the development planning for rural Canada under a scenario where every effort is made by us, albeit against the tide of the previous argument, to stay. A scenario of outcomes and process is presented. I argue that in light of the inadequate and indeed sometimes perverse policy, institutional, and other technologies that we have today, the sustainable development of rural Canada will require a radical transformative praxis. This praxis will have to go to the very roots of the constructed, now deep-structure values that we have inherited from market capitalism and previous sources, and facilitate a rapid and system-wide transformation of most facets of rural society in Canada. The Canadian countryside will look very different, we will organize our precarious lives differently, we will live with the earth differently, we will live together differently, and we will plan our sustenance, our livelihoods, our social services, our built environment, our land use and settlements, and most other facets of our lives in a very different manner than today. Survival will require a radically reconfigured rural society, and a radically informed, development-planning praxis.

Author's note

Much of the inspiration for this chapter has come from the critical and incisive questioning of the graduate students that I have had the privilege to work with since 1985, especially through the Rural Planning and Development Theory course at the School of Environmental Design and Rural Development, University of Guelph. I owe them my respect and sincere thanks. Additional inspiration and insights have come from the numerous rural communities that I and graduate students have worked with over the years through our diverse outreach projects, most recently Mayor Rick Masse and our colleagues in the township and community of Pelee Island, in Lake Erie, Ontario. I extend my gratitude to each and all of them for their trust and collaboration, and my continuing education.

References

Arendt, H. (1958). *The human condition.* Chicago: University of Chicago Press.

———. (1968). *Between past and future.* New York: Viking Press.

Argyris, C., & Schön, D. (1974). *Theory in practice: Increasing professional effectiveness.* San Francisco: Jossey-Bass.

Bruce, D. (2009). *Rural-urban interaction in Atlantic Canada: Toward new opportunities and greater synergies.* Sackville, NB: Rural and Small Town Programme, Mount Allison University.

Brundtland, G. H. (1987). *Our common future.* New York: Oxford University Press.

Cabaj, P. (2009). Good and scary. *Making Waves, 19*(3), 20–21.

Caldwell, W. (2010). Planning and management for rural development: The role of local government. In D. J. A. Douglas (Ed.), *Rural planning and development in Canada* (pp. 110–133). Toronto: Nelson.

Canadian Institute of Planners. (1990). *Reflections on sustainable planning: The implications of sustainable development for planning and the Canadian Institute of Planners.* Ottawa: Canadian Institute of Planners.

Carr, M. (2004). *Bioregionalism and civil society: Democratic challenges to corporate globalism.* Vancouver: University of British Columbia Press.

Cloke, P., Marsden, T., & Mooney, P. H. (Eds.). (2006). *Handbook of rural studies.* London: Sage.

Daly, H. E. (1977). *Steady state economics.* San Francisco: W.H. Freeman.

Daly, H. E., & Cobb Jr., J. B. (1989). *For the common good: Redirecting the economy toward the community, the environment and a sustainable future.* Boston: Beacon Press.

Dewey, John. 1980. *The quest for certainty: A study of the relation of knowledge to action.* New York: Perigree Books (Original 1929).

Douglas, D. J. A. (1996). Taking charge: Planning and development strategies for sustainable communities. In R. D. Needham & E. N. Novakowski (Eds.), *Sharing knowledge, linking sciences: An international conference on the St. Lawrence ecosystem* (pp. 21–25). Ottawa: University of Ottawa.

———. (1997). Rural futures: Some issues, opportunities and challenges. *FORUM, 21*(7), 11–13.

———. (1999). The new rural region: Consciousness, collaboration and new challenges and opportunities for innovative practice. In W. Ramp, J. Kulig, I. Townshend, and V. McGowan (Eds.), *Health in rural settings: Contexts for action* (pp. 39–60) Lethbridge: University of Lethbridge.

———. (2005). The restructuring of local government in rural regions: A rural development perspective. *Journal of Rural Studies, 21,* 231–246.

———. (2006). Rural regional development planning: Governance and other challenges in the new EU. *Studia Regionalia, 18,* 112–132.

Douglas, D. J. A. (Ed.). (2010). *Rural planning and development in Canada.* Toronto: Nelson.

Douglas, D. J. A. (2012). *Sustaining rural Canada?: The exit scenario.* Guelph, ON: Unpublished manuscript.

Douglas, D. J. A., & O' Keeffe, B. (2009). Rural development and the regional construct: A comparative analysis of the Newfoundland and Labrador and Ireland contexts. In G. Baldacchino, R. Greenwood, and L. Felt (Eds.), *Remote control: Governance lessons for and from small, insular, and remote regions* (pp. 77–113). St. John's, NL: ISER Books, Memorial University of Newfoundland.

Douglas, D. J. A., & Annis, B. (2010). Community development: A cornerstone of rural planning and development. In D. J. A. Douglas (Ed.), *Rural planning and development in Canada* (pp. 281–328). Toronto: Nelson.

Douglas, D. J. A., Reimer, B., Bollman, R. D., Bryant, C., Bruce, D., Greenwood, R.,… Annis, B. (2010). Rural planning and development in Canada: Prospects and potentials. In D. J. A. Douglas (Ed.), *Rural planning and development in Canada* (pp. 355–369). Toronto: Nelson.

Ekins, P. (Ed.). (1986). *The living economy: A new economics in the making.* London: Routledge & Kegan Paul.

Ekins, P., & Max-Neef, M. (Eds.). (1992). *Real life economics: Understanding wealth creation.* London: Routledge.

Forester, J. (1989). *Planning in the face of power.* Berkeley: University of California Press.

Freire, P. (1984). *Pedagogy of the oppressed.* New York: Continuum.

Friedmann, J. (1987). *Planning in the public domain: From knowledge to action.* Princeton, NJ: Princeton University Press.

———. (1992). *Empowerment: The politics of alternative development.* Cambridge: Blackwell.

Gouvernement du Québec. (2006). *National policy on rurality: 2007–2014.* Québec ministère des Affaires municipales et des Régions.

Grant, J. (Ed.). (2008). *A reader in Canadian planning: Linking theory and practice.* Toronto: Nelson.

Greenwood, R. (2010). Policy, power, and politics in rural planning and development in the Canadian state. In D. J. A. Douglas (Ed.), *Rural planning and development in Canada* (pp. 86–109). Toronto: Nelson.

Greenwood, R., & Vodden, K. (2011). Rural-urban interaction in Newfoundland and Labrador: Understanding and managing functional regions. *Newfoundland Quarterly, 104*(1), 38–40.

Henderson, H. (1978). *Creating alternative futures: The end of economics.* New York: Berkeley Publishing.

Hodge, G., & Gordon, D. L. A. (2008). *Planning Canadian communities.* Toronto: Nelson.

Hodge, G., & Robinson, I. M. (2001). *Planning Canadian regions.* Vancouver: University of British Columbia Press.

Homer-Dixon, Thomas. (2011.) Growth won't last forever. *Foreign Policy*, No. 184, 56.

Innis, H. A. (1956). *The fur trade in Canada: An introduction to Canadian economic history.* Toronto: University of Toronto Press.

International Union for Conservation of Nature [IUCN]. (1980). *World conservation strategy: Living resource conservation for sustainable development.* Gland, Switzerland: International Union for Conservation of Nature and Natural Resources.

Judt, T. (2010). *Ill fares the land.* London: Penguin.

Krueger, R. R., Sargent, F. O., de Vos, A., & Pearson, N. (1970). *Regional and resource planning in Canada.* Toronto: Holt and Winston of Canada Limited.

Leopold, A. (1949). *A Sand County almanac and sketches here and there.* New York: Oxford University Press.

Organisation for Economic Co-Operation and Development [OECD]. (2010). *OECD rural policy reviews: Québec, Canada.* Paris: OECD.

Partridge, M.D., Ali, K., & Olfert, M.R. (2010). Rural-to-urban commuting: Three degrees of integration. *Growth and Change, 41*(2), 303–335.

Perks, W. T., & Robinson, I. M. (1979). *Urban and regional planning in a federal state: The Canadian experience.* New York: McGraw-Hill Book Company.

Polanyi, K. (1957). *The great transformation.* Boston: Beacon Press.

Rahnema, M. (2003). Participation. In W. Sachs (Ed.), *The development dictionary: A guide to knowledge and power* (pp. 116–131). New York: Zed Books Ltd.

Rees, W. (1991). Economics, ecology, and the limits of conventional analysis. *Journal of the Air and Waste Management Association, 41*(10), 1323–1327.

Reimer, B. (2006). The rural context of community development in Canada. *Journal of Rural and Community Development, 1*(2), 155–175.

———. (2009). Key findings from 20 years of rural research. Summary Paper prepared for the *Reversing the Tide: Strategies for Success Rural Revitalization* project. Montreal: Concordia University.

Reimer, B., & Bollman, R. (2010). Understanding rural Canada: Implications for rural development policy and rural planning policy. In D. J. A. Douglas (Ed.), *Rural planning and development in Canada* (pp. 10–52). Toronto: Nelson.

Rhodes, R. (1996). The new governance: Governing without government. *Political Studies, 44*(4), 652–667.

Rural and Co-operatives Secretariat. (2010). *Rural Canadians' guide to programs and services.* Ottawa: Agriculture and Agri-Food Canada.

Sachs, I. (1984). *Development and planning.* Cambridge: Cambridge University Press; and Paris: Editions de la Maison de Sciences de L'Homme.

Savoie, D. (Ed.). (1986). *The Canadian economy: A regional perspective.* Toronto: Methuen.

Sim, R. A. (1988). *Land and community: Crisis in Canada's countryside.* Guelph: University of Guelph.

Statistics Canada. (Various dates). Rural and small towns' analysis bulletin. Retrieved from www.statcan.gc.ca.

Stoker, G. (1998). *Governance as theory: Five propositions.* Oxford: UNESCO/ Blackwell.

Sumner, J. (2005). *Sustainability and the civil commons: Rural communities in the age of globalization.* Toronto: University of Toronto Press.

———. (2010). From land to table: Rural planning and development for sustainable food systems. In D.J.A. Douglas (Ed.), *Rural planning and development in Canada* (pp. 179–254). Toronto: Nelson.

TWO

Rural Sustainability and the "Lenses" of Place

Don Alexander and Bernie Jones

Introduction

Many rural areas in Canada are experiencing conflict over land use and competing visions of what constitutes rural and small-town sustainability. Much of this conflict is influenced by the different "lenses" or concepts of land that people utilize as they engage in such conflicts (Atherton, 2010). As Learmonth, Whitehead, Boyd, and Fletcher (2007) note,

> [a] land use conflict occurs when there is disagreement or dispute as to the use of land and/or a feeling that a person's rights or well-being or the rights of the environment are being threatened by the action or undertaking of another or the inaction of another.... [T]he root cause of a conflict is when a land use or an action is incompatible with views, expectations and values of the people living in an area. (p. 1)

These conflicts play themselves out in the arena of community planning, sometimes calmly and sometimes rancorously. Using the case study of Echo Heights, a contested piece of land in the unincorporated village of Chemainus within the larger Municipality of North Cowichan on Vancouver Island, British Columbia, we will explore how these lenses influence conflict, how they gain traction respectively (with some thoughts on their origins), and suggest ways for finding common ground among conflicting parties. Our approach is similar to that of Spaling and Wood (1998), who present a case study concerning conversion of farmland on the periphery of Edmonton to examine the underlying conflicting land ethics. As they write,

> Each land ethic is based on a set of deeply held values that an individual, group or society has about the land, and human responsibility for it. It implies application of normative values of right and wrong, good and bad, and duty and obligation to the relationship between humans and the land. Some may value farmland from an economic perspective, so that its allocation and use is determined by market forces. Others may assess the worth of farmland by its inherent biophysical characteristics,. implying that attributes of the land itself should establish its use. Still others may use moral principles (e.g., providing for future generations) or religious beliefs (e.g., Judeo-Christian stewardship of the land) as the ethical basis for directing policy on farmland conversion. These diverging values among stakeholders contribute to land use conflict. (p. 105)

As they go on to note, the "[e]thical dimensions are inherent in all land use decisions, but are seldom made explicit" (p. 105). This is the case with the land-use conflict profiled in our chapter on Echo Heights.

The movement to preserve Echo Heights is a manifestation of rural community sustainability planning in that it places the needs of the community and the ecosystem first, rather than privileging the needs of the development industry or the municipality, as defined by staff or elected officials. The efforts of the Chemainus Residents Association (CRA) have not yet reached the stage of comprehensive planning—in part because of the need to defend the site against municipal proposals for development—nonetheless, the group's orientation manifests some of the hallmarks of Integrated Community Sustainability Planning (ICSP), as defined by the Government of British Columbia (2007): long-term thinking, being broad in scope, and encouraging public engagement and education.

The CRA has sought to collaborate with conservation groups, local First Nations, and local universities, and it has tried to find allies within the local municipal government. It has also begun to implement monitoring and evaluation of the area's ecosystem and recreational values.

Rural community sustainability issues addressed

In its broadest sense, the Echo Heights story has been about (a) growth and land use, (b) varying conceptions of land, and (c) local-government decision making around land use. First, underlying the municipality's drive to develop Echo Heights for residential use is a fundamental commitment to growth, although its articulated land-use and zoning policies are couched in today's de rigueur language of smart growth and sustainability (District of North Cowichan, 2011). The analysis of the conflicting perspectives ("lenses" in our theoretical scheme) between the municipality and the CRA on Echo Heights form the central contribution of this chapter.

Second, the theoretical/ethical approach that has guided the efforts of the CRA in seeking to preserve Echo Heights is that the value of the land as ecosystem, as heritage, as a remnant of a radically transformed bioregion, and as an environment for outdoor recreation and connecting with nature exceeds its value as a commodity (i.e., as a source of revenue for the municipality and the development industry). In this chapter, we attempt to put the value conflict evident in our case study in a broader theoretical context that will help explain land-use conflicts more generally.

Third, this chapter addresses the decision-making process of the municipality relative to land-use matters and the various strategies and tactics employed by the CRA, thus far without success, to affect municipal decision making. In doing so, we offer a typology of strategies for social change. In addressing these three issues, we describe the university–community working relationship, introduce and explain the concept of "lenses," then present the case study. The case study describes the contested area, reviews the history of the conflict, and interprets it using the lenses framework. Following that is a discussion about why some lenses have wider appeal than others, what tools are available for groups seeking to promote a sustainability-oriented lens, and whether a common lens can be found to bring disparate groups together. Conclusions are then drawn about the utility of the lens framework.

The university–community relationship

This chapter does not relate the story of a complete and continuing university–community partnership for community development in the manner of other chapters in this book. The effort to preserve Echo Heights from development began with the formation of the CRA in spring 2006. Early on, the CRA called on the University of Victoria (UVic) Environmental Law Clinic for assistance. Twice it received the assistance of law students, whose work helped the CRA make stronger and more credible arguments for Echo Heights' preservation. Another law student volunteered to produce a 15-minute film about Echo Heights, and UVic and the CRA jointly carried on a biodiversity education project. Staff members from the clinic have remained available to the CRA for general advice and consultation. In addition, in 2010 one of Don Alexander's Vancouver Island University geography classes toured Echo Heights with CRA members and participated in a follow-up discussion about CRA strategies.

The primary outcome of the collaboration between the CRA and UVic to date has been the value of the expertise received and the opportunity for students to apply their knowledge and skills in real situations in the service of the community. These efforts have resulted in the wider education and engagement of the public in the Chemainus area, including through the CRA website. Our collaboration in presenting at the Taking the Next Steps conference and in writing this chapter will also have the effect of disseminating the case to a wider audience in British Columbia and Canada.

The university–community relationship could have been more extensive were it not for the mismatch between the timelines of academia and those of community activism. The nature of the academic calendar, arranged as it is into discrete terms, means that student projects need to be time limited and compact, while community projects are usually lengthy, continuous, loop back and forth, stop and restart, and so on. While unavoidable, these issues hinder the formation and maintenance of a continuing relationship between academic and community partners.

An introduction to the "lenses" of place

As we define them, the "lenses" of place include: land as commodity (financial value), as resource (productive value), as environment

Figure 2.1: Model of the lenses of place.

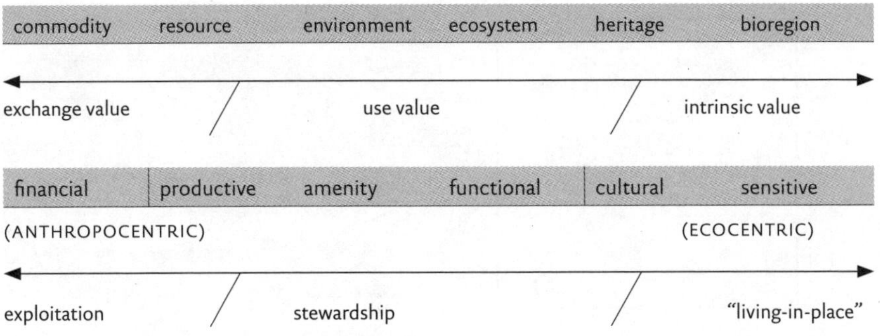

(amenity value), as ecosystem (holistic-functional value), as heritage (cultural value), and as bioregion (involving values that are sensitive to the uniqueness of the local). These can be seen as arrayed along two continua from exchange value through use value to intrinsic value, and from anthropocentric to ecocentric, with varying degrees of exploitation, stewardship and "living-in-place" as the dominant perspective in terms of how land is viewed and used (see Figure 2.1). Clearly, when different stakeholders are viewing the same piece of land or region through these different lenses, conflict is inevitable as each person or group has a different conception of the "highest and best use" to which the land can be put.

In addition, these concepts of land can be correlated with definitions of sustainability. Those embracing a commodity perspective are concerned at best with maintaining the economic viability of a community for the short term but for the most part are not interested in sustainability at all, except perhaps in the sense of "greenwashing" for marketing purposes.

The resource perspective encompasses everything from "cut-and-run" use of the land to long-term, multigenerational stewardship of a resource, such as forest ecosystems or soil. Those with an environment perspective are more concerned about superficial amenities than genuine ecosystem function, but in practice their goals may align with those who seek a more holistic approach (e.g., preservation of open space or wetlands).

The heritage lens focuses on preserving sense of place, a key aspect of social sustainability; it can, but does not always, translate into stewardship

Figure 2.2: Maps of Echo Heights and its geographic context on Vancouver Island.

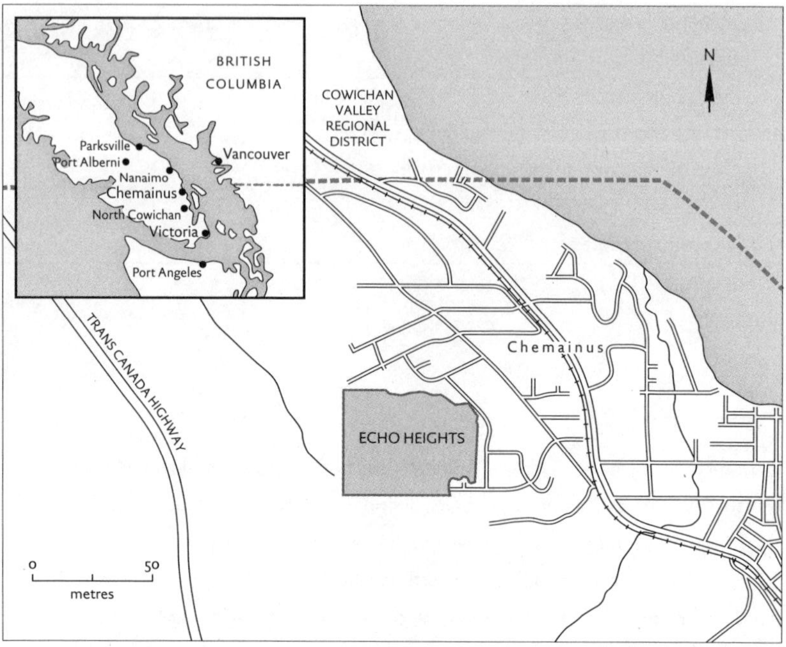

of the land. Finally, the bioregion perspective takes into account how people can live well socially and economically within their respective bioregion while respecting its carrying capacity, but the resulting vision would be one that most North Americans (brought up in consumer culture) might have difficulty embracing.

Municipal land-use planners who play a key role in this case study, and in rural land-use conflicts more generally, vary in their position in the foregoing spectrum. Their sympathies may be with farmland, habitat, and open-space preservation, but their position as employees of often development-hungry municipalities means that they may have to pursue agendas that differ from their own personal orientations (Forester, 1988).

Introduction to the case study

Having described the lens framework, we now examine the Echo Heights area and trace the conflict before interpreting that conflict through the framework. The origins of the 21-hectare piece of land known today

Figure 2.3: Map of informal trails created and maintained by the community.

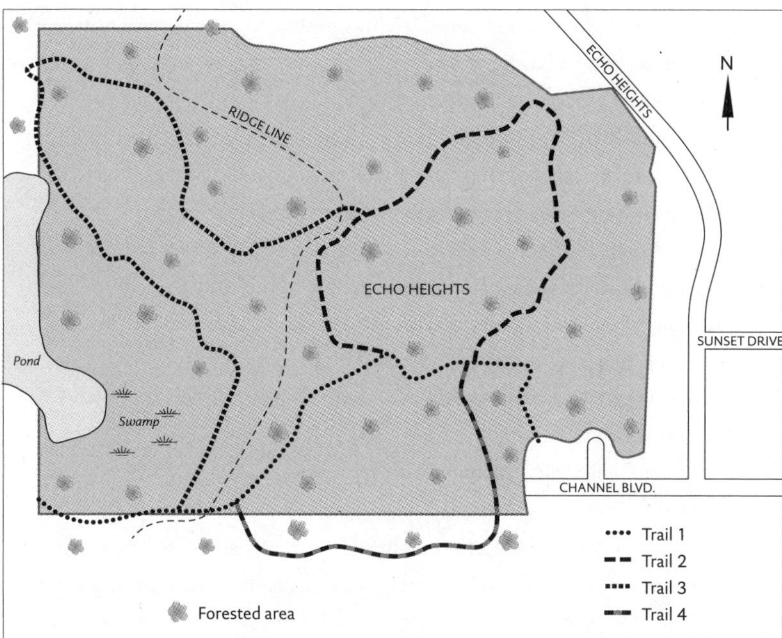

as Echo Heights is enshrouded in unwritten First Nations history (the Penelekut First Nation, in particular). Penelekut Elders talk of their people having made use of the Echo Heights area for ceremonial, recreational, and pharmaceutical purposes for a long period (Sylvester, 2007). Seventy years ago, the Municipality of North Cowichan purchased the site in a tax sale from its previous owner for $71.61 (see Appendix at the end of the chapter). At that time, the land had already been logged. Although initially zoned for 0.8-hectare lots in 1966, the land was never developed except for an eight-unit subdivision in one corner of the site. Significant housing development has occurred adjacent to it, however. For the last 20 years or so, the remainder of the site has been informally used as a park by the Chemainus community. The current Official Community Plan has Echo Heights zoned as R-2 (a relatively low-density, residential zone), and it is also designated as an "urban expansion area" (District of North Cowichan, 2011). To the north and the east are R-3 residential areas now nearing complete development; to the south and west are A-1 agriculturally zoned lands. The first timeline in the Appendix contains the municipality's history of Echo Heights land use and zoning, which sets the stage for the more recent activities outlined in the second timeline.

Echo Heights has been described as one of the last Garry oak meadows in a coastal Douglas-fir ecosystem, and it hosts a wide diversity of flora and fauna. Rocky outcroppings are mixed with marshy areas (three, small, terrestrial herbaceous meadows), all interconnected by a trail system carved out by users over a number of years (see Figure 2.3).

The concept or lens of land as a commodity is in direct opposition to notions of sustainable planning and is seen commonly among developers and real-estate agents, with some notable exceptions. For those who see land this way, farmland and habitat, not to mention community open space, is often conceived of as "raw" land. The goal in this framework is to transform land—even "underutilized" urban land—to its "highest and best use," with the ideal end result of maximizing the financial turnover for land owners.

The concept of land as a resource for human use exists among farmers, and forestry and mining companies (which have varying degrees of commitment to social and ecological responsibility), and the government agencies that regulate them. As noted, the resource perspective encompasses everything from "cut-and-run" practices to long-term, multigenerational stewardship of a resource. Small-scale farmers and forestry companies are more likely to take a stewardship perspective than major forestry and mining corporations, though this is beginning to shift somewhat.

The concept of viewing land as an environment is characteristic of homeowners seeking pleasant views and green space adjacent to their homes. They are still interested in maintaining the property and resale value of their homes, and the "amenities" enhance that, but the environment also enhances their own quality of life. While not unimportant, this perspective is relatively superficial in that it looks at the outward characteristics of a given place and not at the underlying ecological dynamics, though the two may be related. Developers and real-estate agents who market to homeowners or who develop resort communities are also sensitive to these considerations as they enhance the ultimate commodity value of the land.

The ecosystem concept of land is embraced by ecologists and environmentalists, who are concerned with preserving habitat, rare and endangered species, and ecologically important processes. Land that is vital and healthy is often aesthetically appealing as well; thus, it often also scores high on environment/amenity criteria.

The heritage or homeland perspective is characteristic of First Nations, the descendants of pioneers, and history/heritage buffs. For such groups, enduring natural and cultural legacies of the past help define their identities and wider sense of cultural character. Such legacies help provide an essential sense of continuity with the past and provide psychic "fuel" for current struggles and endeavours. Sometimes, these features are also used as marketing devices to "sell" areas to tourists or potential property owners.

A bioregional perspective is shared by those who see the bioregion, however defined, as a place shaped by diverse natural and cultural features that must be "reinhabited" for long-term sustainability (Alexander, 1990; Thayer, 2003). This incorporates elements of the ecosystem and heritage/homeland perspectives, as well as the long-term stewardship component of the resource perspective (for more about different land-use interests and perspectives, see Hite [1998] and Firey [1945]).

Why do some definitions of sustainability have greater traction than others, and is this changing?

Until recently, three major (and closely interrelated) factors have lent far more preponderance to the first three concepts or lenses of land—commodity, human use, and environment—by the fact that our economy is profit- and growth-oriented and "progresses" by transforming "raw" land into a "higher and better use"; by the fact that politicians and political parties are largely judged by their ability to maintain economic growth and boost employment and prosperity; and by the fact that much of the population defines success and happiness in terms of material acquisition and high levels of consumption, which often includes a home in the suburbs (Porritt, 2007).

A fourth possible factor, which has been at play for hundreds of years, is the perception of the "unlimited frontier"—that there is always more land, more resources, more "stuff"—and that we are never really in danger of running out (Brown, 2009). This concept is beginning to change in the forestry and fishing sectors, where renewable resources are starting to prove themselves limited. The rapid decline of species is also beginning to make an impression, as scientists talk of imminent extinctions and as the notion of peak oil begins to register (Dauncey, 2009; Heinberg, 2009).

The balance of forces is changing due to the global ecological crisis that has forced many politicians, and even corporations, into at least paying lip service to sustainability, and to the growing awareness on the part of citizens that the old way of living may not be as tenable and desirable as was formerly thought. However, much of this awareness has yet to be fully reflected in major policy changes, at either a governmental or corporate level, or in a widespread lifestyle change among the general public (Porritt, 2007).

In addition to a slowly dawning ecological awareness, environmental and First Nations groups, among others, have become more adept at lobbying, litigating, and influencing political and economic decision makers at a variety of levels and thus have been able to stop or modify certain developments and enable significant natural areas to be set aside, as well as preserve key cultural artifacts (Mitchell, 2010). Other lenses have also been of assistance: concern for heritage values, desire to preserve environmental amenities, recognition of the importance of ecosystem integrity, and a desire to preserve farmland in the face of food-security issues.

What tools are most effective for formulating and broadcasting definitions of sustainability?

This section will examine the possible tools groups can use for promoting more holistic concepts of land and sustainability and will report on the tools the CRA has employed in its struggle. Some of the customary tools include: lobbying and boycotts, policy work and product certification, education and influencing the opinion makers, and direct action (both political and lifestyle).

Examples of effective lobbying and boycotts include Avaaz (an international online petition organization that gathers signatures for a variety of causes), letter writing to decision makers by concerned citizens, letters to the editor of local or national newspapers, public meetings, boycotts of offending products and companies, and surveys. Lobbying can also take the form of aiding in the election of individuals and parties who stand for the implementation of favoured policies and principles. The CRA has employed lobbying extensively, including presenting to council (e.g., the legal case for using Echo Heights for recreation), letters to the editor, public meetings, and petitioning.

Policy work and product certification includes, for example, formulating alternative land-use planning policies, alternative tax policies, incentives and subsidies of various kinds, energy and traffic-demand management, and certified products (e.g., Forest Stewardship Council–certified timber). The CRA has engaged in policy work with its publication of the *Conservation Alternative*, and its proposals to council for joint-planning work.

Education and influencing the opinion makers usually involves cultivating ties with the media and with educators; raising awareness through websites, leaflets, and social media; celebrity endorsements; and enlisting academic expertise. Education and influencing opinion makers' activities of the CRA have included leading groups on tours of Echo Heights, maintaining a website with many documents and video, publishing leaflets, and utilizing academic expertise.

Direct action can take two forms: political and lifestyle. Political direct action consists of demonstrations, civil disobedience/blockades, and purchases of contested parcels of land, whereas lifestyle direct action involves modelling change through exemplary lifestyles. To date, the CRA has not utilized direct-action strategies, although it has approached conservancy organizations about the possibility of purchasing the land and converting it into a trust. Blockading the land against construction activity could become a possibility in the future.

In general, these strategies for bringing about social change range from the polite (e.g., petitions, letters to the editor, using the electoral process) and the assertive (e.g., legal actions, strikes, pickets) to the militant (e.g., civil disobedience, confrontations, street-level dramatizations, as exemplified by the Occupy movement). Selection among these depends essentially on the degree of consensus among the parties and a sensitive reading of the mood of one's constituents (Jones, 1995).

All of these forms of resistance and social activism have the potential for changing the ideology of society on the ground—reconstructing social reality, as Berger and Luckmann (1966) put it. This is because they lead to specific changes in the way society operates—in the way we interact with and manage nature and land, handle government or corporate accountability, create opportunities for citizen participation, and reallocate society's resources toward transit and alternative energy and transportation. New practices lead to new norms, which can lead to subsequent changes in social behaviour.

Are there concepts of land/sustainability that can provide common ground for competing visions?

In theory, the bioregional concept can be a home for many different groups and perspectives, but it is clearly at odds, as are the ecosystem and heritage concepts, with development as the highest good and a growth-oriented society. Perhaps the imminent crisis being ushered in by climate change and peak oil will change the terms of debate and shift public opinion toward the bioregional perspective (Newman, Beatley, & Boyer, 2009). However, that may take some time.

Nonetheless, while not always using the rubric of bioregion, the concepts of "place" or "community" can provide a common meeting ground for different perspectives so long as the various perspectives are committed to the well-being of place and community, however much their visions of well-being may differ; at least they provide a platform for discussion. There is also evidence to suggest that people are more likely to be willing to consider the regional context in local land-use decisions if there are strong regional symbols that enable them to expand their sense of place beyond the local. Starting a planning process with this identification of "sacred sites" can bring people who would normally be on the opposite sides of issues—such as environmentalists and property-rights advocates—together (Hester, 1999). This certainly proved to be the case in Greater Salt Lake in the context of a comprehensive, regional-planning exercise (Calthorpe & Fulton, 2001). Indeed, all over the world, people are beginning to appreciate and defend those qualities that make their communities and regions—in a word, their places—unique and special, whether it be the landscapes, architecture, cuisine, or a slower pace of life (Honoré, 2004—see also http://www.cittaslow.net).

This idea of using what people care about— the land or the public realm—as a basis for seeking common ground has been discussed by a number of political theorists, including Hannah Arendt (1959) and Daniel Kemmis (1992). Kemmis (1992), the former mayor of Missoula, Montana, has suggested that "the general placelessness of our political thought weakens both our sense of politics and of place.... No real culture—whether we speak of food or of politics or of anything else—can exist in abstraction from place." He goes on to say that "public life can only be reclaimed by understanding, and then practicing, its connection to real, identifiable places" (p. 6), noting that "[i]f people could actually hear the ways in which their neighbors' lives and hopes were rooted in this particular part of the earth that they all call home, they might be able to begin figuring out how to go about living well here..." (pp. 67–68).

While consensus is the ideal—and there are examples elsewhere in British Columbia of where this ideal has been approached in the land-use and resource-planning realms (such as the Co-operative Resource and Environment process, Hodge & Robinson [2001])—in the hardscrabble world of politics, there are usually winners and losers and, in any event, contesting parties are not starting from equal positions of strength. As Berger and Luckmann (1966, p. 109) note, he/she "who has the bigger stick has the better chance of imposing his[/her] definitions of reality." This is why citizens' groups attempt to compensate for their lack of institutional power by mobilizing public opinion and leveraging action through the variety of social-change strategies reviewed above.

Conclusions

In this chapter, we have attempted to show that land-use conflict is fuelled by different lenses concerning land and their associated definitions of sustainability. We have provided a taxonomy of these lenses and have used the Echo Heights story to illustrate them. We believe the struggle over Echo Heights illustrates the different techniques that competing groups—especially citizen organizations—use to advance their agendas, which in turn are based on these lenses. In this case, one can see how emerging concepts of sustainability and place, however contested, provide at least the basis for dialogue, even if the final outcome may yet be decided on the political and ideological battlefield. One area for future research would be to focus on how to make the underlying frameworks and values animating conflict more explicit so that they can become an explicit part of the dialogue; it may yet be possible to do this in the case of Echo Heights.

We have also shown how university researchers and students can go beyond merely studying community group endeavours to actually supporting them and helping them change the world in a more sustainable direction. This provides valuable real-life experience for students even as they lend their research and other skills to strengthening community endeavours.

Appendix

Echo Heights (EH) Timelines

Key Events in Echo Heights Story

1939	Site acquired by the municipality through tax sale
1966	Zoned to allow 0.8-hectare lots, or 0.2-hectare lots with water
1976	68-lot subdivision developed adjacent to property
1978–80	Site designated and zoned for single-family residential lots
1990	Chemainus Comprehensive Development Plan designated area for residential use
1992	Phased development plan prepared for 160+ lots; first phase of 8 lots completed
1993	Second phase of 28 lots tabled due to economic conditions
1999	"Chemainus Planning Chemainus" completed, with site designated as Growth Area
2002	Official Community Plan completed; site designated as Urban Expansion / Growth Centre; municipal lands identified as opportunity to "showcase alternate development standards and housing choices"
2004	Water system upgrade opens up areas above 70 metre-contour for development
2005	Workshop on Chemainus Concept Plan
Spring 2006	Initial Echo Heights Design Charrette
Early 2011	Comprehensive development plan for EH presented to council
Spring 2011	Council has first reading on Echo Heights Comprehensive Development Plan, to be incorporated into draft Official Community Plan

Detailed Timeline and Interpretation of Echo Heights Development Events, 2006–2014

February 2006	Municipality stages Echo Heights Design Charrette. This was potentially an attempt to reconcile the different lenses, but the underlying agenda seems to have been to get people on board with developing the site by offering some protected parcels and innovative "green" features in the development.
April 2006	Council decides to proceed with development but does not release documents on which decision was based. This seems to represent a formalization or institutional endorsement of the commodity lens.
Spring 2006	EH Organizing Committee meets and moves toward formalizing an organization, which becomes the Chemainus Residents Association (CRA). This move created a vehicle that could effectively promulgate an alternative lens.
Spring 2006	The CRA requests assistance from the University of Victoria (UVic) Environmental Law Clinic, constituting an effort to increase the credibility of the CRA's argument for viewing EH through a non-commodity lens.
June 2006	The CRA holds its first AGM and hears from UVic law student challenging the legitimacy of council's secretive decision making about EH, suggesting that a truly dialogic process needs to occur.
October 2006	A consultant's report, *Ecological and Biophysical Assessment Proposed Development Property Echo Heights, Chemainus, BC*, prepared by Madrone Environmental Services, Ltd., October 25, 2006, commissioned by the municipality, is released, analyzing EH's eco-diversity and identifying areas appropriate for conservation. This constitutes validation of an ecosystem lens.
May 2007	The Chemainus Biodiversity Education Project is launched by the CRA in partnership with UVic's Polis Project. This was an effort to increase credibility of the CRA's argument regarding the ecosystem values associated with EH.

July 2009	G. P. Rollo & Associates carries out a *Development Opportunity Study* for the municipality, showing what financial gain could accrue to the municipality from developing EH for residential use. (Only a redacted version has been publicly released.) The study begins from a commodity lens, examining revenue gains only from residential development.
August 2009	UVic law student presents to council the legal case for designating EH a park based on historical, de facto use of the land as a park without any objection from its owner, the municipality. This was a formal attempt to substitute ecosystem, environment (recreation), and heritage lenses for the municipality's commodity lens.
November 2009	At a CRA meeting, Holly Pattison has a premiere showing of her 10-minute film on EH (http://www.chemainiac.ca/). The CRA makes a graphic case for ecosystem and heritage lenses.
December 2009	The CRA formally suggests that council join with it and other potential partners in exploring benefits from scenarios other than those reviewed in the Rollo report in an attempt to get the municipality to entertain discussion of alternative lenses.
January 2010	The CRA presents the document it has prepared, *Echo Heights Forest: The Conservation Opportunity*, to council in an attempt to present a viable way that EH could be preserved without financial loss for the municipality if it were to switch lenses.
Spring 2011	EH Comprehensive Development Plan is prepared without any further community consultation, calling for 40% of land to be housing and 60% to be parkland. With this move, the municipality proposes a compromise between commodity and amenity uses; unacceptable to the CRA.
Spring 2011	Holly Pattison releases an updated and expanded version of her film. Advocates in film express the variety of lenses.

May 2011	Friends of Echo Heights (companion organization to the CRA) brings citizens to EH for a "camas fest." This was an effort by the CRA to broaden support for EH's ecosystem value.
Summer 2011	Public-information session and public hearing scheduled with final adoption projected to occur in September. The public hearing and second reading were postponed indefinitely, i.e., until after November 2011 municipal elections. The public hearing would likely have seen a loud and dramatic clash of competing lenses and perhaps eventual triumph of one lens over another.
Fall 2011	With some changes in council after the election, the situation remains uncertain. There may be an opportunity to recast the debate and entertain other lenses.
June 2014	North Cowichan Council votes 6–1 to designate 91% of Echo Heights as a park, limiting housing development to the other 9%. The CRA supports and applauds the action.

References

Alexander, D. (1990). Bioregionalism: Science or sensibility? *Environmental Ethics* 12(2), 161–73.

Arendt, H. (1959). *The human condition*. Chicago: University of Chicago Press.

Atherton, J. S. (2010). *Frames of reference*. Retrieved September 24, 2011, from http://www.doceo.co.uk/tools/frame.htm.

Berger, P. L., & Luckmann, T. (1966). *The social construction of reality: A treatise in the sociology of knowledge*. Garden City, NY: Anchor Books.

Brown, D. S. (2009). *Beyond the frontier: Midwestern historians in the American century*. Chicago: University of Chicago Press.

Calthorpe, P., & Fulton, W. (2001). *The regional city: New urbanism and the end of urban sprawl*. Washington, DC: Island Press.

Dauncey, G. (2009). *The climate challenge—101 solutions to global warming*. Gabriola Island, BC: New Society Publishers.

District of North Cowichan. (2011). *Draft bylaw 3450: Official community plan bylaw*. Retrieved September 24, 2011, from District of North Cowichan, http://northcowichan.fileprosite.com/Documents/DocumentList.aspx?ID=60504.

Firey, W. (1945). Sentiment and symbolism as ecological variables. *American Sociological Review, X,* 140–148.

Forester, J. (1988). *Planning in the face of power.* Berkeley: University of California Press.

Government of British Columbia. (2007). *The integrated community sustainability planning (ICSP) initiative.* Retrieved September 24, 2011, from ICSP, http://www.cscd.gov.bc.ca/lgd/intergov_relations/library/ICSP_Backgrounder.pdf

Heinberg, R. (2009). *Powerdown: Options and actions for a post-carbon world.* Gabriola Island, BC: New Society Publishers.

Hester, R. T. Jr. (1999). A refrain with a view. *Places, 12*(2), 12–25

Hite, J. (1998). Land use conflicts on the urban fringe: Causes and potential resolution. Retrieved from Strom Thurmond Institute, Clemson University, http://sti.clemson.edu/index.php?option=com_docman&task=cat_view&gid=163&Itemid=310.

Hodge, G., & Robinson, I. M. (2001). *Planning Canadian regions.* Vancouver: University of British Columbia Press.

Honoré, C. (2004). *In praise of slow: How a worldwide movement is challenging the cult of speed.* Toronto: Random House Canada

Jones, B. (1995). Taking action: Community development strategies and tactics. *CD Practice,* 3, 1–9.

Kemmis, D. (1992). *Community and the politics of place.* Norman, OK: University of Oklahoma Press.

Learmonth, R., Whitehead, R., Boyd, B., and Fletcher, S. (2007). *Living and working in rural areas: A handbook for managing land use conflict issues on the NSW north coast.* Wollongbar, AU: Southern Cross University.

Mitchell, B. (Ed.). (2010). *Resource and environmental management in Canada: Addressing conflict and uncertainty.* London: Oxford University Press.

Newman, P., Beatley, T., & Boyer, H. (2009). *Resilient cities: Responding to peak oil and climate change.* Washington, DC: Island Press.

Porritt, J. (2007). *Capitalism as if the world matters.* London: Earthscan.

Spaling, H., & Wood. J. R. (1998). Greed, need or creed? Farmland ethics on the rural-urban fringe. *Land Use Policy, 15*(2), 105–118.

Sylvester, A. (2007, July 22). Why cut down a pharmacy? *Biodiversity Matters 1*(2), 1–2.

Thayer, R. (2003). *LifePlace: Bioregional thought and practice.* Berkeley: University of California Press.

THREE

Engaging the Public in Wildlife and Greenspace Stewardship in Camrose, Alberta

An Analysis of Outcomes, Drivers, and Lessons Learned

Glen T. Hvenegaard and Michael Barr

Introduction

Alberta has undergone tremendous economic growth as it develops its natural resources, especially its abundant oil and gas reserves. In the last two decades, the province's population has increased (mostly through immigration into cities), rural areas have been developed, and municipal development has intensified (Government of Alberta, 2008). The entire province has felt the effects of diminishing natural habitats (Timoney & Lee, 2001) and has launched sustainability-planning initiatives to address this public concern (Alberta Urban Municipalities Association [AUMA], 2011). The city of Camrose, located in east-central Alberta, has experienced similar issues related to development and habitat change (Hvenegaard & Barr, 2010).

A key planning challenge exists related to the extent and management of greenspace areas (Davies et al., 2008). In this chapter, greenspaces will refer to natural and semi-natural lands in urban or semi-urban areas that contain substantial wildlife and amenity values (e.g., Van Herzele & Wiedemann, 2003). Local residents and visitors use greenspaces for a variety of purposes, including recreation, education, ecosystem services, ecological health, and clean water. In the absence of proactive planning and effective management, the quantity and quality of greenspaces will decline over time (James et al., 2009). As a result, there will be fewer opportunities for people to connect and engage with nature provided by greenspaces. This has the potential to reduce the quality of life for residents in urban and semi-urban areas and to limit the full set of opportunities afforded by greenspaces. Planners and managers will promote wildlife and greenspace conservation only if they see obvious community support. In addition, planning and management decisions are more likely to succeed if key stakeholders are involved in those decisions in a meaningful way (Gruber, 2010). Thus, it is important to appropriately engage residents (one of those key stakeholders) in the stewardship, management, and planning related to greenspaces and wildlife (Gruber, 2010).

We have wrestled with several questions regarding the importance of public engagement with residents for greenspace and wildlife stewardship in the City of Camrose. What are the best ways to engage the public? Over which issues is it appropriate to engage the public? How involved is the public willing to become? Is there a critical threshold of potential public support? What are the ultimate measures of success for wildlife and greenspace stewardship? In this context, we define stewardship as "the recognition of our collective responsibility to retain the quality and abundance of our land, air, water and biodiversity, and to manage this natural capital in a way that conserves all of its values, be they environmental, economic, social or cultural" (Land Stewardship Resource Centre [LSRC], 2011).

The purpose of this chapter is to examine the potential and practical role of engaging the public in wildlife and greenspace stewardship. We seek to highlight the challenges, lessons learned, and future opportunities in engaging the public in order to mobilize community support for local environmental stewardship projects, using Camrose as a case study. Moreover, we will demonstrate that increasing community engagement, in the form of stewardship activities such as education programs, enhancement projects, research, and policy development, have aided greenspace and wildlife management in the city.

In order to achieve this purpose, we have reflected on the establishment of a local stewardship project (the Camrose Wildlife and Stewardship Society [CWSS]) and on our involvement in other conservation activities in the city. First, both of us have been on the board of directors of the CWSS since its inception in 2002. Second, we have supervised an annual, summer-staff member in charge of implementing many of the CWSS's activities. We draw heavily on annual reports of this staff member and of the CWSS. Third, in the courses he teaches, Glen connects learning activities about local environmental sustainability (e.g., public involvement in wildlife conservation and data gathering for developing the city's Municipal Sustainability Plan [MSP]) with greenspace and wildlife issues. Michael regularly addresses community stewardship needs in his organization's goal of conserving wetlands. Last, as residents of the city, we regularly interact with wildlife and greenspace issues (e.g., bird watching, nature study, cross-country skiing) and participate in the political process to effectively manage greenspaces (e.g., presentations to city council on issues and progress of the CWSS).

Context and issues

Camrose is located about 100 kilometres southeast of Edmonton. Similar to Alberta, the City of Camrose, has undergone substantial growth in recent times. The population has risen from 15,253 in 2001 to 17,236 in 2011, a 13.0% increase in 10 years (City of Camrose, 2011). Economically, the city is supported by industrial agriculture and serves as a regional centre for legal, financial, retail, and educational services (City of Camrose, 2011). Socially, Camrose has a long history of strong community engagement in the arts, sports, and service clubs (City of Camrose, 2011). Ecologically, Camrose is found within the aspen parkland natural region, characterized by a mosaic of wetlands, aspen forests, and grassland meadows, but these habitats have been largely converted to other uses (Natural Regions Committee, 2006). Fortunately, the city is graced with significant greenspace areas through a fortunate combination of landforms (a creek valley) and visionary effort by early civic leaders. The city maintains over 1,750 hectares of park and open greenspaces, 21 kilometres of paved trails, and 15 kilometres of nature trails (City of Camrose, 2010).

The catalyst for this case study came from anecdotal reports from some local residents about the declining quality and quantity of greenspaces and wildlife populations within the city. This decline has the potential to reduce ecological benefits (e.g., declining wildlife communities) and social benefits (opportunities for connecting people with nature; Patterson, Montag, & Williams, 2003). Greenspace was raised as a concern during Camrose's recent Municipal Sustainability Plan process (City of Camrose, 2010). Indeed, urban greenspace areas are critical for long-term sustainability (Chiesura, 2004) and are a critical component of the ecological pillar of most MSPs. More specifically, the Camrose MSP calls for available and well-maintained, local, accessible greenspaces and facilities. There is no clear policy framework to support greenspace conservation and only minimal greenspace provisions for future city annexations (Hvenegaard & Barr, 2010). As well, there are concerns about the implications of a future in which a public does not identify with or support the value of urban nature conservation (Louv, 2005).

In Alberta the provincial government is responsible for wildlife management (The Constitution Act, 1867, sections 92 and 92A). The City of Camrose, and in particular the Parks Program of the Community Services Department, manages greenspace within the city boundaries. In addition, city officials provide advice and some management action related to wildlife. Other key stakeholders involved in wildlife and greenspace issues include residents, nongovernmental organizations (NGOs), and a variety of community groups. One of those community groups is the Camrose Wildlife and Stewardship Society (formerly called the Camrose Wildlife and Greenspace Stewardship Project). In brief (more background provided later), the CWSS seeks to raise public awareness, knowledge, and support among local residents for abundant wildlife and greenspaces in Camrose, and to emphasize the importance of these features as contributors to quality of life in the community.

Conceptualizing civic engagement

Before using this case study to demonstrate how community engagement can promote local greenspace and wildlife stewardship goals, we will briefly provide some relevant background information. Civic engagement can be defined as "commitment to helping improve one's neighborhood or community" (Tuxill, Mitchell, and Clark, 2009, p. 3). There are many methods of public participation in environmental sustainability, including, for example, citizens' juries, round tables, hearings, volunteerism, and citizen science (Konisky & Beierle, 2001). The "pursuit of sustainability is inextricably linked to civic engagement" (Portney, 2005, p. 583) because it can enhance public interest and value in natural resources, increase appreciation for the value of these resources (Tuxill et al., 2009), increase the effectiveness of problem solving (Robson & Parkins, 2010), increase trust and satisfaction in the decision-making process (Burns, Sperry, & Hodgson, 2003; Robson & Parkins, 2010), and enhance volunteer involvement (Shandas & Messer, 2008). Likely outcomes of civic engagement in sustainable communities, for example, are changed participants (e.g., raised consciousness, changed consumer behaviour) and changed politics (e.g., processes of involvement, communication with local leaders; Portney, 2005).

Civic engagement can be examined within a few conceptual frameworks. Greenberg's (2001) theory of neighbourhood civic participation states "that family history, self-interest, and personal efficacy are foundations of neighborhood civic participation" (p. 41). In terms of family history, civic participation develops when people see family members and close family friends serve as role models in their volunteer positions, receive teaching about important values and opportunities regarding community engagement, and come from family and socio-economic backgrounds (e.g., confidence, education, and affluence) that allow time and opportunity for such participation. In terms of self-interest, people are motivated through, for example, a desire to address perceived threats to their community (e.g., safety, unwelcome developments). In terms of personal efficacy, people are motivated to participate in community activities with which they have some association (e.g., parents volunteering with school councils; Greenberg, 2001).

Second, civic ecology theory is a framework for studying the role that stewardship practices play in integrating "social and environmental values within a social-ecological systems framework" (Krasny & Tidball, 2009a, p. 2). This theory focuses on active engagement with nature, building on concepts such as biophilia (Wilson, 1984) and nature-deficit disorder (Louv, 2005). As people actively engage in nature restoration, they can contribute to their individual well-being (Miles, Sullivan, & Kuo, 1998). As individual actions are examined at the community scale, civic engagement may emerge. Stewardship practices and educational programs can help foster the desired characteristic of resilience in the context of civic engagement (Chapin, Kofinas, & Folke, 2009).

Third, social learning theory suggests that learning occurs as partners participate in the social and biophysical processes within a specific environment (Krasny & Tidball, 2009b). Social learning is defined "as a collaborative process among multiple stakeholders aimed at addressing management issues in complex systems" (p. 2). Social learning occurs as individuals acquire new learning, as they interact with other people and the local environment, as skill level increases within the community, and as stakeholders interact toward a common cause (Krasny & Tidball, 2009b).

Civic engagement in the realm of environmental sustainability can be enhanced through the use of a flagship species, which is typically a popular and charismatic animal species (Smith & Sutton, 2008) "used as the focus of a broader conservation marketing campaign based on its possession of one or more traits that appeal to the target audience" (Verissimo, MacMillan, & Smith, 2010, p. 111). Flagship species are able to "capture the imagination of the public and induce people to support conservation action" (Walpole & Leader-Williams, 2002, p. 544), through, for example, financial donations, stewardship activities, and public support (Verissimo, Fraser, Groombridge, Bristol, & MacMillan, 2009). Thus, flagship species play a critical strategic and public relations role in civic engagement.

Last, civic engagement can be realized through citizen science, or a "method of integrating public outreach and scientific data collection locally, regionally, and across large geographic scales" (Cooper, Dickinson, Phillips, & Bonney, 2007, p. 1). With citizen science, agencies and organizations invite volunteer members of the public to participate in science projects using established methods. Data collected at limited spatial and temporal scales can be pooled to derive information across larger areas and time periods. For example, citizen science has been used effectively to monitor bird populations (e.g., breeding bird surveys, Christmas bird counts; Dunn, Cadman, & Falls, 1997). Citizen science encourages civic engagement by enlisting public participation in science projects that address matters of public interest, increasing public awareness, increasing scientific literacy of participants, and advancing scientific knowledge (Evans et al., 2005; Krasny & Bonney, 2005). These interwoven concepts of civic engagement, public support, flagship species, and citizen science are illustrated by the work of the CWSS, as described below.

Processes and outcomes

The most significant processes and outcomes from the CWSS include stakeholder involvement, baseline research, sustainable funding, weekly nature-education events during the summer months, and increased purple martin (the flagship species) populations. These outcomes culminated in the city undertaking a municipal greenspace planning process in 2011. In 2007 and 2012 the CWSS was also a finalist for an Alberta Emerald Award for environmental leadership, and was a winner in 2015. The discussion below will briefly explain these outcomes and how they relate to the frameworks of analysis for civic engagement.

The first major outcome is the development and maturation of a civil society organization into the CWSS, an Alberta-based registered society. The CWSS began in 2002 in an effort to address the issues of greenspace loss and fragmentation, lack of public awareness of greenspace and wildlife issues, and the lack of sufficient consideration of greenspace and wildlife issues in planning efforts. The vision for the work of the CWSS is "a greenspace network that enhances community values and quality of life for City of Camrose residents" accomplished by a comprehensive greenspace plan and ongoing community-based stewardship activities (Camrose Wildlife and Stewardship Society, 2015). The CWSS advocates community enrichment through an understanding and appreciation of greenspace. It achieves this through conducting nature-based education programs and stewardship projects, scientific research, and supporting and promoting responsible and sustainable greenspace planning and management. The CWSS provides advice (though not as an official advisory group) to the city, service to the community, and support to city staff working on greenspace and wildlife issues (e.g., through policy analyses and volunteer involvement). Since 2003 the CWSS has received an annual grant from the city to hire a staff person and to run its educational programs. This grant has been supplemented by donations from other local community groups to achieve a three-month hiring in the summer.

The CWSS builds on collaborative activities to promote community stewardship among project partners that represent several environmental NGOs, service clubs, municipal agencies, and educational institutions. These partners now include the Wildrose Outdoor Club, Ducks Unlimited Canada, the University of Alberta's Augustana Campus, Camrose Ski Club, Tourism Camrose, Camrose Rotary Club, Alberta Fish and Wildlife, Camrose and District Fish and Game Association, and the City of Camrose. These partners identified areas of common concern that can shape future collaboration, namely greenspace conservation, wildlife management, and outdoor recreation opportunities. The diverse partners are engaged in a form of social learning that has allowed common concerns to arise, sharing of available information, debate about possible solutions, and decisions to move forward.

Second, the CWSS engages with city staff in several ways to promote effective wildlife and greenspace planning and management. The CWSS prepared a preliminary wildlife stewardship plan and an annual budget in 2002, which were endorsed by city council. The coordinator inventoried and evaluated greenspace distribution (using a geographical information system [GIS]) and prepared development options for city staff. Building on these efforts, the city completed a comprehensive municipal greenspace plan in 2014. The CWSS implemented wildlife-enhancement projects for target species (e.g., nest boxes for purple martins) and assisted with city groups that had projects associated with other species (e.g., hummingbirds and butterflies). These processes highlight the role of civic ecology in that individuals affiliated with the CWSS engage in municipal planning, management, and governance processes associated with wildlife and greenspace issues.

Each summer the CWSS hires a coordinator to work on wildlife and greenspace stewardship projects, including weekly summer educational events for the public at a city-owned facility adjacent to a large greenspace area. These events helped catalyze, with leadership from the Camrose Rotary Club, the creation of the Four Seasons Environmental Centre, which hosts grade-school environmental education programs. The CWSS also helps with a variety of educational activities for children through local schools, summer camps, and special events. Many local businesses now support CWSS activities with donations (e.g., free advertising, beverages, and building supplies). The CWSS publishes weekly articles about stewardship topics in local newspapers and responds to many public inquiries. The level of support for these programs by residents, visitors, presenters, organizers, and local businesses illustrates neighbourhood civic participation through the concepts of self-interest (e.g., people wanting more wildlife will participate in wildlife-planning exercises) and personal efficacy (e.g., people with specific skills [wildlife, greenspace, organizational, presentation] are willing to contribute to the broader benefit of the city).

The CWSS also devotes considerable efforts toward a flagship species, the purple martin, which is a large swallow that depends almost completely on human-provided cavity nesting structures. The purple martin is a species of concern in Canada because of its reliance on these structures. Because martins are tolerant of people, they can be observed closely throughout their life cycle. This familiarity and interest has helped develop a subculture of martin enthusiasts in North America that maintains nesting boxes and records information about martin nesting (Tremblay & Hvenegaard, 2008). The CWSS raised funds to construct several "condominium-style" nesting boxes and now facilitates the Purple Martin Landlords, a group of about 20 volunteers who maintain city-owned nest boxes on city land near each landlord's house. These landlords are supported with information, equipment, and mentoring opportunities. A recent study of landlord motivations provided opportunities to maintain interest and increase management effectiveness (Tremblay & Hvenegaard, 2008). The project also educates other Camrose residents about their martin houses. The annual survey of purple martins shows the population has increased from 8 pairs in 2003 to 133 pairs in 2013 (with an all-time high of 177 in 2009; Hvenegaard & Trefry, 2011). In 2010 the CWSS started an annual Camrose Purple Martin Festival, attended by over 130 people in that year and 90 in 2011 (Trefry, 2010).

The purple martin serves as an effective flagship species and is extremely popular in North America for viewing and for assisting with nesting (Rempel & Hvenegaard, 2013). Because the purple martin is largely dependent on human-built nesting structures, they are tolerant of close human presence, so much so that they seem little disturbed by lowering of nesting structures or close inspection of nests. The purple martin is used for conservation marketing in many ways, such as insect control, close contact with nature, connecting with kids, and citizen science. The Purple Martin Landlords have increased support for purple martins and other wildlife in Camrose through their commitment, enthusiasm, citizen science, and innovative management strategies. Many landlords contribute significant amounts of volunteer hours and money to martin management (Tremblay & Hvenegaard, 2008). The purple martin has become the strategic "mascot" of the CWSS in terms of branding and marketing.

The Purple Martin Landlord program also promotes social learning through mentoring, social events, friendly competition, and citizen science (Tremblay & Hvenegaard, 2008). The North American Purple Martin

Conservation Association (PMCA) encourages landlords to collect purple martin data regarding arrival times, nesting success, and management issues (PMCA, 2011). The PMCA reaches out to the public through its website, regional organizations, local experts, and its magazine. Then the association encourages martin landlords to submit data for compilation and assessment at the continent scale. Many Camrose landlords are eager participants in this citizen-science program and derive benefit from the data produced, such as the expected timing of purple martin events in the future. Landlords also derive satisfaction from contributing personally to the larger martin research efforts (Hvenegaard & Fraser, 2014).

Third, to minimize wildlife conflicts, the CWSS evaluated current management practices that affect wildlife, their habitat, and people (e.g., "nuisance" wildlife policies, habitat naturalization). For example, the best management practices produced by the CWSS for "nuisance" or "pest" species have been used locally and by other jurisdictions (Macklin, 2003). The CWSS also serves as a clearinghouse for all greenspace and wildlife issues by advising on, for example, a proposed deer cull, beaver management concerns, and a bridge proposal that would negatively impact greenspace. In this way, the CWSS serves an administrative and educational function on behalf of the city, thus contributing to social learning within public and municipal networks.

Fourth, the CWSS conducts research and monitoring to promote sound and sustainable decisions about wildlife and greenspace. In its first year, the CWSS conducted a benchmark study on bird populations that will be repeated in future years to provide comparable data over time. This study analyzed bird diversity among habitat types that help city managers effectively evaluate potential biodiversity impacts resulting from development and management decisions. In summary, the average species richness was 37 along the riparian areas, 26 in aspen forests, 23 in grasslands, 9 in industrial areas, and 5 in new residential areas (Elliott, Hvenegaard, & Barr, 2002). Since birds are useful indicators of biodiversity in general (Chace & Walsh, 2006), these results can help improve municipal planning for environmental sustainability (Fernandez-Juricic & Jokimaki, 2001). The CWSS also conducted surveys of beaver, fox, and deer, assisted with a black knot fungus inventory, helped with mosquito trapping to document the spread of West Nile virus, and prepared natural and aquatic greenspace maps. Again, while these studies are conducted by biologists and university students, they provide opportunities for civic engagement by skilled volunteers or employees.

The CWSS also found a high level of support for wildlife among Camrose residents. First, in August 2002, surveys were sent along with the city utility bills to solicit public use of, interest in, and support for wildlife in the city. Based on a random sample of Camrose residents (202 respondents), 93% enjoy watching wildlife from their home or on an outing, 76% attracted wildlife to their property, 93% would support wildlife stewardship projects, 33% would volunteer for wildlife stewardship projects, and 17% would sponsor wildlife stewardship projects (Elliott et al., 2002). Second, there is a growing number of letters to the editor of the local paper and inquiries from the public to city officials about greenspace topics. Third, organizers of the Tourism Camrose website indicate that their most commonly visited page is one provided by the CWSS on bird watching around Camrose. The high levels of support for stewardship projects, volunteering, or sponsoring indicate great potential for increasing current levels of civic engagement. How much civic engagement increases will depend on identifying individuals with specific interests and skills, and then matching them with relevant and satisfying opportunities. The high levels of satisfaction among the Purple Martin Landlords (Tremblay & Hvenegaard, 2008) and other CWSS volunteers (e.g., CWSS leaders and the Camrose Purple Martin Festival volunteers) indicate some success because the landlords and other volunteers were well-matched to the work they do as volunteers.

Drivers of the process

The key change we have observed in Camrose is enhanced public involvement in, and supportive attitudes toward, wildlife and greenspace issues. We base this conclusion on sustained CWSS activities over ten years, growing involvement of community organizations and local businesses, ongoing financial support from various sponsors, and increased involvement in promoting the flagship species. There are a few key reasons behind this change. First, early in the project, the CWSS was able to select a flagship species that gave the group an opportunity to identify tangible goals, achieve significant successes, provide benefits to other species and habitats, and serve as a catalyst for education and community support. The interactions between landlords and martins generate a positive public profile of martins in particular, and of wildlife and greenspace in general.

Second, CWSS members have important connections, experiences, and skills to benefit the society and its programs. Members were connected to business and municipal leaders, which allow for better understanding of how communities and municipal governments work and help uncover resources that are needed for the project (e.g., networks, office space, student employees). CWSS members also have substantial experience with community organizations, allowing them to encourage citizen engagement and timely volunteer involvement. In addition, CWSS members have skills in wildlife management and conservation that increase credibility in the process and results.

Third, Camrose residents have a growing desire for knowledge about environmental topics and a need to become personally involved in sustainability projects. This level of interest is demonstrated by the steady participation in the summer environmental education events, growing supply of volunteers for the Purple Martin Landlord program, participation in special tree- or wildflower-planting projects, and involvement in related public meetings (e.g., debates over public use of greenspace).

Fourth, from the beginning of the project, it was possible to create a common vision among partners that was supported by dedicated and energetic volunteers. For example, the long-term collaborative partnerships among organizations and volunteers are important to the success of the project. Early on, the CWSS developed a productive relationship with city staff and the city council that has not only promoted a positive attitude toward wildlife and greenspace but also toward environmental topics in general. A partner (University of Alberta) has enhanced project activities by directing undergraduate research projects on key topics (e.g., beaver distribution, bird diversity, managing Purple Martin Landlords). Overall, this project embraces a collaborative, team-based approach with the support of many agencies and individuals in the community. The project supports existing activities, develops innovations, links long- and short-term action, and strives for effective, long-term planning.

At present, the project has had an impact at the local scale, in terms of growing purple martin populations and awareness among Camrose and area residents. At the regional scale, the CWSS events attract people from across east-central Alberta and serve as a catalyst to explore other nearby attractions, thus leading to further local tourism benefits (Hvenegaard, 2011). At an international level, the purple martins will provide ecosystem benefits along their migratory routes and at their wintering sites. The CWSS's purple martin program was profiled at the 2011 international conference of the Purple Martin Conservation Association in Pennsylvania.

How can the success of this project be scaled up for greater impact or transferred to other communities? A key possibility is to transfer the lessons learned to other locations. To that end, other municipalities in Alberta (e.g., Lakeland County, Town of Bonnyville) have examined how CWSS strategies can be implemented elsewhere. Representatives of nearby communities have asked the CWSS to provide advice about stewardship initiatives and community engagement. Furthermore, the CWSS can engage in important reciprocal support with other stewardship groups (e.g., Ellis Bird Farm near Lacombe and Kerry Wood Nature Centre in Red Deer) in Alberta. Moreover, those involved are willing to share research about stewardship issues such as bird monitoring, Purple Martin Landlord motivations (Tremblay & Hvenegaard, 2008), purple martin populations (Hvenegaard, 2005; Hvenegaard & Trefry, 2011), and beaver activities (Loates & Hvenegaard, 2008). Finally, the CWSS is hosting an annual Camrose Purple Martin Festival with hopes of providing ongoing conservation, educational, community, and economic benefits (e.g., Hvenegaard & Manaloor, 2007).

Lessons learned

Since its inception, members of the CWSS have learned several broad lessons about leadership and stewardship activities in the context of sustainable urban communities. First, diverse partnerships, in terms of resources, expertise, and connections, have been essential in creating the project's public profile. Without these partnerships, the work of the CWSS would proceed very slowly and may have stagnated due to limited resources.

Second, the CWSS continually pushes for greater municipal responsibility of the project; a sustainable internal infrastructure is critical for long-term progress, and the CWSS needs to be patient and persistent. Ongoing reliance on volunteer leadership helps initiate and advise projects such as the CWSS, but institutional support is required, at some point, to take charge of the administrative duties. The CWSS has been able to carve out positions that simultaneously attract and maintain institutional support, and help the CWSS with its administrative needs.

Third, public education has been and continues to be necessary to generate a broad constituency of support for stewardship activities. Attendance at the weekly environmental education events ranges widely, but a committed core of people attends regularly. The CWSS hopes that all attendees, whether they have low or high levels of knowledge, become active in greenspace and wildlife management activities and contribute to the greenspace-planning process.

Fourth, the CWSS capitalizes on high-profile events to raise public awareness of wildlife and greenspace issues. For example, prominent environmentalists give talks as guest speakers, simultaneously generating media attention. In addition, the CWSS was a finalist for the Alberta Emerald Awards (for environmental excellence in the community group category) in 2007 and 2012, and was a winner in 2015. In 2008 a proposal to build a bridge across Mirror Lake in Camrose generated a significant amount of attention for greenspace issues. Attention derived from each of these events helped convince the city of the need for developing its municipal Green Space Master Plan.

Fifth, choosing the purple martin as a flagship species helped the CWSS to focus on activities with measurable gains. The CWSS has succeeded in receiving funding from several sources (e.g., Ross Agri, Alberta Conservation Association, Canadian Tire, Camrose and Region Fish and Game Association) because of the tangible benefits perceived to come from supporting martin populations. In turn, these relationships have developed into partnerships that help strengthen and broaden the project. For example, the martin project has expanded into the nearby County of Camrose, and the CWSS has a very good relationship with the Fish and Game Association in managing the project.

Sixth, instead of rushing into action, the CWSS planned activities carefully and conducted critical baseline research in its first year of operation. This research focused on people's attitudes toward and involvement in stewardship activities with current wildlife populations. This information was important in highlighting the issues that needed to be addressed and the opportunities available for future stewardship activities. In addition, the CWSS conducted a visioning exercise in 2008 to ensure an ongoing focus on common goals and collaborative tasks.

Seventh, the CWSS has learned that any stewardship project needs key people to lead and be champions for the cause. Aside from being resourceful, often using local experts, experiences from nearby municipalities, and in-kind donations (e.g., advertising, office space, and printing), the CWSS relies on prominent citizens to be spokespeople for various aspects of the project. For example, many people play key roles in terms of the martin project, baseline research, conservation advice, administrative support, and marketing.

Conclusion

As the City of Camrose proceeds to implement its municipal Green Space Master Plan, the CWSS hopes to engage citizens even further in the process. The CWSS will promote participation and explain the implications of implementing the plan. This greenspace plan needs to be integrated within other, related city plans (e.g., development, sustainability, transportation, recreation). The CWSS hopes that the weekly environmental activities and the Camrose Purple Martin Festival will generate significant local and regional interest for enhanced stewardship participation. Members continue to push for greater integration of greenspace issues, wildlife management, and stewardship activities into municipal administration (e.g., Patterson et al., 2003). The CWSS seeks to integrate the volunteer activities of other community groups engaging in environmental activities (e.g., Rotary Club developing a local environmental centre, neighbouring municipalities, watershed groups). The CWSS is strengthening its ties with tourism organizations to enhance promotional activities. Finally, there are plans to conduct research on public attitudes, stewardship involvement, and ecological indicators to aid in planning and management decisions (Alvey, 2006; Mahon & Miller, 2003). Overall, the CWSS envisions strong partnerships with other groups in the areas of education, research, and stewardship projects.

Based on the outcomes, drivers, and lessons learned by the CWSS, we can make a few connections between the group and the conceptual frameworks mentioned earlier. First, the CWSS has employed civic engagement (Tuxill et al., 2009) through its efforts of generating support for its activities, learning through its educational events, action for stewardship, advocacy for greenspace issues, and volunteerism in the Purple Martin Landlord program. Second, the CWSS understands the notion of neighbourhood civic participation (Greenberg, 2001), in that CWSS volunteers work on community projects for the broader social good (e.g., future generations, community greenspaces) as well as for self-interest (e.g., personal enjoyment, learning from wildlife). In addition, personal efficacy has been significant in drawing on leaders and volunteers for various tasks. Third, the CWSS offers activities that support individual values, desires, and decisions to engage with nature; collectively these actions generate wildlife and greenspace benefits for all and support the notion of civic ecology (Krasny & Tidball, 2009a). Fourth, social learning (Krasny & Tidball, 2009b) has occurred among the diverse set of individuals and organizations associated with the CWSS, as people collaborate on its vision, objectives, and activities. Fifth, the purple martin (the CWSS's flagship species) has captured the imagination of many active and passive supporters in the community and beyond, allowing Camrose to develop as a nature tourism destination and mentor city for other interested municipalities. Last, some local residents, through the Purple Martin Landlord program, have embraced citizen science by contributing knowledge, becoming even more engaged in greenspace and wildlife stewardship. All of these activities have demonstrated civic engagement in this unique context.

Community support and civic engagement rely on a public that is informed, inspired, and invited to participate in relevant activities. Constructive interactions on critical issues among the interested public, relevant organizations, and the municipal government will improve the problem-solving abilities of all concerned (Saltmarsh, 2008). Community engagement in stewardship activities is crucial to long-term sustainability in many areas, including wildlife and greenspace (Portney, 2005). The involvement of diverse individuals and community partners has helped increase success of the stewardship programs (Shandas & Messer, 2008). Understanding the conceptual foundations of community support and civic engagement can help develop more effective programs, identify individuals to contribute, improve satisfaction with the process, and promote long-term success.

Authors' note

We thank past summer stewardship coordinators for their work in implementing CWSS activities. We also thank past and current members of the CWSS for their financial and logistical support. We thank the many local and provincial businesses and organizations for their helpful, direct, and in-kind support. Nhial Tiitmamer Kur provided helpful research assistance.

References

Alberta Urban Municipalities Association (AUMA). (2011). Municipal sustainability in action. Retrieved May 4, 2011, from http://msp2010.auma.ca/.

Alvey, A. A. (2006). Promoting and preserving biodiversity in the urban forest. *Urban Forestry & Urban Greening, 5*, 195–201.

Burns, S., Sperry, C., & Hodgson, R. (2003). People and fire in western Colorado: Methods of engaging stakeholders. In P. N. Omi & L. N. Joyce (Eds.), *Fire, fuel treatments, and ecological restoration: Conference proceedings* (pp. 213–224). Fort Collins, CO: USDA Forest Service, Rocky Mountain Research Station.

Camrose Wildlife and Stewardship Society (2015). Camrose wildlife and greenspace stewardship project. Retrieved May 13, 2015, from Alberta Emerald Foundation, http://emeraldfoundation.ca/aef_awards/camrose-wildlife-and-greenspace-stewardship-project/.

Chace, J. F., & Walsh, J. J. (2006). Urban effects on native avifauna: A review. *Landscape and Urban Planning, 74*, 46–69.

Chapin, F. S., Kofinas, G. P., & Folke, C. (2009). *Principles of ecosystem steward-ship: Resilience-based natural resource management in a changing world.* New York: Springer.

Chiesura, A. (2004). The role of urban parks for the sustainable city. *Landscape and Urban Planning, 68*, 129–138.

City of Camrose (2010). *Municipal sustainability plan 2010*. Camrose, AB: The City of Camrose.

———. (2011). *City of Camrose 2011 census*. Camrose, AB: The City of Camrose.

Cooper, C. B., Dickinson, J., Phillips, T., & Bonney, R. (2007). Citizen science as a tool for conservation in residential ecosystems. *Ecology & Society, 12*(2), 1–11.

Davies, R. G., Barbosa, O., Fuller, R. A., Tratalos, J., Burke, N., Lewis, D.,... Gaston, K. J. (2008). City-wide relationships between green spaces, urban land use and topography. *Urban Ecosystems, 11*, 269–287.

Dunn, E. H., Cadman, M. D., & Falls, J. B. (Eds.). (1997). *Monitoring bird populations: The Canadian experience*. Canadian Wildlife Service Occasional Paper Number 95. Ottawa, ON: Minister of Public Works and Government Services Canada.

Elliott, C., Hvenegaard, G., & Barr, M. (2002). *Greenspace and wildlife stewardship plan.* Camrose, AB: City of Camrose Wildlife Stewardship Planning Committee.

Evans, C., Abrams, E., Reitsma, R., Roux, K., Salmonsen, L., and Marra, P. P. (2005). The neighborhood nestwatch program: Participant outcomes of a citizen-science ecological research project. *Conservation Biology, 19,* 589–594.

Fernandez-Juricic, E., & Jokimaki, J. (2001). A habitat island approach to conserving birds in urban landscapes: Case studies from southern and northern Europe. *Biodiversity and Conservation, 10,* 2023–2043.

Government of Alberta. (2008). *Water for life: A renewal.* Edmonton, AB: Government of Alberta.

Greenberg, M. R. (2001). Elements and test of a theory of neighborhood civic participation. *Human Ecology Review, 8*(2), 40–50.

Gruber, J. S. (2010). Key principles of community-based natural resource management: A synthesis and interpretation of identified effective approaches for managing the commons. *Environmental Management, 45,* 52–66.

Hvenegaard, G. (2005). Camrose becomes purple martin–friendly. *Edmonton Nature News, 2*(4), 24.

———. (2011). *Birding and nature hotspots around Camrose.* Retrieved May 4, 2011, from Tourism Camrose, http://www.tourismcamrose.com/attachments/view/283/birding_and_nature_hotspots_around_camrose_2011_january_3.pdf.

Hvenegaard, G. T., & Barr, M. (2010). Protecting green spaces in urban areas in oil-rich Alberta. Retrieved May 4, 2011, from Leadership for Environment and Development in Focus, http://www.lead.org/page/544.

Hvenegaard, G. T., & Fraser, L. (2014). Motivations and benefits for citizen scientists engaged in purple martin migration research. *Human Dimensions of Wildlife, 19,* 561–563.

Hvenegaard, G. T., & Manaloor, V. (2007). A comparative approach to analyzing local expenditures and visitor profiles of two wildlife festivals. *Event Management, 10*(4), 231–239.

Hvenegaard, G. T., & Trefry, L. (2011). Integrated purple martin conservation in Camrose, Alberta, Canada. *Purple Martin Update, 29*(1), 22–24.

James, P., Tzoulas, K., Adams, M. D., Barber, A., Box, J., Breuste, J.,... Ward Thompson, C. (2009). Towards an integrated understanding of green space in the European built environment. *Urban Forestry & Urban Greening, 8,* 65–75.

Konisky, D. M., & Beierle, T. C. (2001). Innovations in public participation and environmental decision making: Examples from the great lakes region. *Society & Natural Resources, 14*(9), 815–26.

Krasny, M., & Bonney, R. (2005). Environmental education through citizen science and participatory action research. In E. A. Johnson & M. J. Mappin (Eds.),

Environmental education or advocacy: Changing perspectives of ecology and education (pp. 292–319). Cambridge, UK: Cambridge University Press.

Krasny, M. E., & Tidball, G. K. (2009a). Applying a resilience systems framework to urban environmental education. *Environmental Education Research, 15*, 465–482.

———. (2009b). Community gardens as contexts for science, stewardship, and civic action learning: The Garden Mosaics example. *Cities and the Environment, 2*(1), Article 8. Retrieved May 4, 2011, from Cities and the Environment, http://escholarship.bc.edu/cgi/viewcontent.cgi?article=1037&context=cate.

Land Stewardship Resource Centre. (2011). *Stewardship.* Retrieved May 4, 2011, from Land Stewardship Resource Centre, http://www.landstewardship.org/stewardship/.

Loates, B. M., & Hvenegaard, G. T. (2008). The density of beaver (*Castor canadensis*) activities along Camrose Creek, Alberta within differing habitats and management intensity levels. *Canadian Field-Naturalist, 122*(4), 299–302.

Louv, R. (2005). *Last child in the woods: Saving our children from nature-deficit disorder.* Chapel Hill, NC: Algonquin Books of Chapel Hill.

Macklin, P. (2003). *Final report of the 2003 Camrose wildlife stewardship coordinator.* Unpublished report. Camrose, AB: City of Camrose.

Mahon, J. R., & Miller, R. W. (2003). Identifying high-value greenspace prior to land development. *Journal of Arboriculture, 29*(1), 25–33.

Miles, I., Sullivan, W., & Kuo, F. (1998). Ecological restoration volunteers: The benefits of participation. *Urban Ecosystems, 2*, 27–41.

Natural Regions Committee. (2006). *Natural regions and subregions of Alberta.* Compiled by D. J. Downing & W. W. Pettapiece. Publication Number T/852. Edmonton, AB: Government of Alberta.

Patterson, M. E., Montag, J. M., & Williams, D. R. (2003). The urbanization of wildlife management: Social science, conflict, and decision making. *Urban Forestry & Urban Greening, 1*, 171–183.

Portney, K. (2005). Civic engagement and sustainable cities in the United States. *Public Administration Review, 65*(5), 579–591.

Purple Martin Conservation Association (PMCA). (2011). PMCA research & conservation. Retrieved May 4, 2011, from PMCA, http://purplemartin.org/main/research.html.

Rempel, S., & Hvenegaard, G. T. (2013). Can purple martins be used as flagship species for wildlife conservation? *Purple Martin Update, 22*(3), 18–21.

Robson, M., & Parkins, J. R. (2010). Taking the pulse of civic engagement in forest management. *Forestry Chronicle, 86*(6), 692–696.

Saltmarsh, J. (2008). Why Dewey matters. *Good Society Journal, 17*(2), 63–68.

Shandas, V., & Messer, W. B. (2008). Fostering green communities through civic engagement: Community-based environmental stewardship in the Portland area. *Journal of the American Planning Association, 74*(4), 408–418.

Smith, A. M., & Sutton, S. G. (2008). The role of a flagship species in the formation of conservation intentions. *Human Dimensions of Wildlife, 13*, 127–140.

The Constitution Act (British North America Act). (1867). Section 92 and 92A. 30–31 Victoria, c. 3, UK.

Timoney, K., & Lee, P. (2001). Environmental management in resource-rich Alberta, Canada: First world jurisdiction, third world analogue? *Journal of Environmental Management, 63*, 387–405.

Trefry, L. (2010). *2010 Camrose wildlife and stewardship society wildlife and green-space stewardship project report.* Unpublished report. Camrose, AB: City of Camrose.

Tremblay, C. A., & Hvenegaard, G. T. (2008). For me or the Martins? Motivations for being a Purple Martin Landlord. *Purple Martin Update* (Summer), 2–5.

Tuxill, J. L., Mitchell, N. J., and Clark, D. (2009). *Stronger together: A manual on the principles and practices of civic engagement.* Woodstock, VT: Conservation Study Institute.

Van Herzele, A., & Wiedemann, T. (2003). A monitoring tool for the provision of accessible and attractive urban green spaces. *Landscape and Urban Planning, 63*(2), 109–126.

Verissimo, D., Fraser, I., Groombridge, J., Bristol, R., & MacMillan, D.C. (2009). Birds as flagship species: A case study of tropical islands. *Animal Conservation, 12*, 549–558.

Verissimo, D., MacMillan, D.C., & Smith, R.J. (2010). Toward a systematic approach for identifying conservation flagships. *Conservation Letters, 4*, 1–8.

Walpole, M.J., & Leader-Williams, N. (2002). Tourism and flagship species in conservation. *Biodiversity and Conservation, 11*, 543–547.

Wilson, E.O. (1984). *Biophilia.* Cambridge, MA: Harvard University Press.

FOUR

Peaks and Valleys on the Prairies

Optimism and Resistance to Sustainable Community Development in Craik, Saskatchewan

Sean Connelly, Kelly Green, Sean Markey, and Mark Roseland

Introduction

Economic and political restructuring over the past 25 years, accompanied by less interventionist federal and provincial governments and offloading of responsibility to municipal governments, has increasingly placed the responsibility for community development in the hands of individual communities (McAllister, 2004). Economic restructuring presents a daunting challenge, but it also offers opportunities to re-envision and reshape our communities. Canadian communities can plan for the future in an integrated manner where there is recognition and incorporation of a greater diversity of criteria (social, environmental, and economic) beyond territorial expansion and conventional economic development. Sustainable community development represents both a conceptual and practical process that helps facilitate and guide integrated planning, improve public participation, and generate creative and practical solutions to address shared economic, environmental, and social problems (Connelly, Markey, & Roseland, 2009).

Faced with the economic and population decline common throughout rural Saskatchewan, the Town of Craik realized that something had to be done that would draw attention to the town in a positive sense and raise its profile. Influential outsiders provided the catalyst for Craik by embracing sustainability in response to the need for community revitalization. Rather than embarking on traditional economic development initiatives in competition with surrounding towns (e.g., free land, town marketing, and highway-oriented development), leaders in the community became convinced that sustainable community development provided the key to long-term stability and rural revitalization. In 2003 the town and rural municipality worked together in cooperation with community members under the Craik Sustainable Living Project (CSLP) to build an eco-centre and plan for an eco-village development designed to raise the profile of Craik, spur more environmentally conscious economic development, and provide a model for sustainable living for other rural communities.

Craik provides an inspiring but cautionary example of a community sustainability project. On the one hand, Craik's achievements were made possible with the aid of external expertise and support, as well as through strong community ties (social capital), attachment to place and sense of pride that generated a capacity for change through volunteerism, community leadership, and collective action. On the other hand, resulting changes to the status quo were not universally embraced by all members of the community, which resulted in a change of elected officials. Subsequent lack of political support to follow through with sustainability initiatives left project champions feeling frustrated and disillusioned. As the project stalled, residents further questioned and criticized a sustainable-community development approach, particularly in the context of a newly invigorated and booming Saskatchewan economy. As a result of this growing sentiment, enthusiastic newcomers, drawn to the community as a result of the emphasis on sustainability, faced challenges fitting in and were surprised and frustrated to find that sustainability was in fact not being embraced by the whole community. These tensions took their toll on family and community relationships, with many newcomers moving away.

Despite the challenges and pitfalls, the eco-village continues to expand, the town continues to attract new businesses and residents,[1] and, perhaps most important, the town still offers a glimmer of hope and inspiration to other communities looking to make a positive change. The Craik example provides valuable lessons in the importance of linking tangible physical demonstration projects with investments in social infrastructure: capacity building, discussion of values, trust, and community cohesion.

Drawing from the CSLP, the purpose of this chapter is to identify strategies for moving from physical infrastructure development to building social infrastructure for sustainable community development. Our research identifies the importance of fostering and maintaining the social infrastructure of communities as investments are made to transform physical infrastructure demonstration projects to a platform and trajectory for sustainability. For CSLP members, understanding the peaks and valleys of community involvement and action was a critical, strategic response to change. In this chapter we will briefly highlight some important challenges that arose from moving from sustainability planning to implementation, provide some more detail on the CSLP, and analyze the strategies those involved with the CSLP used to generate physical and social infrastructure investments. We hope that understanding the project in the context of the peaks and valleys of enthusiasm and resistance provides important lessons for how other rural communities can take steps toward sustainable community development.

Sustainable development challenge

Sustainable development is a concept that has achieved widespread recognition following the publication of *Our Common Future* (Brundtland, 1987). While this publication galvanized and elevated attention to matters of the environment, economy, society, it did little to provide direction regarding the appropriate balance between sustainability on the one hand and development on the other. Despite the diverse and contested meanings attached to concepts of sustainability, they all fundamentally begin with the recognition of the mismatch between increasing human demands on Earth and the ability of finite natural systems to cope with those demands (Williams & Millington, 2004).

In very broad terms, the diverse perspectives of sustainable development and related responses to environmental problems can be placed along a continuum from weak to strong sustainability (Hamstead & Quinn, 2005; Williams & Millington, 2004). Those who adopt a process that promotes weak sustainability view the environment-economy challenge largely as an issue of supply. They prioritize the economy and economic growth over ecosystem integrity while seeking to meet sustainability objectives through technological efficiency and investments in "greener" physical infrastructure. The assumption here is that sustainability can be achieved primarily through investments that make the products and services we use greener (e.g., hybrid cars) without addressing the need for those products in the first place (i.e., reducing demand for automobile use). Conversely, those who uphold processes that privilege strong sustainability challenge the material intensity of demand and view a healthy economy as fundamentally dependent upon ecosystem integrity and carrying capacity. From a strong sustainability perspective, well-being can be enhanced through development of different forms of community capital (social, human, cultural, physical, economic, and natural) (Roseland, 2012) and not just through quantitative measures of growth, wealth, and consumption. Recognition of finite limits to growth, collective action, and social innovation are at the core of the strong sustainability perspective, where solutions to local and global environmental problems are rooted in social rather than technological change (Rees, 1995). This is not to say that investments in technology, resource efficiency, and attention to physical infrastructure are not important, but investments in social infrastructure are also required, especially those that can support fundamental changes to individual values regarding the relationship between people and their environment.

Sustainability literature suggests that it is through participatory processes that sustainable solutions to community problems can be collectively determined and implemented (Berke, 2002; Bulkeley, 2006; Conroy & Berke, 2004; Roseland, 2012) and that the tensions between diverse and contested views of sustainability can be addressed through this process. However, research on sustainability initiatives indicates that there are considerable challenges in moving from a discussion of sustainability as a concept to actual transition to a more sustainable community. This gap between conceptual understandings of sustainability and implementation is multifaceted and involves a lack of coherent dialogue about the meaning of sustainability, lack of congruence between different political levels, a lack of political will to change the status quo, and lack of a shared sustainable-development ethos between levels of government and community stakeholders (Dale, 2001; Evans, Joas, Sundback, & Theobald, 2005).

From a structural perspective, the implementation of complex and integrated initiatives associated with sustainability often involves changes in relationships between participants and shifts in power. First, there is an inherent conflict between sustainable community-development processes and principles that focus on collaborative problem solving and participatory approaches while local restructuring processes place greater emphasis on economic networks and private-sector initiatives (Harvey, 1989; Healey, Cameron, Davoudi, Graham, and Madani-Pour, 1995; McAllister, 2004; Osborne & Gaebler, 1993). Second, governance structures often have difficulty integrating formal institutional processes with grassroots initiatives (van Bueren & ten Heuvelhof, 2005), presenting challenges for citizen engagement and social capacity development (Dale & Onyx, 2005; Rydin & Pennington, 2000). Other structural barriers to implementation include the dominant conventional economic rationale, bureaucracy inertia, and the perception that change is unnecessary without a crisis, all of which prevents multiple bottom-line decision making based on a different way of valuing options (Adger et al., 2003).

Related to these structural barriers are the procedural challenges associated with effective multi-stakeholder processes (Clapp & Meyer, 2000; Conroy & Berke, 2004; Gibbs & Jonas, 2000; Mercer & Jotkowitz, 2000; Parkinson & Roseland, 2002; Portney, 2003), navigating the complexity of local sustainability initiatives (Bulkeley, 2006; Guy & Marvin, 1999; Morrison, 2006), and building the capacity of municipal decision makers to link short-term problems with long-term sustainability solutions (Blair & Evans, 2004; Brugmann, 1994; Campbell, 1996; Evans et al., 2005; Newman & Verpraet, 1999; Parkinson & Roseland, 2002).

The CSLP highlights the tensions between the strong and weak approaches to sustainability and highlights these structural and procedural challenges in terms of maintaining political support and citizen engagement as the project shifts in emphasis from providing the physical to social infrastructure for sustainability. In the following section, we look at the CSLP as a case study that illustrates the importance and challenge of investments in physical and social infrastructure for sustainable community development. The case study and subsequent analysis are based on a comprehensive literature review, semi-structured interviews with key stakeholders in 2007, and a review of local secondary sources. One of the authors had firsthand experience with the CSLP, having moved to Craik in 2008 as a result of commitments made to sustainability.

The Craik Sustainable Living Project

The catalyst for the CSLP was Dr. Lynn Oliphant, professor emeritus of the University of Saskatchewan and founding member of the Prairie Institute for Human Ecology. He presented his vision of building an eco-village that captured the interest of members of the councils of the Town of Craik and the Rural Municipality (RM) of Craik (representing the region). In 2001 they joined forces with interested community members to establish a community-based sustainability project that would bring attention to the town, thus attracting new residents and businesses, and provide a model for sustainable living for other rural communities. With support from the town and RM councils, the CSLP was established as a volunteer-based community organization that would be responsible for organizing, planning, and establishing sustainability initiatives in Craik. There are four components to the CSLP project: (a) community outreach and education, (b) community action, (c) an eco-centre demonstration building, and (d) the development of an eco-village. Each of these components relied on volunteer commitments from CSLP members and were identified as a means to raise awareness of sustainability issues, to demonstrate local action, and to build capacity for the ultimate goal of building an eco-village.

In terms of community outreach and education, ongoing initiatives have been undertaken to establish a collection of sustainability reference materials for the local library, and to host an annual solar fair to showcase green initiatives and a series of workshops to demonstrate various techniques and strategies to reduce environmental impact. Examples of community action include an anti-idling campaign, a community-wide compost project, a 4-H sustainability club, a sacred spaces initiative to bring multiple faith-based groups together to address sustainability, an interpretive nature-trail program, and a tree-planting program. While these initiatives are important and have contributed to increased awareness of the CSLP, it was the building of the eco-centre and eco-village that drew widespread (local to international) attention to Craik as a community that was approaching rural-development challenges differently.

The CSLP developed the eco-centre first as a tangible demonstration project. The centre features innovative, energy-efficient building design and integrated heating, cooling, and electrical systems. Passive solar design and the use of heat sinks and ground-source heat exchange provide for most of the building's heating and cooling needs. Water and waste water are collected and treated on site and composting toilets are used for human waste. Building materials consist of recycled local materials such as straw bales and timbers and bricks from local demolitions. The eco-centre serves as a restaurant, meeting space, local-product gift shop, and club house for the adjacent municipal golf course.[2]

Funding for the eco-centre relied on public investments from the town reserve fund and a $100,000 grant and $150,000 loan from the Federation of Canadian Municipalities (FCM) Green Municipal Fund. The project also relied on external, alternative-building expertise, local hired labourers, local and external volunteers, and was aided by a variety of successful, local, fundraising activities (e.g., "Buy a Bale" and a "Green Lottery" that raised $40,000, corporate and organizational sponsorship, and in-kind contributions).

At the heart of the CSLP was a plan to develop an eco-village across the highway from the main community. The eco-village currently consists of 15 residential lots that were made available by the rural municipality. These lots are in various stages of construction, with some already fully developed. The lots are provided unserviced and cost $1 (plus an additional six cents for federal tax). The low purchase price was designed to create an incentive for sustainable housing, loosely defined as being energy efficient and unserviced, to be developed by prospective owners. It is expected that owners will provide their own heat, power, and water and handle sewage and waste water on site. Owners are to start construction within one year of purchasing the lot. In addition, the municipality has made available two-hectare parcels of agricultural land on lease to each lot for eco-business activities that conform to sustainability principles. Plans for the eco-village have been pragmatic and rely on a simple set of criteria to assess the viability and sustainability of development proposals. Those who wish to develop a lot must describe on a simple, two-page form how their home would address energy efficiency in an innovative manner and indicate how heat, power, potable water, sewage, and waste water would be dealt with in an eco-friendly manner.

Peaks: Investments in physical infrastructure for sustainability

The real strength of the CSLP rests with its ability to place sustainability on the agenda as a response to community decline. The link between sustainability and community revitalization provided a project platform that appealed to a cross section of people in the community. The CSLP attempted to define sustainability in very practical and pragmatic terms by focusing on community liveability and resilience, leading to the participation of people from across the political spectrum. The CSLP steering committee had access to local and external expertise to help facilitate project development and access to funding. It was hoped that residents would be able to see the broader developmental benefits of adopting and implementing a vision of sustainability for their community, thereby building capacity and support for further sustainability initiatives.

> There was a feeling that something had to be done, luckily we were able to put our issues in a sustainability context, and then the local councils, and others as well, bought in and took a leadership role, and we have what we have currently. (CSLP member)

Initially, the mayor and councillors who identified with and supported the CSLP received strong electoral support from residents, which provided them with the security they needed to take risks and be innovative. Having political support was critical for changing the perception in the community that sustainability, eco-buildings, and eco-villages were risky, "wing-nut" ideas. The challenge is to have a coherent, long-term vision for change (Parkinson & Roseland, 2002). Sustainability literature refers to the importance of public participation as being critical, particularly in shifting perceptions of innovations for sustainability as being untested and risky (Mercer & Jotkowitz, 2000). The CSLP benefitted from having the right people involved at the right time and in leadership positions with a "learn as we go" mentality.

> It's a council with a vision of more than most politicians, you know, that four-year mentality. These guys think 10 or 20, and a

> couple of the guys said, too, when the decision was made to do this, it was not totally popular with everybody. You know, people weren't convinced, and some of them said, "You know, they put me on council to do what I think is right. I think this is right, and if they don't elect me again, fine. I'm going to do the best I can do for my four years." And everybody that ran again got elected again. (Craik resident)

Leadership figures in the community were able to mobilize community interest and commitment to the CSLP and eco-centre more broadly by focusing energy and investments on a tangible, physical project. Having the eco-centre as a tangible demonstration project provided an opportunity for all community members with a diversity of skills (planning, finance, construction, etc.)—as one interviewee described "the doers and the thinkers"—to engage with the project. While a small segment of the community drove the process, they were able to pull the rest of the community along and were able to draw on an understanding of the community context, the people, the history, and the do-it-yourself mentality that exists in the town.

> It raised the awareness of the rest of the people, even the people on the committee. Because when it all started, it was being driven by Lynn Oliphant, basically, because he is the guy that had the passion and understood the environmental swing of it, and being involved in it now, it's spread out into our community. I would say over 50% of our population, anyway, have an environmental slant to their thoughts now that they never had before. (CSLP member)

The CSLP were able to rely on local volunteer labour, a sense of community responsibility and initiative, and local resources to get the eco-centre built.

> Obviously there's a lot of volunteer help, a lot of people have come out and worked on the building, which is what you get in a small community. You know, you're not going to be getting large sums of capital. We do a lot of tours on the building, and people

> say, "That just wouldn't happen in another community," nobody would work for nothing, you know, you have to pay them, and it just gets out of hand, the cost of it. (CSLP member)

The use of the eco-centre as a demonstration project was another key factor of success. Having a tangible and visible outcome that people could point to as an example made the longer-term vision and goals of the CSLP concrete.

> So that was a major decision, to look at, number one, to get something on the ground for people to come and see, and experience, to show we were serious, to inspire other communities and the community. (CSLP member)

Having a visible demonstration of sustainability alternatives provided the CSLP with the opportunity to scale up the project and link it to broader activities in the town and in the region. Rather than having a planning document that outlined sustainability goals, the CSLP had a building. In the context of a community in decline, any new construction was seen as a symbol of rejuvenation, renewal, and growth that created excitement for the town. Faced with limited human and financial resources, the CSLP made a conscious choice between engaging in a complex, formal planning process and demonstrating sustainability. For example, Craik was successful in obtaining a grant from FCM (that required matching funds) to use The Natural Step (TNS) to guide local action planning, but there was a sense that the CSLP could either do The Natural Step action plan or build the eco-centre; the group did not have the financial or human resources for both. As one resident stated, "If we had decided to go with the plan, we would still be talking about it and wouldn't have the eco-centre." The focus on a physical demonstration of sustainability in the rural context was seen as a critical first step toward building the social infrastructure and capacity for broader community transition to sustainability.

However, political support did not last, and after three terms in office, the mayor was not re-elected in 2010, in part due to the perception that concerns about the viability of the town were no longer of concern in the context of a booming agricultural economy. While the CSLP was able to build on the early success and the goodwill generated during the construction of the eco-centre, maintaining and building on that momentum and interest proved to be more difficult.

Valleys: Investments in social infrastructure for sustainability

Despite the broad support for the CSLP during the construction of the eco-centre, engagement and mobilization of citizens in Craik around the broader concept and practice of sustainability were difficult to maintain as the CSLP struggled to link the principles underlying the eco-centre and eco-village with residents' daily lifestyle choices. Bridging the gap between values and action for sustainability is complex and requires concerted efforts and investments in community mobilization (Kollmuss & Agyeman, 2002). The value–action gap was identified as being critical, yet it was also more difficult and required longer-term investments to demonstrate results. The tensions associated with social change and competing versions of and visions for sustainability in Craik represented the biggest challenge. The local excitement generated by the construction of the eco-centre and the prospect of people moving to Craik after years of population decline masked the fact that local residents were divided over investment in the eco-centre and the value of sustainability as a concept. Although the project had the financial and political support of both local governments (the town's mayor, the RM reeve, and respective councils) at its initiation, local residents were divided on whether or not it was a good idea.

Prior to the CSLP, the approach to revitalizing the town was based purely on standard economic-development initiatives. For example, some residents described the early approaches to sustainability as simply finding ways of getting people to stop in town and spend some money as they drove the highway between Saskatoon and Regina. For those residents, sustainability was interpreted as simply meaning viability of the town and preservation of services (schools, health centre, and RCMP detachment). However, there were also those who believed that a strong sustainability approach was needed, based on concerns about the environmental impact of society. Those with this perspective described their view of the focus of the CSLP being to:

> encompass everything to make living on the Prairies a reasonable thing to do and [is] sustainable into the future. So, we

> weren't exporting our soil, contaminating our water supplies, we weren't, you know, utilizing energy other than our renewable energy. That's where I'd like to see the project go, eventually. (CSLP member)

Despite these different views of sustainability, the underlying motivation for the project was always one of ensuring that the town remained viable by drawing new residents into the town to end the gradual population decline. It was the strong sustainability perspective and expectations associated with the eco-centre and eco-village that attracted environmentally conscious residents to the town. However, upon arrival, these new residents were unprepared for the lack of integration between the eco-centre and eco-village and the town. For example, one resident's attempt to build a straw-bale, eco-friendly home on the main street in Craik was not supported by the community.[3] Some individuals in the community commented that the new residents might be "too eco." Some supportive residents responded, "Well, what kind of folks do you think would be attracted to this kind of project?" As these tensions became more apparent, a few families originally attracted to Craik due to perceived commitments to sustainability became disillusioned and have since left the town.

Despite the fact that the population of Craik has grown from 408 to about 450 people since 2006, it is difficult to determine how many are a direct result from the CSLP activities and and how many were attracted by improved economic conditions. While the population has increased, economic activity in the town has not seen dramatic economic revitalization. The planned hemp-fibre plant did not materialize, and no new businesses have opened on Main Street. In fact, since 2009, Craik has lost a café and Sears outlet on Main Street. While new, small, home-based businesses have been established in the eco-village, as well as a facility to convert biological waste to energy, the eco-centre and eco-village have been unable to address barriers to economic revitalization that were beyond their control.

> You know, we're located about midway between Saskatchewan's two largest cities, and I would suggest that the majority of the

> retail dollars which are generated in this community end up in, you know, the larger centres. So, people's mobility, etc., it's an easy trip, you know. So there was that sense that the economic base of the community was being eroded by factors that really we had no control over. And it became clear to any local retailers that it was going to be very difficult to keep going. (member of Craik town council)

Communication and public engagement was another challenge faced by the CSLP. The project required constant communication and engagement, through informal conversation, information handouts, and attempts to include information in the local media to hold the interest and maintain support of volunteers and the broader community. There was concern from some residents in Craik about the costs to the town for the eco-centre and eco-village and about whether or not the town was facing too much financial risk. This concern culminated in a petition for a special town-hall meeting to clarify the finances and the project. At this point, CSLP members recognized that they had been caught up in promoting the project outside of the community and had not done a good enough job communicating with people locally.

> That, in fact, is one lesson that we have learned, and that is, for something like this, particularly this kind of project, because of the risk, the perception, and just the nature of it, you've really got to educate your public about it right from the get-go. And we probably didn't do enough of that. We've learnt that lesson. (CSLP member)

The community meeting served to inform residents about the project and to dispel misconceptions and also served to remind the CSLP of the importance of public engagement about the project. However, being reliant on volunteers made it difficult to maintain momentum. After the eco-centre was finished, there was a lull in participation as everyone involved needed a break. It was difficult to get people engaged in discussing new ideas and new projects or to engage in the long-term discussion of underlying social values and visions for what a "sustainable" Craik might look like. Avoiding volunteer burnout and managing the need for specific skills and human-resource capacity for the project was another challenge that had to be addressed.

> For every person that worked [for pay] on that building, there's hundreds of hours of volunteerism out there, you know. For every piece of material that went into that building, there's thousands of dollars' worth of building materials that were donated or at a reduced cost or whatever. So I guess, in essence, we take a reduced risk by doing things like that. But it's a challenge; you can only expect people to do so much. (member of town council)

While the eco-centre construction served as a galvanizing moment for the CSLP and generated much support, eventually interest waned as other priorities emerged in the lives of individuals. Therefore, some aspects of the project are only half-done, and it was sometimes difficult to link individual projects together to maintain the long-term vision. In many ways, the challenges associated with the CSLP reflect the difficulty in having critical discussions about the meaning of sustainability and making the necessary investments in the social infrastructure for change. Engaging in a more formal sustainability-planning process could have helped build the social capacity and contributed to greater communication about values and visions, dialogue and trust; this is an area that has been a particular challenge for the CSLP.

While building trust and a sense of community ownership over the eco-centre construction was successful among existing residents, there was not sufficient investment in building the social infrastructure to integrate the values and principles underlying the eco-centre and eco-village development among all residents of the town. Perhaps it is not so much a lack of communication, but selective or exclusive communication. Being a small community where traditionally everyone knows each other, lines of communication in Craik are informal. Like many small communities, there is a combination of inclusion and exclusion operating, and informal power structures exist that are not apparent. Whether it be through "coffee row," word on the street, gossip, or rumour mill, many can be left out of the conversation. Newcomers can find it very hard to become involved, partly because of trust issues, and in the case where they hold opposing views, outright exclusion. This structure makes it easier for the most assertive voices to carry forward. New and innovative ideas to address sustainability are perceived to be additionally risky when they are proposed by outsiders, unless there are leadership figures within the community who are willing to support those ideas. As a result, discussion is controlled by the more powerful, conflicting views are not openly addressed, and viewpoints remain polarized.

Despite the involvement of a select group of people in the community, members of the CLSP made concerted efforts to engage additional community members in both the activities of the CSLP and in the actual construction of the eco-centre. Unfortunately, the town seemed divided, with those who supported the CSLP getting involved and others paying very little attention and seemingly not interested. Despite this fact, the CSLP was able to rely on supporters to build capacity through their volunteerism, their individual skill sets and knowledge, to move the project from an idea to action. However, simply involving residents in sustainability projects without engaging and challenging values and visions for what sustainability means for them limits the ability for projects to have a transformational impact (Selman, 2001). The approach of focusing on the physical demonstration project (i.e., the eco-centre) without engaging community members with the concept of sustainability limited the CSLP's ability to transfer lessons from the eco-centre and eco-village to daily life in the town.

The CSLP has attempted to address these problems by actively encouraging residents to attend and participate in their open meetings, but since the completion of the eco-centre construction, the group has had difficulty raising awareness about its projects and initiatives, and it is sometimes viewed as "exclusive," partly a result of mistrust and a lack of communication and understanding.

Communicating through the local media (the *Craik Weekly News*) might be viewed as a good way to reach the local population, yet neither the town nor the RM used that medium effectively to discuss the CSLP, or any other issue affecting the town. Members of the CSLP have written extensively for the local paper, however, these contributions are viewed with scepticism, as they represent voices that are not seen to be neutral, but rather reflect the views of newcomers or long-time locals who are known to support the CSLP.

The CSLP provided a model for regional cooperation based on sustainability values. There is a history of regional competition between various towns that has intensified with declining rural populations and a desire to maintain existing services in the face of consolidation. However, cooperation is occurring informally around certain types of economic-development opportunities. For example, the opportunity exists for traditional economic development along the corridor between Saskatoon and Regina (much like what Red Deer and other communities between Edmonton and Calgary in central Alberta are experiencing), yet that vision does not match the sustainability vision of the CSLP. The challenge remains to encourage and convince the surrounding communities of the value of a sustainability approach to regional development and to collaborate on defining criteria that lays out what is and is not acceptable for the region.

> So that we don't get pitted against each other by companies or, you know, are we going to allow intensive livestock operations? If so, where? What will be the rules? And the whole region, are we going to allow new subdivisions? If so, where? What are going to be the rules, so that everybody has the same ones. So if you go to Craik, if you go to Davidson or Kenaston, or whatever. So we want to bring in people that will help the whole region, and I think that the popularity of Craik and the publicity we've gotten for our project has helped the entire region, too. (Craik town councillor).

However, without regular communication and discussion between local government, residents, newcomers, business owners, and even academics, media, and others from the outside, addressing the conflicting values and visions of sustainability will not be possible. Some openly wish that the eco-centre would fall into the valley (it's on an unstable hillside) and all the "eco-people" simply move away. Residents and town and RM councils have lost enthusiasm for the CSLP. Outsiders, once-enthusiastic supporters and collaborators, are starting to become disillusioned.

Conclusion

Despite the challenges and pitfalls, there are those in Craik continuing to advance the sustainability agenda. The town is no longer formally involved with the CSLP; instead, CSLP volunteer committee members have managed to carry on programs and projects that build on the sustainability theme and continue to attract attention to the project. There is a recycling, compost, and hazardous-waste collection program; education programs on pesticides and organic gardening/lawn care; an annual Solar Fair trade show; film festivals; a library resource collection; and the developing eco-village.[4]

The eco-centre and eco-village have raised the profile of Craik, with national and international media attention drawing people from around the world to visit the project. The eco-village has eight families as full-time or part-time residents, in addition to an international language school and a modular "eco"-cabin construction business. There is a diversity of innovative buildings: sandbag bee-hive like structures; sunken shipping containers; straw-bale homes; insulated concrete–formed, super insulated, off-grid houses; even take-away modular, off-grid cabins.

There are a lot of things that show promise for Craik and its sustainability goals. However, without investments in the social infrastructure—capacity-building, discussion of values, trust, and community cohesion —investments in physical infrastructure for sustainability will have limited impacts. Making the choice to build the eco-centre as a physical demonstration of sustainability rather than engaging in a sustainability-planning process can be viewed two ways. It is possible that if Craik had engaged in a sustainability-planning process, it might have been able to address some of the conflicts between different values and views for sustainability with the result that sustainability would become more integrated into the daily life of residents of the town. However, it is equally likely that the same tensions would emerge and the resistance to sustainability would not be resolved, and all of the efforts in the planning process would not amount to change. This is an all-too-common result, particularly in rural communities, where the resources for planning are limited, often relying on one-off external consultants and the gap between sustainability planning and implementation is too wide (Markey, Halseth, & Manson, 2008).

The other view is that the decision to forgo a formal planning process and instead build a physical demonstration of sustainability represents a strategic choice based on the understanding of community dynamics. It is impossible to maintain constant effort. The inevitability of peaks and valleys in support for alternative views, coupled with limited resources, meant that when interest and support for sustainability waned, at least there would be a physical demonstration of sustainability that could be used to build on when support returned. Understanding the ebbs and flows of community dynamics has allowed CSLP members to strategically choose their moments and adopt a project-based approach that reinforces residual benefits in values and behavioural change. The challenge the CSLP faces is capturing those shifts in values in a way that will allow members to plan, guide, and inform future project choices. Despite the challenges and resistance to integrating sustainability into the life of all residents of the town, the eco-centre and eco-village represent a daily reminder to residents of possible alternatives. That is something that even the best sustainability plans cannot achieve. CSLP members have recognized the importance of building the capacity of citizens to engage in dialogue about the sustainability of their town, particularly as the complexity of initiatives and the behavioural change required by residents to reduce their ecological footprint increases. They are struggling with an ad-hoc planning process for future initiatives of the CSLP, which is ongoing despite the complete lack of resources and capacity at the municipal level. As is identified elsewhere, rural communities face critical resource constraints that do not enable them to use existing sustainable-planning frameworks and tools designed to manage the complexity of integrated planning (Markey, Connelly, & Roseland, 2010; Halseth, Markey, Reimer, & Manson, 2010).

One of the original strengths of the CSLP was the coming together of the community around shared values and sense of place. Craik was a place worth maintaining and the immediacy of work on the eco-centre provided a focus for that community energy. The social cohesion that was created served as a valuable community resource. However, social cohesion is multidimensional and can also serve to exclude (Jaffe & Quark, 2004). In deciding the future of Craik, the role of community, the relationships, and the sense of place will be challenged and renegotiated. Maintaining social cohesion, quality of life, and community survival will be an undertaking that will not simply be a challenge of economic viability but also of inclusion and equality (Jaffe & Quark, 2004). Craik's CSLP is an example of a small, rural town using the framework of sustainability to address rural decline and to ensure the continued viability of the town. Rather than embarking on conventional economic-development initiatives, the leadership of the town was convinced that sustainable community development offered a way to differentiate Craik from other towns, to draw attention to the town, and to reduce residents' ecological footprint. While the CSLP is guided by a long-term vision of sustainable living on the prairies, it was recognized that a tangible demonstration of what that entails was needed to engage residents. Craik is an inspiring example of a community that has embraced the challenge of sustainability and has been successful in building its eco-centre and establishing an eco-village, but, like many other communities, it has struggled to address more fundamental, values-based change and community action toward sustainability.

Notes

1. Population for the Town of Craik was estimated to be 450 people in 2010. Praxis International Institute, an international private school that offers high-school curriculum and ESL preparation, and Titan Carbon Smart Technologies, a company that recycles biomass, both were attracted to locate in Craik as a result of the commitments to sustainability.
2. The Audubon Society has certified the golf course in recognition of its environmental management initiatives, which include the use of compost material from the restaurant and toilet as a source of organic fertilizer, habitat restoration, and natural pest management.
3. The challenges were documented by the CBC's *The Passionate Eye* in the documentary "Eco-Home Adventures," which demonstrates the deep-seated conflicting views and resistance to sustainability. See CBC, *The Passionate Eye*, retrieved June 15, 2015, from http://www.cbc.ca/player/Shows/Shows/The+Passionate+Eye/ID/1449987664/.
4. See the CSLP website for more details: http://www.craikecovillage.com/.

References

Adger, W. N., Brown, K., Fairbrass, J., Jordan, A., Paavola, J., Rosendo, S., & Seyfang, G. (2003). Governance for sustainability: Towards a "thick" analysis of environ-mental decision-making. *Environment and Planning A, 35*(6), 1095–1110.

Berke, P. R. (2002). Does sustainable development offer a new direction for planning? Challenges for the twenty-first century. *Journal of Planning Literature, 17*(1), 21–36.

Blair, F., & Evans, B. (2004). *Seeing the bigger picture: Delivering local sustainable development*. York: Joseph Rowntree Foundation.

Brugmann, J. (1994). Who can deliver sustainability? Municipal reform and the sustainable development mandate. *Third World Planning Review, 16*(2), 129.

Brundtland, G. H. (1987). *Our common future*. New York: Oxford University Press.

Bulkeley, H. (2006). Urban sustainability: Learning from best practice? *Environment and Planning A, 38*(6), 1029–1044.

Campbell, S. (1996). Green cities, growing cities, just cities? Urban planning and the contradictions of sustainable development. *Journal of the American Planning Association, 62*(3), 296–312.

Clapp, T. A., & Meyer, P. B. (2000). *Managing the urban commons: Applying common property frameworks to urban environmental quality*. Paper presented at the International Association for the Study of Common Property (IASCP), May 31–June 4, Bloomington, IN.

Connelly, S., Markey, S. P., & Roseland, M. (2009). Strategic sustainability and community infrastructure. *Canadian Journal of Urban Research—Canadian Planning and Policy Supplement, 18*(1), 82–104.

Conroy, M., & Berke, P. (2004). What makes a good sustainable development plan? An analysis of factors that influence principles of sustainable development. *Environment Planning A, 36*(8), 1381–1396.

Dale, A. (2001). *At the edge: Sustainable development in the 21st century*. Vancouver: University of British Columbia Press.

Dale, A., & Onyx, J. (2005). *A dynamic balance: Social capital and sustainable community development*. Vancouver: University of British Columbia Press.

Evans, B., Joas, M., Sundback, S., & Theobald, K. (2005). *Governing sustainable cities*. London: Earthscan.

Gibbs, D., & Jonas, A. E. G. (2000). Governance and regulation in local environmental policy: The utility of a regime approach. *Geoforum, 31*(3), 299–313.

Guy, S., & Marvin, S. (1999). Understanding sustainable cities: Competing urban futures. *European Urban and Regional Studies, 6*(3), 268–275.

Halseth, G., Markey, S., Reimer, B., & Manson, D. (2010). The next rural economies. In G. Halseth, S. Markey, and D. Bruce (Eds.), *The next rural economies: Constructing rural place in a global economy* (pp. 1–16). Oxfordshire, UK: CABI International.

Hamstead, M., & Quinn, M. (2005). Sustainable community development and ecological economics: Theoretical convergence and practical implications. *Local Environment, 10*(2), 141–158.

Harvey, D. (1989). From managerialism to entrepreneurialism: The transformation in urban governance in late capitalism. *Geografisker Annaler, 71*(1), 3–17.

Healey, P., Cameron, S., Davoudi, S., Graham, S., & Madani-Pour, A. (1995). Challenge for urban management. In P. Healey, S. Cameron, S. Davoudi, S. Graham, and A. Madani-Pour (Eds.), *Managing cities: The new urban context* (pp. 273–289). Chichester, New York: J. Wiley.

Jaffe, J., & Quark, A. (2004). Now every farm has its own tomcat: New dynamics in social cohesion and cleavage in an agriculturally based community in rural Saskatchewan. *Prairie Forum, 29*(2), 317–328.

Kollmuss, A., & Agyeman, J. (2002). Mind the gap: Why do people act environmentally and what are the barriers to pro-environmental behavior? *Environmental Education Research, 8*(3), 239–260.

Markey, S., Connelly, S., & Roseland, R. (2010). "Back of the envelope": Pragmatic planning for sustainable rural community development. *Planning Practice and Research,* 25(1), 1–23.

Markey, S., Halseth, G., & Manson, D. (2008). Closing the implementation gap: A framework for incorporating the context of place in economic development planning. *Local Environment, 13*(4), 337–351.

McAllister, M. L. (2004). *Governing ourselves? The politics of Canadian communities.* Vancouver: University of British Columbia Press.

Mercer, D., & Jotkowitz, B. (2000). Local Agenda 21 and barriers to sustainability at the local government level in Victoria, Australia. *Australian Geographer, 31*(2), 163–181.

Morrison, H. T. (2006). Pursuing rural sustainability at the regional level: Key lessons from the literature on institutions, integration, and the environment. *Journal of Planning Literature, 21*(2), 143–152.

Newman, P., & Verpraet, G. (1999). The impacts of partnership on urban governance: Conclusions from recent European research. *Regional Studies, 33*(5), 487–491.

Osborne, D., & Gaebler, T. (1993). *Reinventing government: How the entrepreneurial spirit is transforming the public sector.* New York: Plume.

Parkinson, S., & Roseland, M. (2002). Leaders of the pack: An analysis of the Canadian "Sustainable Communities" 2000 municipal competition. *Local Environment, 7*(4), 411–429.

Portney, K. E. (2003). *Taking sustainable cities seriously: Economic development, the environment, and quality of life in American cities.* Cambridge, MA: MIT Press.

Rees, W. R. (1995). Achieving sustainability: Reform or transformation? *Journal of Planning Literature, 9*(4), 343–361.

Roseland, M. (2012). *Toward sustainable communities: Solutions for citizens and their governments.* Gabriola Island, BC: New Society Publishers.

Rydin, Y., & Pennington, M. (2000). Public participation and local environmental planning: The collective action problem and the potential of social capital. *Local Environment*, 5(2), 153–169.

Selman, P. (2001). Social capital, sustainability and environmental planning. *Planning Theory and Practice*, 2(1), 13–30.

van Bueren, E., & ten Heuvelhof, E. (2005). Improving governance arrangements in support of sustainable cities. *Environment and Planning B: Planning and Design*, 32(1), 47–66.

Williams, C., & Millington, A. (2004). The diverse and contested meanings of sustainable development. *Geographical Journal*, 170(2), 99–104.

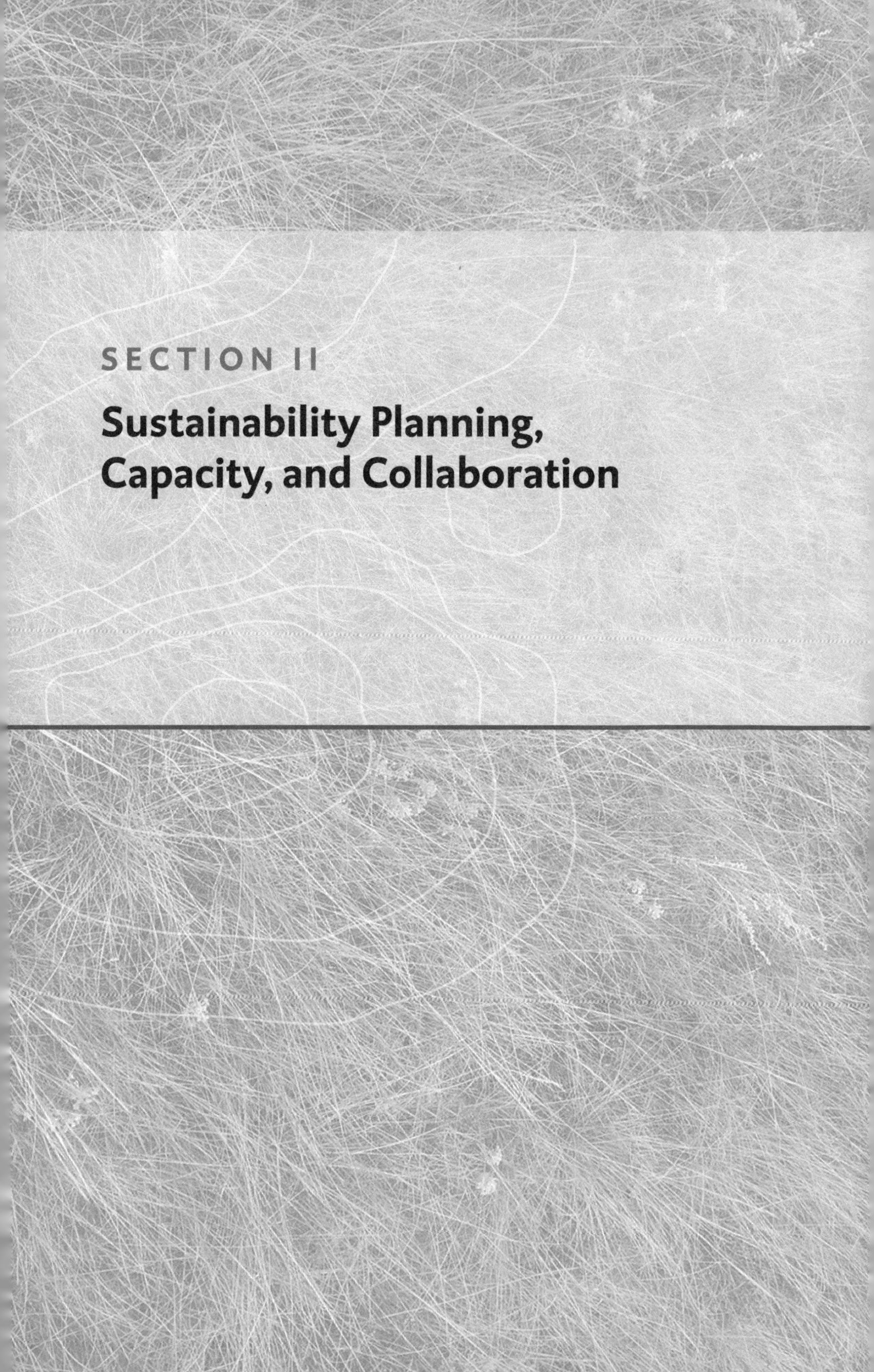

SECTION II

Sustainability Planning, Capacity, and Collaboration

FIVE

Municipal Sustainability Planning, Community Engagement, and Rural Revitalization

A Case Study of Chauvin, Alberta

Moira J. Calder, Mary A. Beckie, and Shelly McMann

Introduction

Community sustainability planning has been formalized in Canada through federal–provincial Gas Tax Agreements (GTAs), initially known as the New Deal for Cities and Communities (Finance Canada, 2005).[1] The Gas Tax Fund, administered by Infrastructure Canada, is meant to address some of the "infrastructure deficit" experienced by Canadian municipalities and First Nations communities as a result of more than two decades of downloading and offloading of responsibilities to municipalities by the federal and provincial governments, without sufficient transfer payments (Federation of Canadian Municipalities-McGill University, 2007; Mirza & Haider 2003). Between 2005 and 2014, $13 billion will have been spent on this program (Infrastructure Canada, 2011).

In western Canada, integrated sustainability plans are a requirement for local government eligibility of the infrastructure fund in British Columbia (Canada, British Columbia, & Union of British Columbia Municipalities, 2005), Alberta (Government of Alberta, 2009), and Manitoba (Infrastructure Canada, 2009), but not in Saskatchewan (Government of Saskatchewan, 2009). Identified as Integrated Community Sustainability Plans (ICSP), or Municipal Sustainability Plans (MSP) in Alberta, these high-level, strategic, and non-statutory plans are distinguished from other municipal plans by a long-term, holistic approach integrating environmental, cultural, social, and economic dimensions (Planning for Sustainable Communities Round Table, 2005).

A "culture of community involvement" (Connelly, Markey, & Roseland, 2009, p. 4) is essential to creating a shared vision of a more sustainable future and generating the commitment needed to move the community forward on this path. Democratic dialogue is therefore at the core of sustainability planning (Markey, Connelly, & Roseland, 2010; Roseland 2005). It is critical not only to citizen participation and collaboration but also in establishing the legitimacy, transparency, and accountability of the process (Cooper & Vargas, 2004; Nelson, 2001). Some research has shown that mechanisms and success of citizen engagement in policy and planning vary considerably, depending on both micro-level (individual attitudes and relations) and macro-level (socio-political) variables (e.g., Masuda, McGee, & Garvin, 2008; McCann 2001). Processes that promote and facilitate citizen engagement and community transformation, therefore, are worthy of study, as findings can identify areas of focus and practices that might be helpful to other communities addressing issues of sustainability. In this chapter we address the research question: what role do communication strategies and social networks play in shaping a dialogue-based, MSP process?

We situate this study in the Village of Chauvin, a small east-central Alberta community that came into being more than a century ago but, similar to many other resource-based communities, is struggling to survive in a period of rural decline. To Chauvin's municipal leaders, sustainability meant "staying alive." In 2007 the village took the opportunity to participate in a municipal sustainability planning pilot project launched by the Alberta Urban Municipalities Association (AUMA) to access infrastructure funding and other resources that would help Chauvin's citizens revision and revitalize their community. Chauvin's MSP process evolved as part of the AUMA pilot but was unique to its context, including location, resources, and time frame. An analysis of Chauvin's experience provides an opportunity to explore the methods by which small-scale communities, with limited resources, engage citizens in sustainability planning. By using a variety of communication and engagement methods, community members accessed and enhanced social networks within the community and outside it. These created opportunities for information sharing and access to information and resources, much of which was linked to their involvement in the AUMA pilot program. Despite the advantages of being a small community and a participant in the pilot, reliance on volunteers and ongoing issues of affordability made it challenging to gather community input and achieve a consensus of vision within the given time frame of the AUMA program. However, the process was completed and tangible results were accomplished that have created momentum toward a more sustainable future.

The second author (MB), a university professor, became involved in the AUMA's sustainability-planning pilots through her work with The Natural Step and discussed with them the possibility of a follow-up study. The first author (MC) conducted the research for her master's degree after the study communities had been selected in conjunction with the AUMA. The third author (SM) is the village administrator at Chauvin. This chapter was developed as a collaborative case study (Creswell, 2009) and is based primarily on community members' perspectives on their MSP experience as revealed through qualitative interviews with MSP participants, Chauvin's MSP report, and a conference presentation prepared by SM.[2] Benefits of the collaboration to the Chauvin community include an opportunity to reflect on past and current practices, and opportunities to present to and discuss the community's efforts and achievements with a larger audience through conference presentations and journal or magazine articles.

MC conducted in-depth, semi-structured interviews in person from October to December 2009 with three Chauvin community members, two community-development officers, and two AUMA representatives. At the time of the interviews, Chauvin had completed the MSP and was in the fourth of five phases in the MSP process. Interviews were conducted with stakeholders directly involved with the MSP process, identified through purposive and snowball sampling. The number of interviewees was limited by the availability of participants, and time and funding constraints. Federal and provincial documents related to the GTA and ICSPs were also reviewed, as well as related scholarly literature. This literature provided background information on sustainability planning, citizen engagement, and the role of dialogue in planning and democratic decision making, which was important in the development of interview questions and also in data analysis.

We begin by embedding Chauvin's story within the literature on public engagement, focusing on communication strategies and social networks as factors that can either limit or empower citizen involvement. We use this theoretical context throughout the remainder of the chapter to frame and guide our analysis of the community's experiences. Our aim in merging theoretical and applied perspectives in this community–university collaboration is to generate a rich description and assessment of the engagement process that will have relevance for both practitioners and academics. Following the literature review, we provide an overview of the AUMA MSP guide and pilot project then focus on a description and analysis of Chauvin's experience during the five phases of the MSP process. Based on these findings, a set of recommendations is provided for other communities involved in sustainability planning.

Defining a theoretical framework: Public involvement in planning and decision making

In recent decades, Western democracies have experienced a gradual decline in citizen engagement (Fischer, 2009); in Alberta voter turnout in provincial elections declined from 60.2% in 1993 to 40.6% in 2008 (Elections Alberta, 2010). To regain citizens' trust in government and create "more robust, effective and equitable planning," there has been a "trend away from expert-driven policy-making models towards processes that facilitate two-way information flow" (Masuda et al., 2008, p. 360). Recent emphasis on engagement in sustainability planning is also a response to the complexity and interconnectedness of many contemporary issues (Innes & Booher, 2004) that cannot be solved by government alone (Cooper & Vargas, 2004). Sustainability is a normative, value-laden concept (Davidson, 2002) that is best defined and operationalized within specific social and biophysical contexts, by local stakeholders (Roseland, 2005): "Effective and acceptable local solutions require local decisions, which in turn require the extensive knowledge and participation of the people most affected by those decisions" (p. 222). In practice, Canadian federal–provincial–municipal relations have been characterized by ongoing negotiations surrounding power sharing rather than by the subsidiarity principle, which implies that "any particular task should be decentralized to the lowest level of governance with the capacity to conduct it satisfactorily" (Marshall, 2008, p. 80). However, since the

1960s, pluralistic approaches involving civil society and business in policy-making have emerged in Canada (Parkins & Davidson, 2008).

Although public participation in decision making can help overcome some issues such as trust, concerns remain related to how to achieve citizen involvement, what citizens' roles should be, and who sets the agenda. As well, participation necessitates learning political skills, so capacity building must be built into the structure (Fischer, 2009), which might make decision making slower and more expensive. Even where choices are relatively clear, however, a tension exists between the rights of the individual and the "good" of the community. Some scholars have questioned whether it is possible to achieve community consensus without excluding some voices (Mouffe, 2009). Related to this is the question of what constitutes expertise. Scientific knowledge is increasingly seen as "a necessary resource of policymaking even though it may be contested and open to interpretation in a specific case" (Maasen & Weingart, 2005, p. 4). Some (e.g., Fischer, 2009) have argued for a redefinition of the relationship between "experts" and citizens, for a co-construction of scientific knowledge, and for a redefinition of expertise based on experience rather than formal qualifications. Although the public might wish to be involved in knowledge creation, the scientific community might not be receptive to this (Fischer, 2009; Maasen & Weingart, 2005).

The International Association of Public Participation (IAP2) (IAP2, 2007) has identified five levels of increasing community participation with different communication methods linked to each: (a) informing (e.g., fact sheets, websites, or open houses); (b) consulting (e.g., public comment or meetings, focus groups, and surveys); (c) involving (e.g., workshops or deliberative polling); (d) collaborating (e.g., citizen advisory committees, consensus building, and participatory decision making); and (e) empowering citizens (e.g., citizen juries, ballots, or delegated decisions). Each level corresponds to a different degree of information or knowledge sharing, from one-way information transfer to two-way or multidirectional dialogue and collaboration.

Communication enacted through interactions of individuals and groups within a social network is fundamental to engagement (Newman & Dale, 2005) and to the generation of new knowledge, a critical factor in creativity (Sawyer, 2007). The relationships of trust and reciprocity formed within a community are characterized as strong ties or bonding relationships (Portes, 1998) and are distinguished from the weak ties, or bridging relationships, formed with external actors and agencies (Granovetter, 1982). Although bonding relationships help generate social cohesion or social capital (Cuthill, 2003), constraints and relations of power can also form that inhibit community change (Newman & Dale, 2005). Governments might endorse engagement, for example, yet provide limited opportunities and/or retain control over the process, sometimes through the use of external experts as facilitators (McCann, 2001). Furthermore, engagement processes might be dominated by business and community elites, and special interest groups might be overrepresented (Rydin & Pennington, 2000). In smaller communities with strong bonding ties, where participation is driven by a desire to foster and build social capital (Reddel & Woolcock, 2004), commitment might not last as engagement "takes time, effort and resources" (Rydin & Pennington, 2000, p. 161). Bridging relationships can bring new knowledge to the network that stimulates innovation and positive community transformation but might also exert control (McCann, 2001; Newman & Dale, 2005). Thus, how knowledge and power are mobilized through social networks influences the engagement process, possibly enhancing or inhibiting it (Masuda et al., 2008).

The New Deal and Alberta's response

Following the signing of the Alberta GTA, the AUMA was quick to endorse municipal sustainability planning, which was a requirement of the Alberta agreement. In collaboration with The Natural Step (TNS)—an international, not-for-profit organization that assists in sustainability planning and development[3]—the AUMA developed an MSP guide (AUMA, 2006, 2007) to provide support for its member municipalities in establishing an inclusive and integrative approach.[4] The MSP guide incorporates the TNS systems-based and participatory framework for sustainability planning (James & Lahti, 2004), which also emphasizes community-asset mapping (Mathie & Cunningham, 2003) and collaboration through dialogue (Innes & Booher, 2004). Its framework is systems-based and consists of four sustainability principles that aim to reduce and eventually eliminate (a) dependence on fossil fuels, rare minerals, and metals; (b) production of synthetically manufactured and persistent chemicals and compounds; (c) degradation of natural ecosystems; and (d) barriers to meeting human needs "fairly and efficiently" (James & Lahti, 2004, p. 9). Sustainability principles serve as a framework for envisioning a sustainable future as well as the lens through which the current situation is assessed; then, steps are determined to move the community strategically toward sustainability (James & Lahti, 2004). The MSP guide delineates five phases, acknowledging that these will not necessarily follow a linear path as sustainability planning is an iterative process:

1. Structuring the planning process;
2. Creating a shared understanding of success;
3. Collectively determining and analyzing issues related to community success;
4. Planning actions using principles developed in the previous steps; and
5. Implementation, monitoring, and ongoing reporting of progress. (AUMA, 2006)

In 2007 the AUMA launched a pilot project to test the guide and provide further support for small to medium-sized urban municipalities (hamlets, towns, and villages), with limited resources, in the MSP process. Five communities were selected based on their interest and need, as well as AUMA criteria of diversity in size and location: the towns of Claresholm, Olds, and Pincher Creek (with populations approximately 3,600, 7,200, and 3,600, respectively, at the time; AltaPop, 2009); and the villages of Thorhild and Chauvin (with populations of 505 and 321 respectively, at the time; AltaPop, 2009). The AUMA provided assistance from its own staff for educational and networking events, arranged for a full-time secondment from Alberta Environment to assist with coordination and information dissemination, and also enlisted community development officers (CDOs) from the Alberta Ministry of Municipal Affairs to serve as facilitators in community consultations and help identify resources both internal and external to the pilot villages. The towns used their own personnel and/or consultants.

By facilitating interactions and knowledge exchange between these pilot communities at events and through online venues, the AUMA pilot program assisted in establishing a municipal sustainability network in the province that was embedded at the local level but also had links to broader national and international sustainability initiatives. Through the pilot the AUMA also aimed to provide examples of successful MSPs for other communities, demonstrating the importance of public involvement in sustainability planning and how it could foster a sense of common purpose, and build community capacity by expanding social networks. One AUMA participant noted that by the time the AUMA's formal involvement in the process had wound down, most communities in Alberta had been able to access some of the resources through either local or higher-level planning (e.g., municipal districts). We will now describe and examine how the Village of Chauvin used communication strategies to strengthen citizen engagement and expand social networks in order to achieve dialogue-based community sustainability planning.

Chauvin begins its sustainability journey

> Chauvin is a small community with a population of 321 people and located in east-central Alberta about 80 kilometres south of Lloydminster, near the Saskatchewan border. Being a rural community, we don't have a lot of pollution or many of the problems that larger communities have to deal with. Our council will probably never have to consider a bylaw to disallow drive-throughs to cut down on vehicle emissions! We are able to view star-filled skies and have the security of caring neighbours. (2a)[5]

> In our application [to the AUMA], we outlined our desire to prepare such a plan but expressed our concern as to funding and time requirements for our staff. We knew it was something that had to be done, but we needed a push to get it going. Being chosen as a pilot gave us incentive to get started, and the help we received made the process possible. (2a)

Chauvin's economy depends on agriculture and oil, and consequently has been subject to the ups and downs of commodity markets. Community leaders were attracted to the provincial municipal sustainability initiative because of the infrastructure funding available but also saw the pilot project as a way of accessing resources. The village has a paid administrator and foreman in addition to a mayor and four unpaid councillors who meet monthly. It has a primary/secondary school that produces a community newsletter, and as the village owns its utilities, it can also send information to residents through bill inserts. There is a seniors' centre and several grazing associations but no formal organizations outside of village administration aimed at community planning or promotion, although activism has led to ad hoc group formation. For example, when the school burned down in 1978 and the school board decided to close it, the community successfully lobbied to have it rebuilt (Village of Chauvin, 2008).

Chauvin's MSP

In this section we describe the MSP process and relate the specific activities to communications and engagement methods and to IAP2 (2007) levels of engagement. In reality, the process was less linear than that set out in the AUMA guide, with the community action group revisiting the steps as they worked on different sustainability goals. For community planning to be sustainable, it must be iterative, for example, with ongoing input from the community and consideration of options that might not have been previously possible throughout and not just at the beginning of the planning process.

1. Structuring the planning process

> Chauvin Village Council adopted an official resolution to do an MSP on April 19, 2007. This was an important step as it demonstrated that there was the necessary leadership and commitment of resources from the municipal authority to steer the process through problems that may arise. (2c)
>
> *The Shock!* What did we get ourselves into? But the community felt they had to do an MSP to gather ideas to keep the small community of Chauvin going, now called village sustainability. (2c)
>
> Determining the plan parameters of the Chauvin MSP led to a number of good discussions. Was Chauvin a community defined by natural features, economic network, intermunicipal region, or political boundary? (2c)

- *Activities:* Recruitment and training of leaders
- *Communication and engagement methods:* Direct contact, word-of-mouth, workshop
- *Levels of engagement (IAP2):* Inform, consult, collaborate

Once the village council lent support to the MSP—and community members emphasized the importance of village council's involvement and support—the first step was to identify leadership and provide education as the leaders needed a level of comfort in understanding sustainability concepts to be able to promote them (AUMA, 2006).

> The process leader...was needed to initiate and lead the overall process, be highly respected, and know the community well. Chauvin was fortunate in that they had two people that carried out that role...In addition other technical support was secured for the Chauvin MSP. (2c)

Council members attended initial educational (train-the-trainer) sessions led by the CDOs in Chauvin, who had received training from the AUMA. Members of the Chauvin council stayed directly involved throughout the MSP process, providing leadership and oversight. The CDOs had time commitments in addition to work at Chauvin, which was compounded by their time spent travelling. AUMA staff felt that having someone in place at least half of the time would have been preferable: "We really were dependent on the community development officers, which was excellent. They did a great job. But they almost wore themselves out, I think. It was, like, they have other jobs as well" (2b).

To access additional information and expertise, the CDOs made connections—"weak ties" (Granovetter, 1982)—with council members, individuals, and organizations. An AUMA representative observed that capacity building was a particular issue in the pilots given that these MSPs were developed during a provincial boom time, when smaller communities were experiencing high staff turnover because of employment opportunities elsewhere. AUMA involvement gave the communities indirect access to the AUMA's network, such as the ImagineCalgary visioning process[6] and organizations such as the British Columbia Centre for Sustainable Cities, thereby expanding the resources on which they could draw. The CDOs, seconded from the Alberta government, offered their own network of resources, for example, arranging a workshop in Chauvin on cooperatives in response to villagers' concerns about the loss of their hardware store. Outside resources—for example, visits to other communities—were considered important for generating new ideas, but attending AUMA workshops in other locations was difficult and costly for members of this fairly remote community, particularly in the winter. AUMA funding for travel did not cover all expenses, and village councillors were not compensated for time off work.

A citizen advisory group (CAG) was established to facilitate learning, receive and process community input, and later to implement projects identified under the various goals (IAP2, 2007). There was selective recruitment of "strategically positioned people who had expertise" (2b) and existing community connections that could be leveraged (McCann, 2001). Interviewees underlined the importance of key individuals in the community who took a leadership role, who kept the process moving by working within existing social networks but also helped modify these networks as needed (Giddens, 1984). Village council members were represented in the CAG, which aided communication between the CAG and the council.

> A Citizen Advisory Group (CAG)...provided community expertise, resources, coordination, and continues to be very active implementing the Chauvin MSP. Most important, the group has passion, believes in each other, and truly feels they can make a difference in their community. (2c)

Community members noted the importance of this ongoing communication to the success of the process. They also described the importance of social networks—"getting the right connections" (2b)—in engaging the public (Rydin & Pennington, 2000) and in building social and intellectual capital (Cuthill, 2003). They leveraged existing strong ties (bonding relationships) within the community through personal contact but also created new ones (bonding and bridging relationships) that increased community capacity by adding knowledge and skills (Granovetter, 1982). The existence and extent of bonds of group identity have also been linked to participation in community deliberation but might work to make deliberative groups homogeneous or open to only certain types of participants (Ryfe, 2002). However, individuals who participate in community dialogues tend to be longer-term residents with higher socio-economic status and who occupy central positions in social networks (Laurian, 2004). In Chauvin they consciously worked to include those who might not step forward on their own.

In Figures 5.1 and 5.2, the AUMA and Chauvin networks are outlined, with additions to pre-existing networks shown by outlining of text boxes (Granovetter, 1982). This can only be an approximation as particularly informal relationships might not have emerged in the written or interview data. Interactions between different contexts are shown clearly, and in most cases, introduction of members into a different context—for example, TNS input to AUMA on their guidebook—was made through an existing contact.

2. Creating a shared understanding of success

> To us, sustainability meant "staying alive." We were (and still are) looking to attract more businesses and residents to Chauvin. When we started into the process, we were not fully prepared for the concept of sustainability as in The Natural Steps program. Along the way, we realized that both concepts are closely linked. (2a)

> We asked the question [to the community]: What do we need to do in Chauvin over the next 15, 20 years to make sure the community survives, thrives, and is environmentally sustainable? That was the wording we came up with. Originally we sort of were just going to say "sustainable"...the community struggled with the wording...they really wanted the words "environmentally sustainable" put in there. And I know that sustainability isn't just environment. But they thought to trigger people's thoughts and understanding, they really needed that word in there. So that was a community negotiation. We thought, "That's their community, you know. This is about asking what's most important to them, the question that's going to be really important." (2b)

Figure 5.1: Chauvin village administration communications network.

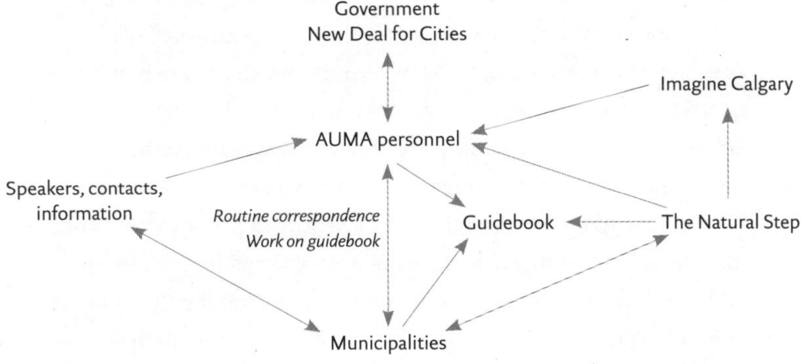

Figure 5.2: Alberta Urban Municipalities Association communications network.

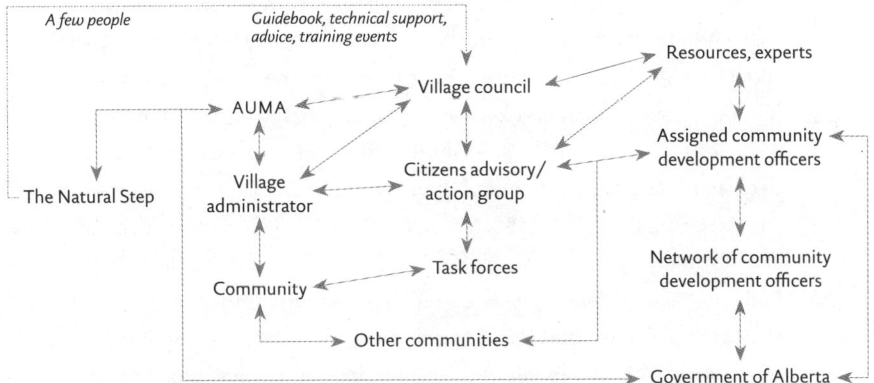

- *Activities:* Open house and participants writing down their vision of the future of Chauvin; input sessions also contained education component
- *Communication and engagement methods:* Public meetings, surveys, public comment
- *Levels of engagement (IAP2):* Inform, consult, involve

Creating a common understanding and language for sustainability, through education and dialogue, is an essential step in sustainability planning (James & Lahti, 2004; Ling, Dale, & Hanna, 2007). Informing and educating citizens about sustainability and the MSP process was carried out through the use of various communication methods: radio, print, public presentations, and word of mouth. Initially Chauvin CAG used the school newsletter and utility-bill inserts but later began publishing a quarterly village newsletter. Posters placed in the village office were considered less effective than other methods such as radio. At the time of the pilot, Chauvin did not have high-speed Internet access in homes or private businesses, although it used the village website to provide information to outsiders. A survey and questionnaire were also conducted with students and people from outside the community, but neither the CDOs nor the community members wanted to rely on surveys because of their experiences with low response rates and sense that a survey might not "get to the heart of what people are thinking" (2b).

The first open house included an asset-mapping exercise (Mathie & Cunningham, 2003), in which attendees were asked what they valued in their community and would not consider changing, and what aspects they thought might be worth re-examining, changing, or expanding upon. This input was used to then develop a vision for a preferred future. Community visioning is an increasingly popular method in planning that creates a detailed picture of a community's future through dialogue and consensus (McCann, 2001; Walzer & Hamm, 2010). Citizens engaging with one another in the visioning process become informed, exchange ideas, and build the relationships, sense of ownership, and commitment needed to put the plan into action, thus transitioning from the present toward a more sustainable community. Public input for the visioning process was solicited at public events (community barbeque) and gathering places (restaurant, public library) (Reddel & Woolcock, 2004). People were handed cards and asked to use words, pictures, or both to describe a preferred future for the community. The CDOs noted the ease of communication within the community: "They just have a natural web, aided by being a small community" (2b).

> At the first meeting we were asked to list our assets. It was amazing how quickly the ideas came forward and how many there were. Even though we had some negative people in the room, they even seemed to come around when the positive ideas came forth. (2b)

Public education took place alongside the gathering of input on the community vision. One individual described educational material included in the school newsletter but also noted "crossover" between education and action-focused sessions. Responsibility for education gradually shifted from the CDOs to community members educating each other: "They were making the connections to maybe if somebody wasn't seeing something….They were educating each other." This person observed that "the group got more creative and more creative as we went along" (2b).

> We had input from all parts of our community….We received about 250 [cards] for consideration at our October workshop and we considered *all of them* in developing our goals. (2b)

A shared vision ("Chauvin is the community of choice to live, grow, work, and play!" [2c]) was important for plan implementation (i.e., motivation for momentum; Bronfenbrenner, 1979), and participants described the importance of the process in changing what people think and talk about. Higher-level strategizing developed through the visioning process as the community identified goals that could not be reached by one village. For example, Chauvin does not have the population to support in-place elder care, but CAG members began thinking in terms of partnering with nearby communities (e.g., the ICE [Irma-Chauvin-Edgerton] communities). Chauvin has successfully positioned itself as a local hub, earlier by preventing the school closure, and in 2010 by rebuilding the district fire hall.

Response rates and representation for visioning input were considered good, but there were challenges. Young adults, who often worked away from the town or village, "stay-at-home moms," and seasonal residents such as cottage owners were identified as difficult to engage. Chauvin aimed to involve the entire community in the visioning process, and, because the oil and gas industry is a major contributor to the economy, the group "wanted to make sure all the oil and gas people were contacted" (2b). However, the industry raised concerns over the presentation of the environmental dimension in the guide, which they felt cast a negative light on the energy industry. Despite this reaction, the main public-input event took place at a barbeque hosted by a major energy firm, selected because it was an event that almost the entire community attends.

3. **Collectively determining and analyzing issues related to community success**

   One point that came out early in our sustainability process was that *yes* we want to grow enough to keep the amenities that we have but we also want to keep the small community advantage.... By changing or modernizing some of our facilities, we could recognize our assets and make them more usable. (2a)

   I remember one fellow came to me and said: "You know, we're talking about some things here that we don't generally talk about in our community, which I think is good." (2b)

   Not all suggestions were positive, but all were considered, and we tried to come up with ways to solve the negative problems. (2b)

- *Activities:* Workshops and small-group work, open houses to inform of progress
- *Communication and engagement methods:* Workshop, Open houses
- *Levels of engagement (IAP2):* Involve, inform

Public input was synthesized at a weekend workshop, or charrette, attended by approximately two dozen people and facilitated by the CDOs. This information was reviewed and sorted into categories based on the five dimensions of sustainable communities outlined in the AUMA guide: environmental, economic, cultural, social, governance. Although only a small percentage of the community was present at this synthesis event, those who did participate considered the community's views to be represented in the data that had been collected.

4. **Planning actions using principles developed in the previous steps**

   At our community workshop, we identified...goals and people volunteered to be on task forces to accomplish some of those goals. We aren't working on all the goals yet, but focusing on the ones that the group felt were the most important. (2a)

- *Activities:* Subgroup formation
- *Communication and engagement methods:* Citizen advisory committees, task forces
- *Levels of engagement (IAP2):* Involve, collaborate

Task forces were created for each goal identified in the charrette (Figure 5.3). This initially involved members of Chauvin council and citizens at the meeting identifying the areas where they wanted to contribute. Task force participation was seen as different from involvement in other types of community organizations: "If you go to the arena board meeting, you have to be a president or a secretary. You have to do something. You have to work, work, work, work. Being on a task force is mostly working your mind" (2b). Recruitment took place primarily by word of mouth at events that were mostly social in nature and encouraged but did not require attendees to commit immediately to aspects they wanted to be involved with. People with specific skills were also identified for recruitment to task forces through asset mapping (James & Lahti, 2004), translating human capital to social capital (Cuthill, 2003). A participant said that in ongoing recruitment for the advisory committee, the CDOs encouraged the community to look beyond "the same people all the time" (2b). One interviewee noted that newcomers were directly approached (i.e., increase social capital; Cuthill, 2003). New residents were seen as bringing fresh and different perspectives on things that might have been taken for granted by long-term members. Conflicts between new and long-time residents did arise, however, over attachment to cultural and heritage aspects of the community. This required dialogue and negotiation to achieve mutual understanding.

Chauvin recognized the importance of setting realistic goals, not trying to take on too much too quickly, and acknowledging that working toward sustainability is an ongoing project. By prioritizing goals, the village was able to achieve some early successes that helped build confidence and encouraged continued pursuit of longer-term projects. To date, successes have been achieved in recycling, ecotourism, and infrastructure improvements. Some issues were seen as too big for a small community to handle in the short term, such as the water issue at Chauvin, which would involve the local gas companies because of industrial water use

Figure 5.3: Chauvin municipal sustainability plan task forces.

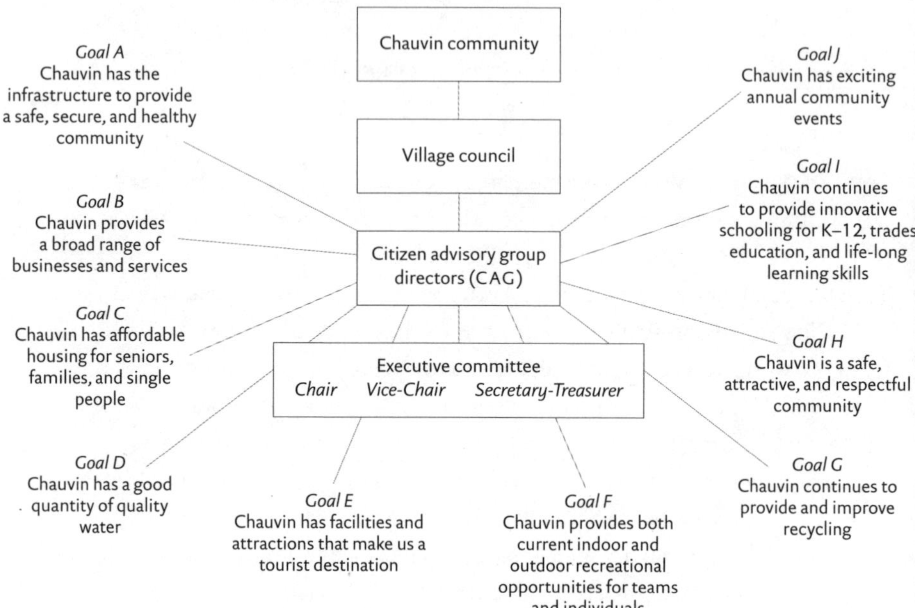

(National Round Table on the Environment and the Economy, 2010) and "take more of an advocacy, lobbying piece" (2b).

5. Implementation, monitoring, and ongoing reporting of progress

We came a million miles. (2c)

The mind set has changed to "We can and want to go forward!" We realize that even though people may not want a leadership role, they are willing to help if asked. (2c)

The plan has brought forth a discovery of talents within our community which have provided participation and imagination from long time and new residents….We have discovered people with expertise in many areas of which we were not aware and this is helpful now and will be in the future. (2c)

- *Activities:* Depended on the citizen advisory group (CAG) and task forces; communications with oversight body informal (council members' direct involvement in CAG); ongoing communication with citizens
- *Communication and engagement methods:* Recycling program; ICE (Irma-Chauvin-Edgerton) local partnership; new fire hall; task forces: "Small pieces of the plan are being worked on by various groups to spread out the workload. Each group is looking into funding for their own projects" (2c); "Citizen Advisory Group meets regularly to receive and discuss reports from task forces" (2c)
- *Levels of engagement (IAP2):* Consulting, involving, empowering

Participants described accomplishments and project implementations under all of the AUMA's pillars of sustainability (social, culture, governance, environment, and economy) but noted the need for ongoing negotiation and discussion concerning prioritization and implementations of initiatives. One stated that it was important to start actions quickly, selecting the "low-hanging fruit"—an AUMA (2006) guide recommendation—to maintain motivation of volunteers, who face time constraints. Participants described adapting the vision to current reality, at times having to scale back desired plans. For example, the recycling system had to be revamped because the centre was not being used properly. Funding was a primary consideration when reviewing initiatives being proposed, although the CDOs helped locate free resources where possible. Village councillors are not paid, so the MSP process added to their unpaid workload. In general, resources were limited or at least finite, and therefore decision making and prioritizing were critical.

Monitoring progress and reporting back to the community was done face to face at social gatherings. The CAG reported back to the community at the same barbeque where a year earlier they had collected community input. Task forces report monthly to village council. They also had a potluck dinner, at which

> we didn't attract a whole bunch of new ones, but I think there was about four, which was four more than we had before, so it was great. And it was a really nice evening. It was no training, and you didn't have to take on a position or anything. You just had to come and enjoy yourself. (2b)

Communication was central to prioritizing plans, as the community could not implement all plans simultaneously because of resource constraints. Community members actively "bridged" visioning and implementation through such means as managing the engagement cycle and consulting experts (Connelly et al., 2009). They also described monitoring progress and recording successes or else adjusting plans when necessary. At the time of the interviews, pilot communities were implementing action plans developed through the first round of community input. Chauvin continued its focus on communication through social avenues by initiating drop-in sessions with village council. With a community cohort having followed through the process previously, rather than having it led by "outsiders," comes an opportunity to involve more community members through personal contacts and so help develop the momentum needed for a sustainable process (Bronfenbrenner, 1979).

Overall, there was a lack of conflict in the MSP process. Although the AUMA MSP guide promoted dialogue at the condensation stage among advisory group members rather than at the input stage, participants mentioned the importance of listening to negative input and noted that "it was discussed" at the workshop. If conflict did occur, it tended to be at the implementation rather than MSP stage, related to issues such as (at least perceived) lack of follow-through, who is responsible for implementation, the effectiveness of a planned action, or differing perspectives between long-time and more recent community members: for example, a newcomer's decision to remove the community's mascot was overturned following protests from citizens who felt the mascot reflected village history.

Recommendations

Even a community the size of Chauvin, with access to external resources and support provided by the AUMA and related agencies, struggled to obtain community input and achieve consensus of vision within the time frame of the MSP pilot program. Described above, these challenges related to volunteer recruitment and commitment, time, and ongoing access to affordable resources. As a result of its MSP experience, the Village of Chauvin recommends that the following points be considered by communities embarking on a sustainability-planning process.

1. **Structure the planning process: Secure local government leadership and support**

   If the council isn't kind of united, doing this in a united way, that can impact the governance and leadership dimension of sustainability and make it difficult to put things forward. (2b)

2. **Create a shared understanding of success: Engage the community through ongoing communication and networking**

   Be sure to keep the community informed and welcome people to join all along the process (not just at the beginning)....We found that by having regular meetings and making an effort to keep everyone informed, the community seems more interested in the process and are more willing to provide feedback. (2c)

   Encourage leadership and participation from everyone in the community. (2c)

3. **Colletively determine and analyze issues related to community success: Recognize assets and build on them**

   When we got into the asset-mapping exercise, people became involved in depth. When you engage a community about their community, they are the experts! Lots of great ideas about what they wanted to share about their community and what they wanted to keep intact about their community came forward. We discussed community history and values. (2c)

4. **Plan actions using principles developed: Set realistic goals and don't try to do too much too soon (2a)**

> Developing an MSP does not necessarily have to be costly, but the time of community members and staff members is an expense.... Remember, it does not all have to be done at once. Prioritize and put into bite-sized, manageable pieces.
>
> Take baby steps, then bigger steps. (2c)
>
> One of our biggest challenges is obtaining funding for some of the projects we would like to accomplish. As a small village, our staff is stretched very thin and don't always have time to research and apply for grants. In our area we have recently joined with our neighbouring villages to work cooperatively on some projects. This has proved to be very, very beneficial. (2a)

5. **Implementation, monitoring, and ongoing reporting: Be prepared to be in this for the long haul**

> Be aware that this is an ongoing process and be prepared for that....Now that we have established our task forces and started to work on several of the projects, we realized we are in this for the long haul—not just the one-year pilot project—but now at least we have a road map to go by. I think that many of the residents also realize that if they want something done, it's not just up to the members of council—everyone in the community has to work for worthwhile projects. (2a)

Conclusion

The GTAs and the promotion of integrated sustainability planning in Canada were "designed to accelerate the shift in local planning and decision-making toward more long-term, coherent and participatory approaches to achieve sustainable communities" (Planning for Sustainable Communities Round Table, 2005, p. 4). In Alberta the AUMA contributed to this collaborative process by creating a guide, a resource for all urban municipalities in the province, and developing the pilot program as a way to provide additional support for small-scale communities with limited resources. Rather than rename a standard strategic plan or have administration "fill in the blanks," sustainability planning was intended to be an opportunity to "broaden the scope of factors considered, lengthen the timeframe, and encourage participation and collaboration through participatory techniques" (p. 4). Finally, through the pilot program, the AUMA initiated the development of a community sustainability network in Alberta, through which communities can share knowledge and expertise on an ongoing basis at the AUMA's annual conference and through online venues.

To residents of Chauvin, a rural community in east-central Alberta, sustainable development initially meant "staying alive," growing enough to maintain the community but keeping the advantages of a small community. As they engaged with AUMA resources, they came to understand and appreciate that a deeper understanding of the concept and principles of sustainability could assist in addressing a broader range of community goals. The Village of Chauvin's MSP produced tangible results and provided momentum toward sustainable practices. Using a variety of communication and engagement methods, MSP leaders accessed and enhanced social networks within the community and outside it (Granovetter, 1982). These created opportunities for information sharing and access to information and resources unavailable within the community, primarily through their connections with the AUMA, TNS, and the CDOs. Despite challenges of volunteer recruitment and commitment, time and ongoing access to affordable resources, Chauvin has embarked on a process of social engagement in planning and action that is essential to creating more sustainable and democratic communities.

Authors' note

Shelly McMann would like to thank the AUMA, Debbie Hagman, and Scott Vaughn for their assistance and hard work, which has enabled us to reach this point. We also thank all participants in the research on which this chapter is based.

Notes

1. Parts of this research were previously published as: Calder, M. J., & Beckie, M. A. (2011). Engaging communities in municipal sustainability planning: The use of communication strategies and social networks in Alberta. *Local Environment, 16*(7), 671–686. doi: http://dx.doi.org/10.1080/13549839.2011.589432.

2. For a more detailed description of the research study, see Calder and Beckie (2011).
3. See www.naturalstep.org.
4. The AUMA's MSP microsite is http://msp.auma.ca.
5. We will refer to community reflections through the current village administrator's presentation (Calder, Beckie, & McMann, 2010), labelled 2a, participants words from the qualitative research study (Calder & Beckie, 2011), labelled 2b, and the Village of Chauvin's (2008) MSP report, 2c.
6. The blueprint for Calgary, Alberta, is available at http://www.imaginecalgary.ca.

References

Alberta Urban Municipalities Association (AUMA). (2006). *Guidebook for municipal sustainability planning*. Edmonton, AB: AUMA.

———. (2007). *Municipal sustainability initiative: Analysis and recommendations*. Edmonton, AB: AUMA.

AltaPop. (2009). *Alberta population*. Retrieved from http://www.altapop.ca/urban.htm.

Bronfenbrenner, U. (1979). *The ecology of human development*. Cambridge, MA: Harvard University Press.

Calder, M. J., & Beckie, M. A. (2011). Engaging communities in municipal sustainability planning: The use of communication strategies and social networks in Alberta. *Local Environment, 16*(7), 671–686. doi: http://dx.doi.org/10.1080/13549839.2011.589432.

Calder, M. J., Beckie, M. A., & McMann, S. (2010, October). *Engaging the community: Communications strategies in municipal sustainability planning in Alberta*. Paper presented at the Taking the Next Step conference, Camrose, Alberta.

Canada, British Columbia, & Union of British Columbia Municipalities. (2005). *Agreement on the transfer of federal gas tax revenues under the New Deal for Cities and Communities, 2005–2015*. Retrieved from http://CDOs.civicnet.bc.ca.

Connelly, S., Markey, S., & Roseland, M. (2009). Strategic sustainability: Addressing the community infrastructure deficit. *Canadian Journal of Urban Research, 18*(1 Suppl.), 1–23.

Cooper, P. J., & Vargas, C. M. (2004). *Implementing sustainable development: From global policy to local action*. Lanham, MD: Rowman & Littlefield.

Creswell, J. W. (2009). *Research design: Qualitative, quantitative, and mixed method approaches* (3rd ed.). Thousand Oaks, CA: Sage.

Cuthill, M. (2003). The contribution of human and social capital to building community well-being: A research agenda relating to citizen participation in local governance in Australia. *Urban Policy & Research, 21*(4), 373–391.

Davidson, J. (2002). Sustainable development: Business as usual or a new way of living? *Environmental Ethics*, 22(2), 25–42.

Elections Alberta. (2010). *Voter turnout in recent Alberta provincial elections.* Retrieved from http://www.elections.ab.ca/public%20website/927.htm.

Federation of Canadian Municipalities-McGill University. (2007). *Danger ahead: The coming collapse of Canada's municipal infrastructure.* Ottawa: FCM-McGill.

Finance Canada. (2005). *A new deal for Canada's communities.* Retrieved from http://CDOs.fin.gc.ca/budget05/pamph/pacom-eng.asp.

Fischer, F. (2009). *Democracy and expertise: Reorienting policy inquiry.* Oxford, UK: Oxford University Press.

Giddens, A. (1984). *The constitution of society: An outline of the theory of structuration.* Oxford, UK: Polity.

Government of Alberta. (2009). *Municipal sustainability initiative 2009 actual allocations.* Retrieved from http://CDOs.municipalaffairs.gov.ab.ca/wp_municipal_sustainability_initiative.cfm.

Government of Saskatchewan. (2009). *Federal gas tax program.* Retrieved from http://CDOs.municipal.gov.sk.ca/Funding/Federal-Gas-Tax-Program.

Granovetter, M. (1982). The strength of weak ties: A network theory revisited. In P. V. Marsden & N. Lin (Eds.), *Social structure and network analysis* (pp. 105–130). Thousand Oaks, CA: Sage.

Infrastructure Canada. (2009). *Gas tax agreement: Canada-Manitoba.* Retrieved from http://CDOs.infc.gc.ca/ip-pi/gtf-fte/agree-entente/agree-entente-mb-eng.html#tphp.

Infrastructure Canada. (2011). *Gas tax fund.* Retrieved from http://CDOs.infc.gc.ca/ip-pi/gtf-fte/gtf-fte-eng.html.

Innes, J. E., & Booher, D. E. (2004). Reframing public participation: Strategies for the 21st century. *Planning Theory & Practice*, 5(4), 419–436.

International Association of Public Participation (IAP2). (2007). *IAP2 spectrum of public participation.* Retrieved from http://CDOs.iap2.org/associations/4748/files/spectrum.pdf.

James, S., & Lahti, T. (2004). *The Natural Step for communities: How cities and towns can change to sustainable practices.* Gabriola Island, BC: New Society.

Laurian, L. (2004). Public participation in environmental decision making: Findings from communities facing toxic waste cleanup. *Journal of the American Planning Association*, 70(1), 53–65.

Ling, C., Dale, A., & Hanna, K. (2007). Integrated community sustainability planning tools. Retrieved from http://CDOs.crcresearch.org/files-crcresearch/File/PlanningTool(1).pdf.

Maasen, S., & Weingart, P. (2005). What's new in scientific advice to politics? In democratization of expertise? In S. Maasen & P. Weingart (Eds.), *Exploring novel forms of scientific advice in political decision-making* (pp. 1–19). Dordrecht, NL: Springer.

Markey, S., Connelly, S., & Roseland, M. (2010). "Back of the envelope": Pragmatic planning for sustainable rural community development. *Planning, Practice & Research*, 25(1), 1–23. doi: 10.1080/02697451003625356.

Marshall, G. R. (2008). Nesting, subsidiarity, and community-based environmental governance beyond the local level. *International Journal of the Commons*, 2(1), 75–97. Retrieved from http://www.thecommonsjournal.org.

Masuda, J. R., McGee, T. K., & Garvin, T. D. (2008). Power, knowledge, and public engagement: Constructing "citizenship" in Alberta's industrial heartland. *Journal of Environmental Policy & Planning*, 10, 359–380.

Mathie, A., & Cunningham, G. (2003). From clients to citizens: Asset-based community development as a strategy for community-driven development. *Development in Practice*, 13(5), 474–486. doi: 10.1080/0961450320001258 57.

McCann, E. J. (2001). Collaborative visioning or urban planning as therapy? The politics of public–private policy making. *Professional Geographer*, 53, 207–218.

Mirza, M. S., & Haider, M. (2003). *The state of infrastructure in Canada: Implications for infrastructure planning and policy*. Retrieved from http://CDOs.regionomics.com/infra/Draft-July03.pdf.

Mouffe, C. (2009). *The democratic paradox*. London, UK: Verso.

National Round Table on the Environment and the Economy. (2010). *Changing currents: Water sustainability and the future of Canada's natural resource sectors*. Retrieved from http://CDOs.nrtee-trnee.com/eng/publications/changing-currents/changing-currents-water-report-eng.pdf.

Nelson, L. S. (2001). Environmental networks: Relying on process or outcome for motivation. In M. P. Mandell (Ed.), *Getting results through collaboration: Networks and network structures for public policy and management* (pp. 89–102). Westport, CT: Quorum.

Newman, L., & Dale, A. (2005). The role of agency in sustainable local community development. *Local Environment*, 10(5), 477–486. doi: 10.1080=13549830500203121.

Parkins, J. R., & Davidson, D. J. (2008). Constructing the public sphere in compromised settings: Environmental governance in the Alberta forest sector. *Canadian Review of Sociology*, 45(2), 177–196.

Planning for Sustainable Canadian Communities Roundtable. (2005). *Integrated community sustainability planning: A background paper*. Retrieved from http://CDOs.cultureandcommunities.ca/downloads/FINAL_ICSP-Discussion-paper.pdf.

Portes, A. (1998). Social capital: Its origins and application in modern sociology. *Annual Review of Sociology, 24*(1), 1–24.

Reddel, T., & Woolcock, G. (2004). From consultation to participatory governance? *Australian Journal of Public Administration, 63*(3), 75–87.

Roseland, M. (2005). *Toward sustainable communities: Resources for citizens and their governments* (Revised ed.). Gabriola Island, BC: New Society.

Rydin, Y., & Pennington M. (2000). Public participation and local environmental planning: The collective action problem and the potential of social capital. *Local Environment, 5*(2), 153–169.

Ryfe, D. M. (2002). The practice of deliberative democracy: A study of 16 deliberative organizations. *Political Communication, 19*(3), 359–377. doi: 10.1080/01957470290055547.

Sawyer, K. (2007). *Group genius: The creative power of collaboration.* New York: Basic Books.

Village of Chauvin. (2008). *Shaping Chauvin's future: Chauvin municipal sustainability plan as of April 16, 2008.* Unpublished manuscript.

Walzer, W., & Hamm, G. F. (2010). Community visioning programs: Processes and outcomes. *Community Development, 41*(2), 152–155.

SIX

Developing Assessment and Adaptation Capacity

Integrating Climate Change Considerations into Municipal Planning in Newfoundland and Labrador

Melanie Irvine, Robert Keenan, and Kelly Vodden

Introduction

Concerns continue to mount worldwide about climate change and its local impacts. Communities in Newfoundland and Labrador (NL) are no exception and are likely to experience changes in climate that include an increase in the magnitude and frequency of storms, more variable conditions, increased flooding, rising sea levels, and increased rates of coastal erosion (Vasseur & Catto, 2008). Communities are at risk to these changes, with potential direct and indirect implications for infrastructure, natural resources, industries, social and cultural practices, and ways of life.

Planning is an important adaptation tool for communities facing changes in climate and in other aspects of their social, political, economic, and natural environments. Limited formal planning experience and capacity presents a challenge for adaptation planning in NL. The province is composed of mostly small municipalities (fewer than five thousand people) that provide a few core services such as snow clearing, garbage collection, fire protection, tax collection, and representative local government (Keenan, 2011). Limited municipal capacity can be linked to the relative infancy of the municipal sector in NL and a reliance on the provincial government, where centralized decision making has been the norm, leaving most municipalities responsible for only the most basic services (Baker, 1984; Baker & Pitt, 1988; Dunn, 2003). Since the late 1980s many NL towns have faced severe economic and demographic decline combined with pressures associated with an era of neoliberal restructuring and new public management. Experienced by municipalities across the country, these pressures include increased responsibilities, often without corresponding increases in financial resources, and rising service-delivery standards (Friedmann, 2008; Hebdon & Jalette, 2008; Kitchen, 2002; Plant, Agocs, Brunet-Jailly, & Douglas, 2005).

In this context, adapting to climate change, or even understanding climate change, is often perceived as outside the mandate and/or the capacity of municipal government. Furthermore, the distinction between climate change adaptation and mitigation is often misunderstood at the municipal level. Municipal governments may want to play a role in mitigation by constructing green buildings and cleaner, more efficient water systems, but few understand their critical role in adaptation. Municipal leaders, for example, may understand the risks of building homes at the edge of the coast or in a flood zone, but, with an undeveloped municipal-planning culture, they lack the tools to address both current and future vulnerabilities posed by permitting such construction. NL communities are not alone. A study by the Federation of Canadian Municipalities in 2002 conducted in six municipalities across the country found that formal risk management was unfamiliar to many communities. Financial and human-resource constraints, three-year council mandates, and lack of awareness of the importance of climate-change issues were identified as key barriers to incorporating climate change–related considerations into infrastructure decisions (Federation of Canadian Municipalities, 2002). Concerns about limited municipal resources and awareness related to climate change and its impacts suggest the importance of hands-on assistance and resources to assist communities to undertake risk and vulnerability assessments and to explore adaptation options.

In 2009 Memorial University of Newfoundland (MUN) geographers, Department of Environment and Conservation staff, and Municipalities Newfoundland and Labrador (MNL) began a collaboration to develop a practical reference and assessment package to support municipal decision making, raise awareness of existing and emerging climate change–related hazards, and identify opportunities and constraints in responding to these challenges. This was a new relationship between the three groups, although there was a history of MUN reseachers working with the Department of Environment and Conservation and MNL, individually. MUN has a long track record of climate-change and community-development research, and it connected experts on climatology, community development, and climate change with municipal leaders, who had the contacts and intimate knowledge of the municipal sector, and with government officials, who had climate change—and policy and program—related experience. This chapter describes the collaborative development, piloting, and preliminary assessment of a climate-change adaptation workbook and resource guide by these partners. The project ran from 2009–2011 as a significant component of the larger Atlantic Climate Adaptations Solutions (ACAS) process and national Regional Adaptation Collaboratives (RAC) initiative.

Project rationale

Challenges facing municipalities in Newfoundland and Labrador

Though all municipal systems are unique to some degree, NL's municipal system stands apart in Canada due to the province's distinct geography, settlement pattern, isolation, and historic over-reliance on one industry—the fishery. With the lowest population density of all Canadian provinces, NL has a large land base relative to a small population of approximately 509,000 (Economics and Statistics Branch, Department of Finance, the Rural Secretariat, Executive Council, and Memorial University, 2007).

While NL has relatively few people in relation to its size, it has a large number of municipalities. Currently, NL has 276 municipalities, which is more municipalities than the remaining Atlantic Canadian provinces combined. This large number of incorporated municipalities is related to the province's size and historical economy. For hundreds of years, the province's settlement pattern was driven almost exclusively by the fishery. Settlers selected their homes based on their access to bountiful fishing grounds and isolation from other competing fishers. Over the centuries, these settlements developed into mostly small, coastal communities, many of which continue to exist. The province underwent a significant period of government-sponsored resettlement, which affected 250 communities from the 1950s to 1970s, but this program did little to alter the overall settlement pattern (Royal Commission on Employment and Unemployment in Newfoundland and Labrador, 1986).

NL was the last province to join Confederation in Canada and the last to develop a modern municipal system. In the late 1940s, NL had fewer than 30 municipalities, but by the mid-1980s there were 314 (Baker & Pitt, 1988). This tenfold increase was not the result of local demands for democratic representation; rather it was the result of a need for a local structure through which provincial funding could be provided. Municipal governments became convenient agents to assist the provincial government in bringing the benefits of modernity, such as roads and water and sewer systems, to rural and remote areas.

For decades the provincial government provided municipalities with most of their annual revenue to provide municipal services and infrastructure, but little effort was made to strengthen local governments. Municipalities were not empowered to conduct future planning, to help diversify the local economy, or to be innovative in service delivery and infrastructure development and maintenance. The collapse of the cod fishery in the early 1990s challenged the entire raison d'être for many municipalities and the pillars of support for the municipal system. The province's long and profound economic recession, which preceded the cod moratorium and continued throughout the 1990s, resulted in significant changes in the level of provincial government support available to municipalities. For example, the provincial government stopped providing planning services for municipalities, requiring all municipalities to conduct their own planning at their own cost. Provincial operating grants available to municipalities were also cut by 60% (Government of NL, 2007). With many still reeling from the decline of the fishery, municipalities were not prepared for these cutbacks. Having relied on provincial government support for decades, municipalities had not developed into economically sustainable, or even responsible, entities. Most municipalities imposed either very low or no municipal property tax. As a result, they had no means to make up for the services or revenue once provided to them by the provincial government. Moreover, with many areas of the province economically depressed, it was uncertain whether a shrinking number of residents would have the capacity to pay an increased property tax.

Therefore, when the province pulled its support for municipal planning, most municipalities simply stopped planning. As of 2007, less than half had an emergency-preparedness or capital-works plan, less than one third had a land-use plan, and very few had sustainability plans. When the provincial government cut back on operating grants, municipalities tried to cope by altering operations, and services and infrastructure maintenance and the provision of services suffered as a result. Municipalities found themselves in increased financial difficulty, their debts ballooning to such levels that the provincial government was compelled to establish a debt-reduction program (Braun-Jackson, Feehan, Penney, & Tomblin, 2009).

The municipal system has not yet recovered from the dual shock of reduced provincial government services and reduced provincial government funding. For decades, a municipal office did not need more than one full- or part-time employee; any support not available at the local level was usually available at the provincial level. Now, many municipalities need more staff to conduct planning, economic development, and to maintain infrastructure, but they cannot afford more than one full-time clerk. Of the 276 municipalities in NL, 239 have fewer than 2,000 people, and over half (143) of those have fewer than 500. Few of these 239 municipalities have the resources to be considered sustainable according to increasing standards for municipal operations or to adapt to the many changes they face, including climate change.

Considering climate change impacts and adaptation in community planning

Residents of NL have a long and intimate relationship with weather- and climate-related issues. Storms that endanger people working at sea or ice conditions that allow for winter travel in some instances while serving as a barrier to travel in others are just two examples. As climate conditions change so do these interconnected aspects of life in the province.

The nature and seriousness of the climate change–associated risks impacting communities varies based on factors that include climate, location, topography, and geology. Most communities in NL are built along the coast. During extreme weather events, strong winds and waves can damage coastal infrastructure and flood low-lying areas. Slow, ongoing processes such as erosion also threaten roads, houses, and other structures built along coastlines (Vasseur & Catto, 2008). Many communities are also vulnerable to river flooding, particularly during periods of heavy rain and throughout the spring snowmelt. The impacts of climate-related issues extend beyond infrastructure damage, however, having social, economic, and environmental consequences. Communities in NL are often built on top, at the face, or at the base of steep slopes, and rockfalls, landslides, mudflows, and other forms of slope movement have claimed the lives of at least 50 people in the province, and injured many others, since the 1880s (Liverman, Batterson, Taylor, & Ryan, 2001). Dry springs and summers occurring in conjunction with limited snowmelt have resulted in water shortages in communities whose key economic industries rely on fresh water, such as fish-processing plants.

Climate change—long-term changes in weather conditions[1]—is expected to result in increased climate variability and more extreme weather in the near future, as well as long-term changes in climate variables such as precipitation and temperature. This will translate into environmental changes, which may increase the magnitude and/or frequency of climate-related impacts. For instance, communities in NL have observed a decrease in the extent and duration of sea ice, which increases shoreline exposure to the erosive power of tides and waves. These threats are not consistent throughout the province, and there are areas of higher and lower risk based on local geography. Such exposure also raises the potential for damage to coastal infrastructure such as wharfs, breakwaters, roads, and buildings. Certainly, the projected rise in sea level will impact areas at risk of coastal flooding and erosion (Batterson & Liverman, 2010). Local knowledge in many communities suggests that winters are now warmer and more variable than they have been, making winter travel over lakes and ponds to reach fishing, hunting, and cabin areas more challenging and dangerous. Increased variation in temperatures will also cause an increase in the frequency of freeze-thaw cycles (which is the freezing and expansion of water) thereby increasing the risk of slope movement (Batterson, McCuaig, & Taylor, 2006). It is important to note, however, that changes in climate may also result in opportunities, notably longer construction and growing seasons and increased potential for marine transportation between Labrador and the Island of Newfoundland due to a decrease in the spatient extent and duration of ice cover.

The impacts of climate-change issues on communities are dependent on multiple factors, including the nature, frequency, and magnitude of the risk, the perception of how the risk will impact communities, and the ability to cope or adapt (Dolan & Walker, 2003; Hopkin, 2010). Through adaptations, communities can modify their operations, management, infrastructure, and land uses to respond to risks. Effective adaptation, however, requires an understanding and examination of the local impacts of climate change on different sectors of the community and the integration of climate-related issues in community-level planning and decision making (Kelly & Adger, 2000).

Most of the province's municipalities have suffered through a prolonged and severe wave of out-migration since the early 1990s. For many of these municipalities, planning for and adapting to a long-term future are difficult when it is hard to imagine these municipalities remaining in their current form in 15 to 20 years. Instead, the preoccupation of town leaders is with how to fulfill their responsibilities while managing significant economic and demographic constraints.

Though municipalities in NL have limited planning resources, all municipal governments were required to submit to the provincial government by the end of March 2010 Integrated Community Sustainability Plans (ICSPs) pursuant to the Canada–Newfoundland and Labrador Gas Tax Agreement. While, for many municipalities, planning is an unaffordable luxury, the provincial government compelled municipal cooperation in the planning effort by making continued access to gas-tax funding dependent on the completion of an ICSP. The intent of the ICSP process was to encourage more long-term, coherent, participatory, community planning and decision making across the country (Planning for Sustainable Canadian Communities Roundtable, 2005). Underlying this goal was the premise that even, and perhaps especially, small, threatened communities can benefit from addressing their sustainability challenges through an effective planning process.

Gas-tax funds are designated for two main purposes: capacity building and environmentally sustainable, municipal infrastructure, emphasizing the importance of the ecological pillar of sustainable communities and community efforts to minimize their ecological footprint. A provincial framework for ICSPs specifically noted reduced greenhouse-gas emissions as an example of the types of environmental benefits that should result from gas-tax investments (Department of Municipal Affairs Newfoundland and Labrador [MA], 2009). As a result many NL communities mention energy use and/or greenhouse-gas reduction within their ICSPs. Few, however, refer to climate-change adaptation. In a review of a sample of 16 ICSPs representing 27 communities of varying sizes, for example, 11 refer to greenhouse-gas emission reduction but only two mention the need to adapt to climate change. This reflects a low level of awareness of and/or priority placed on climate change–related impacts in planning, despite the municipalities' intimate relationship with weather and climate described above. The ICSP process appears to have been a missed opportunity by municipalities to raise climate-change issues. This is consistent, however, with the situation across Canada, where "municipal government adaptation strategies are at an early stage" and a consistent approach and resources and tools to assist municipalities with assessing vulnerabilities and adaptation options are lacking (Federation of Canadian Municipalities, 2009, p. 5).

The climate-change assessment tool process

The players

At both the provincial and federal government levels, climate-change adaptation policies are being pursued with a needed sense of urgency. Within the past few years, significant resources have been devoted to assist adaptation efforts at the provincial and municipal levels. Following up on its 2008 "National Assessment of Climate Change Impact in Canada," Natural Resources Canada announced a program for the development of Regional Adaptation Collaboratives (RACs) to support the advancement of climate-change adaptation in six regions across Canada.

In Atlantic Canada, the RAC is referred to as Atlantic Climate Adaptations Solutions (ACAS), which is managed by the Atlantic Climate Adaptations Solutions Association (ACASA). The ACASA, headquartered in Halifax, is a partnership between all four Atlantic provincial governments and the Atlantic Canadian municipal associations, planning associations, and engineering associations. The ACASA is also supported by various post-secondary institutions in the Atlantic provinces, with MUN playing a significant role in NL.

With a mandate derived from the Council of Atlantic Environment Ministers' Climate Change Adaptation Commitment, the ACASA is working to:

1. Pursue collaboration among the Atlantic provinces and others to develop effective, regional, long-term, climate-change adaptation responses;
2. Deliver significant, on-the-ground "mainstreaming" of climate-change adaptation considerations in decision making through education and engagement of professional organization networks and decision makers;
3. Support the development and deployment of environmental information, technologies, and innovation practice to inform decisions; and
4. Develop and implement climate-change adaptation measures, including toolkits that actively support a range of adaptation initiatives. (Atlantic Environment Ministers, 2008)

Within the ACASA each province has its own steering committee and projects. One of NL's primary commitments for the Atlantic RAC is to develop a tool kit to assist municipalities with climate-change adaptation. Development of the tool kit is being led by the provincial Department of Environment and Conservation, with several contributing individual components (including the project discussed in this chapter) development and piloting of a climate-change adaptation workbook and accompanying resource guide.

The creation and implementation of the workbook and resource guide has been a collaborative effort involving a number of organizations and communities. The project was led by the Geography Department at MUN, working in partnership with the Provincial Department of Environment and Conservation, Municipalities Newfoundland and Labrador (MNL), Professional Municipal Administrators (PMA), and six pilot communities. Representatives from the Atlantic Planners Institute, the Rural Secretariat, and the Department of Municipal Affairs were also involved in an advisory role, providing valued input into the materials created.

The approach

The overall project approach involved three key elements: (a) partnerships, (b) the tool kit approach to planning assistance, and (c) an integrated, community-risk and -vulnerability assessment methodology that considers risk and vulnerability within a broader resilience and integrated community-planning framework (Parewick, Vodden, Catto, & Renaud, 2010). This collaborative, resilience-centred approach is contrasted with the more technocratic and physical hazards–focused tradition in risk and hazards assessment (Chester, 1993; Hewitt, 1983).

The goal of the project was to make climate change–related information available, useful, and relevant to communities to provide them with a basis for decision making. But, in the spirit of collaboration, the project would benefit all partners by providing provincial agencies with a better understanding of the issues and challenges being faced by municipalities and by filling a gap in the literature with respect to climate-change adaptation in small communities in peripheral regions, particularly in NL.

In recent decades, compendia of reference materials referred to as "tool kits" have become increasingly popular as resources to guide readers through demanding or unfamiliar tasks. "Tools" typically include checklists, questionnaires, and other content users can work through selectively and at their own pace. Appropriate for a collaborative endeavour such as this project, tool kits often straddle the domains of theory and practice. Tool kits can be a versatile means of creating awareness of priority issues and good practices in use to address them. They may also be incomplete, however, or lead to inappropriate "Band-Aid" or "cookie-cutter" solutions and in turn lead to serious problems. Tool kits must be contextualized and are best utilized in concert with hands-on support and collaboration among scientific, government, and community sectors (Parewick et al., 2010).

Community-risk and -vulnerability assessments (CRVAs) "are used by communities to determine the vulnerability of people, property, and the natural environment to the risks posed by hazards" (NOAA Coastal Services Centre, n.d.). A review of CRVA frameworks revealed a relatively standard array of methods, some apparently better-suited for application in NL communities. In particular, approaches that are participatory, help build capacity, are situated in place, and recognize community strengths and opportunities as well as threats were considered most appropriate.

The traditionally dominant risk-assessment approach is criticized for heavy reliance on scientific and technical expertise and solutions, emphasizing physical hazards (Chester, 1993; Hewitt, 1983). In contrast, vulnerability assessment tends to consider a wider range of factors.

In the context of climate change, vulnerability is "the degree to which a system is susceptible to, or unable to cope with, adverse effects of climate, including climate variability and extremes" (Public Infrastructure Engineering Vulnerability Committee [PIEVC], Canadian Council of Professional Engineers, 2007). The character, magnitude, and rate of change in climate to which a system is exposed, together with its capacity to adjust practices, processes, or structures in response to or anticipation of changes in conditions all contribute to both vulnerability or resilience, meaning "the capacity to buffer perturbations, self-organize, learn and adapt" (Folke et al., 2002, p. 51).

Processes of planning for community sustainability must involve an appreciation of the unpredictable nature of complex social-ecological systems (SES) and an effort to build the capacity to adjust (adapt) to unexpected external shocks or disturbances (Gunderson & Holling, 2002). Resilience literature emphasizes continual interactions and interdependence between social and ecological systems and an evolutionary notion of sustainability that incorporates concepts such as self-organization and complex adaptive systems into the understanding of vulnerability and resilience (Holling, Gunderson, & Peterson, 2001; Iyer-Raniga & Treloar, 2000; Scoones, 1999).

In this project, we drew from each of these three key elements—partnerships and collaboration, tool kits used in concert with hands-on support, and integrated community-risk and -vulnerability assessment within a resilience framework—in a way that was deemed appropriate for the NL community context. The intent was to generate, through this combination, cross-disciplinary types of knowledge and related approaches to planning practice that would be applied in NL but also in other ACASA member provinces that would adapt and utilize this appoach.

The process

Following a review of CRVA frameworks, municipal consultations were conducted as a first step in the process of creating a municipal tool kit for climate-change adaptation. Through the consultations, feedback was sought from municipal leaders on what kinds of tools and information, including both format and content, would be most appropriate for community decision makers. The Government of NL, through the Department of Environment and Conservation, provided a grant to MNL to conduct four consultations, in partnership with Memorial University, between November 2009 and February 2010. The sessions were held in St. John's, Corner Brook, Gander, and Labrador City. A report on the consultations was released in June 2010. The consultations provided important insights and experience to the facilitators and project partners. Further, feedback form data indicated that all of the participants would recommend the session to a colleague. The majority of participants strongly agreed that the sessions were infomative and vaulable, and many volunteered their communities as potential participants in the assessment pilot phase that followed (Parewick, Keenan, Vodden, & Catto, 2010).

As was discussed earlier, NL is composed of many small municipalities and few municipalities with more than five thousand residents. One distinction between larger and smaller municipalities that was emphasized during the consultations is the level of capacity and sophistication that most larger municipalities possess relative to smaller towns. Larger municipalities have several staff members, many of whom have post-secondary degrees and provide specialized services such as engineering or land-use planning. In contrast, no municipality in NL of fewer than five thousand residents has a land-use planner, and the vast majority have no engineers on staff.

These significant differences in capacity affected the municipal consultations in two related ways. The first involved perception. The consultations were poorly attended, despite significant promotional efforts: the consultation dates and locations were announced at least two months in advance, an invitation letter and registration form were faxed to every municipality, the consultations were advertised on a weekly basis by MNL, and follow-up phone calls were made to municipalities during the week before the consultations. Nonetheless, the Newfoundland consultations were attended by only six municipalities (staff and council members), a consultant, and two provincial government planners. Of the six municipalities that attended the Newfoundland sessions, three were from the 16 municipalities in the province with a population over five thousand. The

Labrador consultation was the best attended. This event benefitted from a partnership with the Combined Councils of Labrador Annual General Meeting, which attracted an additional six municipalities.

The low turnout was linked to a perception among small towns that they have no role in climate change or managing its impacts (an opinion that seems to slowly be changing, particularly since Hurricane Igor in September 2010). For smaller municipalities, climate change is seen as a global issue that is outside of their capacity to affect change. Leaders of small municipalities note changes in sea levels, increased coastal erosion and flooding, and shorter winters, but they often lack the resources to react to these changes and/or do not see links between individual weather-related events and climate change. For example, two municipalities, Gambo and Badger, that had been severely affected by weather-related issues were contacted regarding attending MNL's climate-change consultations. Both replied that they thought that the consultations did not apply to them. This small-town perception of climate change highlighted a particular challenge that the developers of a municipal climate-change tool kit would face: how to make climate change and climate-change adaptation relevant and practical to small municipalities.

MNL's consultations also highlighted the impact that capacity differences have on the extent and ways in which municipalities can pursue adaptation policies. The three larger municipalities that attended the consultations were all represented by municipal staff—a town manager, a municipal engineer, a land-use planner, and a sustainability officer—who were professionals with some planning background, knowledge of or exposure to technical tools, and were familiar with climate change. In contrast, the three smaller municipalities were represented by mayors, deputy mayors, or councillors, who were motivated to learn more about climate-change adaptation and did not have the level of technical knowledge or tools available to large municpalities. As a result, the consultations tended to be dominated by the former group discussing tools, particularly geographic information systems (GIS), which were not understood by the other municipal leaders in attendance and are not currently available to the vast majority of municipalities.

This raised a second challenge for developing a climate change–related tool kit for municipalities. The tool kit would have to carefully account for the significant technological and expertise differences that exist between large and small municipalities. It was stressed by everyone involved in the consultations that the tool kit has to empower, not intimidate, municipalities. To achieve this result, those creating the tool kit would have to boil down vulnerability considerations and municipal adaptation options to an appropriate level so that climate-change threats and adaptation solutions could be identified and understood with nothing more than a map, some markers, and the tool kit.

With this guidance in mind, the team set out to create and pilot a climate change–adaptation tool that can be used by communities to aid in the identification and assessment of current and future climate-related issues. The process also assesses the feasibility of adaptation options that will help users best cope with or take advantage of issues identified. The tool, a workbook and accompanying resource guide, is intended to be suitable for communities across NL and guides users through a process to identify the implications of climate change for their communities, including implications for community operations and management, infrastructure, and social, economic, and environmental impacts.

An array of adaptation tool kits have been implemented in other provinces and territories in the country, but through the consultations and previous experience of the project team, a need to create an adaptation tool specifically designed for communities in NL was identified. Having a local adaptation tool ensures that the issues and options discussed in the tool are relevant and suitable given the needs and capacities of communities, that applicable resources and case studies are provided, and that the format and language used are appropriate. Because their needs and circumstances differ, the tool was written for communities on the Island of Newfoundland and modified for communities in Labrador.

The workbook consists of an introduction in which types of climate-related issues are described and explored, followed by seven, individual, issues-based sections: coastal issues (primarily coastal flooding and erosion), land-based flooding, slope movement, winter issues, forest fires, and drinking water. An "other" section was also included in the event that a community is experiencing issues not included in one of the six sections already mentioned.

Within each issue-based section, users are guided through a seven-step process:

1. Identifying the types of issues impacting a community
2. Mapping the location(s) impacted (or will be impacted)
3. Examining which infrastructure will be affected
4. Looking at the residents who will be most affected and who can help
5. Evaluating the economic sectors most impacted and any potential economic opportunities
6. Looking at the impacts on the natural environment
7. Assessing ways to address concerns and opportunities that have been identified.

The workbook concludes with a "moving forward" section, where past adaptation efforts are described, and the feasibility of future strategies that users can adopt to help them best cope with, or take advantage of, the issue are explored.

The seven-step process was adapted from the National Oceanic and Atmospheric Administration's (NOAA) Community Vulnerability Assessment. The NOAA tool kit was selected as a model due to its strong use of visuals, straightforward, step-by-step process, inclusion of all aspects of a community (facilities and infrastructure, society and culture, economy and environment), and strong focus on adaptations, which are all characteristics considered suitable for communities in NL.

The step-by-step, issue-based workbook includes a series of short questions and tables to guide users through identifying climate-related issues and their implications on communities. Checklists are in place to ensure that users understand and complete each section. The text is supported by photos, figures, and tables. Local case studies are used to illustrate potential implications and adaptation options. Prior surveys of municipal councillors provide a good understanding of the average education level of municipal leaders, therefore the tool employs non-technical language at a grade level considered appropriate (Grade 8). As well, scientific terms or concepts are defined. As access to computers is limited for some towns and potential users, the tool is available in both digital and paper format.

A resource guide accompanies the workbook. It includes local case studies describing the impact of climate-related issues on other communities and adaptation solutions pursued, with details such as the steps, cost, time, resources, material, and personnel required for specific adaptations; a list of financial resources; sources of information and technical support; concepts and definitions; and examples of assessment, prioritization, planning, and evaluation methods.

The tool was piloted in six communities across the Island of Newfoundland in 2010–2011. Communities were selected based on expressions of interest following the consultation sessions discussed above as well as consideration of their varied characteristics (e.g., size, location, capacity, climate-change issues). All pilot communities were coastal. They included the city of Corner Brook and the town of Irishtown-Summerside in western Newfoundland, the town of Indian Bay in central Newfoundland, the town of Fortune on the Burin Peninsula, and Ferryland and Logy Bay-Middle Cove-Outer Cove on the Avalon Peninsula in eastern Newfoundland.

Following each municipal council's approval to participate in the project, a key contact was selected. The key contact was generally the town clerk or mayor, who was critical to the project's success by ensuring proper communication between the project team and the community, and by providing guidance and background information. Select community members such as seniors, long-term residents, and municipal staff and councillors were then interviewed to gain local information. When available and appropriate, experts were also interviewed (academics, scientists, engineers).

In addition, literature reviews were conducted for each community and compiled in the form of a community background report. The literature explored included peer-reviewed papers and studies, government reports, historical information, municipal self-assessments, plans, and stories from the media. The project team also analyzed relevant data such as stream flow, relative sea-level rise, and temperature and precipitation patterns, and presented results to community members.

After background information was collected, reviewed, and synthesized, a topic and date for a community workshop was chosen. Project team members facilitated a three-hour workshop in each community, where one topic in the workbook was explored in detail. Workshops were interactive and aimed to engage participants to explore climate change–related issues. Community members worked with various maps of their communities, which enabled them to circle areas that were or may become at risk of being effected by climate-related issues. The project team later returned to the community to further explore adaptation options and to obtain feedback on a community report. Communities were encouraged to put the constraint map that had been created as part of the process on the wall in their townhall as a reminder of the areas at risk, and three communities agreed.

Based on the pilot project, three, dominant, climate-related issues emerged as having significant implications: coastal erosion, flooding, and slope movement. Coastal erosion and flooding are occurring in all of the six pilot communities. For example, in Ferryland, coastal erosion and flood events are damaging the road access to the Colony of Avalon, a 17th-century archaeology site, in addition to several homes, and the Lighthouse Picnics enterprise, which is an economically important tourist site for the area. Despite efforts to protect the shoreline with a breakwater, winter storms continue to cause damage. The loss of access to these areas of the community would have significant economic, social, and cultural implications for Ferryland.

Inland flooding is also a concern for most of the communities, primarily as a result of heavy rain, storms, and snowmelt. In Indian Bay rapid snowmelt in the spring and heavy rains in the fall have resulted in river flooding in a portion of the community where a church, homes, a town park, a water pump station, and a historic and current graveyard are at risk. Flooding in Indian Bay has been increasing in both magnitude and frequency in recent years. Slope movement, in particular avalanches, landslides, and rockfalls, were also stressed as significant climate-related concerns.

Issues of more minor concern discussed with pilot communities included the quality of the drinking water, both within communities and in the backcountry. Causes of poor water quality were primarily associated with aging or inadequate infrastructure and lack of qualified water-treatment personnel, and not with climate-related issues. Winter issues, or more precisely the change in winter conditions, is a concern in some of the pilot communities, in particular for those whose residents travel to cabins and fishing areas during the winter months. Forest fire was not noted as a major concern in the pilot communities.

Options for adaptation

Education and dissemination of knowledge and information was voiced as a critical necessity for climate-change adaptation in the pilot communities. Project participants in Corner Brook suggested, for example, there is still disbelief in the community that climate change is real, and will have implications for people living there. Workshop participants felt that residents need to understand how climate change will impact them on a personal level, and what they can do about it. Drainage and slope issues need to be explained in non-technical ways. Creating brochures or flyers that do not necessarily focus on climate change but require residents to think about whether or not a place is a safe one in which to live, is one avenue. Other suggested ways to transmit information include the facilitation of focus groups and workshops, and efforts focused on banks and other sources of development financing.

Communities also expressed the need for increased monitoring, assessment, and data collection to allow for a greater understanding of the current conditions and characteristics of the physical environment. More data, such as geotechnical analysis and flood-risk mapping, would be useful for Corner Brook to better cope with slope movement and river flooding, for example. In order to inform residents about which areas may be too dangerous for travel, the Indian Bay municipal council discussed a desire to monitor the ice conditions of ponds used in the winter for ice fishing and transportation routes to cabins. Project participants expressed the need for province-wide regulations and legislation to provide backing for councils to make difficult, preventative zoning decisions. There is also a need for education about the building policies and regulations that do exist. For instance, in Irishtown-Summerside members of council are unsure of the legal limits of building on floodplains, and if they are legally able to not allow development in areas at high risk of flooding, slope movement, or erosion. Members of council are not sure which existing acts, legislation, or bylaws could provide backing and support for decision making regarding land-use and landscape risks.

Another important adaption strategy mentioned was land-use changes and restrictions. For instance, restricting wood cutting near riverbanks would decrease the risk of flooding and aid in slope stabilization and soil retention. Slope stabilization through planting vegetation was noted as a relatively low-cost option, with plants such as alder, ground juniper, red-osier dogwood, bearberry, lance-leaved and rough-leaved goldenrod being options that establish quickly, develop a strong and widespread root system to stabilize soils, and can grow in a variety of nutrient-poor and well-drained soils.

The maintenance, upkeep, and replacement of aging or inadequate infrastructure was an option mentioned by most pilot communities as critical to being prepared for climate-related issues. For example, Irishtown-Summerside feels an extension to the town marina would prevent coastal erosion and slumping, which is currently threatening residential homes and property in the area. The town of Fortune installed gabion walls along its shoreline, which was eroding, and project participants feel this has prevented significant shoreline erosion.

Increased communication among communities, between communities and outside agencies, and between relevant agencies was also suggested. In order to better deal with drainage problems enhanced by upstream development, participants from Logy Bay-Middle Cove-Outer Cove would like to see improved communication between their community and the neighbouring City of St. John's. Ferryland representatives voiced the importance and need for communication among groups coming into the community to ensure that the needs and priorities of Ferryland are addressed in an appropriate manner and to ensure that financial resources are being distributed effectively.

Conclusions

Based on the pilot project, there was agreement from all project participants that the climate is changing. Conditions are generally more variable and less predictable, and this will impact communities in a diversity of ways. What communities did in the past to cope with climate-related issues will not be sufficient in the future.

Project participants felt there is a need to increase the inclusion of climate-related issues in community planning and management. This is in part because, as one councillor pointed out, communities are sometimes unaware that they have an issue, or they do not realize that climate change can actually impact them until they talk about it.

It is too early to discuss long-term project outcomes, but initial feedback suggests an increased interest in, awareness of, and, we hope, understanding of, climate change and its impacts. As a caveat though, increased interest will not likely translate into incorporation into municipal decision making without measures to address the many other challenges faced in both planning and adaptation.

Contributions to communities

Potential benefits for communities demonstrated through the project include access to tools and information to support community-level decision making about climate-related issues. This can lead into increased awareness, knowledge, and inclusion of these issues in community planning, operations, and management. In order to increase the understanding of the types, causes, and seriousness of climate-related issues, we analyzed relevant data such as temperature, precipitation, and stream flow. As most communities in the pilot project lacked the time, resources, and often the ability to examine such information, project participants benefitted from having support from university and government partners to help them gain an increased understanding of local trends.

Each community had a facilitated workshop to explore and discuss climate-related issues and adaptation options. The majority of project participants felt the workshops were a valuable exercise, and the participatory mapping process was particularly beneficial in stimulating discussions and increasing the understanding of specific locations where issues are occurring and where residents may be vulnerable. Project participants feel that increased awareness of climate and climate change–related issues will translate to increased consideration of these issues when municipalities make planning and management decisions in the future.

While the completed workbook provides the beginnings of a community climate change–adaptation strategy, it also provides information that can be used directly for ICSPs, land-use planning, economic development, infrastructure planning, emergency preparedness, and other local planning efforts. Integration of climate-change considerations into these existing processes, rather than viewing them as yet another task, is seen as critical.

Difficulties encountered

Community engagement and commitment was a challenge throughout the project. Community leaders and volunteers are busy, have limited resources, and face many immediate concerns that take precedence over longer-term considerations. In addition, many community leaders do not see the connection between their communities and climate change. For those communities that did express interest in participating in the project, one concern in some cases was a potential lack of genuine commitment to the entire process, with some communities participating for a specific purpose (e.g., documentation in support of a particular project). For risk and vulnerability assessment to reach its full potential, communities need to be willing to undertake the process with an open mind, considering all potential issues and options.

As anticipated, planning-capacity challenges had to be taken into account in the project. Most communities in the pilot project did not have the staff or personnel to adequately assess the feasibility of adaptation options, or the economic means to carry out identified solutions. This process is also time intensive, taking a year or more to complete, thus maintaining initial community interest was a challenge in some communities. Yet time limitations resulted in the community workshop having a focus on climate-related issues rather than adaptation options and primarily on understanding the impacts of a single priority issue. A longer workshop, or series of workshops, would have allowed a greater exploration of solutions and other important concerns. The long-term viability of the workbook and resource guide as a useful tool is likely to require a delivery mechanism that can shorten the overall process of assessment and developing a climate-change adaptation plan for communities unwilling to enter into a longer-term process. ACASA partners in New Brunswick are currently piloting a more rapid assessment approach, adapting the NL tools and process. Comparisons of the results of this process in the two provinces promises to be informative.

Most project participants felt the workbook was written in a suitable manner with clear and concise questions. However, some participants felt portions of the workbook were either not suitable, or not presented and explored in sufficient detail. For some participants from smaller communities, the issues were relatively new, and discussed in plain language. While larger pilot communities had suggested early in the pilot process that one tool could suit towns of all sizes as a starting point, this feedback highlights the difficulty of creating a resource that is suitable for users with varying backgrounds, expectations, and capacities.

Guidance for future work

One critical element in the climate-change assessment and adaptation process described here was facilitation of the process. A facilitator, or facilitators, who have a background in both community planning and an understanding of climate change is required. Both the project team and community members felt that without someone from outside the community guiding the workshop and other stages of the project, community engagement would have been reduced. The involvement of outside agencies and resource people helped to stimulate and maintain interest in the project. In addition, community members felt that the project team provided them with very important, local information.

Planning for climate change requires sufficient information on past climate events and trends, together with causes and impacts of climate-related issues on municipal infrastructure and operations (Canadian Council of Professional Engineers, 2008; Federation of Canadian Municipalities, 2002). The project team conducted a review and synthesis of local information (past studies, interviews, data) to assist in the assessment process. Some information needs, such as future scenarios for climate variables at the local level, involve data analysis such as climate downscaling that requires expertise not generally found in communities. Therefore, this process is not feasible for many communities without outside support from university and/or government partners. At the same time, residents, municipal staff, and political leaders contributed necessary knowledge related to previous local events and community conditions.

Thus, a collaborative approach was essential, incorporating what Burke (2000), Friedmann (2008) and others have referred to as "knowledges." The expertise, experience, and knowledge of each project contributor, and the range of backgrounds, were critical in ensuring the project methodology and products were applicable, relevant, and suitable for communities on the Island of Newfoundland. Community reviews of the workbook resulted in modification of its content, and advice from provincial officials and municipal associations improved the format and content of the workbook and the facilitated assessment process.

The project also demonstrated the need for continuing education on climate-related issues within the municipal sector. Climate-related issues are likely to intensify, and there is the need to continue to raise awareness and keep climate change and its impacts "on the radar" of municipal leaders. Yet with so many other priorities facing communities in NL, and so few resources, greater awareness and increased municipal vulnerability will not necessarily result in the greater integration of climate-change considerations and municipal planning. Communities need external support such as facilitation and scientific advice, together with guidelines and examples, to ensure sustainable, long-term planning and to assist with the use of scientific information. Developing tool kits with the expectation that most municipalities will then be able to conduct risk and vulnerability assessments and develop adaptation plans on their own is an example of the "fend for yourself" approach common within a neoliberal era. The experience of this project suggests instead that collaborative planning and governance models are more appropriate for dealing with complex challenges such as climate change and community sustainability (Healy, 1997; Vodden, 2009).

Senior government support may be technical or financial, but incentives or even requirements that are taken seriously by government agencies are also beneficial, particularly when combined with other supports. Current funding for adaptation is lacking and represents a major barrier for many towns. Tying infrastructure funding to a requirement to consider climate-change impacts is one example of an approach that could be used to reward communities for having given climate-related issues consideration within their planning. Examples of ICSPs and emergency preparedness plans in the province demonstrate that unless the need for planning and consideration of climate-change adaptation is emphasized by the provincial government and tied to funding, support, and deadlines, it is likely to remain in the hands of only the most proactive and well-resourced communities.

During the course of the project, relationships were built between Memorial University and the communities. Factors contributing to sucessful partnerships included repeated visits by the research team to the communities over a period of over one year and continuity on the side of both the research team and the communities. If the key researcher changed, or if the key community contact was no longer able to participate in the project, this had negative implications on the partners' relationship. Time and continuity contributed to building trust and familiarity between project players.

Finally, the NL pilot project illustrates that, with appropriate supports and incentives in place, it will be important to continue to work at integrating climate-change adaptation into existing planning processes such as ICSPs and emergency preparedness plans (often referred to as "mainstreaming climate change"). Situating climate-change adaptation within an overall community-development framework, provides the critical benefit of integrating information and tasks in environments where planning requirements are increasing without corresponding increases in human and financial resources. This leaves community leaders with difficult decisions to make about how to allocate limited resources among a growing range of priorities and challenging planning issues.

Note

1. Climate describes variables such as temperature and precipitation over a long time period (30 years or more). Weather is the term used to describe these same variables over a short period of time.

References

Atlantic Environment Ministers. (2008). Climate change adaptation strategy for Atlantic Canada. Retrieved June 2, 2011, from http://www.gnb.ca/0009/0369/0018/0002-e.pdf.

Baker, M. (1984). Local government in Newfoundland and Labrador before 1982. *Encyclopedia of Newfoundland and Labrador, Vol. 2.* Retrieved June 8, 2011, from http://www.ucs.mun.ca/~melbaker/LocalGovtNLpre1982.pdf.

Baker, M., & Pitt, J. (1988, October 7–9). *The third tier: A historical overview of the development of local government in Newfoundland and Labrador.* Presented at the Convention of the Newfoundland and Labrador Federation of Municipalities, St. John's, NL.

Batterson, M., & Liverman, D. (2010). Past and future sea-level change in Newfoundland and Labrador: Guidelines for policy and planning. *Current Research Geological, Newfoundland and Labrador Department of Natural Resources, Geological Survey Report, 10-1,* 129–141.

Batterson, M. J., McCuaig, S. J., & Taylor, D. (2006). Mapping and assessing risk of geological hazards on the northeast Avalon Peninsula and Humber Valley, Newfoundland. *Current Research, Newfoundland and Labrador Department of Natural Resources, Geological Survey Report, 06-1,* 147–160.

Braun-Jackson, J., Feehan, J. P., Penney, R., & Tomblin, S. (2009). Newfoundland and Labrador. In A. Sancton and R. Young (Eds.), *Foundations of governance:*

Municipal government in Canada's provinces (pp. 453–486). Toronto: University of Toronto Press.

Burke, P. (2000). *A social history of knowledge: From Gutenberg to Diderot.* Cambridge, UK: Polity Press.

Canadian Council of Professional Engineers. (2008). *Adapting to climate change: Canada's first national engineering vulnerability assessment of public infrastructure.* Retrieved December 20, 2011, from http://www.pievc.ca/e/Adapting_to_climate_Change_Report_Final.pdf.

Chester, D. (1993). *Volcanoes and society.* London: Edward Arnold.

Department of Municipal Affairs Newfoundland and Labrador (MA). (2009). *Integrated community sustainability plan.* Retrieved June 26, 2011, from http://www.ma.gov.nl.ca/ma/publications/icsp/newfoundland-and-labrador-icsp-framework.pdf.

Dolan. H., & Walker, I. (2003). Understanding vulnerability of coastal communities to climate change related risks. *Journal of Coastal Research,* Special Issue 39. Proceedings of the 8th International Coastal Symposium, Itajaí, SC, Brazil.

Dunn, C. (2003, May 9–10). *Provincial mediation of federal–municipal relations in Newfoundland and Labrador.* Presented at the Institute of Intergovernmental Relations Conference, Kingston, ON: Queen's University.

Economics and Statistics Branch, Department of Finance, the Rural Secretariat, Executive Council, and Memorial University. (2007). *Regional demographic profiles Newfoundland and Labrador.* St. John's: Government of Newfoundland and Labrador.

Federation of Canadian Municipalities. (2002). *Final report on Federation of Canadian Municipalities municipal infrastructure risk project: Adapting to climate change.* Ottawa: Natural Resources Canada.

———. (2009). *Partners for climate protection: Municipal resources for adapting to climate change.* Ottawa: Federation of Canadian Municipalities.

Folke, C., Carpenter, S., Elmqvist, T., Gunderson, L., Holling, C. S., Walker, B., & Svedin, U. (2002). *Resilience and sustainable development: Building adaptive capacity in a world of transformations.* Scientific background paper on resilience prepared for the process of the World Summit on Sustainable Development on behalf of The Environmental Advisory Council to the Swedish Government, Stockholm: Environmental Advisory Council, Ministry of the Environment.

Friedmann, J. (2008). The uses of planning theory: A bibliographic essay. *Journal of Planning Education and Research, 28,* 247–257.

Government of Newfoundland and Labrador. (2007). *Annual report 2005/06, Department of Municipal Affairs.* Retrieved January 2010 from http://www.ma.gov.nl.ca/ma/publications/annual_reports/annualreport2005_06revisedapril202007.pdf.

Gunderson, L., & Holling, C. S. (2002). *Panarchy: Understanding transformations in human and natural systems.* Washington, DC: Island Press.

Healey, P. (1997). *Collaborative planning: Shaping places in fragmented societies.* London, UK: Macmillan.

Hebdon, R., & Jalette, P. (2008). The restructuring of municipal services: A Canada–United States comparison. *Environment and Planning C: Government and Policy, 26,* 144–158.

Hewitt, K. (Ed). (1983). *Interpretation of calamity: From the viewpoint of human ecology.* Boston: Allen.

Holling, C. S., Gunderson, L. H., & Peterson, G. D. (2001). Sustainability and panarchies. In L. H. Gunderson & C. S. Holling (Eds.), *Panarchy: Understanding transformations in human and natural systems* (pp. 63–103). Washington, DC: Island Press.

Hopkin, P. (2010). *Fundamentals of risk management: Understanding, evaluating and implementing effective risk management.* Philadelphia: Kogan Page Limited.

Iyer-Raniga, U., & Treloar, G. (2000). FORUM: A context for participation in sustainable development. *Environmental Management 26*(4), 349–361.

Keenan, R. (2011). *Census of municipalities in Newfoundland and Labrador 2011.* St. John's: Municipalities Newfoundland and Labrador.

Kelly, P. M., & Adger, W. N. (2000). Theory and practice in assessing vulnerability to climate change and facilitating adaptation. *Climate Change 47,* 325–352.

Kitchen, H. (2002). Municipal revenue and expenditure issues in Canada. In *Canadian Tax Paper 107.* Toronto: Canadian Tax Foundation.

Liverman, D. G. E., Batterson, M. J., Taylor, D., & Ryan, J. (2001). Geological hazards and disasters in Newfoundland. *Canadian Geotechnical Journal 38,* 936–956.

NOAA Coastal Services Centre. (n.d.). Vulnerability assessment techniques and applications (VATA). Retrieved January 29, 2009, from http://www.csc.noaa.gov/vata.

Parewick, K., Keenan, R., Vodden, K., & Catto, N. (2010). *Climate change adapation tool development: Community consultations.* St. John's: Municipalities Newfoundland and Labrador.

Parewick, K., Vodden, K., Catto, N., & Renaud, N. (2010). *On the receiving end: Reconciling contemporary perspectives on community risk and vulnerability assessment.* Unpublished draft report for the Atlantic Regional Adaptation Collaborative. Department of Geography, Memorial University of Newfoundland.

Planning for Sustainable Canadian Communities Roundtable. (2005, September 21–23). Integrated community sustainability planning: A background paper. Report to the prime minister's external advisory on cities and communities, Ottawa: Ontario.

Plant, T., Agocs, C., Brunet-Jailly, E., & Douglas, J. (2005). From measuring to managing performance: Recent trends in the development of municipal public sector accountability. *New Directions Report*, 16. Toronto: Institute of Public Administration of Canada.

Public Infrastructure Engineering Vulnerability Committee (PIEVC), Canadian Council of Professional Engineers. (2007). *Adapting infrastructure to a changing climate: Glossary/definitions*. Retrieved May 31, 2011, from www.pievc.ca.

Royal Commission on Employment and Unemployment in Newfoundland and Labrador. (1986). *Building on our Strengths: Final report of the Royal Commission on Employment and Unemployment*. St John's: Government of Newfoundland and Labrador.

Scoones, I. (1999). New ecology and the social sciences: What prospects for a fruitful engagement? *Annual Review of Anthropology*, *28*, 479–507.

Vasseur, L., & Catto, N. (2008). Atlantic Canada. In D.S. Lemmen, E.J. Warren, J. Lacroix, and E. Bush (Eds.), *From impacts to adaptation: Canada in a changing climate* (pp. 119–170). Ottawa: Government of Canada.

Vodden, K. (2009). *New spaces, ancient places: Collaborative governance and sustainable development in Canada's coastal regions*. Ph.D. dissertation, Department of Geography, Simon Fraser University, Burnaby, BC.

SEVEN

The Creative Economy

An Opportunity for Rural Community Sustainability

Yolande E. Chan and Jeff A. Dixon

Introduction

Rural economies are undergoing dramatic transition. Many of Canada's rural communities are in economic, demographic, educational, and social decline, according to the 2006 Interim Senate Report on rural poverty (Senate Standing Committee on Agriculture and Forestry, 2006). Their low population density leads to a lack of critical mass for service and infrastructure. This in turn leads to a lower rate of business creation, fewer jobs, and, ultimately, out-migration that lowers the population density even further. Rural Ontario, home to Queen's University, is not exempt from these common rural challenges: youth out-migration, an aging population, lower incomes, a smaller tax base to pay for services delivered over long distances, fewer educational and cultural opportunities, a less-educated workforce, and an employment base whose traditional agricultural and manufacturing roots are undermined by globalization. As traditional economic bases erode, rural communities are seeking new solutions to economic sustainability.

The 2009 provincial government report, *Ontario in the Creative Age,* proposes key strategies to foster knowledge-based jobs concentrated in largely urban mega-regions (Martin Prosperity Institute [MPI], 2009b).

This shift in economic-development policy creates new challenges for rural communities. To remain competitive in a creative economy, rural communities must attract and develop the skilled labour required in this emerging sector. While rural communities' quality of place is appealing to many in the "creative class," they face unique hurdles in attracting this segment of the workforce. To develop vibrant, knowledge-based economies, rural communities are increasingly looking for ways to expand access to new technologies, to nurture the development of innovative business ventures, and to assist businesses in building critical links to urban markets.

In 2008, The Monieson Centre at Queen's School of Business launched a three-year Knowledge Impact in Society (KIS) project to support rural, eastern Ontario's economic development and sustainability through mobilizing academic tools and resources. The project was built on partnerships with almost 40 community organizations and businesses, and it succeeded on the basis of collaboration between academics and community partners.

Through a series of 24 community consultations in eastern and southwestern Ontario, the creative economy was identified as a key knowledge gap related to rural economic sustainability and vitality. Partnerships among The Monieson Centre, other academic institutes, and community organizations enabled a multifaceted approach to addressing this key research need. By matching academic resources with community priorities, the centre achieved increased engagement and opportunities for ongoing collaboration and research beyond the scope of the initial KIS project. This chapter explores how such collaborations can support the economic sustainability of rural communities and how the creative economy operates as a strategy for building ongoing rural economic health.

The changing face of rural Ontario

By definition, rural regions contain low population densities spread over large distances. Rural economic-development agencies therefore focus on reducing the "price of rurality" by decreasing the price of distance and reducing the disadvantages of low population density and their accompanying lack of economies of scale (Reimer & Bollman, 2006). In the past, these agencies have focused on traditional sources of rural economic competitiveness: access to natural resources and relatively lower costs of production. However, these advantages have been nullified over the past 20 years by global competition caused by declining transportation costs and reduced trade barriers (Munnich, Schrock, & Cook, 2002).

Compounding these economic challenges is a shift in political interest away from rural issues. According to the 2006 Interim Senate Report *Understanding Freefall: The Challenge of the Rural Poor*, the rural poor are under-researched and under-represented since most academic and activist communities are preoccupied with studying the plight of the urban poor (Senate Standing Committee, 2006).

The rural economy's traditional economic base, agriculture, has been battered by food-safety issues, border closures, the transition of the family farm into large-scale farming corporations, and decreasing commodity prices. Indeed, farms are more dependent on rural communities than rural communities are on farms; farming families rely on neighbouring populations to buy their products and provide employment to maintain the family income (Johnson, 2001).

Likewise, there have been challenges in the manufacturing sector. As industrialization reduced the need for labour in natural resource–based sectors, economic developers looked to maintain tax bases and drive the service economy by attracting manufacturing to their communities (Johnson, 2001). Beginning in the 1970s, many rural communities benefitted from an urban-to-rural shift in manufacturing employment, concurrent with growth in small and medium enterprises (Jarvis & Dunham, 2003). While rural manufacturing in Canada saw growth as late as 2000 (Rothwell, 2001), by 2007 the sector was declining faster than in urban communities, a process compounded both by distance from urban communities and resource reliance (Rothwell & Bollman, 2011). Globalization, decreased transportation costs, and corporate decision making that is far removed from the local community have undermined the factors that first drew manufacturing to rural communities, such that most of eastern Ontario's "company towns" have lost their mainstay corporate employers. These include, for example, the 2008 closures of the Hershey and Stanley Tools plants in Smiths Falls, Domtar leaving Cornwall in 2006, and General Mills moving out of Quinte West in 2008.

These changes negatively affect incomes: rural eastern Ontario family incomes are almost 20% lower than the Ontario average (MPI, 2009a). Lower incomes and smaller tax bases challenge rural municipalities to provide services that were once provincial responsibilities such as road infrastructure, boosting local primary healthcare, and meeting more stringent water/wastewater regulations.

Eastern Ontario is also experiencing demographic shifts. Although all of Canada is aging, rural communities are aging more rapidly, which compounds their economic challenges. For example, eastern Ontario's Prince Edward County's recent annual net in-migration of 256 people largely consisted of 45 to 64 year olds (Donald, 2008). Retirees possess experience and external networks that can serve their adopted communities well. However, retirees need more government services such as health care and, if they are not locally engaged, add little economic support in terms of purchasing power and labour capacity. Youth out-migration from rural areas reinforces the shortage of skilled labour in eastern Ontario, which is projected to worsen within the next five years and restrict subsequent economic growth (Harris, 2006). The youth that are remaining in rural eastern Ontario are less educated than their urban peers.

Rural eastern Ontario is also lagging in terms of its residents' health. Eastern Ontario has higher mortality rates than the Canadian average due to cancers, circulatory and cardiovascular diseases, and industrial accidents. Prince Edward County's strategic plan concludes that eastern Ontario's rural residents' health is suboptimal, partly as a result of healthcare centralization, which has caused significant barriers to service access (Harris, 2006, p. 20).

Eastern Ontario is not alone—these problems are typical symptoms of the rural cycle of decline as outlined in a 2006 Organisation for Economic Co-operation and Development (OECD) report (OECD, 2006). The rural community's low population density leads to a lack of critical mass for services and infrastructure. The lack of critical mass discourages business attraction and creation, which means fewer jobs for rural residents. Fewer jobs put pressure on youth and young families (especially those with marketable skills) to migrate away from rural communities, resulting in an even lower population density.

Growing economies are the foundation of vital rural communities. In comparison to stagnant or declining communities, vital rural communities have stronger social and knowledge networks, more services, volunteers and programs, a more educated workforce, enhanced cultural opportunities, and better access to health-care services. Ultimately, such communities deliver a better quality of life to their citizens. Eastern Ontario's demographic, labour force, population health, and economic shortcomings all point to a need for careful study and targeted support to help the area escape the cycle of rural decline and become a more socially vibrant, healthy, and productive region. Community–university research partnerships can assist in addressing this need. For instance, faculty can conduct high-impact studies and report findings directly to decision makers. These projects can be funded by the municipal, provincial, or federal government; community agencies, foundations, and other non-profits; and private investors. Students are able to carry out projects as part of their course requirements, learning by doing. Community representatives can provide campus lectures and presentations to increase the awareness of problems faced and discuss potential solutions. As information is shared, relationships are built, and a positive knowledge-sharing cycle is created.

Supporting economic development through knowledge mobilization

Founded in 1998 and located in the heart of eastern Ontario, The Monieson Centre at Queen's School of Business supports community sustainability by enabling businesses and communities to harness their knowledge capital. The centre works with organizations and researchers to explore how to generate value through knowledge. By connecting leading researchers directly with key business and community representatives, The Monieson Centre improves knowledge mobilization and transfer. The centre's research teams investigate issues related to knowledge-based enterprise (e.g., economic development) that directly benefit clients. The research teams and Monieson Centre staff translate findings into effective, practice-based recommendations to ensure research results make timely, real-world impact.

In April 2008, The Monieson Centre received funding, via its director, from the Social Sciences and Humanities Research Council of Canada (SSHRC) for a three-year Knowledge Impact in Society (KIS) project to support economic development in rural eastern Ontario through knowledge mobilization. SSHRC identifies knowledge mobilization as a pathway, "to increase the positive impact of social sciences and humanities research on individuals, businesses and communities…as it helps integrate the campus and community, and creates new avenues for discussion and understanding" (SSHRC, 2008). In this capacity, universities play a crucial role in fostering community sustainability, as they, "not only produce codified knowledge and human capital, but also participate actively as important institutional actors in building and sustaining local networks and flows of knowledge, and in linking them with global ones" (Bramwell & Wolfe, 2008, p. 1178). By creating the relationships, the channels, and the communications products to find, translate, and deliver academic knowledge, the KIS project was a valuable knowledge-mobilization initiative, designed to increase the economic vitality and sustainability of rural eastern Ontario communities.

The Monieson Centre collaborated with two lead partners—the Prince Edward / Lennox & Addington Community Futures Development Corporation (PELA CFDC) and the Eastern Ontario CFDC Network, Inc.—and almost 40 supporting community partners. The partnership network involved federal government organizations including FedNor and the Rural Secretariat; provincial partners such as the Ontario Ministry of Agriculture, Food and Rural Affairs (OMAFRA); a wealth of municipal governments and ecoomic-development organizations; as well as chambers of commerce and small businesses. Over the life of the project, this broad partnership network proved critical for engaging the 15 communities across the region.

The KIS project sought to address economic-development challenges and research gaps in a number of ways. First, it provided public access to a series of six faculty research studies initially developed to assist PELA CFDC in building a renewed, sustainable, economic base. These included reports on the knowledge economy, the emerging wine industry, regional networks, and health-care issues (e.g., physician attraction).

Second, the KIS project sponsored 15 student consulting projects for small businesses and community organizations. These projects supported economic sustainability by helping organizations develop business plans and strategies to remain competitive in a changing economic environment. In Hastings County, for example, a team of fourth-year Bachelor of Commerce students developed an investment plan for developing a micro-brewery cluster. This tool analyzed the local agricultural and market capacities for micro-breweries and is now being used by the county's economic-development office to attract investors to launch such businesses in the community. Students also worked with businesses like Holiday Manor Fishing Lodge. Shifting generational vacation preferences, combined with the rapid decline of American tourists due to increased border security measures following September 11, 2001, had resulted in declining visits and revenues to this established tourism business. The student team developed a marketing plan to help the owner better understand current market conditions, identify key potential customer bases, and target those customers with effective promotions.

Third, a series of 19 knowledge syntheses targeted key research gaps that threaten the region's long-term economic health and sustainability. These four- to five-page reports summarize leading academic research and government reports in an accessible format for small businesses and rural economic developers. Topics include youth retention, community economic development, investment attraction, and the creative economy. The reports are designed to be primers on these key economic-development issues that allow local leaders to understand how the issues might affect their community, receive guidance on how they might respond to the challenges based on best practices, and find resources for more in-depth learning. As a gateway to research and resources, the reports are an effective means of bridging the academic and practitioner communities.

Fourth, the project profiled 18 business success stories from across the region through a series of case studies developed by fourth-year Commerce students. These highlight businesses finding new ways to compete in traditional rural industries, including agricultural businesses like La Gantoise beef and tourism businesses like Wolfe Springs Resort. They also feature examples of modern industries such as video producer WhistleStop Productions, and restaurant franchisor Wild Wing, which has developed sustainable business models in a rural context. Each case study provides insight into the respective business's existing market conditions and the innovative practices they employed to succeed in a changing economy.

To disseminate these resources, The Monieson Centre developed a multifaceted engagement strategy. The project website (now archived at www.economicrevitalization.ca) provided free access to all of the aforementioned resources. Web content was designed for low-bandwidth usage as many rural Ontario communities lack high-speed Internet access. The project web presence expanded into several social media outlets. The *Creative Communities* blog served as a forum for graduate students to present research in a conversational forum, allowing communities to post comments and feedback. One blog article discussing new federal-government funding for infrastructure development and attracted over two thousand readers. The blog was expanded to include articles by rural economic-development experts from the region and across Canada, building further integration between the academic and practitioner communities. In the second year of the project, a Twitter account was launched to support ongoing—often daily—dialogue with researchers and community leaders. To date, the account has grown to over four hundred followers. The project's YouTube page features over a hundred videos of seminars and conference presentations related to rural economic development. Facebook is also used to promote events.

In addition to the web presence, the project hosted three annual KIS Showcases, free conferences hosted at Queen's University to promote dialogue on priority economic-development issues between researchers and practitioners. The three conferences drew together over four hundred participants and engaged senior delegates from both the university and community, including (former) University Principal Tom Williams, Member of Parliament (MP) Gord Brown, and Member of Provincial Parliament (MPP) Jim Brownell. Both the web-engagement strategy and the annual conferences were critical to building the knowledge networks necessary in a sustainable, growing economic environment.

Using discovery workshops to identify economic-development research priorities

As university–community knowledge networks are critical to sustainable economies, the project also directed significant resources into community consultations through a series of Discovery Workshops offered in eastern Ontario. The project team hosted a total of 16 workshops over two years, with at least one workshop in each of the CFDC partner communities across the region. The purpose of the Discovery Workshops was to determine local knowledge needs, identify community knowledge resources, and build opportunities for academic–community collaborations. All of these goals served the overarching purpose of building a long-term, sustainable vision for the region's economy.

The Discovery Workshop planning process was collaborative in nature, acting as a catalyst for ongoing partnerships between the university and community partners. The Monieson Centre teamed with the Queen's Executive Decision Centre to provide electronic-based facilitation for the consultations. The Executive Decision Centre's technology consists of laptops and presentation hardware to support team-planning and decision-making tasks, allowing efficient, anonymous brainstorming. Community partners provided suitable local meeting places and identified key local participants for the workshops.

The workshops asked four central questions. First, they addressed burning economic-development issues, asking, "What are your challenges and needs with respect to rural economic development and making the community sustainable?" Second, they enabled participants to develop a research wish list, asking, "If you had access to our researchers for a year, what would you ask them to study? What are your rural research priorities?" Third, they assessed local capacity to support academic research by exploring, "What local resources (organizations, reports, past work, etc.) might contribute to addressing the issues identified above?" Finally, the workshops challenged participants to define success for the project, inquiring, "If this project is to be successful, what would you see in place in the next two years? What must happen in order to ensure that the KIS project makes a positive impact?"

The Monieson Centre received funding from OMAFRA through the University of Guelph School of Environmental Design and Rural Development to extend the Discovery Workshops into southwestern Ontario. This project, entitled *Identifying Rural Research Priorities through Community Engagement*, involved partnering with Dr. Wayne Caldwell and Dr. Jennifer Ball at the University of Guelph, and Harold Flaming and Suzanne Ainley of The Ontario Rural Council (TORC, now the Rural Ontario Institute) to further consult with the 23 CFDC communities in southwestern Ontario to determine their economic-development issues and knowledge gaps through a series of eight Discovery Workshops.

For question one, workshop participants brainstormed local-development challenges. Most workshops identified 20 to 30 unique challenges faced by their communities. Each participant was then given six, equally weighted votes to identify the top issues in the list. The voting resulted in a prioritized list of challenges faced by the represented communities. The resulting top ten priorities from each of the 24 workshops were given a weighted ranking, where the top issue in a community was given ten points, the second issue nine points, and so on. These scores resulted in a ranked list of economic-development challenges across rural southern Ontario, and more specifically, across eastern Ontario and southwestern Ontario (see Table 7.1 in the Appendix). The process was repeated for question two, resulting in a similar list of related knowledge gaps across the region (see Table 7.2 in the Appendix).

From these lists, a picture of the overall region's economic-development challenges, as well as differences between the east and southwest regions, emerged. The results made it clear that for rural southern Ontario to be sustainable, key issues to be addressed currently include youth retention, skills training, the provision of economic opportunities, economic diversification, transportation, and infrastructure. In eastern Ontario, there is a keen awareness of the need for regional strategies and collaboration. In southwestern Ontario, agriculture and farm revitalization issues are also critically important.

The resulting inventory of research gaps highlighted three prominent themes: *build it deep, build it unique, and build it wide.* "Build it deep" refers to the need for research on sustainable economic-development strategies, that is, how to build jobs that will remain in the community for the long term. The second theme, "build it unique," speaks to the need for research on how a community or region can identify its comparative advantage relative to other communities. This includes identifying the unique social fabric and turning it into an identifiable brand to attract investment, residents, and tourists. The third, "build it wide," addresses the growing recognition of the importance of economic diversity. Economic resilience requires a move from single-industry dependency (e.g., on manufacturing, tourism, or natural resources such as forestry and agriculture) toward a broader economic base that can weather the ups and downs of market cycles. While some differences emerged between the regions (e.g., a focus on small-business development in the eastern part of the province, and on farm revitalization and land use in the southwest), these three themes were consistent across rural southern Ontario. Further, they address many of the more specific issues identified in the workshops, including youth retention and labour attraction.

What arises from the identified knowledge gaps, and the three themes in particular, is an impression of rural economies in transition. Many communities are seeking to move beyond traditional models of "smokestack chasing" toward a diversified economy built on a skilled, entrepreneurial labour force that will build jobs and industries that can sustain the economic vitality of the community in the long term. In short, communities in the region have found that old models of economic development, particularly wherein a community is reliant on one or a small handful of employers governed by multinational corporations, are no longer viable. Such models leave the majority of jobs at risk, under the control of decision makers often removed from the community. Communities are envisioning a sustainable economy built with deep, local roots, and are looking for related economic-development models.

This perspective reflects a broadening understanding of business and economic sustainability. Lo and Sheu (2007) have suggested that corporate sustainability is "a business approach that creates long-term shareholder value by embracing opportunities and managing risk from economic, environmental and social dimensions" (p. 245). Some scholars, however, argue that a more dynamic view of the firm, with a reduced emphasis on shareholder value, is necessary to achieve economic sustainability. In this view, businesses must accept

> the scarcity of natural resources and the notion of business and society's co-responsibility related to the use and development of social resources...and support the idea that firms should create sustainable value (that is to say, economic, social and environmental value) in the double sense of the word sustainable: in a persistent way and coherently with the principles of sustainable development. (Rodriguez, Ricart, & Sanchez, 2002, p. 137)

Communities are recognizing that such dynamic firms are vital to their long-term economic health.

Not surprisingly, then, as identified above, the need for "sustainable economic development strategies" was identified as the top research priority across the region as a whole and in southwestern Ontario, and ranked second in eastern Ontario. While sustainability was referred to in many contexts, the communities of southern Ontario discussed economic sustainability primarily in terms of five key themes: economic sustainability, economic-development models, balancing local and regional strategies, community resilience, and social enterprise. The first, economic sustainability, speaks to the need for economic-development strategies that will be viable in the long term, particularly in the light of peak oil and climate change. The second highlights the challenges of applying economic-development models designed for urban areas in rural contexts. This leads to the third theme, wherein rural communities are often encouraged to band together and pursue regional economic-development strategies. Many small communities, however, find such approaches fail to recognize their unique cultures and needs. These communities are thus seeking ways to balance regional strategies with local needs. The fourth theme asks what components—such as knowledge-transfer models, infrastructure, supports, attitudes, and beliefs—are necessary to foster community resilience. The final theme addresses how rural communities should factor social enterprise into economic planning. In particular, what economic indicators can be used by policy makers to foster and assess the growth and impact of social enterprises.

The desire to identify and leverage comparative advantage reflected a unique emphasis in eastern Ontario, as it was the top priority among the communities in that region. By contrast, it ranked 13th in southwestern Ontario. Eastern Ontario residents wished to see communities understand their unique strengths and then use those strengths to build a healthy local economy attractive to investors. This priority also consists of five general themes defined by related research questions: identifying a community's niche, developing a community brand, building asset inventories, fostering pride of place, and developing cultural assets. In the first theme, communities are seeking to understand how they can define their local comparative advantages, be they cultural assets, natural resources, or otherwise, and leverage those into dynamic, competitive advantages that can be used to attract investment. The second, developing a community brand, reflects a desire to understand processes and tools by which rural communities and regions can communicate their niches in a cohesive brand. It also addresses the tension individual communities face in developing regional brands, and how they can cooperate with nearby communities without losing their unique identities. The third theme demonstrates the value of tools for community leaders to help them assess their core assets and strengths. The fourth, pride of place, relates to the role that quality of place plays in attracting investment to rural regions, and the need to engage residents as champions of their communities. The fifth theme is related, asking how communities can identify, value, and market their cultural assets.

This priority issue reinforces the shift from smokestack chasing to creating an economic-development model based on the unique cultural and economic fabrics of the community. If corporate sustainability depends on co-responsibility between the community and the firm, then a clear understanding of local comparative advantage is critical to building such sustainability. A community whose branding reflects its natural resources, labour pool, quality of place, and other local strengths is better equipped to foster businesses connected to the long-term viability of the community. Its failure to rank as a top-ten priority in southwestern Ontario may be a result of that region's more robust manufacturing sector. This emphasis in eastern Ontario signals a broader trend in the region to tailor investment attraction activities to a given community's economic strengths.

The question of the rural creative economy

In seeking economic development strategies that foster community resilience and build on local strengths and culture, southern Ontario has voiced an increasing interest in the creative economy as a source of economic sustainability. Although it was not a top-ranking economic-development issue or research gap, it is an emerging subject of inquiry by rural communities. Richard Florida of the Martin Prosperity Institute (MPI) has initiated a growing body of research around this economic-development theory, which, he argues, offers a new path to economic sustainability (Gertler, Florida, Gates, and Vinodrai, 2002, p. 25). Ontario's communities have been given a distinct impetus to better understand this issue following the publication of *Ontario in the Creative Age*, an MPI study commissioned by the Ontario government to explore provincial policy implications of this emerging sector, namely, to "provide recommendations to the Province on how to ensure Ontario's economy and people remain globally competitive and prosperous" (MPI, 2009b, p. iv).

The study traces the overall decline of traditional, physical labour–intensive jobs in Ontario, including both industrial jobs like manufacturing and traditional rural jobs in the agricultural and forestry sectors. The new Western economy, Florida argues, is based on the rise of the service sector and the creative sector—those jobs in which people are paid to produce intellectual capital (MPI, 2009b). Jobs in the creative economy, then, would include:

1. Professional occupations in natural and applied sciences
2. Technical occupations related to natural and applied sciences
3. Teachers and professors
4. Professional occupations in art and culture
5. Technical occupations in art, culture, recreation and sport
6. Finance and insurance administration occupations
7. Professional occupations in health
8. Nurse supervisors and registered nurses
9. Technical and related occupations in health
10. Judges, lawyers, psychologists, social workers, ministers of religion, and policy and program officers. (MPI, 2009a, p. 29)

Rural communities have wrestled with the implications of government policy regarding the creative economy for their local economies. The Discovery Workshops uncovered difficulties in defining the creative economy, building a broader understanding of its nature, and developing an awareness of the issue beyond economic-development circles. Definitions of the creative economy do vary; however, a consensus does seem to be emerging. An early definition from the UK proposed, "those industries which have their origin in individual creativity, skill and talent and which have a potential for wealth and job creation through the generation and exploitation of intellectual property" (United Kingdom Department for Culture, Media and Sport , 2001, p. 5). The United Nations (2008) suggested,

> at the heart of the creative economy lie the creative industries. Loosely defined, the creative industries are at the crossroads of the arts, culture, business and technology. In other words, they comprise the cycle of creation, production and distribution of goods and services that use intellectual capital as their primary input. (p. iv)

In eastern Ontario, a collaboration led by the Eastern Ontario CFDC Network, Inc., studied the local creative economy and defined it as, "A major shift in the structure of the global economy—from one based on the production of goods to a more knowledge based economy driven by ideas and innovation" (MPI, 2009a, p. 15). As an economic-development strategy, then, the creative economy does not focus only on those occupations traditionally branded "creative"—namely those related to arts and culture—but, rather, casts a broader net encompassing all knowledge-based occupations.

Beyond defining the creative economy, the communities of rural southern Ontario raised a variety of research questions related to this economic-development issue. Topics ranged among a variety of themes:

1. *Theory*
   "How do you use [Richard] Florida's work in urban settings and transfer it to rural settings?"
2. *Methodology*
   "What economic development methodologies can be applied (or adapted) to the creative and/or knowledge economy?"
3. *Practical issues, including planning*
   "How do we create a long-term strategic plan to attract and maximize [the benefits of] the 'creative economy'?"
4. *Labour attraction*
   "What support, rewards, and incentives will attract the creative class?"
5. *Skills development*
   "What changes must be made in our education system so our rural youth are prepared for future knowledge-based jobs?"

Questions also reflected varying definitions of the creative economy. Some communities treated it as largely cultural and artistic in nature, such as Mitchell, ON, where leaders asked, "How do we capitalize on cultural economic development?", and Smiths Falls, ON, where leaders questioned, "What are best practices in Cultural Community Planning and how can we implement it?" Others took a broader approach. For instance, Northumberland County in the east and Orillia in the southwest, among others, asked questions pertaining to knowledge-based jobs including, "What can the community do to attract knowledge-based industry?" and "How do we transition from old industry to the knowledge-based economy?" Others, such as leaders from Kawartha Lakes, recognized the role of innovation in the creative economy asking, "What are the factors/conditions that are important to attract innovation (people, organizations, start ups)?"

These questions highlight how forward-thinking communities see the creative economy as a potential key to building a sustainable economy. It remains, however, an emerging issue, as it did not rank highly in either eastern or southwestern Ontario's research priorities. In southwestern Ontario, it ranked 12th, in eastern Ontario 18th, and overall it was ranked the 15th most pressing research need. Delegates at the 2009 KIS Showcase, however, identified it as the single most important issue for further research. This may be a reflection of the creative economy theory receiving greater exposure among policy-makers and researchers, as represented by the 2009 KIS Showcase participants, compared with the grassroots business and economic-development networks reflected in the community-based Discovery Workshops. As an emerging economic-development issue for rural communities, then, significant opportunities remain for communicating strategies to harness its benefit at the community, and not just the policy, level.

While the promise of high-paying creative occupations is attractive to rural communities seeking new models for sustainable economic development, the existing body of knowledge is largely urban based. This challenge is compounded by the core recommendations of the MPI (2009b) report for the provincial government, whose policy recommendations focus on four key strategies, including a labour shift toward analytical and social intelligence skills; building the "3 Ts" of social *tolerance*, labour force *talent*, and *technology* innovation and adoption; and creating education-based social safety nets to protect vulnerable groups (pp. 2–3). While each of these three recommendations raises unique challenges for rural communities, the fourth recommendation creates a potential significant threat to rural sustainability. Indeed, MPI recommended building a province-wide geographic advantage by focusing development initiatives on three "mega-regions": the Greater Toronto Area, Kitchener-Waterloo, and the National Capital Region. While mega-regions focus economic development efforts on geographical industry clustering—locating traditionally competitive organizations in close proximity to each other to encourage collaboration and foster innovations that would not occur in isolated firms—they are largely urban-centric. While rural communities adjacent to these urban centres can benefit, those outside of a government-supported mega-region fear they may be left out of this new economy.

This policy shift creates challenges for Ontario's rural communities, particularly in eastern Ontario. Already, at $53,345, eastern Ontario's average full-time annual wages lag behind the provincial average of $55,626. Likewise, the region's employment rate of 58.5% is lower than the provincial rural average of 61% (MPI, 2009a). In addition to these current disadvantages, the education and skills-training issues were identified as part of the top-ten research gaps and economic development issues in the Discovery Workshops, and were also noted as a challenge in the Senate Standing Committee on Agriculture and Forestry (2006) report on rural poverty, place rural communities at great risk in this new economic landscape. Without access to education, rural communities fear they may simply fall victim to the new social safety nets discussed in these policy recommendations. Compounding this difficulty is rural Ontario's geographical relation to the developing mega-regions. If provincial economic-development efforts are targeted at the three mega-region urban areas, rural Ontario will be at an even greater disadvantage. Thus, while growing the creative economy creates possibilities for sustainable economic development, these urban-centric policy developments pose a significant threat to the province's rural communities.

Fostering the rural creative economy

Despite these challenges, several eastern Ontario case studies, completed by The Monieson Centre as part of the KIS project, demonstrate how creative economy theory can apply in rural contexts and offer lessons for developing economic sustainability in both traditional and emerging industries. Fifth Town Artisan Cheese[1] is an innovative cheese producer in Prince Edward County. Founded in 2008, the business exemplifies the value intellectual capital and innovation can bring to a traditional industry. Despite ceasing production in 2012 due to cash-flow challenges, the business re-emerged in 2014, offering useful lessons for those seeking to initiate creative enterprises.

Fifth Town is an environmentally and socially responsible business, positioned as a niche producer of quality, handmade cheeses made with locally produced goat and sheep milk. The market for artisan cheese is growing at 20% per annum, far exceeding the industrial cheese growth rate of 1–3%, and the industry is underdeveloped in Ontario, with only ten Ontario producers in 2008, compared with over 85 in Quebec (DesRoches, Habkirk, Reid, Robinson, & Zhou, 2009).

Capitalizing on this market opportunity, Fifth Town exhibits key characteristics of creative economy–based businesses, all of which contributed to its initial growth and success. First, its geographical context nurtures the 3 Ts: tolerance, talent, and technology. While the county has a small minority population of 1.3% vs. the provincial average of 22.8%, the community developed social tolerance in other forms. Programs like the Arts Trail encourage a thriving arts scene. Likewise, the healthy tourism industry actively targeted a diverse urban audience through grassroots organizations like Out in the County, which targets tourism products to LGBT audiences. While ethnic diversity takes long-term efforts to develop, these short-term initiatives help attract a broad range of perspectives and ideas to the region. This is also reflected in Fifth Town's management philosophy. For example, staff profiles on the company's website highlight the unique personalities, interests, and talents of each team member.

Second, Fifth Town places a strong emphasis on developing talent. Previous owner Petra (Cooper) Kassun-Mutch related, "We decided to do this because we wanted a bit of a change in lifestyle. We looked at the County as a 'place,' and we were interested in authentic foods as a theme, and we were interested in the environment as a challenge to sort of say, 'what could we do to build the greenest enterprise out there?'" (Kassun-Mutch, 2009). This approach to business is reflected in the company's employee-development programs. Many of the initial, core team members were recruited from urban communities, with backgrounds in publishing, hotel management, and cheese making. As the team grew, the company recruited several new staff from within Prince Edward County. Petra placed a strong focus on employee retention, understanding that a talented, engaged workforce can generate new ideas to help create long-term business sustainability.

Third, the business's environmental commitment has led it to embrace technological development. Integrating environmental sustainability into every process requires creative solutions to many everyday business processes. Energy is produced on-site by a windmill and solar panels, with added energy sourced through the Bullfrog network. Despite paying higher energy rates, Fifth Town's energy use is 30% compared with the industry baseline. This is due both to operational practices and because of the design of the facility, which received LEED Platinum certification. Many other small cheese manufacturers have struggled with increased regulation of waste disposal; however, Fifth Town's innovative use of bio-digestion, which reflects its sustainability-based philosophy, enables them to overcome this hurdle.

Beyond exemplifying the 3Ts, Fifth Town has also benefitted from industry clustering. Resources and programs from the county, including co-marketing through the Taste of the County—a regional event designed to cross-promote local food producers and restaurants—as well as access to the Royal Winter Fair and Ontario Food & Wine Show, have helped Fifth Town access markets beyond its immediate community. Petra commented, "Sometimes there's an overemphasis on rural partnerships. We're close to three major markets and to ignore them is to your peril" (Kassun-Mutch, 2009). While it can be difficult for one business to access these markets in isolation, support from the county made this possible. Likewise, the county's Taste of the Trail initiative has developed a roadmap to discover the many local food-related businesses in the region. This has helped Fifth Town successfully co-brand with other food producers, wineries, and restaurants to promote themselves to urban tourists. Fifth Town also built a strategic partnership with a nearby cheddar-cheese manufacturer, the Black River Cheese Company. Rather than viewing each other as competitors, the companies have cooperated to achieve economies of scale in accessing rural markets.

While Fifth Town has integrated creative-economy principles into a traditional agricultural-based business, WhistleStop Productions is an example of a digital business operating in a rural context. In the 1980s David Hatch was working in television production in Toronto, starting out as an audio engineer, later supporting the launch of The Sports Network, and then moving into daily news reporting for Global Television. In 1989 he branched out and founded his own video-production company, WhistleStop Productions. Following its 10th anniversary, WhistleStop began a series of dramatic changes. First, David's partner Stacey, a producer, director, and writer, joined the team in 2000. They then relocated the business to Prince Edward County, two hundred kilometres east of Toronto.

WhistleStop responded to the arrival of high-definition (HD) video technology, as new technologies like digital television signals and Blu-Ray Discs offered higher-quality images than that produced by DVDs and older television signals. Over the past decade, WhistleStop has grown into a leading HD production house and is now one of the first-movers into 3D video production, as well. From a home office, the company has produced sports-television content, documentaries, and custom-commercial programming. Much like Fifth Town, WhistleStop's success has depended on links with urban markets. Following the move to Prince Edward County, the company's initial growth was built on David and Stacey's industry contacts in Toronto. Their new location allowed them to access other urban markets, as well, as they were located within two to three hours of Toronto, Ottawa, and Montreal.

As video production has become an increasingly digital technology, web connectivity has become of greater importance than geographical proximity to markets. One of WhistleStop's primary business partners is based in Europe, and their relationship has been developed and maintained virtually. The introduction of HD and 3D video technologies has dramatically increased the company's data-transfer capacity needs, making high-speed broadband technology crucial for the ongoing viability of the business. Support for technological development, thus, has been and continues to be a key to WhistleStop's success.

Although initially operated as a home-based business, WhistleStop is now an active partner in the development of Headlands, a rural multimedia technology incubator. By locating in the incubator, WhistleStop is supporting new multimedia start-ups, serving as a mentor, supplier, and customer. Headlands has also partnered with Loyalist College to offer an industry-leading 3D-video production program, launched in September 2011. This program enables skill development and helps address the critical issue of rural youth retention.

While Fifth Town and WhistleStop have operated in very different industries, they both illustrate the role the creative economy can play in creating viable, sustainable rural economies. The creative economy should not be treated as an urban phenomenon. Rather, as research demonstrates, rural and urban Canada are interdependent, particularly in metro-adjacent rural regions that deal with workforce mobility, urban sprawl, environmental protection, and transportation issues (Olfert & Partridge, 2005). In this economic model, quality of place is a key to attracting the creative class (Hall & Donald, 2009). Fifth Town and WhistleStop are located in Prince Edward County, now described as a "gastronomic treat," "countylicious," and "one of Canada's top 5 family vacation destinations" (Prince Edward County, 2011). Attracting skilled employees has not been difficult. Rural communities offer the creative class attractive living environments. To retain their businesses, however, also requires supporting innovation through tolerance, talent, and technology. Rural-based creative businesses also require support in accessing urban markets through marketing support and industry clustering. By supporting these principles, rural communities can make the creative economy a vital component of a sustainable economy.

Conclusions and lessons learned

Sustainable economic development recognizes the linkages between firms and communities, and the need for both to cooperate and share responsibility in creating economic, social, and environmental value for the greater common good. "Sustainability is ultimately about creating economies of place, quality, authenticity and lasting value" (Dickerson Hartsock, 2007, p. 5). With traditional sources of rural employment in decline, southern Ontario's communities are a reflection of a broader search for new sources of economic sustainability that build on a community's cultural, environmental, and economic strengths.

In addition to renewed economic-development strategies, robust knowledge networks are a critical element in generating the innovation and creativity necessary for economic sustainability in the 21st century. Universities, community colleges, and other tertiary institutions can play a critical role here as they partner with communities for mutual benefit. As a research centre dedicated to the study of knowledge and the knowledge economy, with a commitment to real-world impact, The Monieson Centre has operated as a local catalyst for dialogue and research on the rural creative economy. Rather than being a top-down initiative driven by the university, the creative economy research priority has been developed in eastern Ontario through dialogue with community partners. There has been mutual "skin in the game," with researchers and students spending time in rural communities, learning about and documenting these communities for academic purposes, and with community members determining the issues to be investigated and receiving timely reports and presentations. By engaging community leaders to identify critical emerging research gaps, the centre has been able to produce research that is timely and relevant to local needs. This process has reinforced relevance and trust, and resulted in vibrant relationships and communication. The centre has also been able to create efficiencies for researchers, taking care of administrative details (e.g., research ethics clearance, making travel arrangements, and assisting with practitioner-oriented reports). The centre has been able to assist members of the community, directing them to researchers across Canada and internationally who have expertise in the issues with which they are wrestling. Such collaborations between researchers and communities enhance the region's capacity for economic growth and ongoing viability.

As southern Ontario's traditional industries decline, new ways to create economic sustainability are being explored. It has been necessary to innovate and "think outside the box." This chapter has described a community–university alliance that permitted just this —brainstorming in 24 communities across southern Ontario regarding the key economic-development challenges and knowledge needs. Emerging from these discussions have been requests for more information on sustainable economic-development and economic-diversification strategies. Specifically, the creative economy has significant economic-development potential that has not yet been exploited in many rural areas. Recent research is documenting how, "new business start-ups have been generated by in-migrants moving into rural areas and by enterprises moving out of urban centers to take advantage of improved transport and communications infrastructure and reduced congestion" (Bosworth & Atterton, 2012, p. 255). The creative economy encourages this trend as seen in the Fifth Town and WhistleStop cases. The focus on the 3 Ts attracts youth and new business, fostering innovation, the arts, and cultural contributions. For rural communities facing potential economic and social decline, the creative economy provides a new way to promote community sustainability.

Appendix

Table 7.1: Ranked lists of economic-development challenges in rural southern Ontario.

Rank	*Combined*	*Eastern Ontario*	*Southwestern Ontario*
1	Youth retention	Youth retention	Youth retention
2	Skills training / education/literacy	Skills training / education/literacy	Agriculture / farm revitalization
3	Transportation improvement	Labour migration & attraction	Sustainable economic development
4	Economic diversification	Infrastructure	Transportation improvement
5	Infrastructure	Regional strategies & collaboration	Economic diversification
6	Employment opportunities	Economic diversification	Skills training / education/literacy
7	Agriculture / farm revitalization	Small-business support	Employment opportunities
8	Sustainable economic development	Strategic planning & implementation	Health-care issues
9	Efficient, cooperative government	Transportation	Efficient, cooperative government
10	Regional strategies & collaboration	Efficient, cooperative government	Infrastructure

Table 7.2: Ranked lists of knowledge gaps in rural southern Ontario.

Rank	*Combined*	*Eastern Ontario*	*Southwestern Ontario*
1	Sustainable economic-development strategies	Comparative advantage	Sustainable economic-development strategies
2	Comparative advantage	Sustainable economic-development strategies	Youth retention
3	Economic diversification	Economic diversification	Farm revitalization
4	Youth retention	Small-business development	Labour migration & attraction
5	Labour migration & attraction	Labour migration & attraction	Environment & land use
6	Farm revitalization	Regional-development strategies	Skills training / education
7	Regional-development strategies	Learning from best practices	Economic diversification
8	Small-business development	Tourism	Governance models
9	Skills training / education	Youth retention	Emerging/green industries
10	Learning from best practices	Skills training / education	Transportation

Authors' note

The authors thank the Social Sciences and Humanities Research Council of Canada for funding the research described in this chapter. They also thank The Monieson Centre, Queen's School of Business, Queen's University, for the research support provided. They thank the anonymous reviewers for their helpful comments.

Note

1. The Fifth Town and WhistleStop Productions cases are also described in Yoland Chan and Jeff Dixon's 2012 article, "The creative economy: An opportunity for rural revitalization," in EcDevJournal.com.

References

Bosworth, G., & Atterton, J. (2012). Entrepreneurial in-migration and neoendogenous rural development. *Rural Sociology, 77*(2), 254–279.

Bramwell, A., & Wolfe D. A. (2008). Universities and regional economic development: The entrepreneurial University of Waterloo. *Research Policy 37*, 1175–1187.

Dickerson Hartsock, L. (2007, April). *The role of universities in regional and local economic development.* Symposium conducted at Cornell University, Ithaca, NY.

DesRoches, R., Habkirk, J., Reid, A., Robinson, L., & Zhou, M. (2009). Fifth Town Artisan Cheese. *Community success stories.* Kingston, ON: The Monieson Centre.

Donald, B. (2008). *Growing the creative-rural economy in Prince Edward County: Strategies for innovation, creative and sustainable development.* Kingston, ON: The Monieson Centre.

Gertler, M. S., Florida, R., Gates, G., & Vinodrai, T. (2002). *Competing on creativity: Placing Ontario's cities in North American context.* Toronto: Ontario Ministry of Enterprise, Opportunity and Innovation.

Hall, H., & Donald, B. (2009). *Innovation and creativity on the periphery: Challenges and opportunities in northern Ontario.* Toronto: Martin Prosperity Institute.

Harris, B. (2006). Strategic plan for PELA CFDC. (Personal communication.)

Jarvis, D., & Dunham, P. (2003). Conceptualising the "competitive" strategies of rural manufacturing SMEs. *Tijdshrift voor Economische en Sociale Geografie, 94*(2), 246–57.

Johnson, T. G. (2001). The rural economy in a new century. *International Regional Science Review 24*, 21–37.

Kassun-Mutch, P. (2009, April). Fifth Town Artisan Cheese. Lecture conducted at 2009 KIS Showcase, Queen's School of Business, Kingston, ON.

Lo, S.-F., & Sheu, H.-J. (2007). Is corporate sustainability a value-increasing strategy for business? *Corporate Governance, 15* (2), 345–358.

Martin Prosperity Institute (MPI). (2009a). *Canada's creative corridor: Connecting creative urban and rural economies within eastern Ontario and the mega region.* Toronto.

———. (2009b). *Ontario in the creative age.* Toronto.

Munnich, L. W., Schrock, G., & Cook, K. (2002). Rural knowledge clusters: The challenge of rural economic prosperity. *Reviews of Economic Development Literature and Practice: No. 12.* Minneapolis: Humphrey Institute of Public Affairs, University of Minnesota.

Organisation for Economic Co-operation and Development (OECD). (2006). The new rural paradigm: Policies and governance. Paris: OECD.

Olfert, R., & Partridge, M. (2005). *Urban sprawl shows rural–urban interdependence: New governance needed to bridge rural–urban divide.* Policy brief. Saskatoon: University of Saskatchewan.

Prince Edward County. The official tourism website. Retrieved November 11, 2011, from http://prince-edward-county.com/.

Reimer, B., & Bollman, R. D. (2006). The new rural economy: Key observations for research and policy in the Canadian context. In M. F. Rogers & D. R. Jones (Eds.), *The changing nature of Australia's country towns.* Ballarat: VURRN Press.

Rodriguez, M. A., Ricart, J. E., and Sanchez, P. (2002). Sustainable development and the sustainability of competitive advantage: A dynamic and sustainable view of the firm. *Creativity and Innovation Management, 11,* 135–146.

Rothwell, N. (2001). Employment in rural and small town Canada: An update to 2000. *Rural and Small Town Canada Analysis Bulletin,3*(4).

Rothwell, N. & Bollman, R. (2011). Manufacturing firms in rural and small town Canada. *Rural and Small Town Canada Analysis Bulletin, 8*(6).

Senate Standing Committee on Agriculture and Forestry, Canadian Parliament. (2006). *Understanding freefall: The challenge of the rural poor.* Ottawa: Queen's Printer.

Social Sciences and Humanities Research Council of Canada (SSHRC). (2008, Summer). Scholarship in action: Knowledge mobilization and the academic process. *Dialogue.* Retrieved from http://www.sshrc-crsh.gc.ca/newsletter-bulletin/summer-ete/2008/knowledge_mobilization-eng.aspx.

United Kingdom Department for Culture, Media and Sport. (2001). *Creative industries mapping document.* London: HMSO.

United Nations Conference on Trade and Development. (2008). *Creative economy report 2008. The challenge of assessing the creative economy: Towards informed policy-making.* Geneva: UNCTAD.

EIGHT

University–Community Partnerships to Support Small-Town Economic Transition

Laura Ryser, Marc von der Gonna, and Greg Halseth

Introduction

Pressures limiting community development and community economic development in rural and small-town places include challenges related to human resources, infrastructure, industrial capacity, policy supports, and environmental assets (Herbert-Cheshire & Higgins, 2004; Ryser & Halseth, 2010). Addressing these pressures and challenges often means accessing information and research capacity (McDonald, 2004). Building community–university relationships is one way by which small places can access such needed information and research. Unfortunately, the top-down approach adopted by many research partners (Holkup, Tripp-Reimer, Salois, & Weinert, 2004), and the limited capacity of rural and small-town places to be receptors and mobilizers of research (Minkler, 2005), have been identified as key issues inhibiting action and support for community renewal.

Drawing upon the relationship between the town of McBride, British Columbia, and the University of Northern British Columbia's (UNBC) Community Development Institute (CDI), this chapter will explore some key lessons for developing and maintaining university–community partnerships in order to equip small communities with the information they need to respond to rural restructuring. McBride provides an excellent opportunity to explore the development and deployment of a community–university partnership as the community has been affected by economic and social change.

After a brief review of the impacts of restructuring on rural and small-town places, we explore the role that "engaged" post-secondary institutions can play in supporting community renewal. This includes a discussion of some of the problems and constraints that affect the development of effective university–community partnerships. Based upon a long relationship between UNBC's CDI and various community groups in McBride, we then discuss six key lessons for developing successful community–university relationships that can meet current needs and endure over the longer term.

Rural restructuring

Since the 1980s, pressures driving rural change have ranged from industrial consolidation to the adoption of labour-shedding technologies (Hayter, 2003; Ryser & Halseth, 2010). Fluctuations in currency and commodity prices, uncertainty surrounding international trade agreements, as well as increasing global competition have all made it difficult for Canadian resource industries to remain competitive (Prudham, 2008). Such challenges have had a significant impact in rural and small-town Canada where primary production remains a large part of local economies (Markey, Halseth, & Manson, 2008).

Also since the 1980s, neoliberal policy decisions aimed at reducing government expenditures are compounding the challenges of economic restructuring (Halseth & Ryser, 2006; Meinhard & Foster, 2003). The state has been actively downsizing, offloading, regionalizing, or closing many forms of services and supports (Halseth & Ryser, 2007; Tonts, 2000). Unfortunately, this retrenchment of government supports has also meant a withdrawal of economic development and community-development tools at a time when they are needed most (David Curran Associates, 2009; Halseth, Killam, & Manson, 2008a, 2008b). Such service closures can have profound impacts on residents and the viability of rural places.

Community–university partnerships: The challenge

The engaged campus

As communities prepare for, and respond to, economic, social, and political change, they need timely, relevant, and useful information to help them make decisions. Post-secondary research institutions can be an important source of this information. As part of an "engaged campus" strategy, these institutions can provide knowledge that supports innovation and competitiveness, informs strategic-planning exercises and community-development initiatives, mobilizes resources, builds local capacity, facilitates local and regional networks, empowers community engagement, and improves the quality of life in small places (Halseth, 2002; Honadle, 2001; Kniazev, 2002; Ostrander, 2004). They can provide credible information to inform and support debates. The university can also be an "honest" broker of arrangements and agreements between communities, community-service groups, industries, and various levels of government (Feld, 1998).

Unfortunately, many university tenure and promotion committees still do not accord enough consideration to the time, support, and long-term benefits to faculty development of long-term university–community relationships and partnerships (Israel, Schulz, Parker, & Becker, 2001). Policies and pressures associated with tenure and promotion systems can direct faculty attention away from these long-term investments in university–community relationships in favour of short-term "product" creation that can be linked directly to faculty career security. This becomes more complicated where faculty work under different norms and cultures with respect to the role, process, and supports for research (Ryser & Halseth, 2009). Due to tenure and promotion pressures, as well as organization and training constraints, academics enter research tasks seeking to build theory and improve questions for future research (Sá, Li, & Faubert, 2010). This results in a mismatch of expectations as communities want answers while academics want questions. In some cases, by the time research results become available, they may no longer be relevant to the community context or be a key priority for policy-makers (Williams, Labonte, Randall, & Muhajarine, 2005). With a mismatch of expectations, researchers must consider how knowledge will be mobilized (Cooper & Levin, 2010) or incorporated into the day-to-day operations of community groups.

Different expectations about how university and community partners will engage throughout the collaborative process may also exist. Some community partners may be frustrated by limited input into the design of research questions (Ostrander, 2004). Others may lack an understanding of the capacity that universities can contribute to community-development efforts (Le Gates & Robinson, 1998). Rather than adopting a community-driven approach that builds local capacity and guides implementation, researchers may also pursue community work as short-term consulting contracts (Feld, 1998). As a result, communities may be skeptical about the commitment of universities to support community-renewal efforts (Rubin, 2000).

Constraints to knowledge mobilization

The last decade has witnessed a rise in interest in how to more effectively put research knowledge to use in society. In Canada, federal funding agencies have increasingly called for knowledge-mobilization activities that link research with policy and practice as a part of their mandates (Sá et al., 2010). While previous work highlights a range of knowledge-mobilization strategies (Jacobson, Ochocka, Wise, & Janzen, 2007), many of these "strategies" are rarely more than a diverse range of communication tools used to promote research results. To be effective, researchers need to play a greater role in facilitating and guiding the implementation of the knowledge produced. Knowledge must be mobilized by producing new processes, policies, products, and skills. In other words, knowledge mobilization must produce some form of change.

Receptor capacity

Greater efforts are needed by post-secondary institutions, funding partners, and other government agencies to assist rural and small-town community partners to be better consumers of research. Many small municipal offices have a limited staff complement who must take on increasing responsibilities downloaded by federal and provincial/territorial governments (Halseth, Sullivan, & Ryser, 2003; McMillan, 2006; Smith & Stewart, 2006). Some places may have limited human capital, skills, and experience to mobilize new knowledge. In times of economic uncertainty, there may be labour turnover and hence a leakage of capacity and institutional memory from the community (Lackey, Freshwater, &

Rupasingha, 2002). Furthermore, municipalities may have limited local technical capacity, support, and resources to fulfill these roles (De Loe, Di Giantomasso, & Kreutzwiser, 2002; Honadle, 2001). These constraints can make it difficult to obtain mutual commitment in community–university partnerships. Relationship demands can be difficult to maintain with limited time and staff, not to mention that many small communities cannot afford a financial commitment to research projects/partnerships during periods of fiscal crisis.

Senior levels of government and post-secondary institutions need to realize that the bottom-up side of the knowledge-mobilization equation may not have the receptor capacity to take up their side of a research or knowledge relationship. Ongoing supports are needed to enable small places to build relationships and capacity that can be mobilized to pursue new ideas and processes. This will serve communities well during positive and challenging economic conditions. Unfortunately, this is not well understood by funding programs. While academic and funding institutions talk the "engaged" language, they often are not equipped to follow through with the infrastructure and support needed to transition from producing knowledge to producing change in communities (Baum, 2000; Williams et al., 2005; Wolff & Maurana, 2001).

Academic institutions, for example, may have inadequate resources allocated to support the development and evaluation of university–community partnership work (Williams et al., 2005). Incentives or requirements to pursue community-based research may not be incorporated into hiring and tenure/promotion policies. Standards of practice for engaging with communities and community-based research ethics protocols may be underdeveloped (Roche, 2008). Peer-reviewed publications may also place an emphasis on theoretical work, thereby undermining faculty interest in community-based research (Savan, 2004). There may be few community-based scholarships to encourage student interest in community-based research. Furthermore, community partners may have limited access to funding resources, mentoring and training supports, and research processes that are allocated to, and controlled by, university partners (Roche, 2008).

With short-term grants, funding institutions do not provide the resources necessary to nurture university–community partnerships (Flicker, Savan, McGrath, Kolenda, & Mildenberger, 2007). While more funding programs are being delivered to support community-based research (Levesque, 2007), the broader range of grants for traditional scholarship can discourage university–community partnerships (Savan, 2004). Few granting programs are designed to incorporate the decision-making processes of community groups throughout the research process (Williams et al., 2005).

University support for economic renewal: The case of McBride, British Columbia

To demonstrate how a community–university relationship can effectively support economic renewal, the remainder of our attention in this chapter will focus on some initiatives undertaken between UNBC and groups in McBride, British Columbia. Located approximately 210 kilometres from Prince George (Figure 8.1), McBride is a small community of roughly 660 people (Statistics Canada, 2006). It serves as the local centre in the Robson Valley,[1] a population of about four thousand people.

While the McBride area has historically benefitted from a mixed economy based upon agricultural, forestry, and service sectors, economic and political restructuring has jeopardized the stability of the local economy. For example, forest operations have been impacted by the mountain pine beetle epidemic, the softwood lumber dispute with the United States, rising stumpage fees, the increasing value of the Canadian dollar, and slow markets (Estabrooks, 2004). After losing its employment outreach office and government agent, the community experienced further job losses with the closure of the McBride-Robson Valley Forest District Office (*The Valley Sentinel*, January 31, 1996; November 27, 1996; December 11, 1996). The agricultural sector has been affected by the bovine spongiform encephalopathy crisis and new processing and water-management regulations (Leeson, 2004). The community needed to find new ways to support employment and entrepreneurial opportunities in the region, as well as ways to enhance the quality of life to attract new residents and businesses. This prompted several groups within the community to engage with faculty at the UNBC in order to obtain information that would support and inform new initiatives, programs, policies, and investments.

In this context, it is worth noting that the UNBC is a newer university that emerged out of a grassroots movement from residents across

Figure 8.1: Location of McBride within the Regional District of Fraser-Fort George.

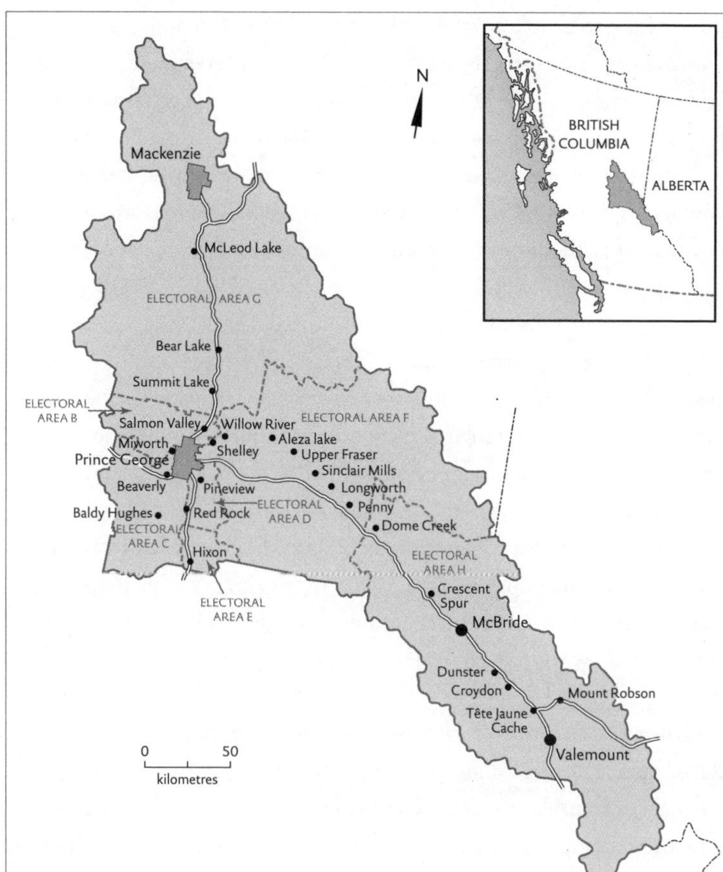

northern British Columbia's small communities in the 1980s and 1990s. Despite opposition from within the provincial government and other universities, residents initiated a petition drive that collected $5 from each signatory, which was used to conduct a feasibility study for the university (McCaffray, 1995). Designated as a university "in the north, for the north," a key component of UNBC's strategic research plan was to function as an "engaged campus" to support the sustainability of these small communities.

Formed in 2003, the CDI provides one of the venues to fulfill the university's "engaged campus" role by supporting research and providing information to enable northern British Columbia communities to make informed decisions about their futures. With an interest in supporting community capacity[2] and community development,[3] there are three foundations that drive the CDI's activities, including research, education, and outreach. Since 2003 the CDI has delivered these three activities as a part of their work with local groups in McBride in order to support actions toward economic renewal (see Appendix). To support community renewal, these projects have been designed to develop a greater understanding of the community, to explore the impacts of restructuring and policy changes on community viability, to take stock of community assets and resources, to identify service and capacity gaps, to link local groups with a broader range of resources and supports, and to identify appropriate policy and program supports that are needed to support local and regional initiatives. This would not have been possible without a long-term, effective collaborative working relationship with a broad range of local and non-local groups. In the remainder of this chapter, our discussion about university actions to support community-renewal processes draws upon our experiences working with local groups.

Lessons for community–university relationships

Based upon a research approach adopted by the CDI and community partners in McBride, we identify six key lessons important for building effective community–university relationships. These lessons are drawn from the experiences, conversations, and meetings that the authors have had with many local leaders, community groups, and residents (see Appendix). Topics identified in the literature were used to provide a basis for developing themes for key issues that have been raised over the years. In addition to situating the themes within a broader literature on university–community partnerships, these themes have been reviewed by both academic and community partners to enhance the reliability and validity of the work (Grinnell & Unrau, 2011). The six key lessons include:

1. Creating and maintaining a relationship,
2. Linking community partners with appropriate university resources,
3. Developing bottom-up research ideas,

4. Adopting a research design driven by community partners,
5. Involving community partners in the execution of research projects, and
6. Active co-mobilization of knowledge.

These lessons enhance the capacity of both researchers and local organizations during community and economic change, and they enable local groups to be better consumers of research.

Creating and maintaining a relationship

Community–university partnerships take time to develop and nurture (Halseth, 2002; Wolff & Maurana, 2001). While they may start with some tentative partnering "baby steps" or specific projects, the creation of robust relationships requires an investment of time and resources from the multiple stakeholders. Through routine interaction, this long-term working relationship will enable universities and community partners to develop a foundation of trust and credibility; share power, responsibility, and accountability; and facilitate mutual learning (Le Gates & Robinson, 1998; Rubin, 2000; Wiewel & Lieber, 1998).

The long-term relationship between the CDI and local groups in McBride was first established with a series of meetings with local civic and business leaders, service providers, and community groups. During these inaugural meetings, the CDI team provided information about its mandate and areas of expertise. These meetings also provided a venue for local groups to identify information and research gaps that needed to be addressed in order to guide local policy, program, and investment decisions. As such, these early discussions were critical to determine and plan for the needs, capacities, and expectations of both university and community partners throughout the research process (Gearheard & Shirley, 2006).

The success of early research projects conducted by the CDI team provided a foundation of trust upon which further research partnerships evolved (see Appendix). In addition to these initial meetings and research projects, routine visits were organized as part of the CDI's outreach mandate to enable members of the CDI team to continue to strengthen this relationship and to be privy to emerging issues and needs within the McBride area.[4] It is important to note, however, that many of our partners in McBride visit the CDI on a routine basis as they conduct other business in Prince George, thereby demonstrating the mutual commitment and importance that our community partners have assigned to matching and reciprocating outreach communication and dialogue activities (Maiter, Simich, Jacobson, & Wise, 2008). Of course, due to the significant distance, costs, winter weather, and safety associated with travel between Prince George and McBride, several other mechanisms have been used to maintain dialogue between the CDI and local groups, including video conferencing, informal phone calls, e-mails, a newsletter, and a website.

Link community partners with appropriate university resources

While community partners strive to discover what types of research and expertise universities offer, it is often not easy to quickly browse university websites or accurately identify specific research capacities. More outreach activities are needed to promote areas of research expertise to communities. This should include matching community stakeholders and needs with valuable contacts and information.

While CDI outreach activities have linked community development and community economic-development expertise with local groups in McBride, UNBC's vice-president and provost asked the CDI to execute a community-dialogue process in 2008 to identify a wider range of research needs and link other research capacities at the university with northern British Columbia communities (Manson & Halseth, 2008). Despite other Canadian examples that highlight the need to provide resources that support outreach work for developing university–community partnerships (Roche, 2008; Savan & Sider, 2003), the North First Community Dialogue Project did not include a budget to follow through with linking research capacities across northern British Columbia communities. As community needs are constantly changing, it will be important for the university to both revisit this exercise on a routine basis and allocate adequate resources for outreach activities in order to ensure that research continues to be relevant and useful for places like McBride.

Through its Community Speakers Series, the CDI has developed a venue to showcase UNBC's research capacity both at its main campus in Prince George and at venues across northern British Columbia. Recognizing the restructuring challenges facing the local forest sector, for example, the CDI sponsored a Community Speakers Series in McBride in October 2008 featuring Dr. Kathy Lewis, a UNBC faculty member who specializes in forest-management practices. Again, the CDI's newsletter and website, as well as informal discussions, have helped to link McBride groups with a broader range of research capacity and expertise at UNBC. Supporting the use of a broad range of communication tools is critical to build the university's capacity as an "engaged campus" and to link a breadth of community organizations and residents with appropriate university resources (Michael Smith Foundation for Health Research, 2010).

Meetings of the Omineca Beetle Action Coalition's (OBAC) Future Forest Summit, the BC Community Forest Association, the BC Inland Rainforest Conference, and the Forest History Association of BC have provided additional opportunities for the CDI to connect research capacity and expertise with local economic- and community-development groups in McBride and the surrounding rural areas. Despite these successes, rural infrastructure is largely underutilized in the support of conferences and other outreach activities that would not only provide another venue to build relationships with rural stakeholders and provide access to research expertise but would also support the ongoing operations and maintenance of rural facilities. Many rural health, economic-, and community-development meetings continue to be concentrated in urban areas, resulting in an economic leakage of potential benefits that could be accrued to rural research partners and other local stakeholders. It may also continue to undermine the receptor capacity of community partners who have limited resources and are unable to commute to distant regional centres.

Develop bottom-up research ideas

Perhaps the most important lesson for developing university–community partnerships is the need for research to be truly collaborative and community driven (Viswanathan et al., 2004). This will help ensure that research is relevant and useful to support decisions. By way of example, the UNBC has been working with the McBride Community Forest Corporation (MCFC). At this writing, the MCFC is a key local tool for community development and economic diversification. Established in 2002, the MCFC's goal is "to provide the village and the surrounding community with a greater socio-economic diversity within the scope of a healthy environment" (Personal communication, 2009). The net income generated from the MCFC has produced a number of benefits for the community, including financial support for a new community hall, a community foundation, an economic-development officer position, and projects initiated by nonprofit community groups. Revenue generated from the MCFC is paid to the Village of McBride as a dividend. The village then uses the money as leverage to obtain other financial support, as well as for community projects that are providing a foundation for renewal and long-term capacity.

Critical to local decision making about how to operate the MCFC and how to invest local benefits is knowledge about the fundamentals of community and economic renewal. The relationship with the CDI at the UNBC provides a platform for ongoing dialogue and exchange of ideas on both these topics. Through previous discussions with MCFC staff, a range of research and information needs have been identified that will provide a foundation for future local initiatives and community transition. These include:

1. *Energy (waste-wood bio-energy)*
   Business cases / models; technology options; environmental impacts/ monitoring; waste, transport, emissions, ash, etc.; feasibility studies for new power lines; and bio-fuel for other industrial plants.
2. *Forestry*
   International market surveillance, maximizing wood values, and possibilities for non-timber products (i.e., devil's club, mushrooms, medicinal plants / herbs).
3. *Transportation*
   Alternatives for moving wood / forest products, traffic studies, impacts of changing traffic mix, highway and "off-highway" safety, and truck and traffic impacts on highway maintenance.
4. *Business infrastructure and development*
   Key trends for small and medium-sized businesses, human-resource needs, and infrastructure needs.

5. *Marketing and exporting products*
   Market/product options, case studies of successful small places/ exporters, marketing/distribution models for local products, and use of / access to e-commerce.
6. *Quality of life*
   Role of a healthy, diversified economy in attracting residents/ businesses, and services to improve quality of life.

A first area of community research needs focused upon developing viable and secure alternative-energy options that can support a variety of industrial activities. Second, our community partners identified knowledge gaps that inhibit the efficient and wiser use of a broader range of forest resources by multiple stakeholders. With increased activity associated with the MCFC, questions are emerging about transportation infrastructure needs, including the impact of community forest activities on highway safety and maintenance.

Information is also needed to develop opportunities and capacity within the business sector. Bringing new products and innovations to market requires timely access to information and supports. While the MCFC has already pursued innovative approaches to promoting and marketing its products through various small-market logger programs and its initiative to donate wood to the Olympic podium project, additional supports are needed for market surveillance and to assist new partners and entrepreneurs to establish market strategies and tools. Furthermore, to attract and retain investors, businesses, and a stable workforce, information is needed to inform community-development strategies that can enhance local quality of life. While this only provides a sample of research and information needs, it gives a sense of the critical need and opportunities available to extend community–university relationships.

Research design should be driven by community partners

Once university and community partners have identified research priorities, it is important to continue to collaborate with local groups in the design and execution of the research project. During the design phase, for example, it is important to clearly define the problem as groups may have different interests and perspectives of the problem (Monk, Manning,

& Denman, 2003). The design of the research project should fit with the community goals as well as the larger processes of relationship and capacity building, and change (Maiter et al., 2008). Researchers should work with community partners to ensure they understand the purpose of each question and how results can be used in their daily activities and decision-making processes. They can help university–community collaborations to obtain a greater response from residents and capture authentic representations of key issues under investigation (Roche, 2008).

In April 2003 the McBride Industrial Adjustment Committee was formed in response to the closure of provincial government offices and a downturn in the forest industry. Shortly after, a partnership was formed with the UNBC's CDI to conduct a survey to assess employment skills and capabilities of area residents. Through telephone calls and videoconferencing, the CDI met with local groups to draft and review a door-to-door survey. The CDI also provided feedback and guidance to the committee for a funding proposal submitted to Human Resources and Skills Development Canada.[5] It is important to note that during this funding application exercise, the main applicant on the proposal, and subsequently the holder of funds, was the McBride Industrial Adjustment Committee. This approach was critical to empower community groups as fully engaged partners in the collaboration (Wolff & Maurana, 2001) and to build the capacity of local groups to work with senior government agencies. Through this capacity-building exercise, local leaders and groups attained a greater understanding of the research design process.

Involve community partners in the execution of research projects

Community participation in the execution of research projects is important to build local capacity, strengthen the trust and working relationship with the research team, and educate community groups about the execution-related aspects of the research process. Meaningful involvement in the execution of research projects can also allow local groups to become more invested in mobilizing research results (Viswanathan et al., 2004). Community partners can also, however, contribute considerable research support by providing logistical support (i.e. access to records, office space, and equipment) and in-kind support to alleviate field and accommodation costs (Gearheard & Shirley, 2006).

With the McBride Skills Inventory survey, local groups not only helped to design the study, they also provided drop-off locations and boxes for completed surveys, promoted the project's purpose and ongoing research activities, wrote the final report based on data compiled by the CDI team, and promoted the results. Their involvement in every aspect of the research, from design to the writing of the final report, led to a greater sense of ownership of the project and its report. Although the degree of community involvement may vary from place to place, the successful lessons in executing collaborative research have been replicated in other research initiatives across northern British Columbia (e.g., the Community Transition Toolkit developed in partnership with the District of Mackenzie; the inclusion of youth in the execution of the Village of Old Masset Economic Development Strategy; and the inclusion of seniors in the execution of work for the Tumbler Ridge Mayor's Task Force on Seniors' Needs: www.unbc.ca/cdi/research.html).

Guide knowledge mobilization

Once a project is completed, a key element to mobilizing knowledge is to widely communicate the research results and identify their importance for informing community actions in order to broaden community support for change (Jacobson et al., 2007). Incorporating a diversity of community partners throughout the research process helps to generate wide interest in the results, support for the project, and will provide a broad foundation of networks in which to promote action for change. The CDI has used multiple methods to reach a diversity of audiences through letters, newspaper articles, radio interviews, posters in community centres, copies of research products in public libraries, websites, e-mails, community forums, and presentations. Posting research results on a university website alone does not work.

Knowledge mobilization, however, is about more than just using a diverse range of communication tools to promote results. It is about sharing decision making and project responsibilities in order to increase ownership, understanding, and mobilization of new knowledge, new relationships, or new processes (Mitton, Adair, McKenzie, Patten, & Perry, 2007). By incorporating a diversity of local stakeholders throughout the research process, a greater sense of ownership and action may emerge over the knowledge that is produced to support renewal activities.

The creation of a research relationship with communities must have at its core a sense of respect, patience, and flexibility in assisting communities to reach their goals. Most of all, researchers must follow-up with communities on a regular and routine basis to assist local leaders to bridge the results with short-term, medium-term, and long-term actions that will be required to mobilize the knowledge into practice. There are always questions and the need for interpretation, and it is important, therefore, to maintain mechanisms for dialogue. In this respect, the CDI team has provided advice to community partners in McBride during, after, and between research projects. These actions are critical to strengthen relationships and trust with community partners and build momentum for change, ensuring that this will not just be another study that sits on the shelf. Small, immediate success breeds further success as it can generate wider community support and participation as people see the benefits of deliverables.

To further mobilize resources and actions, university partners can act as brokers of dialogue and relationship building between various groups in rural and small-town places, industries, and senior levels of government (Cooper, 2010; Holmes & Harris, 2010). The MCFC was one of several representatives from small communities across northern British Columbia that participated in the Future Forest Summit coordinated by the CDI, Timberline Natural Resource Group, and the OBAC. This workshop brought together representatives from First Nations groups, community forest organizations, local government, industry, and various provincial and federal government agencies to develop a future forest and fibre strategy for the region. After participants reviewed research and best practices about forest and non-timber forest practices and products, the goal of the workshop was to foster interaction across multiple stakeholders and prioritize the key actions that need to be undertaken to address capacity and policy issues in order to support future opportunities in the OBAC region.

Conclusion

Community–university relationships can be an effective tool for building community-development and economic-development foundations. In rural and small-town places, they can enhance and supplement human-resource capacity, expertise, and the local ability to be better consumers of knowledge that is produced in partnership with the research community. They can also strengthen the development of civil-society groups and be a surrogate for interaction, developing common values and trust, and mobilizing networks and resources to respond to emerging challenges and opportunities (Putnam, 2001; Reimer, 2002). Research, however, is not only important to assist timely decisions but it can also spur innovation and small-scale economic-development options, and enhance competitiveness. In the case of McBride, British Columbia, obtaining access to needed knowledge has also been important for addressing the environmental goals for the community and its surrounding forested landscape. The collaboration between the CDI and groups in McBride has also led to many successful outputs such as sharing information and advice, enhancing the capacity for both academic and community partners to engage in partnership work, delivering joint presentations, producing publications, brokering new relationships for both academic and community partners, and fostering future research initiatives.

However, rural and small-town places can experience considerable information, economic, and capacity leakage during the course of traditional research projects. While researchers obtain grants, data, and publications to support their career development, the short-term, top-down research approach does not enable rural and small-town places to maximize the potential benefits and assets available through university partnerships to support economic transition.

If universities are going to fulfill their role as "engaged campuses" that can support rural development, some key changes are needed to ensure that knowledge is mobilized and that rural and small-town places benefit from more than just the export of survey responses. First and foremost, community stakeholders must be treated both with respect and as equal partners during the development of research ideas and during the design and execution of research projects. This will not only strengthen the capacity of community stakeholders to engage in future research endeavours with the research team, but it will also broaden support and commitment for change. Over time, trust and routine interaction between universities and rural and small-town places will increase the efficiency and timeliness of research products and advice. In this respect, researchers can no longer ignore their responsibility to facilitate the mobilization of new knowledge that is produced. In an "engaged campus" strategy, the focus should not be the completion of projects and publications but rather that relationships with communities must endure and change must be supported. Providing ongoing advice, education, and training; brokering dialogue between different stakeholders; and providing assistance to community partners to strategically plan short-, medium-, and long-term actions is a part of this commitment. Given limited resources and the vast size of northern British Columbia, the CDI has been very resourceful and has benefitted from many forms of in-kind community support in order to fulfill its role in responding to the North's research and information needs. Long-term resources, however, are needed to bring stability to staff and outreach activities.

As part of the tenure and promotion system, universities can strengthen the "engaged campus" by rewarding faculty who engage in community-based research (Moses, 2002). Developing university–community partnerships should also be a key component of doctoral training in academic research and community service (Le Gates & Robinson, 1998). Furthermore, long-term infrastructure and funding supports are needed to bring stability to collaborative initiatives with rural and small-town places in order to sustain momentum. In this respect, funding agencies and universities should ensure that both research and outreach activities are well supported. Some institutions have also created offices with the sole mandate to facilitate and mobilize university partnerships with communities (Sá et al., 2010).

In this chapter, we have described some of the approaches used by the UNBC's CDI and local groups in McBride to build a community–university relationship to enhance local capacity to support community and economic transition. It is based on the idea that research-project partnerships can lead to robust research relationships. Such relationships are needed to assist in nurturing knowledge mobilization and action in small places where capacity constraints and pressing local needs underscore the value of a platform for dialogue, checking, and sharing that such a relationship can provide. Through a relationship approach, not only can research projects and knowledge-mobilization activities be more successful compared to non-collaborative and researcher-controlled approaches, but university and community commitments to supporting positive change can be more successful.

Appendix

Timeline of CDI research activities in McBride.

2003 • *Historical guide to local events*
A collection of issues and stories to be used for later references and analysis. The purpose was to provide some background information for research into issues from the recent past.

2003, 2005, 2008 • *Service inventory*
Explores the relationship between changes in services and local capacity in McBride.

2004 • *Quality-of-life study*
Explores the relationship between changes in available services and residents' perceptions of their quality of life. Information collected was provided to help residents, businesses, service providers, and policy-makers adjust to changing conditions.

2004 • *McBride skills inventory assessment*
Identifies skills, education, experience, and local interests of the work-force in the McBride area. The information collected was used by existing businesses and was provided to potential business interests in the region.

2004 • *Northern Economic Development Vision and Strategy Project*
Meetings, workshops, and interviews were coordinated to collect input and recommendations from stakeholder groups that would inform supportive policy development, community and infrastructure investment, and regional coordination.

2005/2006 • *Innovative services and voluntary organizations*
Explores how innovative service providers and voluntary groups in McBride contribute to local capacity and community development, and how they sustain themselves during periods of transition.

2008 • *North First Community Dialogue Project*
Conducted at the request of UNBC's vice-president and provost, community-based interviews in small places across northern British Columbia

to better connect a broad range of UNBC's activities with the needs of its service region. Information was collected about "what do our communities need to know?" and "what would they like the university to do?"

2008/2009 • *Northern British Columbia service sector study*
Identifies labour market issues and practical solutions to address short-term and long-term gaps and needs.

2008/2009 • *Omineca Beetle Action Coalition (OBAC) Community Transition Toolkit*
A suite of tools that were completed in McBride to assist with community transition and preparedness planning.

2009 • *Videoconferencing at McBride Secondary School*
Identifies lessons and capacity gaps concerning the application of distance-teaching video technologies in McBride Secondary School.

2009 • *United Way project*
Interviews conducted with local service providers and community service groups to identify service pressures and gaps that need to be addressed. Feedback obtained was used to inform funding strategies, fundraising initiatives, and program investments.

2009 • *OBAC's Future Forest Summit*
In partnership with OBAC and Western Economic Diversification Canada, the CDI hosted a future forest summit with community and forest-industry representatives from around the OBAC region, including McBride. Information was collected about capacity and policy issues that need to be addressed in order to strengthen and support future opportunities in the region. Recommendations were used to inform OBAC's Future Forest Products and Fibre Use Strategy.

Notes

1. The Robson Valley consists of many small communities that engage in agricultural and forestry activities such as Dunster, Tête Jaune Cache, and Dome Creek.

2. The CDI refers to community capacity as the ability of residents to organize their assets and resources to achieve objectives they consider important (www.unbc.ca/cdi/description.html).
3. The CDI refers to community development as improvements to social and cultural infrastructure, including the development of skills, knowledge, and abilities of residents to access information and mobilize resources that can be used to create strategies and partnerships to help them adjust to change in the new economy (www.unbc.ca/cdi/description.html).
4. CDI community visits to McBride were conducted in June and December 2007, October 2008, and May and October 2009.
5. Another key element to the success of this application was HRSDC's knowledge of the prior success the CDI team had working with HRSDC and other communities. Developing and sustaining a relationship with funders is clearly another key component to successful university–community partnerships.

References

Baum, H. (2000). Fantasies and realities in university–community partnerships. *Journal of Planning Education and Research, 20*(4), 234–246.

Cooper, A. (2010). *Knowledge brokers: A promising knowledge mobilization strategy to increase research use and its impact in education.* Toronto: Ontario Institute for Studies in Education.

Cooper, A., & Levin, B. (2010). Some Canadian contributions to understanding knowledge mobilization. *Evidence & Policy, 6*(3), 351–369.

David Curran Associates. (2009). *Municipal economic crisis response program: A municipal guide for economic recovery.* St. John's, NL: Municipalities of Newfoundland and Labrador. Retrieved from http://www.nlreda.ca/system/filestore/OM%20resource%20materials/ECRP%20Draft%20Final.pdf.

De Loe, R., Di Giantomasso, S., & Kreutzwiser, R. (2002). Local capacity for groundwater protection in Ontario. *Environmental Management, 29*(2), 217–233.

Estabrooks, J. (2004, November 24). Mill owner says MFI will be back up to speed soon. *The Valley Sentinel*, 1.

Feld, M. (1998). Community outreach partnership centers: Forging new relationships between university and community. *Journal of Planning Education and Research, 17*(4), 285–290.

Flicker, S., Savan, B., McGrath, M., Kolenda, B., and Mildenberger, M. (2007). "If you could change one thing..." What community-based researchers wish they could have done differently. *Community Development Journal, 43*(2), 239–253.

Gearheard, S., & Shirley, J. (2006). Challenges in community–research relationships: Learning from natural science in Nunavut. *ARCTIC, 60*(1), 62–74.

Grinnell, R., & Unrau, Y. (2011). *Research and evaluation: Foundations of evidence-based practice.* 9th edition. New York: Oxford University Press.

Halseth, G. (2002). Practical steps for community–university links. *The Bulletin of the Association of Commonwealth Universities,* May(No. 151), 20–21.

Halseth, G., Killam, S., & Manson, D. (2008a). Economic emergency toolkit for smaller municipalities: Background and triage (part 1). *Municipal World, 118*(3), 35.

———. (2008b). Economic emergency toolkit for smaller municipalities: Following through (part 2). *Municipal World, 118*(4), 35.

Halseth, G., & Ryser, L. (2006). Trends in service delivery: Examples from rural and small town Canada, 1998 to 2005. *Journal of Rural and Community Development, 1*(2), 69–90.

———. (2007). The deployment of partnerships by the voluntary sector to address service needs in rural and small town Canada. *Voluntas, 18*(3), 241–265.

Halseth, G., Sullivan, L., & Ryser, L. (2003). Service provision as part of resource town transition planning: A case from Northern British Columbia. In D. Bruce & G. Lister (Eds.), *Opportunities and actions in the new rural economy* (pp. 19–46). Sackville, NB: Rural and Small Town Programme.

Hayter, R. (2003). The war in the woods: Post-Fordist restructuring, globalization, and the contested remapping of British Columbia's forest economy. *Annals of the Association of American Geographers, 93*(3), 706–729.

Herbert-Cheshire, L., & Higgins, V. (2004). From risky to responsible: Expert knowledge and the governing of community-led rural development. *Journal of Rural Studies, 20*(3), 289–302.

Holkup, P., Tripp-Reimer, T., Salois, E., & Weinert, C. (2004). Community-based participatory research: An approach to intervention research with a Native American community. *ANS, 27*(3), 162–175.

Holmes, J., & Harris, B. (2010). Enhancing the contribution of research councils to the generation of evidence to inform policy making. *Evidence & Policy, 6*(3), 391–409.

Honadle, B. (2001). Theoretical and practical issues of local government capacity in an era of devolution. *The Journal of Regional Analysis and Policy, 31*(1), 77–90.

Israel B., Schulz, A., Parker, E., & Becker, A. (2001). Community-based participatory research: Policy recommendations for promoting a partnership. *Approach in Health Research. Education for Health, 14*(2), 182–197.

Jacobson, N., Ochocka, J., Wise, J., & Janzen, R. (2007). Inspiring knowledge mobilization through a communications policy: The case of a Community University Research Alliance. *Progress in Community Health Partnerships: Research, Education, and Action, 1*(1), 99–104.

Kniazev, E. (2002). The role of higher education in regional development: The Russian experience. In *Universities project final report, 1997-2002* (pp. 28–32). Salzburg, AT: Salzburg Seminar.

Lackey, S., Freshwater, D., & Rupasingha, A. (2002). Factors influencing local government cooperation in rural areas: Evidence from the Tennessee Valley. *Economic Development Quarterly, 16*(2), 138–154.

Leeson, B. (2004, January 21). Regulation would make meat inspection mandatory. *The Valley Sentinel*, 1.

Le Gates, R., & Robinson, G. (1998). Institutionalizing university–community partnerships. *Journal of Planning Education and Research, 17*(4), 312–322.

Levesque, P. (2007). *Network: The key to acting on knowledge*. Ottawa: Knowledge Mobilization Works.

Maiter, S., Simich, L., Jacobson, N., & Wise, J. (2008). Reciprocity. *Action Research, 6*(3), 305–325.

Manson, D., & Halseth, G. (2008). *North first initiative: Building toward a northern BC research and development cluster*. Prince George, BC: University of Northern British Columbia. Retrieved from http://www.unbc.ca/assets/cdi/north_first_initiative_project_report_sept_08.pdf.

Markey, S., Halseth, G., & Manson, D. (2008). Challenging the inevitability of rural decline: Advancing the policy of place in northern British Columbia. *Journal of Rural Studies, 24*(4), 409–421.

McCaffray, C. (1995). *UNBC, A northern crusade: The how and who of BC's northern university*. Duncan, BC: CJ McCaffray.

McDonald, J. (2004). The Tsimshian protocols: Locating and empowering community-based research. *Canadian Journal of Native Education, 28*(1–2), 80–91.

McMillan, M. (2006). Municipal relations with the federal and provincial governments: A fiscal perspective. In R. Young & C. Leuprecht (Eds.), *Canada: The state of the federation. Municipal, federal, and provincial relations in Canada* (pp. 45–82). Montreal: McGill-Queen's University Press.

Meinhard, A., & Foster, M. (2003). Differences in the response of women's voluntary organizations to shifts in Canadian public policy. *Nonprofit and Voluntary Sector Quarterly, 32*(3), 366–396.

Michael Smith Foundation for Health Research. (2010). *Knowledge translation/exchange discussion paper*. Vancouver, BC: Michael Smith Foundation for Health Research.

Minkler, M. (2005). Community-based research partnerships: Challenges and opportunities. *Journal of Urban Health, 82*(Supplement 2), ii3–ii12.

Mitton, C., Adair, C., McKenzie, E., Patten, S., & Perry, B. (2007). Knowledge transfer and exchange: Review and synthesis of the literature. *The Milbank Quarterly, 85*(4), 729–768.

Monk, J., Manning, P., & Denman, C. (2003). Working together: Feminist perspectives on collaborative research and action. *ACME, 2*, 91–106.

Moses, Y. (2002). The moral purpose of higher education. In *Universities Project Final Report, 1997-2002* (pp. 23–25). Salzburg, Austria: Salzburg Seminar.

Ostrander, S. (2004). Democracy, civic participation, and the university: A comparative study of civic engagement on five campuses. *Nonprofit and Voluntary Sector Quarterly, 33*(1), 74–93.

Prudham, S. (2008). Tall among the trees: Organizing against globalist forestry in rural British Columbia. *Journal of Rural Studies, 24*(2), 182–196.

Putnam, R. (2001). *Bowling alone: The collapse and revival of the American community*. New York and Toronto: Simon and Schuster.

Reimer, B. (2002). A sample frame for rural Canada: Design and evaluation. *Regional Studies, 36*(8), 845–859.

Roche, B. (2008). *New directions in community-based research*. Toronto: Wellesley Institute.

Rubin, V. (2000). Evaluating university–community partnerships: An examination of the evolution of questions and approaches. *Cityscape: A Journal of Policy Development and Research, 5*(1), 219–230.

Ryser, L., & Halseth, G. (2009). Building student research capacity: Faculty perceptions about institutional barriers in Canadian universities. *Research Management Review, 17*(1), 1–19.

———. (2010). Rural economic development: A review of the literature from industrialized economies. *Geography Compass, 4*(6), 510–531.

Sá, C., Li, S., & Faubert, B. (2010). Faculties of education and institutional strategies for knowledge mobilization: An exploratory study. *Higher Education, 61*(5), 501–512. doi: 10.1007/s10734-010-9344-4.

Savan, B. (2004). Community–university partnerships: Linking research and action for sustainable community development. *Community Development Journal, 39*(4), 372–384.

Savan B., & Sider, D. (2003). Constrasting approaches to community-based research and a case study of community sustainability in Toronto, Canada. *Local Environment, 8*(3), 303–316.

Smith, P., & Stewart, K. (2006). Local whole-of-government policy making in Vancouver: Beavers, cats, and the mushy middle thesis. In R. Young & C. Leuprecht (Eds.), *Canada: The state of the federation. Municipal, federal, and provincial relations in Canada* (pp. 251–272). Montreal: McGill-Queen's University Press.

Statistics Canada. (2006). Community profiles. Ottawa: Statistics Canada.

Tonts, M. (2000). The restructuring of Australia's rural communities. In B. Pritchard & P. McManus (Eds.), *Land of discontent: The dynamics of change in rural and regional Australia* (pp. 52–72). Sydney, AU: University of New South Wales Press, Ltd.

The Valley Sentinel. (1996, January 31). Food bank gets start, 1.

———. (1996, November 27). McBride loses government agent, 3.

———. (1996, December 11). Forestry office loses a quarter of its staff, 5.

Viswanathan, M., Ammerman, A., Eng, E., Gartlehner, G., Lohr, K., Griffith,... Whitener, L. (2004). *Community-based participatory research: Assessing the evidence.* Rockville, MD: Agency for Healthcare Research and Quality.

Wiewel, W., & Lieber, M. (1998). Goal achievement, relationship building, and incrementalism: The challenges of university–community partnerships. *Journal of Planning Education and Research, 17*(4), 294–301.

Williams, A., Labonte, R., Randall, J., & Muhajarine, N. (2005). Establishing and sustaining community–university partnerships: A case study of quality of life research. *Critical Public Health, 15*(3), 291–302.

Wolff, M., & Maurana, C. (2001). Building effective community–academic partnerships to improve health: A qualitative study of perspectives from communities. *Academic Medicine, 76*(2), 166–172.

SECTION III

Implementation and Action

Lessons from the Front Lines

NINE

Taking the Next Steps Toward Environmental Sustainability

Implementing the Official Plan on Pelee Island

Jennifer Sumner and Claire Sanders

Introduction

Located in the middle of the west end of Lake Erie, the Township of Pelee Island is made up of one main island (Pelee Island) that is approximately four thousand hectares and eight smaller islands with no permanent population. It forms the southernmost point in Canada and hosts a variety of Carolinian flora and fauna not found elsewhere in the country. Its southerly latitude, combined with the relative warmth of Lake Erie, make it home to a unique variety of rare insects, snails, mammals, birds, reptiles, and amphibians. Glaciation left a variety of habitats for this wildlife: wetlands, sand dunes, alvars (areas of limestone with a shallow overburden), and deep soils suitable for the trees of the Eastern Deciduous Forest zone (Pelee Island, 2011a). Pelee Island attracts a range of people as well. Farmers find that the mild climate makes the island suitable for growing grapes and other crops. Many residents cater to the tourists who come to watch birds, participate in the annual pheasant hunt, or simply enjoy island life. Summer residents swell the small full-time population, some of whom are descendants of the earliest European settlers. Given its sensitive ecological niche and the negative impacts humans can create, the

Municipality of Pelee Island has drawn up what it calls the Official Plan, which aims to protect its environmental heritage.

Development of the Official Plan

In recent years a vision for this island community has emerged, which the official website of the Municipality of Pelee Island maintains is based on a longstanding tradition of balanced interests: "For Islanders a healthy community always has meant a combination of job opportunities, a degree of self reliance, a clean environment, a significant place for wildlife, opportunities in education for our youth, and a vibrant cultural life" (Pelee Island, 2011b). In tandem with the emergence of this vision came a recognition that it would not be realized on its own—it had to be planned. According to the official website:

> As representatives of the community, Pelee Island's Municipal Council has authorized the preparation of an Official Plan that addresses these issues, paying special attention to sustainability of the Island's economy, environment, and cultural traditions. While the Municipality is looking to increase the population to ensure the provision of community services and of vital social infrastructure needs, it also wishes to ensure that the Island's biodiversity is not merely protected, but indeed enhanced. To this end protected sensitive natural areas are being expanded as additional economic opportunities, ones in keeping with the sought after balance, are pursued. (Pelee Island, 2011b)

To implement the Official Plan, the island community has been careful not to encourage polluting industries such as chemical factories that might damage its ecological uniqueness and the tourism it attracts. Instead, it aspires to become a model of environmental sustainability by supporting organic agriculture, developing bike trails, dedicating land to conservation, piloting an alternative vehicle project, and proposing an international eco-school.

But what exactly is sustainability and how do rural communities like Pelee Island know if they are becoming more or less sustainable? This chapter will begin with an examination of the concept of sustainability and link it to the civil commons—cooperative human constructions that protect and/or enable universal access to life goods. It will then briefly discuss the new meanings that emerge from compound terms such as "sustainable development" and "sustainable rural communities." It will go on to explain how the subcategories of economic, social, and environmental sustainability also reside in the civil commons, providing, respectively, economic, social, and environmental life goods.

The chapter will then concentrate on examples of environmental sustainability on Pelee Island, using five cases: Meadowlark Organic Farm, Pelee Island and the Nature Conservancy of Canada, the Pelee Island Bird Observatory, Pelee Island and the Ontario Endangered Species Act, and the Ecological Trail System. The cases will be analyzed in terms of community development, collaboration, rural community sustainability, and decision making. In addition, the cases will be assessed with respect to benefits, costs, and lessons learned. The chapter will conclude with a consideration of the unsustainability of our current way of life and the importance of the civil commons.

Sustainability

Although the word "sustainable" has been used in the English language since 1290, the term "sustainability" did not appear until 1972 (Simpson & Weiner, 1989). It emerged as a response to the ecological destruction at "the nexus between economic activity and the natural environment" (Common, 1995, p. 4). Before such destruction became unavoidably apparent, sustainability was not an explicit goal, but it was certainly implicit: "no human society has ever consciously promoted its own unsustainability" (Bossel, 1999, p. 1).

The term slowly gained recognition in the 1980s, culminating with what came to be known as the Brundtland Report in 1987, published as *Our Common Future*. The report centred on the concept of sustainable development—development that meets the needs of the present without compromising the ability of future generations to meet their own needs (World Commission on Environment and Development [WCED], 1987). Although many criticized the vacuity of this definition (Lohmann, 1990; Rees, 1990; Sumner, 2005; Visvanathan, 1991), it undoubtedly catapulted the term "sustainability" to world-wide recognition.

In the years since the Brundtland Report, sustainability has dominated the world stage, requiring at the very least minimal adherence to its inherent demands. And yet it remains a fuzzy term without a clear definition or commonly recognized criteria for judging whether a policy or action will lead to more or less sustainability. The concept of the civil commons, however, opens the possibility of providing clarity, criteria, and community participation to this pivotal term.

The civil commons

Conceptualized by McMurtry (1999b), the civil commons is "any co-operative human construction that protects and/or enables the universal access to life goods" (p. 1). In this way, the civil commons is cooperative, not competitive. It does not occur naturally but is built by human agency. The civil commons protects through rules and regulations, and it enables by opening up spaces and opportunities. It involves universal access, not paid access, to life goods, such as food, water, shelter, education, and health care. The civil commons can be described as "society's long-evolving system of conscious human protection of the larger life-host humanity lives from" (McMurtry, 1999a, p. 213). Examples of the civil commons are all around us, but they have never been collectively named: public-education systems, universal health-care programs, building regulations, water and power installations, bridges, environmental accords, social-safety protections, laws, libraries, the Canadian Broadcasting Corporation (CBC), sewage systems, and social assistance. In essence,

> [t]he nature of the civil commons can be expressed as follows: It is society's organized and community-funded capacity of universally accessible resources to provide for the life preservation and growth of society's members and their environmental life-host. The civil commons is, in other words, what people ensure together as a society to protect and further life, as distinct from money aggregates. (McMurtry, 1998, p. 24)

Sustainability and the civil commons

The civil commons, and the life-support systems it offers, provides not only the basis of a definition for sustainability but also the criteria by which to judge matters of sustainability. Keeping in mind cooperative human constructions that protect and/or enable universal access to life goods, sustainability involves building and maintaining the civil commons

(Sumner, 2005, 2009, 2011). The more we build and maintain the civil commons, the more sustainable we become. The more we enclose and dismantle the civil commons, the less sustainable we become. For example, the more we protect public education, public health care, and public pensions, the more sustainable we become. The more we allow the erosion of these projects to provide life goods, the less sustainable we become.

Tightly tying the meaning of sustainability to the civil commons results in new understandings of familiar compound terms. For example, sustainable development becomes development that spreads the civil commons, not the promotion of private entrepreneurship or mega-projects that benefit a few wealthy investors. And sustainable rural communities become rural communities anchored by the civil commons, not by private business development or cash crops for export markets.

Sustainability is generally divided into environmental, social, and economic components. Some picture sustainability as a three-legged stool that needs all three components in order to stand firmly. But this metaphor treats these three components equally, obscuring the understanding that without environmental sustainability, we cannot have social and economic sustainability. To convey the primacy of the environment, we can employ the concept of "nested hierarchies," with the economic component nested within the social component, which is in turn nested within the environmental component.

Using the framework of nested hierarchies, environmental sustainability involves building and maintaining cooperative human constructs that protect and/or enable universal access to environmental life goods, such as organic certification, clean-water bylaws, and public spaces (e.g., provincial parks and town squares). Nested within environmental sustainability is social sustainability, which involves building and maintaining cooperative human constructs that protect and/or enable universal access to social life goods, such as laws ensuring old-age pensions, declarations of women's rights, and neighbourhood palliative-care teams. And nested within social sustainability is economic sustainability, which involves building and maintaining cooperative human constructs that protect and/or enable universal access to economic life goods, such as fair-trade initiatives, minimum-wage laws, legislation guaranteeing the right to form unions, and the establishment of producer, worker, and consumer cooperatives. With the civil commons as the focus of a nested hierarchy of sustainability, we can now turn to the question of environmental sustainability on Pelee Island.

Environmental sustainability on Pelee Island

If environmental sustainability involves building and maintaining cooperative human constructs that protect and/or enable universal access to environmental life goods, then we must look to examples of the civil commons to describe and judge environmental sustainability in rural, and other, communities. Pelee Island offers five cases that can help us understand how to apply this conceptualization of sustainability: Meadowlark Organic Farm, Pelee Island and the Nature Conservancy of Canada, the Pelee Island Bird Observatory, Pelee Island and the Endangered Species Act, and the Ecological Trail System.

Case 1: Meadowlark Organic Farm

The establishment of Meadowlark Organic Farm highlights the civil commons, environmental sustainability, and access to the life good of vital soil. Soil is the basis of the holistic philosophy of organic agriculture, and the pioneers of the organic movement shared an ethic in which soil, crop, livestock, human, and community health were all interconnected (Howard, 1943). For this reason, organic farmers do not apply synthetic pesticides and fertilizers to the soil, which kill microorganisms and render the soil inert. Instead, they build it up with manure and other natural inputs and protect it with cover crops so it provides a range of nutrients to plants and withstands climate extremes.

The organic philosophy dovetails with the sensitivity of the ecological niches on Pelee Island, so much so that the Official Plan includes the provision to attract organic farmers to the community in order to protect this heritage. The Official Plan itself was a massive undertaking by the Township of Pelee, which is still not complete. Its development to date has included many open, public sessions, facilitated by a planner. To help operationalize the organic aspect of the Official Plan, and to encourage local conventional farmers to convert to organic agriculture, Meadowlark Organic Farm was proposed. Funded by a donation from Canadian author and seasonal island resident Margaret Atwood, the plan to establish the farm was initially opposed for a number of reasons, including some politics regarding a previous, unrelated sale of land, a perception on the part of some islanders that the demonstration farm was unfairly receiving government money through the Canadian Nature Federation, and fear by some conventional farmers that they would be sued if their pesticide spray drifted into the organic crops. In addition, some residents were simply uncertain about change, especially in the face of the arrival of different people on the island, such as organic farm volunteers facilitated by organizations or showing up on their own to work on the farm. However, the problems were overcome through negotiation, and the dream of a demonstration farm was realized in 2003. Since the establishment of Meadowlark Organic Farm, the Pelee Island Winery has begun to follow suit, dedicating an expanding number of acres to organic production.

The goals of this community-owned demonstration farm include healthy food production for local consumption, the encouragement of community self-reliance through crop experimentation, local job creation, and the provision of greater promise for wildlife (Municipality of Pelee Island, 2011). As one of the conservation programs under way on the island to promote environmental sustainability, Meadowlark Organic Farm "fosters the ongoing expansion of alternative and organic agriculture. We know that in the past conventional farming practices have reduced wildlife diversity in our countryside and that organic farming can reverse that trend to some degree. Meadowlark aims to support local, healthy food production and bring more economic opportunity to the Island while supporting local wildlife. Perhaps in time we will see the return of species at risk like Fowler's Toad, and the once common Eastern Meadowlark" (Pelee Island Heritage Centre, 2011).

Meadowlark Organic Farm promotes sustainability by instantiating the civil commons in action and providing an example of environmental sustainability. As a community-owned demonstration farm, it is clearly a cooperative human construct that protects and/or enables universal access to life goods—in this case, the life good of vital soil. But Meadowlark Organic Farm also does much more than this. According to Mayor Richard Masse, the municipality didn't just start another farm operation:

- we created job opportunities for our young people
- we added another dimension to our tourist base

- we have given some help to our wildlife
- we have used our land more intelligently with more intensive production
- we have become self-reliant
- we eat more healthy and tasty food
- we are doing our part in reducing our carbon footprint
- we are supporting our neighbours. (Sumner, 2010, p. 184)

Summing up the benefits of this innovation in community development, the mayor maintains:

> When you care about your neighbour, whether human or non-human, and when you care about relationships, and when you care that the earth is to be respected for the sake of future generations, you are in fact building a community. This may be the most exciting thing which all of these gifts add up to. This may be our greatest achievement in starting Meadowlark Organic Farm.... It is of the utmost importance that we support one another in building sustainable and sensible food systems that serve our respective communities. (p. 184)

In this way, this grassroots initiative supports environmental sustainability by protecting wildlife diversity and healthy soil. In addition, it also supports social and economic sustainability on Pelee Island by enabling self-reliance and job opportunities.

Case 2: Pelee Island and the Nature Conservancy of Canada

The case of Pelee Island and the Nature Conservancy of Canada (NCC) highlights the civil commons, environmental sustainability, and access to the life good of wildlife habitat. Habitat is crucial to wild species for basic requirements such as nesting, water, and food. When habitat is destroyed by human encroachment, wildlife faces hardship and extirpation.

Initially, Pelee Island residents were skeptical of NCC because of its historically poor relationships with the Ministry of Natural Resources and the Endangered Species Act (see Case 4 below). Given this original skepticism, NCC has worked very hard to gain the confidence of islanders over the last six to seven years, employing islanders when possible for small contracts, and continuing to allow both turkey and pheasant hunting on its property. And although it was not in the business of creating trails, NCC knew that the trail system, and the tourism it attracts, was important to Pelee Island, so it worked cooperatively with islanders on this issue.

As a private, nonprofit organization, NCC works for the direct protection of Canada's biodiversity through the purchase, donation, or placing of conservation easements on ecologically significant lands (NCC, 2011). To earmark such lands, it creates indices of biodiversity then correlates them with threats to biodiversity across the country. Pelee Island is seen as "globally significant" in this regard and is considered "a biodiversity hotspot for a myriad of bird, plant, and reptile species" (CNW Newswire, 2007). According to its website, NCC "has protected almost 1,000 acres (390 hectares) on Pelee Island alone. NCC manages these lands to ensure that the natural habitat that was protected is properly maintained or restored—this is the 'forever' part of our work" (NCC, 2011).

Like Meadowlark Organic Farm, NCC promotes environmental sustainability by building the civil commons and providing environmental life goods. This benefit is evident in the continuing range of biodiversity found on the island.

But the "forever" part of NCC's work also comes with costs—it is undermining the economic sustainability of the island. NCC now owns about 10% of Pelee Island but is exempt from paying municipal taxes. This reduces the already small tax base for the island and frustrates residents who know that the island could benefit from these lost revenues. Since much of the civil commons is built on taxes (e.g., municipal water treatment), such an exemption compromises the overall sustainability of the island. To begin addressing this problem, NCC has promised that it will not purchase any more land under this "no-tax" loophole agreement.

Case 3: The Pelee Island Bird Observatory

The establishment of the Pelee Island Bird Observatory (PIBO) highlights the civil commons, environmental sustainability, and access to the life good of bird diversity. The conservation of birds contributes not only to the preservation of natural cycles but also directly to human betterment. Rachel Carson's (1964) classic, *Silent Spring*, for example, is a cautionary tale about the folly of failing to protect birds from the overuse of pesticides, as well as other species, including ourselves.

Established in 2003, PIBO is a nonprofit organization devoted to the study and conservation of birds (PIBO, 2011). As the only conservation organization with a permanent presence on the island, PIBO has a mandate for migration-monitoring research, breeding-bird studies, environmental education, and ecotourism, which illustrates the interconnectedness among the environmental, social, and economic aspects of sustainability planning. It is managed by a board and reaches out to create partnerships with other municipal, provincial, national, and international groups. In this way, this grassroots initiative supports environmental sustainability and contributes to social and economic sustainability through its educational programs and tourism mandate.

Case 4: Pelee Island and the Endangered Species Act

The case of Pelee Island and the Endangered Species Act highlights the civil commons, environmental sustainability, and access to the life good of abundant wildlife populations. Like bird conservation, wildlife protection is crucial to a sustainable and biodiverse future. The webs of life on this planet are more interconnected than we will ever understand, so it behooves us to keep them as intact as possible by creating cooperative human constructions—in this case, legislation—that will protect and/or enable universal access to this vital life good (McMurtry, 1999a; Sumner, 2005). Such legislation is a clear example of environmental sustainability.

One piece of legislation created to protect wildlife is the Ontario Endangered Species Act, first passed in 1971 and amended in 2007. A product of the Ministry of Natural Resources (MNR) of the province of Ontario, the act focuses on the protection and recovery of species at risk—defined as any naturally occurring plant or animal in danger of extinction or of disappearing from the province (MNR, 2011). Like its federal counterpart, the Species at Risk Act (SARA), the Endangered Species Act was created to protect vulnerable plants and animals. And while SARA pertains to federal public (Crown) land, the Endangered Species Act pertains to private and provincial public (Crown) land.

Overall, the Endangered Species Act has two aims: (a) to identify species at risk based on the best available scientific information, including information obtained from community knowledge and Aboriginal traditional knowledge; and (b) to protect species that are at risk and their habitats, and to promote the recovery of species that are at risk (MNR, 2011).

It is important to note that the province of Ontario is home to more than 30,000 species, of which more than 180 are currently identified as being at risk. In addition, Pelee Island is one of the most biologically diverse habitats in all of Canada, supporting over 45 species at risk, some of which are globally rare. Thus, it makes sense to promote environmental sustainability by applying the Endangered Species Act to this fragile ecosystem.

Along with these benefits, however, the act has produced some unexpected costs. In 1998, for example, the MNR hired a researcher to map endangered snake habitats, ostensibly to allow residents to claim a tax rebate. In reality, the maps marked off large areas of private property and restricted development, causing a major backlash from the community—a classic confrontation of property rights versus environmental protection. Thus, this application of the Endangered Species Act may be an example of environmental sustainability, but it is fracturing social cohesion on the island—the very basis for future civil commons constructions.

Case 5: The Ecological Trail System

The building of the Ecological Trail System highlights the civil commons, environmental sustainability, and access to the life good of interaction with nature. As humanity becomes more urbanized and increasingly mediates its experience of the world through technology, nature becomes less a part of who we are and what we understand as our ultimate life-support system. Encouraging interaction with nature reminds us of the primacy of environmental sustainability and the importance of protecting it. Civil commons projects to support this interaction are vital to environmental sustainability (McMurtry, 1999a; Sumner, 2005).

On Pelee Island, one of these forms of the civil commons is the Ecological Trail System. Built with funds from the MNR Species at Risk Program, the Ecological Trail System provides access to beaches, forests, sand dunes, marshes, and alvars found nowhere else in Canada. The trail system includes 34 kilometres of on-road bicycle trails, ten kilometres of ecological multi-use trails, and five kilometres of walking trails (Municipality of Pelee Island, 2011). This example of environmental sustainability also generates a number of other benefits—for example, bicycling and ecotourism reduces roadkill and connects green spaces.

But the benefits are tempered by a set of challenges in the form of private landowners and their opposition to the Endangered Species Act. The first stage of the project took place on property owned by the NCC and included approximately two kilometres of trail with interpretive signage. During the second stage of the project, which connected public spaces with a trail across private property, landowners initially agreed to the project in theory. But when it came time to sign agreements, they balked. The Ecological Trail System included plans to plant trees and connect habitat along corridors, and island residents worried that if these changes attracted endangered species, then the Endangered Species Act would restrict them from doing anything on their property. In one salient example, an islander was trying to build a very small extension on his house, but the MNR sent him a letter reminding him that he had an endangered plant on his property (which the homeowner himself had planted), so he had to negotiate major bureaucratic obstacles in order to get approval to build.

In the end, between the delay in obtaining landowner agreements and the rather laborious funding process, at this writing, most of the trail-system project has yet to be completed. However, the mayor is committed to finishing at least a portion of the trail at the north end of the island and has continued to seek funding for the project.

Discussion

These five cases of environmental sustainability on Pelee Island offer some valuable lessons in terms of sustainability planning, citizen participation, and public policy in rural Canada. First, they teach us lessons about community development. While development is often understood as growth, Herman Daly (1990), a former senior economist with the World Bank, separates these two concepts:

> *to grow* means "to increase naturally in size by the addition of material through assimilation and accretion." *To develop* means "to expand or realize the potentialities of—that is, to bring gradually to a fuller, greater, or better state." In short, growth is

> quantitative increase in physical scale, while development is qualitative improvement or unfolding of potentialities. (p. 1)

Following Daly, community development involves the qualitative improvement or the unfolding of potentialities in communities, not growth. Using this framework, all five cases contributed to community development, although some contributed a great deal more than others, depending on the amount of citizen participation. Meadowlark Organic Farm opened up opportunities for increased food security and social-capital formation. The protection of wildlife habitat by the NCC spurred a qualitative improvement in biodiversity. The conservation of birds by PIBO offers the potential of increased encounters with avian species. The protection of wildlife by the Endangered Species Act improves the potential of an enhanced relationship with wildlife such as the blue racer snake, and the establishment of the Ecological Trail System leads to a qualitative improvement in human connections with nature. These examples of community development can help to guide choices in future sustainability planning and public-policy formation in rural Canada.

Second, the five cases provide lessons about collaboration, or lack thereof. Out of all five initiatives, only the establishment of PIBO occurred without controversy, not only because it did not open up questions of land ownership and ways of farming, but also because it included more direct community involvement. The rest of the cases lacked collaboration in varying degrees, some so much so that they have yet to be accomplished. When taking the next steps, it is important to remember that collaboration (literally, labouring together) is at the heart of the civil commons and crucial to the success of sustainability planning, participation, and public-policy development in rural Canada. Dialogue is one of the vital building blocks for sustainability (Sumner, 2005)—without it civil commons projects would be merely top-down impositions. Although top-down methods have their place (witness the immediate positive effect of the province of Ontario imposing a price of five cents on plastic bags at point-of-sale in shops), long-term sustainability planning needs a balance between top-down regulation and bottom-up citizen engagement.

Third, the five cases offer valuable lessons about rural community sustainability and decision making. As examples of environmental sustainability—cooperative human constructions that protect and/or enable universal access to environmental life goods—these cases contribute to overall rural community sustainability on Pelee Island, keeping in mind that sustainable rural communities are anchored by the civil commons. In this way, they have all involved cooperation, collaboration, and participatory decision making at some level. However, without subsidiarity—the principle that a central authority performs only those tasks which cannot be performed effectively at a more immediate or local level (Blacksell, 2000)—a project can stall or fail for lack of local understanding and buy-in. This realization can inform future sustainability planning and participation in rural Canada.

One final consideration involves the tensions and conflicts that can arise among questions of environmental, social, and economic sustainability. As the case of Pelee Island and the Endangered Species Act illustrates, environmental sustainability can sometimes be achieved at the cost of social or economic sustainability. And yet, as nested hierarchies, these forms of sustainability need to complement each other, not cancel each other out. While the environment is the real bottom line in any considerations of sustainability, social sustainability is crucial to the formation of the civil commons and the cooperative human constructions it entails. Similarly, economic sustainability is vital to any vision of a sustainable rural community, and environmental and social initiatives must be created in such a way that they do not block access to economic life goods. The pursuit of sustainability can be complex and time-consuming, but the long-term rewards are undeniable, especially in an era of uncertainty at all levels of life.

Conclusion

Islands, unlike other rural communities, are bounded spaces without immediate connection to the outside world. This isolation creates quasi "laboratory" conditions for studying questions of sustainability. But it also raises the issue of general applicability to other communities—do the lessons from Pelee Island apply more universally? We think the answer is affirmative.

As questions of sustainability become ever more pressing, the civil commons continues to offer its promise of life-support systems—universal human needs. The life goods provided by the civil commons are required by everyone. How that provision is organized may change, however, depending on location. For example, the life good of health care can be provided through the civil commons construct of a national health-care system that operates out of hospitals in urban areas and community-run clinics or health-care cooperatives in rural and remote communities. Connecting sustainability to the civil commons prioritizes cooperation over competition, universal access over paid admission, and the provision of life goods over private, for-profit opportunities. The more we promote the former priorities over the latter, the more sustainable we become. For example, the lack and/or disrepair of public services and emergency management programs in New Orleans after Hurricane Katrina resulted in delayed response, widespread misery, and preventable deaths (see Cooper & Block, 2006). In contrast, the small, poor island of Cuba has developed a sophisticated hurricane-response program, a "culture of safety," civil-defence organizations, a high literacy rate, and disaster-preparedness education (Taylor Martin, 2005)—all hallmarks of an advanced civil commons that can make communities more resilient in the face of disaster.

According to William Rees (2002), co-founder of the concept of the ecological footprint, "unsustainability is an emergent property of the systemic interaction between techno-industrial society and the ecosphere" (p. 250). In other words, when techno-industrial society meets the ecosphere, unsustainability inevitably results. In such a society, the sheer quantity of throughput—defined by Daly (2009) as the metabolic flow of useful matter and energy from environmental sources, through the economic subsystem (production and consumption), and back to environmental sinks as waste—overwhelms the ecosphere, resulting in unsustainability.

From here, we can argue that sustainability can be an emergent property of the systemic interaction between a new kind of society and the ecosphere. This new society would be centred on the civil commons—not the "common future" of the Brundtland Report, but our future as a commons (Visvanathan, 1991). Anchored by the civil commons, rural communities would become environmentally viable, socially just, and economically sound, a firm foundation for what has been called sustainable place-making (Marsden, 2011).

References

Blacksell, M. (2000). Subsidiarity. In R. J. Johnston, D. Gregory, G. Pratt, and M. Watts (Eds.), *The dictionary of human geography*, Fourth Edition (p. 804). Malden, MA: Blackwell Publishers, Ltd.

Bossel, H. (1999). *Indicators for sustainable development: Theory, method, applications*. Winnipeg: International Institute for Sustainable Development.

Carson, R. (1964). *Silent spring*. London: Hamish Hamilton.

CNW Newswire. (2007, November 25). Acquisition of globally significant habitat on Pelee Island by Nature Conservancy of Canada to receive government support. Retrieved January 12, 2012, from http://www.newswire.ca/en/story/7867/acquisition-of-globally-significant-habitat-on-pelee-island-by-nature-conservancy-of-canada-to-receive-government-support.

Common, M. (1995). *Sustainability and policy: Limits to economics*. New York: Cambridge University Press.

Cooper, C., & Block, R. (2006). *Disaster: Hurricane Katrina and the failure of Homeland Security*. New York: Time Books.

Daly, H. E. (1990). Toward some operational principles of sustainable development. *Ecological Economics*, 2, 1–6.

———. (2009). Foreword. In T. Jackson. *Prosperity without growth: Economics for a finite planet* (pp. xi–xii). London/Sterling, VA: Earthscan.

Howard, Sir A. (1943). *An agricultural testament*. New York: Oxford University Press.

Lohmann, L. (1990). Whose common future? *The Ecologist*, 20(3), 82–84.

Marsden, T. (2011, March 4). Sustainable place-making: Towards new spatial imaginations for agri-food and urban-rural relations. Policy workshop, Sustainable Local Foodsystems in Europe and the Americas: Lessons for Policy and Practice, Canada–Europe Transatlantic Dialogue, Ottawa.

McMurtry, J. (1998). *Unequal freedoms: The global market as an ethical system*. Toronto: Garamond.

———. (1999a). *The cancer stage of capitalism*. London: Pluto Press.

———. (1999b, June 7). The lifeground, the civil commons and global development. Paper presented at the annual meeting of the Canadian Association for Studies in International Development, Congress of the Social Sciences and Humanities, Sherbrooke, Quebec.

Ministry of Natural Resources (MNR). (2011). Retrieved April 14, 2011, from http://www.mnr.gov.on.ca/en/Business/Species/index.html.

Municipality of Pelee Island. (2011). Retrieved April 14, 2011, from http://pelee.org.

Nature Conservancy of Canada (NCC). (2011). Retrieved April 14, 2011, from http://www.natureconservancy.ca/site/PageServer?pagename=ncc_main.

Pelee Island. (2011a). Natural heritage. Retrieved December 27, 2011, from http://www.pelee.org/i?page=naturalheritagethings&sid=1413249313864D.

———. (2011b). Our vision. Retrieved December 27, 2011, from http://www.pelee.org/i?page=ourvision&sid=1413249313864D.

Pelee Island Heritage Centre. (2011). Retrieved April 14, 2011, from http://www.peleeislandmuseum.ca/i?page=natural.

Pelee Island Bird Observatory (PIBO). (2011). Retrieved April 14, 2011, from http://www.pibo.ca/02-who.html.

Rees, W. E. (1990). The ecology of sustainable development. *The Ecologist, 20*(1), 18–23.

———. (2002). Globalization and sustainability: Conflict or convergence? *Bulletin of Science, Technology and Society,* 22(4), 249–268.

Simpson, J. A., & Weiner, E. S. C. (1989). *Oxford English dictionary,* Second Edition. Oxford: Clarendon Press.

Sumner, J. (2005). *Sustainability and the civil commons: Rural communities in the age of globalization.* Toronto: University of Toronto Press.

———. (2009). Sustainable horticulture and community development: More than just organic production. *Journal of Sustainable Agriculture, 33,* 461–483.

———. (2010). From land to table: Rural planning and development for sustainable food systems. In D. Douglas (Ed.), *Rural planning and development in Canada,* (pp. 179–224). Toronto: Nelson Education Limited.

———. (2011). Serving social justice: The role of the commons in sustainable food systems. *Studies in Social Justice, 5* (1), 63–75.

Taylor Martin, S. (2005). Can we learn from Cuba's lesson? *St. Petersburg Times.* Retrieved December 28, 2011, from http://www.sptimes.com/2005/09/09/Worldandnation/Can_we_learn_from_Cub.shtml.

Visvanathan, S. (1991). Mrs. Brundtland's disenchanted cosmos. *Alternatives, 16,* 377–384.

World Commission on Environment and Development (WCED). (1987). *Our common future.* New York: Oxford University Press.

TEN

Rural First Nations Tourism

Examining the Relationship Between Sustainable Tourism and Capacity

Rhonda Koster and Kirstine Baccar

Introduction

For many rural communities across Canada, constant and sometimes dramatic change in their economic and social structure is a common experience, especially for single-industry, natural resource–based communities such as those based on forestry and mining. Communities in northwestern Ontario are no exception, where the result of these changes is out-migration, loss of youth, loss of businesses and employment opportunities, and a search for other economic-development opportunities to diversify and stabilize the economy (Southcott, 2006). Such changes also have negative impacts on First Nations communities (the focus of this paper), whose economies are often intricately tied to the forestry industry and the socio-economic structure of neighbouring towns.

For those communities located adjacent to protected areas (e.g., national parks), tourism can offer enhanced opportunities for economic diversification (Butler & Hinch, 2007; Zeppel, 2006); the establishment of Parks Canada's Lake Superior National Marine Conservation Area (LSNMCA) in northwestern Ontario is a case in point (Lemelin, Koster, Woznicka, Metansinine, & Pelletier, 2009). The market for Aboriginal tourism both domestically and internationally is growing (Aboriginal

Tourism in Canada [ATTC], 2003; Aboriginal Tourism Team Canada & Canadian Tourism Commission [ATTC & CTC], 2000; Budke, 2000; Hart, Steadman, & Woods, 1996; Williams & Dossa, 1996; Williams & Stewart, 1997), and this, in combination with the opportunities provided by a national park designation, market, and infrastructure (Good, 2000; Stein, Anderson, & Thompson, 1999), has created an opportunity for proximal First Nations communities to explore their tourism potential, as a strategy to diversify their economy, create and explore ways to retain traditional culture, and contribute to the sustainable development of their communities (Bennett & Lemelin, 2009; Bennett, Lemelin, Ellis, & Enzoe, 2010; Bennett, Lemelin, Koster, & Budke, 2012; Koster, Lemelin, & Davar, 2005).

For many rural communities, however, the capacity for tourism development is limited, which challenges the potential opportunities offered through tourism (Budke, 2000; Eagles & McCool, 2002; Nepal, 2000; Shackley, 1998; Standing Senate Committee on Aboriginal Peoples, 2001; Wellings, 2007). Most residents of resource-based communities readily understand and accept the requirements of their industry (such as forestry) and the associated investments required for implementing any changes within that industry. In contrast, they do not fully understand the requirements of tourism development—often both at a local-government / economic development–office level and at the community-member level (Carson & Carson, 2011; Koster, 2010). Tourism development requires capital and infrastructure investment, community beautification, development of businesses and attractions, and training to develop a culture of customer service and hospitality. All of these items are based on a certain set of capacities that often do not exist within a given rural or First Nations community.

This chapter explores the challenges of developing tourism and its associated capacities and offers suggestions for how to overcome them, based on a four-year collaborative research partnership between the Red Rock Indian Band (RRIB) and Lakehead University, in northwestern Ontario. The chapter begins by providing an overview of our project and partnership, highlighting the lessons we learned as collaborators, the guiding principles grounded in an Indigenous paradigm that framed our research approach, and the important outcomes of the project. We also provide a frank discussion of the challenges we faced and how we overcame them. We then discuss the outcomes of our tourism project and illustrate how they are connected to Integrated Community Sustainability Planning (ICSP) utilizing the *CCP Handbook: Comprehensive Community Planning for First Nations in British Columbia* (Okanagan First Nations et al., 2006) as an appropriate reference for our study.

Building capacity for First Nations tourism: A summary of our project

Our project, Building Capacity for Tourism, began in 2007. At the time, Harvey Lemelin and Rhonda Koster were both new professors at Lakehead University in Thunder Bay, Ontario. We were interested in examining how Appreciative Inquiry (an asset-based planning method) could be used to develop experiential tourism in a rural community, in the absence of tourism-related infrastructure (Koster & Lemelin, 2009). We met with an experiential tourism provider in Manitoba, who also provides workshops for communities and regions interested in developing this tourism niche.[1] We put together a proposal and received funding from Parks Canada, and in the spring of 2007, we attended a regional community meeting where we presented our idea and invited participation.

Hoss,[2] a member of the RRIB (located at Lake Helen Reserve, 115 kilometres east of Thunder Bay—Figure 10.1) indicated that his community would be interested and received approval from the chief and council to engage in the project, along with the economic development officer at the time. While the initial research idea was formulated by the researchers, the resulting partnership evolved based on the common interests of the community, which was in the process of exploring economic-diversification options. The opportunity to work with Lakehead University in building capacity for tourism development came at a good time, as we were trying to determine how to best benefit from the establishment of the Lake Superior National Marine Conservation Area.

In October of 2007 representatives from Lakehead University and RRIB worked with the operator from Manitoba to create the Experience Superior Workshop. The focus of the workshop was to teach the participants from 12 different communities in the region (both towns and reserves) ways of creating and delivering experiential tourism, based on the cultural and environmental assets available within the region. It was a two-day event that highlighted the language (Ojibway/Cree), culture

Figure 10.1: Location of Red Rock Indian Band at Lake Helen First Nation, Ontario.

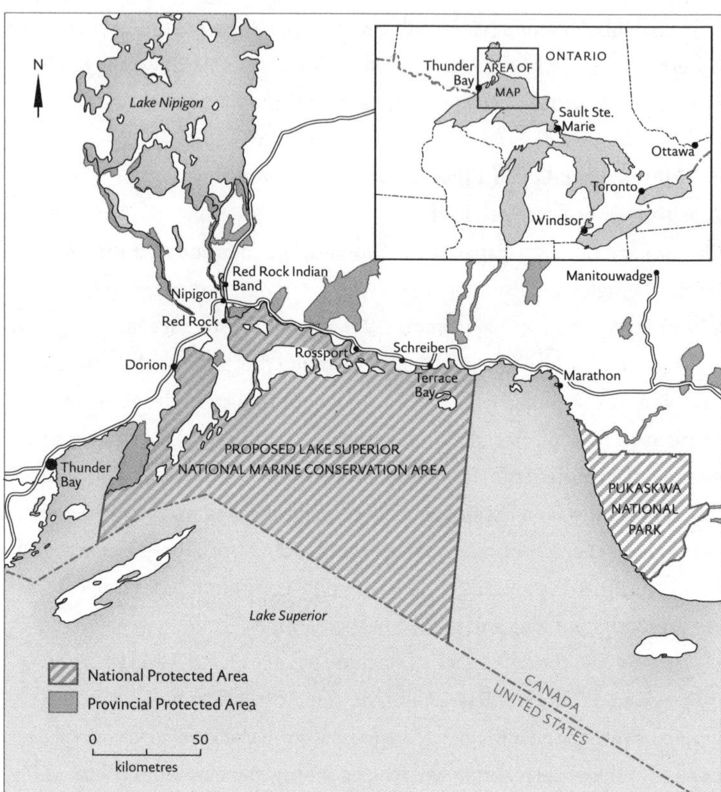

(porcupine-quill crafting), spirituality (sweatlodge and medicine bags), and traditional foods (all local provided by local caterers from the reserve) as examples of products available for tourism in the region, but in particular, within the Lake Helen Reserve. The workshop provided participants with evidence that tourism developments based on locally available assets were possible, as they imagined possibilities based on the features of their own communities.

Although the original research plan was to develop a tourism plan using the Appreciative Inquiry method with the RRIB, after the workshop was over, we asked RRIB representatives how they would like to proceed. They identified that planning for tourism was not appropriate at this stage for their community and instead we needed to begin by determining the interests of community members in tourism, and what kinds of training they would need to get started. Through collaboration over the next two years, we:

1. developed a survey to identify the interests and needs of community members in engaging in tourism;
2. completed an inventory of training opportunities and, through the economic development office on the reserve, began offering various workshops;
3. undertook an extensive inventory of tourism-related assets;
4. assisted in determining how experiential tourism might be developed following acquisition by the band of a tourism lodge;
5. co-created a handbook (Metansinine, Koster, & Lemelin, 2009a[3]) for experiential tourism development for the RRIB;
6. co-created a summary report/development document (Metansinine, Koster, & Lemelin, 2009b); and
7. provided updates to the community through their weekly newsletter, hosted an open house, and at the end of the project provided a presentation at a band meeting.

It was important to all of us to ensure that the project was moving forward in a way that met each partner's expectations, and as such, the four of us agreed to meet and have a discussion to allow everyone to express their views. In addition to determining that everyone was equally satisfied with how the project was proceeding, we also established a set of six guiding principles that formed the basis for our partnership and project. The first of these we termed *trust, follow-through, and commitment.* In combination these elements mean that each partner is committed to designing and meeting the deliverables associated with the project, that each person will complete the tasks they have taken on, and that everyone is working equally hard to achieve the end goal.

We identified *transparency and communication* as critical elements requiring all involved to openly share the intent and objectives of the research and what each party expects to receive as a result of the project. It also means that budget information should be shared; being clear on the expectations of the funding agencies, university, and chief and council;

asking questions and not making assumptions about anything; and having tough discussions when things go wrong and working through problems.

The third guideline we identified is *reciprocity*. Each member of the partnership should be able to learn from the others, and each should be willing to do whatever he/she can to support the project and the community. Reciprocity recognizes that each member of the group will receive benefit from the project, though those benefits will be different for each partner.

Fourth, through *engagement, involvement, and input,* all partners get to share in the creation, execution, evaluation, and outcomes of the project, with no one party having authority to dictate any aspect of the project. It means that opinions and ideas are sought from all partner members to develop and work through the project. It also means including everyone in any academic outputs, such as publications and presentations.

We also identified that *finite projects* are important. Projects must be tangible, have real value to the community (not just an "ivory tower" academic exercise), and have a distinguishable start and end point. It ensures that both parties will be able to meet the expectations of the project and benefit from participation.

Finally, we found that *humour and friendship* form the foundation of a partnership. Treating one another with respect, as friends, being sensitive and caring and laughing together creates an atmosphere in which you are able to negotiate through tough parts and achieve project objectives. It also means that the process is fun.

Since 2008 we have attended three conferences together where we co-presented our research project. Our work has been recognized by Lakehead University with the inaugural Aboriginal Research Partnership Award in 2010. We have published together (Koster, Baccar, & Lemelin, 2012; Lemelin et al., 2009) and have worked for one another on a number of additional projects.

1. In 2009 members from the band used their learning from the Experience Superior Workshop to provide an experiential-tourism half-day program for a delegation attending the International Lakes Tourism Conference. All three of us assisted in developing the programming.

2. In 2010 the community was invited to provide a shore excursion for ten expedition cruise ships that were visiting the regional harbour. All three of us assisted in the creation of this experience, which was provided by the RRIB's women's drum group.
3. Kirstine has served as a committee member for one graduate student and has provided assistance with culturally sensitive issues that both Rhonda and Harvey have experienced in their teaching and other research projects.
4. Between 2010 and 2011, Kirstine worked with Harvey on a photo voice research project.
5. Other community members have contacted Harvey and Rhonda for assistance with other community projects. For example, they were contacted to assist with the development of RRIB content for a regional tourism website.
6. All of us, but in particular Kirstine and Rhonda, have developed a strong friendship that extends beyond the research into other aspects of our personal and professional lives.

Community–research collaborations: Lessons learned

In 2011 we were asked to contribute a paper for a special issue of *The Canadian Geographer* (2012) focused on community-based participatory research involving First Nations. In our contribution (Koster et al., 2012) we critically reviewed our research partnership by examining if it fit the parameters of community-based participatory research and found that, in fact, we had followed an Indigenous research paradigm and that doing so resulted in a successful research partnership and outcomes.

Although many researchers agree that community-based participatory research is a positive way of engaging in research with Indigenous peoples, it is still grounded in dominant Western ways of thinking about and conducting research (Louis, 2007; Wilson, 2008). As a result, Indigenous scholars suggest that incorporating Indigenous ways of knowing and doing research (i.e., an Indigenous paradigm) is important (Fletcher, 2003; Louis, 2007; McGregor, Bayha, & Simmons, 2010; Wilson, 2008). There is no single Indigenous research paradigm, as ways of knowing and sharing that knowledge are specific to each culture. However, there are four concepts that are commonly described by researchers, which help to explain the foundations of Indigenous research methods (Louis, 2007): relational accountability, respect, reciprocal appropriation, and rights and regulation.

Relational accountability acknowledges that Indigenous ways of knowing are based upon relationships between all life forms. When applying this concept to research, the researcher approaches his or her project understanding that all parts of the research process are interconnected, which requires a sincere and authentic investment in the community to develop a true partnership between the researcher and the community (Kovach, 2005; Louis, 2007). Respect requires researchers to co-create the research process with Indigenous people, accepting the decisions of the community and working openly and honestly from the outset to determine how the knowledge gathering will be conducted, shared, and used (Louis, 2007). Reciprocal appropriation recognizes that "all research is appropriation" (Rundstrom & Deur, 1999, p. 239) and requires adequate benefits for both parties involved in the research; this does not mean that the benefits will be the same for both parties. Kovach (2005, 2009) explains that Indigenous culture is based on a collective approach to community, where everyone is responsible for maintaining reciprocal and accountable relationships to one another, the community, clan, and nation, resulting in a sense of belonging. Consequently, the outcomes of the research must help and/or serve the collective. Finally, rights and regulation refers to developing and adhering to a research process that is co-created and based on Indigenous protocols, defined goals, impacts of research consideration, and how the knowledge gathered will be used (Louis, 2007; Smith, 1999). It also means collectively determining how the community will approve the results, how the data will be published and reported, and how the information will be written up to ensure accessibility for the community.

While there is no single process for conducting research within Indigenous paradigms, there are some general steps that can be followed (Fletcher, 2003; Louis & Grossman, 2009), based on the principles identified. In reflecting on our own research process, we found that we took the following four steps.

1. Form a partnership with Indigenous peoples and co-create the research process. Despite the initial researcher-driven intent, asking

the community partners how they wanted to proceed resulted in a jointly created research project that allowed both academic and community benefits. Simply following the initial research idea would not have resulted in the same benefit for the community.

2. Discuss how the benefits of the research should flow to the community, and how the community should control the information generated, how it is to be used, and how it will be disseminated. The four of us spent a good deal of time discussing what kinds of information we would need to collect, who would "own" that data once gathered, and how it could be used. The community became the sole proprietors of the information, and any time research publications or reports were being developed, permission was always given by the community. Further, we agreed at the outset that all presentations and written publications would be jointly authored.
3. Develop a mechanism for Indigenous partners to review and revise drafts of findings and ensure access to the final product. All information was shared among the project team members and verified by Kirstine and Hoss. All final products resulting from the project were kept by the community and not provided to anyone else without permission.
4. Develop and maintain relationships within both Western ethics protocols and within Indigenous cultural frameworks. We followed the ethical research regulations required by the university, and, as previously discussed, we have continued to work together beyond the parameters of the initial project and have developed personal relationships. Clearly, our own guiding principles reflected the principles and processes associated with Indigenous research paradigms. When we experienced any challenges, we returned to these jointly determined guidelines for assistance.

Our project did encounter some challenges. It was difficult to get community members to participate in our interviews, surveys, and focus group meetings. To address this problem, we started to use traditional practices such as having a feast in advance of meetings and offering gifts or incentives for participation. We also changed the way we communicated in the newsletters by using language that was meaningful to residents (i.e., we deleted academic jargon).

As a team we also experienced some difficulties, including meeting the administrative and timeline requirements of our external funding agency, the competing demands we each had on our time, and some communication challenges between team members. In all cases these challenges were addressed by returning to our guiding principles of talking about the issue and finding amenable solutions to the situation. In some cases, it meant taking a bit of time to allow cooler heads to prevail.

We found that it was somewhat easier for the researchers to participate in the project, as their job requires and allows time for research. In contrast, for the community members, participation is not part of their full-time job, and even when the chief and council allows participation as part of the workload, that really just means adding extra work. One of the ways we dealt with this challenge was to be flexible and ensure that meetings or events fit within the timelines of the community partner's competing demands. Creating presentations, reports or publications is especially time consuming for the community partner as this work rarely can fit within a normal workday. We tried to minimize the extra work while still maintaining full participation by having an initial team meeting to discuss the overall content; in this process, the researchers would create/write the first draft of the documents and the community member would later review, revise, and edit, as this takes less time. We found this worked reasonably well, as long as the researchers did not procrastinate. Overall, we found that the challenges are far outnumbered by the benefits we have collectively gained by working in partnership on the project.

Building capacity for tourism development: Sustainable tourism planning

In keeping with our commitment to following the community's protocols, we conducted our project within the established, community-based planning method of working with the community through the chief and council. The RRIB has developed this process of planning and decision making to ensure transparency and community engagement, and it includes the following steps. First, an idea is presented to the community at one of the monthly band meetings. The idea may have come from a community member or organization or from the chief and council. During and following the meeting, the community provides feedback and suggestions to the chief and council on how to proceed. The chief and council then seek out the appropriate experts to create a plan. The "experts" may come from within the community or may be hired from outside, depending on the nature of the project. The selected group of experts will then create a plan and present it to the community, usually first to the chief and council and then to the community through a band meeting. Following all presentations and information provision, the community will advise the chief and council on what action to take.

This framework links directly with two of the ICSP principles of transparency, accountability and reporting, and public involvement (Prime Minister's External Advisory on Cities and Communities, 2005). Other principles within the ICSP include comprehensive analysis, integrated and strategic planning, focus on goals, performance indicators and outcomes, consideration of equity, market principles, precautionary principle, conservation ethic, and continual improvement—all of which influence the way the RRIB Chief and Council develop recommendations to bring forward to the community.

Within their discussion paper, the authors acknowledge that in 2005 there had been no defined concept or process for community planning within First Nations communities, and that the Department of Indian Affairs and Northern Development was working on the development of a framework that would incorporate community planning with traditional Aboriginal practices (Prime Minister's External Advisory on Cities and Communities, 2005). The result of this process was the *CCP Handbook: Comprehensive Community Planning for First Nations in British Columbia* (Okanagan First Nations et al., 2006).

The goals of the handbook are to outline what comprehensive community planning is, develop a process of how it can be undertaken, and illustrate its successes and challenges through five case-study communities that participated in its development. The authors (Okanagan First Nations et al., 2006) define a comprehensive approach as one that

> enables the community to establish a vision for its future and implement projects to achieve this vision; helps to ensure that community projects and programs are thought through, make sense and are the best use of resources; and integrate and link all

> other plans the community has produced. It is a new approach to planning, where the process is steered by the community rather than a small group or committee. (p. 6)

The handbook is comprehensive in that it addresses all the interdependent areas of planning within First Nations communities, including governance, land and resources, health, infrastructure development, culture, social issues, and the economy.

The approach is based on a number of principles including an explicit recognition that community engagement and support are fundamental elements of planning. Instead of having a small committee undertake the planning process, the intent is to engage as many community members as possible. Building community capacity is another critical principle, with the intent to utilize outside assistance only to increase the capacity and training of community members. Effective communication both within the community and with external organizations is another principle, with the intent being to keep everyone informed and to create a network that can support the community's efforts. Finally, effectively understanding the resources required to undertake and implement the comprehensive planning process is important to ensure success.

The handbook outlines the phases associated with community planning, which follows other planning processes such as Reid (2003), where pre-planning and the integration of the community are critical elements that differ from conventional planning methods. There are four stages, with steps to be undertaken in each phase (Okanagan First Nations et al., 2006). We have summarized the characteristics of each of these stages below.

1. Pre-planning: assess community readiness (p. 19). The purpose of this stage is to assess whether or not the community is ready to begin planning, provide the community and leadership information about the planning process and gain their support, and lay the groundwork for an open and inclusive process.
2. Planning: gather background information (p. 29). As part of the planning process, the community identifies its vision and values, and the steps to be undertaken to realize it. As such, during this stage the community gathers to describe itself, conduct a Strengths, Weaknesses,

Opportunities and Threats (SWOT) analysis, decide upon the community's vision and values, build a comprehensive planning framework that addresses all areas of community life, and create a detailed plan for implementing activities and monitoring progress.

3. Implementation: build work plans (p. 49). The purpose of this stage is to undertake and complete all the actions and projects outlined in the planning stage. This is generally the longest phase as projects are implemented over time.
4. Monitoring and evaluation: analyze results (p. 55). This is a critical phase in that it provides an opportunity to assess implementation progress, make necessary revisions to the plan to maintain its relevance and to adjust to external and internal changes, and to keep the community informed and excited about what is being achieved.

The CCP process provides a valuable and user-friendly planning framework that First Nations communities can use to develop a comprehensive plan that addresses the complex needs of their communities. We were not aware of this framework prior to undertaking our project, and the focus of our project was not comprehensive community development. The RRIB, through its economic development office, did however undertake a strategic planning process that was comprehensive in nature, involving the leadership, staff, youth, Elders, the women's drum group, and all departments—including education, health, economic development—that were focused on developing a vision and direction for the community. Tourism development was but one aspect of the economic-development discussion.

The initial intent of our research project (from the researcher perspective) was to develop tourism as part of an economic-diversification plan with the RRIB, which would have followed the kind of process outlined in the *CCP Handbook*. Instead, the community partners suggested that we needed to begin by determining the interest community members had in tourism, understanding what kinds of training and support they might need, conducting an inventory of the various tourism assets the community already possessed, establishing the level of development they might require, and outlining how the community might want to proceed should tourism development become a priority. In doing so, we did follow the pre-planning phase outlined in the *CCP Handbook*.

The survey we conducted illustrated that a limited number of people were interested in tourism or developing a tourism business. We were able to identify the kinds of tourism they were interested in (crafts, guiding, traditional foods), and the kinds of training they needed to start and support a business. We then conducted a survey to determine availability of training services, and these were subsequently offered through the economic development office of the RRIB. We also conducted an inventory of the various tourism-related assets of the band and region, determining that although there are many tourism-related elements present, many of them require development or improvement.

The development of tourism within a rural community, whose economy is historically based on natural resource extraction, requires the presence or development of certain tourism-related capacities. Various researchers have investigated what elements this may include (see for example Budke, 2000; Chaskin, 2001; Frank & Smith, 1999), but none have determined a method to assess how these capacities are related to the level of tourism readiness of a community. Bennett, Lemelin, Koster and Budke (2012) have utilized the theoretical basis of the Sustainable Livelihoods model (Carney, 1998; Chambers & Conway, 1992; Ellis, 2000; Scoones, 1998) and the applied elements of asset-based community development (Green & Haines, 2002, 2008; Kretzmann & McKnight, 1993) to determine a community's level of capacity for tourism development by identifying a variety of what they term "capital assets." These capital assets include *natural assets* found within the naturally occurring resource base; *social assets,* which are made up of the networks, partnerships, and memberships within the community; *human assets,* comprised of the skills, knowledge, physical abilities, and positive attitudes present with the community membership; *physical assets,* represented by the infrastructure of the community; *financial assets,* referring to community-member access to financial resources; and *cultural assets,* which are grounded in the level of traditional practices and language present in the community.

Using the research we conducted in the community, we have evaluated the RRIB based on these capacities to determine the community's readiness for tourism development. We found that although the RRIB does possess all of the capital assets, in many cases, they are underdeveloped. The existing natural assets are appropriate for tourism development but require the development of guiding and interpretation businesses to make them accessible to visitors. The physical assets of the community are limited in terms of the actual land space available for development, though the community does have good road, water, power, and sewage infrastructure. The community has strong social networks that allow people to undertake new developments due to the network of support that they can access. Band members are also able to apply to a variety of funding sources to support business developments, some that are exclusively available to First Nations. Human resources are also good, with high graduation levels and many opportunities for others to access upgrading and training related to the tourism industry. The limitation associated with these three assets (social, financial, and human) is the lack of interest in entrepreneurial developments connected with tourism. Although there are several members of the band who have the knowledge associated with cultural traditions, practices, crafts, food, and language, the majority of residents have lost their culture. As a result, reviving and regaining these cultural assets are a priority for the band, some of whom see the opportunities tourism developments associated with culture may provide. Although this is commonly offered as one of the benefits of tourism developments for Indigenous people (see for example Butler & Hinch, 2007), there are others who caution that such cultural revival may not be authentic when it is staged for visitors (Notzke, 2006).

Despite the lack of some of these assets, there are opportunities to support the development of tourism. In 2008 the band acquired the Chalet Lodge, an accommodation originally built by the Canadian Pacific Railway and later privately owned and developed for hunters and anglers. At present, no developments can take place on this property as the band only owns the buildings and is currently going through the Addition to Reserve process to purchase the land. Once this is complete, they will be able to move ahead with their business plan to utilize green construction and energy sources in their redevelopments, with plans to create accommodations for visitors, a conference centre, food and beverage services, and other tourism-related businesses (such craft sales and outfitting services).

Further supporting tourism development is the presence of the Parks Canada office in the region. Although the National Marine Conservation Area was announced in 2007, it was only in 2009 that staff had a physical presence. The office has been working hard to develop relationships in the region and ascertain the various cultural and natural assets present that will aid in the development of visitation to the region. In addition, there are four communities within 20 kilometres of each other that make up the North of Superior Region (Dorion, Red Rock, Nipigon, and Lake Helen First Nation); these communities worked together to provide shore excursions for 11 cruise ships for the first time during the summer of 2010. As a result of this experience, there has been increasing collaboration among the businesses and entrepreneurs in the region (including those from the RRIB) to develop tourism products and services. We anticipate these various positive developments will result in increased interest in tourism, though the development of the Chalet Lodge is likely to be the best catalyst for those who indicated an interest in developing a tourism business on our survey.

We have learned valuable lessons through our project process, and certainly these lessons are foundational principles of the comprehensive community-planning framework (Okanagan First Nations et al., 2006). The importance of having wide community participation (youth, Elders, the chief and council, and everyone in between) and providing them with the education/knowledge they need to fully understand what tourism is and what it can mean for the community is critical. We have come to recognize the importance of having workshops where experienced people can come and share their knowledge; it is critical to have a wide range of community and band council members—these are the best ambassadors for new ideas—present at such events, so they can share their newly gained knowledge and excitement with those unable to attend. Fundamental to this process is to situate the learning within the natural, cultural, and physical assets that are present, as these assets illustrate to community members the value of their own community, thus boosting community pride and self-esteem. In turn, this provides an opportunity to see the community in a different light, and reinforces the importance of First Nations culture, language, and traditions. Finally, we have learned that any development requires a champion within the community to ensure that people are involved and that projects keep on target. Champions are able to encourage participation and to communicate in ways that the broader community can understand.

Conclusion

Our project has spanned four years, and much has changed within the RRIB. The band has undertaken a variety of economic-development projects that have provided different employment options for band members. These include a hydroelectric project involving four other First Nations, where capacity is being built through the provision of high-school completion programs, followed by hydro industry–specific training, allowing band members to become employable in the industry. Another example is a community-mapping project that has trained two community members in geographic information system (GIS) mapping. The community has developed a Consultation Protocol Package that includes a work plan to further develop economic opportunities for the RRIB. The band has conducted a professional business complex study, and a business plan has been developed to address the huge demand for business development on the reserve. The RRIB and Fort William First Nation are partners in a wind-farm project in the region. Finally, the band has purchased several properties off reserve in nearby communities, which have all been renovated for office space and all are filled with tenants.

Given these developments, it is not surprising that our investigations indicated that members of the RRIB were not ready to move into tourism planning and development. The other economic-development, training, and education opportunities that have occurred for the band during this time period are more obvious to the band members as they related to resource development and industry—areas where band members had experience and that were "ready made" in the sense that people could undertake specific training and/or education and have employment opportunities, rather than creating their own new business. The project has, however, helped to educate RRIB leaders and community members about tourism and the opportunities within the community. It has provided the RRIB with useable data for the development of various community-based projects, not just tourism, which has further assisted in the identification of other possibilities for diversifying the economy. The project has shown the community the value of its culture and traditions, which has increased community pride.

Further, we found that while the community possesses many cultural and natural assets that are important for tourism development, it lacks a number of critical capacities for the development of tourism at this time, relating to infrastructure and funding, and limited entrepreneurial interest in tourism. Some of these will be overcome once the RRIB obtains the rights to the land upon which the Chalet Lodge rests, as they will be able to offer tangible tourism-related employment to interested members. The foundation for the development of tourism capacities has been established through our project—it is now a matter of time to see if tourism will grow into a viable element of a diversified and sustainable economy for the RRIB.

While the intent of this volume is to make connections between community–university projects and the ICSP framework, as we have illustrated, the framework has limited value within a First Nations context. The ICSP was not designed to take into account the unique position of First Nations communities in Canada; they are not municipalities and are not beholden to the province in the same ways. Indeed the authors of the ICSP acknowledge that it has not been developed to address the unique context of First Nations. Secondly, the ICSP process is based on principles that are appropriate within Western ways of thinking and are not based on culturally applicable processes for First Nations communities. In contrast, the *CCP Handbook,* developed by First Nations in British Columbia, is based on a process that follows the holistic approach to community and development that is appropriate within First Nations communities. Additionally, by adapting the ICSP into the *CCP Handbook,* it provides an opportunity to address the complexity of First Nations communities and the social, political, economic, and environmental context (historic and current) in which they function. The *CCP Handbook,* at its core, is fundamentally about building and developing capacity with a First Nations community to create a vision for the community based on wide participation of members, develop a plan that is realistic and that can be implemented based on logical and reasonable timelines.

As we have outlined, our project was one of several ongoing projects within the RRIB that did not fit within the priorities of the community at present. This illustrates the importance of one of our challenges—getting community involvement—which only happens when people are actually interested in, and arguably, knowledgeable about, the project. There is far more interest and participation in meetings regarding hydroelectricity, forestry, and mining potentials, where education and training equals jobs, rather than the far less tangible and more risky opportunities provided by developing a tourism business.

Finally, our project has illustrated to us the importance of developing a partnership between the researchers and the community members—what we term "working with" rather than "on" a community (Koster et al., 2012). "Working with" means figuring out what the right research question is, how to best go about collecting the information, determining who owns that data once collected, and working collaboratively on creating reports, publications, and presentations. We have also found that identifying and working within a set of guiding principles assisted the team in dealing with any challenges that arose. We also acknowledge that "working with" presents challenges to all members of the team, not the least of which is the time commitment associated with such a process. However, we are in agreement that the benefits, especially the development of friendship, far outweigh the costs.

Notes

1. See http://www.earthrhythms.ca/; owner, Celes Davar.
2. During the second year of our project, Hoss received a new employment opportunity external to the community. This meant that he could no longer continue with the project, but he did continue to contribute when possible.
3. For clarification, in 2009 Kirstine Metansinine married and became Kirstine Baccar.

References

Aboriginal Tourism in Canada (ATTC). (2003). *Part I: Economic impact analysis. Final report.* Prepared for ATTC by Bearing Point LP, Goss Gilroy Inc. & Associates.

Aboriginal Tourism Team Canada & Canadian Tourism Commission (ATTC & CTC). (2000). *Demand for Aboriginal culture products in key European markets 2000.* Canada: PricewaterhouseCoopers.

Bennett, N., & Lemelin, R. H. (2009). *Maximizing benefit from the creation of a national park through capacity building and the social economy*. Research report prepared for the Lutsel K'e Dene First Nation, Lakehead University.

Bennett, N., Lemelin, R. H., Ellis, S., & Enzoe, G. (2010). Building local capacity for Indigenous tourism development. In N. McIntyre, R. L. Koster, and R. H. Lemelin (Eds.), *Lake tourism: Towards sustaining communities—and—lake environments* (pp. 47–51). Proceedings from the 4th International Lake Tourism Conference, Making Conservation Work for Communities and Lakes, June 22–25, 2009, Centre for Tourism and Community Development Research, Lakehead University.

Bennett, N. J., Lemelin, R. H., Koster, R., & Budke, I. (2012). A capital assets framework for appraising and building capacity for tourism development in Aboriginal protected area gateway communities. *Tourism Management, 33*(4), 752–766. doi: 10.1016/j.tourman.2011.08.009.

Budke, I. (2000). *Aboriginal tourism in Canada's national parks: A framework for cooperation.* Summary report prepared for Parks Canada. Vancouver, BC: School of Resource Management, Simon Fraser University.

Butler, R., & Hinch, T. (Eds.). (2007). *Tourism and Indigenous peoples: Issues and implications* (2nd ed.). London: Butterworth-Heinnemann.

Carney, D. (1998). *Sustainable rural livelihoods: What contribution can we make?* London: Department for International Development (DFID).

Carson, D., & Carson, D. (2011). Why tourism may not be everybody's business: The challenge of tradition in resource peripheries. *The Rangeland Journal, 33,* 373–383. doi: 10.1071/RJ11026.

Chambers, R., & Conway, G. (1992). *Sustainable rural livelihoods: Practical concepts for the 21st century. IDS discussion paper 296.* Sussex: Institute for Development Studies (IDS), University of Sussex.

Chaskin, R. J. (2001). Defining community capacity: A definitional framework and case studies from a comprehensive community initiative. *Urban Affairs Review, 36,* 291–323.

Eagles, P., & McCool, S. (2002). *Tourism in national parks and protected areas.* New York: CABI Publishing.

Ellis, F. (2000). *Rural livelihoods and diversity in developing countries.* Oxford: Oxford University Press.

Fletcher, C. (2003). Community-based participatory research relationships with Aboriginal communities in Canada: An overview of the context and process. *Pimatziwin: A Journal of Aboriginal and Indigenous Community Health, 1*(1),27–62.

Frank, F., & Smith, A. (1999). *The community development handbook: A tool to build community capacity.* Hull, QC: Labour Market Learning and Development Canada.

Good, J. (2000). *Benefits of parks and protected areas. Canadian parks council. Report 251-e.* Economic Framework Project. Amherst Island, ON: The Outspan Group.

Green, G. P., & Haines, A. (2002). *Asset building and community development* (1st ed.). London: Sage.

———. (2008). *Asset building and community development* (2nd ed.). London: Sage.

Hart, F., Steadman, A., & Woods, P. (1996). *A market analysis for Aboriginal themed tourism products in Saskatchewan.* Project report and summary report. Prepared for the Federation of Saskatchewan Indian Nations. Saskatoon: KPMG.

Koster, R. L. (2010). Local contexts for community economic development strategies: A comparison of rural Saskatchewan and Ontario Communities. In D. G. Winchell, D. Ramsey, R. Koster, & G. M. Robinson (Eds.), *Geographical perspectives on sustainable rural change* (pp. 461–483). Brandon, MB: Rural Development Institute.

Koster, R. L., & Lemelin, R. H. (2009). Appreciative inquiry in rural tourism. *Tourism Geographies, 11*(2), 256–269.

Koster, R. L., Lemelin, R. H., & Davar, C. (2005). *Aboriginal values, protected areas and tourism: The possibilities for rural Canada.* Prepared under contract for Parks Canada.

Koster, R. L., Baccar, K., & Lemelin, R. H. (2012). Moving from research on, to research with and for Indigenous communities: A critical reflection on community-based participatory research. *The Canadian Geographer, 56*(2), 195–210. doi: 10.1111/j.1541-0064.2012.00428.x.

Kovach, M. (2005). Emerging from the margins: Indigenous methodologies. In L. Brown & S. Strega (Eds.), *Research as resistance: Critical Indigenous, and anti-oppressive approaches* (pp. 19–36). Toronto: Canadian Scholars Press / Women's Press.

Kovach, M. (2009). *Indigenous methodologies: Characteristics, conversations, and contexts.* Toronto: University of Toronto Press.

Kretzmann, J. P., & McKnight, J. L. (1993). *Building communities from the inside out: A path toward finding and mobilizing a community's assets.* Evanston, IL: Center for Urban Affairs and Policy Research, Northwestern University.

Lemelin, R. H., Koster, R. L., Woznicka, I., Metansinine, K., & Pelletier, H. (2009). Voyages to Kitchi Gami: The Lake Superior National Marine Conservation Area and regional tourism opportunities in Canada's first national marine conservation area. *Tourism in Marine Environments, 6*(2/3), 101–118.

Louis, R. (2007). Can you hear us now? Voices from the margin: Using Indigenous methodologies in geographic research. *Geographical Research, 45*(2), 130–139.

Louis, R., & Grossman, Z. (2009). Discussion paper on research and Indigenous peoples. Prepared for the Indigenous Peoples Specialty Group of the Association of American Geographers (AAG). Retrieved from http://www.pacificworlds.com/ipsg/Discussion_paper.pdf.

McGregor, D., Bayha, W., & Simmons, D. (2010). "Our responsibility to keep the land alive": Voices of northern Indigenous researchers. *Pimatziwin: A Journal of Aboriginal and Indigenous Community Health, 8*(1), 101–123.

Metansinine, K., Koster, R. L., & Lemelin, R. H. (2009a). *Experiential tourism in Aboriginal communities: Assesment handbook.* Prepared under contract for Parks Canada.

———. (2009b). *Developing experiential tourism in Lake Helen region: A foundational document.* Prepared under contract for Parks Canada.

Nepal, S. K. (2000). Tourism, national parks and local communities. In R. W. Butler & S. W. Boyd (Eds.), *Tourism and national parks: Issues and implications* (pp. 73–94). New York: John Wiley & Sons.

Notzke, C. (2006). *The stranger, the native and the land: Perspectives of Indigenous tourism.* Concord, ON: Captus Press.

Okanagan First Nations, Lytton, Squiala, We Wai Kai (Cape Mudge) and Yekooche First Nations, & First Nations / INAC Comprehensive Community Planning Working Group. (2006). *CCP handbook: Comprehensive community planning for First Nations in British Columbia.* Retrieved April 8, 2011, from http://www.ainc-inac.gc.ca/ai/scr/bc/proser/fna/ccp/ccphb/pub/ccphb-eng.asp.

Prime Minister's External Advisory on Cities and Communities. (2005). *Integrated community sustainability planning: A background paper.* Planning for Sustainable Canadian Communities Roundtable. Ottawa: Prime Minister's External Advisory on Cities and Communities.

Reid, D. (2003). *Tourism, globalization and development: Responsible tourism planning.* London: Pluto Press

Rundstrom, R.A., & Deur, D. (1999). Reciprocal appropriation: Toward an ethics of cross-cultural research. In J. D. Proctor & D. M. Smith (Eds.), *Geography and ethics,* (237–250). New York: Routledge.

Scoones, I. (1998). *Sustainable rural livelihoods: A framework for analysis. IDS working paper 72.* Sussex: Institute for Development Studies (IDS), University Of Sussex.

Senate Standing Committee on Aboriginal Peoples. (2001). *Northern parks: A new way.* A report of the Subcommittee on Aboriginal Economic Development in relation to northern national parks. Ottawa: The Senate.

Shackley, M. (1998). Conclusions. In M. Shackley (Ed.), *Visitor management: Case studies from world heritage sites* (pp. 194–205). Oxford, UK: Butterworth-Heinemann.

Smith, L. (1999). *Decolonizing methodologies: Research and Indigenous peoples.* Dunedin, NZ: University of Otago Press.

Southcott, C. (2006). *The North in numbers: A demographic analysis of social and economic change in northern Ontario.* Orillia, ON: Lakehead University Centre for Northern Studies.

Stein, T. V., Anderson, D. H., & Thompson, D. (1999). Identifying and managing for community benefits in Minnesota State Parks. *Journal of Park and Recreation Administration*, *17*(4) 1–19.

Wellings, Peter. (2007). Joint management: Aboriginal involvement in tourism in the Kakadu world heritage area. In R. Bushell, & P. F. J. Eagles (Eds.), *Tourism and protected areas: Benefits beyond boundaries* (pp. 89–100). Cambridge, MA: CABI.

Williams, P., & Dossa, K. (1996). *Ethnic tourism: Native interest travel markets for Canada*. North Vancouver, BC: Aboriginal Tourism Association of British Columbia.

Williams, P., & Stewart, J. K. (1997). Canadian Aboriginal tourism development: Assessing latent demand from France. *The Journal of Tourism Studies*, *9*(1), 25–41.

Wilson, S. (2008). *Research is ceremony: Indigenous research methods*. Winnipeg, MB: Fernwood Publishers.

Zeppel, H. (2006). *Indigenous ecotourism: Sustainable development and management*. Wallingford: CABI.

ELEVEN

Netukulimk Narratives

Pathways to Rebuilding Sustainable Indigenous Nations

L. Jane McMillan, Kerry Prosper, Morgan E. Moffitt, and Anthony Davis

Indigenous rights recognition and the Mi'kmaq peoples of Nova Scotia

In the past two decades, Indigenous peoples' rights in Canada and abroad have received increasing global attention. In particular, national and international organizations have, through documents and assemblies such as the Royal Commission on Aboriginal Peoples (1996), the United Nations Rio Declaration on Environment and Development (1992), and the United Nations Declaration on the Rights of Indigenous Peoples (2007), highlighted the need for governments to recognize Aboriginal rights and work in conjunction with Indigenous peoples toward creating more equitable and respectful relationships. Yet, despite these efforts, Indigenous peoples continue to struggle to achieve the benefits that are inherent to their rights. Often these struggles are played out within judicial settings, wherein "reliable evidence" is a requirement for decisions that affirm rights. Evidence utilized to support Indigenous communities engaged in legal conflicts with state powers and/or treaty negotiations may evolve out of long-term research collaborations between university researchers and Indigenous communities. Social-research collaborations have the capacity to contribute to these processes and have the potential to create strong ties between communities and researchers. They may also develop important data to be employed by communities to attain social justice and rights recognition, and to implement culturally aligned governance strategies. This is not to say that collaborations are without difficulties; strong relationships take time, mutual understanding, and respect, and they must be grounded in community desires.

This chapter explores the research relationships that are supporting Mi'kmaq rights recognition and their expansion in the province of Nova Scotia, Canada. We outline key attributes of successful social-research collaborations between university researchers and Paqtnkek, an Indigenous Mi'kmaq community in rural Nova Scotia. The strengths and limitations of social-research processes and the contributions that these collaborations have to make are discussed through the lens of cultural sustainability framed by Indigenous resource use and local ecological knowledge. We are a group of anthropologists concerned with the potential constructive role that research partnerships play in documenting resource-use practices and local ecological knowledge to advance Indigenous peoples' legal rights and empowerment. Collectively we work toward building community capacity for long-term, integrated, public engagement in the management of Mi'kmaq moose harvesting as part of a broader movement in mobilizing Indigenous knowledge for environmental, social, and cultural sustainability.

Presently, strong social-research collaborations between the Mi'kmaq and university researchers work at the grassroots level to develop programs and provide the data necessary to support current community-development projects. This research is founded on participatory-action principles and decolonizing methodologies. As Smith (1999) advises, "the methodologies and methods of research, the theories that inform them, the questions which they generate and the writing considered carefully and critically before being applied. In other words, they need to be 'decolonized'" (p. 39). Far from rejecting traditional research principles, decolonizing methodologies pertains to a reworking of research objectives, methods, and techniques to formulate a research design that is based on community desires, involves community members, and is subject to community approval or rejection. Thus, decolonized research is not research *on* an Indigenous community; it is research *for* an Indigenous community in collaboration *with* community members. In our research, our collaborators revealed that the rights to fish commercially or to hunt moose are not merely newly recognized rights granted by the Supreme Court but rather a set of communal rights with tremendous historical privileges that had associated customary governance strategies forged on culturally aligned principles of resource-use sustainability.

Decolonized-research relationships are an essential step toward self-government and autonomy. As Smith (1999) argues, imagining self-determination is "...to imagine a world in which Indigenous peoples become active participants, and to prepare for the possibilities and challenges that lie ahead" (p. 126). The participation of Mi'kmaq peoples in the creation and transmission of research projects is an important step en route to creating sustainable communities and conscious actions toward social justice. Transferring power and control over research goals, outcomes, and methods is as necessary to creating sustainable communities and culturally relevant programs as the devolution of power and control from the state to the Mi'kmaq. Thus, in order for effective and meaningful research to transform and rejuvenate Mi'kmaq communities, strategic research agendas must be formulated through profound and multilevel partnerships rooted in mutual respect and fixed in community control of the determination of research goals and full participation in their outcomes and implementation. Most important, as McMillan and Davis (2010) point out, inclusive research collaborations between the Mi'kmaq and university researchers have the potential

> to contribute meaningfully to thorough documentation of Mi'kmaq customary intellectual property, as well as the association of these with legal interpretations and affirmations of treaty rights, the development of sustainable natural resource-based livelihoods and economic development, and the achievement of self-governance informed by Mi'kmaq culture and customary knowledge. (p. 6)

In this study we found that researching customary laws and cultural concepts such as *netukulimk* are critical to developing and contributing to

Indigenous knowledge mobilization and sustainability planning in rights-implementation work.

Netukulimk narratives

Against colonial encounters, Mi'kmaq peoples are exploring their customary relationships with land, sea, and air to re-establish the nature and form of their treaty rights. *Netukulimk* is a conceptual framework of laws recognizing the interconnection of every animate life form and inanimate object according to Mi'kmaq local knowledge. The teachings of *netukulimk* provide some guidance for uniquely Mi'kmaq approaches to resource utilization and regulation that have the potential to frame sustainable natural-resource management and inform culturally aligned governance strategies against those imposed upon the Mi'kmaq by the state and its agents. The narratives reinvigorating the principles embedded in *netukulimk* reflect shifting balances of power as Mi'kmaq negotiate their rights internally and externally. In some narratives, practicing *netukulimk* is presented as the answer to environmental exploitation and crises, and are told in ways that illuminate the impacts of colonial denial of Indigenous knowledge and practice.

Many *netukulimk* narratives articulate Mi'kmaq treaty rights and demonstrate jurisdictional hitches that interfere with living in a good way with each other, and are permeated with tales of injustice. Aggressive fisheries officers, militant natural-resource patrols, and overzealous sport hunters and fishers, whose claims to traditional rights remarkably have tremendous political and economic leverage, perpetuate systemic discrimination and facilitate the extensive oversurveillance and criminalization of Mi'kmaq harvesting practices (McMillan, 2012). In other narratives, *netukulimk* is part of the story of reconnection with land, language, and culture, particularly in reconciliation narratives—of which we are listening to many and learning of the profound intergenerational impacts of residential schools on Indigenous cultures as we work to mobilize pathways to reconciliation through Indigenous-knowledge mobilization (Prosper, McMillan, Davis, & Moffitt, 2011). In this chapter we detail *netukulimk* narratives at work in the creation of the Mi'kmaq Moose Management Initiative in the context of nation rebuilding after the Supreme Court of Canada R. v. Marshall (1999) decision affirmed Mi'kmaq treaty rights.

Respectful research in Mi'kmaq territory: Collaborative methodologies and participatory action

Two particular research collaborations between Mi'kmaq communities and university researchers illustrate the significant contextual considerations we take as we work to decolonize communities and establish processes that facilitate and enhance strategic cultural sustainability. The Social Research for Sustainable Fisheries (SRSF) project and the Indigenous Peoples and Sustainable Communities (IPSC) program are two examples. Together, these partnerships represent over a decade of collaboration and commitment to developing and supporting healthy and sustainable Mi'kmaq communities. Both of these research partnerships are linked to the release of the R. v. Marshall decision (1999) and the subsequent clarification issued in the fall of 1999.

R. v. Marshall (1999) affirmed that the Mi'kmaq possess a treaty right to participate in commercial fisheries as a means of acquiring a "moderate livelihood" (p. 2), but limiting the accumulation of wealth. Defining "moderate livelihood" is a legal and cultural challenge in the creation, implementation, and justification of sustainable resource management. Limiting Mi'kmaq entitlements creates an uneven playing field and disadvantages Mi'kmaq positions and beliefs in negotiating with multiple resource users. The court decision forced the creation of a framework relationship to govern the process of Aboriginal- and treaty-rights negotiations between the three governments involved in the decision: the Mi'kmaq, the Government of Nova Scotia, and the Government of Canada. Court cases, especially those that are appealed to the Supreme Court of Canada, are often extremely long, cost millions of dollars, and can end with parties dissatisfied with the outcomes. In the R. v. Marshall (1999) decision, the protracted and contentious legal battle resulted in the federal and provincial governments' forced recognition of the contemporary applicability of historical treaties (Coates, 2000; Wicken, 2004). Consequently, both parties were compelled to find new avenues through which to negotiate further conflicts and to implement Mi'kmaq treaty rights. As Coates (2000) testifies, "The R vs. Marshall (1999) decision was not just about lobster or even fishing rights. It was about recognizing the legitimacy of eighteenth-century treaties and rebuilding trust relationships between First Nations and other Canadians" (p. 206). While the relationship between the three governments remains tense at times, and in some cases certain fishing communities have been negatively affected by the decision, it has generally evolved in a constructive manner toward a negotiation process in which the Mi'kmaq are granted a voice and a space to articulate the legitimacy of customary practices, such as *netukulimk*, for contemporary employment. These articulations are often framed against the colonial system that continues to restrain Indigenous rights to sovereign control over subsistence resources. The R. v. Marshall (1999) decision has therefore played a pivotal role in developing the social, economic, and political foundations that are essential to the realization of successful self-government, and vibrant, sustainable communities in Mi'kmaq territory (Davis & Jentoft, 2001).

The SRSF project began in February 1999 with the assistance of the Social Sciences and Humanities Research Council of Canada (SSHRCC) through the Community–University Research Alliances (CURA) program. The SRSF was developed by Mi'kmaq and university partners and involved both Mi'kmaq and non-Aboriginal fisheries organizations throughout Nova Scotia (McMillan & Davis, 2010). This partnership was founded during a very hostile and uncertain time in the Atlantic fisheries. With the collapse of the cod fisheries in the mid-1990s, and the closure and downsizing of multiple fisheries, thousands of families had lost their livelihoods, and the subsequent reshaping of coastal communities fuelled a massive out-migration of working-aged men and women (McMillan & Davis, 2010). The small-boat fleets that remained were able to work for only short periods of the year in highly regulated, limited-entry fisheries often specializing in one or two marine resources (McMillan & Davis, 2010) and with mounting tension between Aboriginal and non-Aboriginal fishers. Igniting this already strained situation was the September 17, 1999, release of the R. v. Marshall (1999) decision; the relationships between non-Aboriginal and Mi'kmaq fishers were dangerously escalating toward violence. The necessity of a workable collaboration between the two parties and reinforced by outsider researchers was paramount to protecting Indigenous rights and played a decisive role in the creation of a strong partnership. Mi'kmaq partners identified the primary focus of SRSF's research as documenting local ecological knowledge of Mi'kmaq and small-boat fishers' knowledge of American eel (McMillan & Davis, 2010). Marshall was fishing eel, a culturally significant food, and a social, commercial, and ceremonial fish, at the time of his charges.

The SRSF research addressed specific issues that were identified by each partner organization. The equal participation of partners throughout the whole engaged process was embedded within the research design and methodology (McMillan & Davis, 2010). The Mi'kmaq-centred aspects of the SRSF methods began with a series of broad and holistic workshops relating to the function of social research and the results that research could and could not deliver in these contexts (McMillan & Davis, 2010). Early in the workshop process, participants (university researchers, Mi'kmaq community members, and Mi'kmaq members training to be research assistants) identified themes that they agreed should guide program design. Through the workshop process, partners agreed upon a three-phase, integrated approach to the research design: building a socio-economic context, systematically gathering reliable and specific background information and detailed documentation of Mi'kmaq knowledge and experiences eel fishing along with community-specified experts (McMillan & Davis, 2010). Throughout these phases, Mi'kmaq community researchers were active in the interview process, analysis, and dissemination of research outcomes. As a result of this in-depth and comprehensive study, a reliable body of evidence detailing Paqtnkek's relationship and experience with *ka't* (eel) is available and can be used for future projects, public engagement, and education, and if necessary, legal conflicts (McMillan & Davis 2010).

The Indigenous Peoples and Sustainable Communities research initiative, supported by the Canada Research Chairs Program at St. Francis Xavier University, is an ongoing collaborative process that examines the intersections of Indigenous knowledge and legal anthropology, with the distinct goal of developing strategies for implementing treaty and Aboriginal rights. Grounded in deep ethnographic work and participatory-action research, the program examines social change, social processes, and social conflicts that relate to the communal structures and relationships emerging from the Supreme Court of Canada decision R. v. Marshall (1999). The research taking place through the Indigenous Peoples and Sustainable Communities program enables comprehensive and participatory studies that are focused on Mi'kmaq strategies of treaty implementation, local ecological knowledge, rights negotiation, jurisprudence, and socio-cultural perceptions and practices. Through SSHRC Aboriginal Research Grant funding, the film *Seeking* netukulimk: *Mi'kmaq knowledge, culture, capacity and empowerment* generated opportunities for capacity building, research training, and knowledge mobilization, which we recognize as imperative to culturally aligned resource-use management and sustainability (Prosper et al., 2011; Stiegman, Prosper, & McMillan, 2013).

Netukulimk: **A strategy for integrated Aboriginal rights sustainability**

Emerging from the SRSF research was a desire from Paqtnkek to explore their cultural and spiritual connection to natural resources and frame their economic ventures around their special connection. The combination of rights that flow down from R. v. Marshall (1999) and R. v. Sparrow (1990), a Supreme Court decision that, like Marshall, clearly states the best way of resolving Aboriginal rights issues is arranging self-government through negotiation (Isaac, 2004), helped us to identify priorities of rights to resources in the event of availability, conservation, and commercial economic activity. The court held that Aboriginal fishing rights are protected under the Constitution and the Crown cannot impose unjustifiably unreasonable limitations (Borrows, 2010). The R. v. Sparrow (1990) test outlines how priority access to a resource may be affected by conservation-management needs set out by the federal government, ranking Indigenous food fishery first, followed by recreational fishery, and commercial access third.

The R. v. Marshall (1999) decision recognizes the right of the Mi'kmaq to earn a moderate livelihood. The Mi'kmaq are challenged with defining what a moderate livelihood means with respect to the interpretation of individual and communal rights with regard to community sustainability planning. The right to earn a moderate livelihood is subdued by a perceived limitation to accumulate wealth from this treaty right. This limit to wealth accumulation is often viewed as a measure of oppression designed to interfere with the full expression of Mi'kmaq rights and thus adds to the socio-legal complexity as Mi'kmaq develop economic ventures or try to plan sustainable economic management mechanisms within their communities.

In the last decade, Mi'kmaq peoples have experienced an intense period of local and provincial institution building and intergovernmental negotiation. This has far-reaching consequences for community sustainability and community empowerment. The Nova Scotia Mi'kmaq are determining value systems and codes of conduct to regenerate cultural identities, increase social cohesion, and manage new relationships with each other, their natural resources, and the larger society. A key area in which the Mi'kmaq are working to re-establish and rebuild cultural connections is in their relationship with natural resources. Colonization had a tremendous impact on Mi'kmaq traditional subsistence strategies, limiting their access to hunting and fishing territories and criminalizing traditional subsistence activities. The result was the endangering of traditional beliefs and concepts such as *netukulimk* and the expansion of socio-economic marginalization of Mi'kmaq peoples. *Netukulimk* is a cultural concept that has been held by Mi'kmaq since time immemorial and is today being put forward as a model for sustainable resource use.

The *netukulimk* narratives are fluid, transformative, intersubjective, situated in process and performance, and grounded in everyday life, and they have political consequences. We explore the Mi'kmaq concept of *netukulimk* as a reference point for illustrating the connection of Mi'kmaq culture and spirituality in their relations with the changing environment while ensuring their survivance. This culturally rooted concept operates as a guide to responsible co-existence and interdependence. It is considered as a body of living knowledge that underpins the moral and ethical relationships that explain their world in the past and provides for the present by sustaining the future. *Netukulimk* provides a roadmap to meaningful expressions of rights and entitlements, and shapes the governance required to generate sustainable values of interaction and livelihood. The accounts of the concepts and practices of *netukulimk* are emergent in land-claim agreements and community-controlled resource management plans. The narratives are about reallocating land, resources, and political power, and are rooted in the broader issues of everyday, common sense, taken for granted categories and practices.

Indigenous knowledge (IK) of the Mi'kmaq posits that they come from the land or they were sprouted from the land. Kerry Prosper explains the tangible and intangible significance of *netukulimk* as follows:

> The Mi'kmaq term "Weji-sqalia'tiek" is interpreted in English as "We sprouted from the land." Mi'kmaq origin beliefs explain and express the development of their relationship to the lands

> and resources through the concept *netukulimk*. *Netukulimk* frames the interconnected relationship Indigenous peoples have to their land, animals, and biomaterial as a result of thousands of years of constant interaction. This interconnected relationship forged each life form into its own niche of survivability and existence since creation. Different life forms that live on land, in water and the sky, for thousands of years, are connected in ways that transcend physical and spiritual boundaries. The Mi'kmaq evolved with their environment and interacted within it for well over 12 thousand years and thus created a special relationship that transcends the spiritual and physical boundaries and connects Mi'kmaq to all the biomass that exist within in their traditional territory to this day.
>
> The life and death cycle as expressed in the nutrient exchange demonstrated by all things is the everlasting gift of creation that is in a constant circle of recycling. It is from within this cycle that the Mi'kmaq have sprouted. This ongoing cycle of life and death is an exchange that results in constant creation. Creation has no beginning and no end, a circle that is forever perpetuating life from one state of being to another. The spiritual connectedness developed in these interrelationships are bound together in the process of transferring nutrients from one life form to another, a cycle that the Mi'kmaq were and are still a part of today. Embedded in this concept is the idea that the ancestors are in everything, and one day your essence will also be providing for future generations so we must be mindful of how we interact with the world around us. (Prosper, 2009)

Universalizing classification systems that accompanied colonial expansion threatened to dislodge or trivialize local systems of meaning. Indigenous knowledge continues to be presented as an object for science rather than as a system of knowledge that could inform science. *Netukulimk* narratives are emerging as rights and responsibility discourses that are informing governance strategies in Mi'kmaq country. The research team decided to explore and animate the *netukulimk* concept and its resource-management potentials as it is operationalized through the Mi'kmaq Moose Management Initiative.

Integrated Community Sustainability Planning: The Moose Management Initiative

There are many challenges to cultural and community sustainability for Indigenous communities. Long-term thinking, resilience, and capacity building are constantly challenged by policies and laws favouring assimilation, narrow treaty interpretations, resource-consuming bureaucracy, litigation uncertainty, and complicated and inadequate funding arrangements. Systemic discrimination and internal colonization are also formidable obstacles to effective implementation of Indigenous models of environmental, social, and cultural sustainability, which are further hindered by jurisdictional conflicts and the inefficient maze of fiduciary responsibility and accountability perpetuated by the state and its agents. Non-Aboriginal resistance to Aboriginal rights is well-documented (Asch, 1997; Blaser, Feit, & McRae, 2004; Boldt, 1993; Borrows, 2010; Cornell, 1988; Niezen, 2003; Royal Commisson on Aboriginal Peoples [RCAP], 1996; Warry, 2007). The Mi'kmaq have a long history of dispute regarding their liberty to exercise their treaty rights. The assertion of Mi'kmaq rights through treaty litigation and protest was and remains extremely difficult and tense for both Mi'kmaq and non-Mi'kmaq throughout the province of Nova Scotia. Despite its tremendous cultural significance, many Mi'kmaq had never participated in the moose hunt because of restrictive government legislation that reduced or ignored Mi'kmaq rights or criminalized customary activities. The Mi'kmaq who hunted moose did so discreetly and tried to avoid any contact with the any Department of Natural Resources (DNR) wardens.

The Simon v. The Queen (1985) decision affirmed the Treaty of 1752 and upheld Mi'kmaq hunting rights off reservation. With the security of treaty rights affirmed, many Mi'kmaq who exercised their rights had very little experience hunting and were unaware of safety regulations and other laws, causing them to be highly susceptible to charges for hunting offences and safety-regulation violations (Moffitt, 2010). In addition, these new hunters hunting under the treaty faced many challenges and contradictions. Within and between communities there was a diverse interpretation of what was considered "proper" treaty-rights implementation, increasing debate about the role of moose as a subsistence resource and whether or not moose should be sold for profit (as in earning a moderate livelihood), and concerns over the laws that should govern Mi'kmaq hunters (Moffitt, 2010). Discourses within communities raised contentious issues of whether or not Mi'kmaq rights are collective or individual treaty rights. It is within this context that the rejuvenation of traditional ecological concepts like *netukulimk* were looked to for guidance.

In a political strategy to protect their treaty rights, the 13 Indian Act–elected Mi'kmaq chiefs of Nova Scotia, under the direction of the grand chief and the grand council, the customary governing body of the Mi'kmaq nation, set out interim guidelines as customary laws that the Mi'kmaq were going to follow as they exercised their treaty right to hunt moose. The guidelines followed the direction and concept of *netukulimk*. The unspoken concept *netukulimk* held in the consciousness was now spoken and written into a document. On Mi'kmaq Treaty Day, October 1, 1986, the majority of the leadership in Nova Scotia ratified a set of guidelines as a first step toward this end (Richardson & Erasmus, 1989). The guidelines stated:

> Until the Mi'kmaq people can come to some agreement with Canada and Nova Scotia on changes to their legislation and regulations, it will be necessary to adopt some interim *netukulimkewe'l* (laws) of our own—both for our own protection and the protection of the animals and fish which form part of our inheritance from the creator. The Treaty of 1752 belongs to all the Mi'kmaq, and we must all work together to keep it strong. We therefore call upon all Mi'kmaq to understand and respect the following guidelines for the treaty right to *netukulimk* under the 1752 Treaty. These guidelines embraced the old concept *netukulimk*. The treaty was brought forward to endure and welcome the 21 century, with it came the old values and traditions of our ancestors. The Mi'kmaq culture shifted to embrace not only a renewed treaty but renewed modern and traditional law ways. (*Mi'kmaq Treaty Handbook*, 1987, p.14)

It is imperative to understand the impacts of colonization on Indigenous knowledge and ways of life in order to produce effective mechanisms for change today. The cultural and spiritual connection of the Mi'kmaq to their territory and resources is critical to the current period of nation rebuilding and cultural revitalization. Mi'kmaq peoples are creating original, culturally relevant programs and initiatives to implement their treaty rights and establish healthy, strong relationships with their customary resources based on the objectives of *netukulimk* and thus must be considered and integrated in community sustainability planning. The following section focuses on a particular case where Mi'kmaq peoples are successfully designing and implementing their own management plans to rebuild community relationships with moose through the principles enshrined in *netukulimk*.

As noted in earlier, rather than continue to have the courts decide Mi'kmaq rights, the Mi'kmaq peoples and the provincial and federal governments created a framework agreement in 2001, the Made-in-Nova Scotia Process, as a way to negotiate effective implementation of Mi'kmaq treaty rights and self-governance within the province of Nova Scotia. Following the 2001 agreement, the tripartite forum, which is a federal/provincial/Mi'kmaq partnership, established from the Marshall Inquiry Recommendations (Royal Commission on the Donald Marshall, Jr., Prosecution, 1989), to mediate and resolve outstanding issues between these governments, was reorganized into working committees focused on specific social–community oriented and rights-based issues addressed throughout the intergovernmental negotiation process. Mi'kmaq interests in these negotiations are represented by Kwilmuk Maw-klusuaqn (KMK) or the Mi'kmaq Rights Initiative Negotiation Office. The goal of KMK is to define, recognize, and implement Mi'kmaq rights for the benefit of Mi'kmaq communities and peoples. Consequently, KMK plays a tremendously important role in ensuring that Mi'kmaq communities achieve recognition, acceptance, implementation, and protection of treaty, title, and other rights. Our research is designed to examine the values of the KMK in the development of Mi'kmaq systems of governance and resource management; to revive, promote, and protect a healthy Mi'kmaq identity; to obtain the basis for a shared economy and social development; and to negotiate toward these goals with community involvement and support.

Control over subsistence activities affirms Mi'kmaq jurisdiction and is therefore a highly contentious issue at negotiations between the Mi'kmaq, the Nova Scotia government, and the Canadian government (Moffitt, 2010). As part of the governance strategies emerging in the post-Marshall negotiation era, the expansion of Mi'kmaq jurisdiction to resource utilization has the potential to become a jumping point from which the KMK and the newly formed Mi'kmaq House of Assembly can negotiate further self-government projects.

The Moose Management Initiative (MMI) officially created in 2006, is paving the way for treaty rights implementation in Nova Scotia (Moffitt, 2010). The project is spearheaded by the Unama'ki Institute of Natural Resources (UINR), an organization that is Mi'kmaq owned and operated, and is a direct result of community working groups established throughout the ongoing negotiations between the KMK, the Government of Canada, and the Province of Nova Scotia. Recognizing that the Simon v. The Queen (1985) and R. v. Marshall (1999) decisions established Mi'kmaq peoples' rights to access traditional resources and, in light of the new framework for rights and governance negotiations, the KMK and the UINR sought to put these rights to work in fostering culturally aligned economic development (Moffitt, 2010). After conferring with federal and provincial representatives and agreeing to proceed with the expansion of Mi'kmaq jurisdiction over the moose harvest, the KMK assigned the UINR the responsibility to develop a comprehensive moose-management plan that would govern the Mi'kmaq hunt. The program is deeply rooted in Mi'kmaq cultural beliefs, their historic *netukulimk*-based relationship with the moose, and the effect that the arrival of European settlers had on this relationship.

Today, Hunters Mountain, located in the Cape Breton Highlands, hosts the main moose population in Nova Scotia. Cape Breton enjoyed a large population of moose as did the mainland of Nova Scotia during contact. With the establishment of the settler society, the moose populations declined. By the mid- and late 1700s it was obvious that the moose herd could not accommodate the constantly growing demands for meat and hides by Natives, settlers, and market hunters (Pulsifer & Nette, 1995). The colonization of Nova Scotia deeply distressed the relationship that Mi'kmaq peoples have with moose and other customary subsistence resources (another excellent example is the collapse of Atlantic salmon stocks over the last century). Overhunting led to the decline in moose population throughout the province and subsequently triggered the criminalization of Mi'kmaq access to moose, the creation of a licence system, and sport hunting, which further separated the Mi'kmaq from their customary resource. Consequently, the Mi'kmaq were disconnected from a culturally significant subsistence resource, impeding the transference of traditional skills and values intrinsic in the moose hunt and its management (Moffitt, 2010). The devastating effects of this separation cannot be underestimated.

The shift in resource availability and its commodification changes the context of resource use and the continued practices of sustainability. Mi'kmaq were forced into survival mode, and the changing economic position shifted customary natural resource management into a world of market-driven competition and food as commodities. The province, ignoring Mi'kmaq treaty rights, continued to intimidate and molest Mi'kmaq exercising their rights. In 1887 six Mi'kmaq were charged with fishing "violations," 23 were charged for hunting deer and moose, and three were charged in connection with commerce and taxation matters (Richardson & Erasmus, 1989, p. 93–94). Such charges were in direct conflict with the Treaty of 1752, which protected Mi'kmaq rights to hunt and fish as usual. The meat supplied by a single moose is abundant and can provide one small family with a year's supply of food. The right to hunt "as usual" as specified in the Treaty of 1752 was the same as hunting "as usual" under the concept of *netukulimk* during contact and the signing of the treaties. The double standards and treaty denial practiced by the province created two competing and conflicting ideas of sustainability. The Mi'kmaq were disempowered and removed from decision making due to institutionalized assimilation processes and discriminatory Indian Act policies, and settler society made determinations regarding resource use to favour non-Aboriginal recreational access to resources over the customary, treaty-protected access of the Mi'kmaq. This situation forced the Mi'kmaq to litigate, and through the long and hard-fought legal battles that ensued, won their rights back. As a result, the Mi'kmaq are working to reinvigorate the principles of *netukulimk* as a foundation of sustainability in the governance of their resource-management strategies.

Pathways to rebuilding a sustainable Indigenous nation

The KMK established the MMI to demonstrate to the federal and provincial governments, as well as their constituents, that the Mi'kmaq have the capacity to create culturally aligned resource-management strategies to benefit their membership. Based on customary governance practices, the MMI used a dynamic community-based, consensus-building model to develop guidelines for governing resource use (Moffitt, 2010). The program coordinator set up numerous workshops to discuss community priorities regarding the moose hunt with Mi'kmaq communities. The MMI, after holding at least two community sessions in each of the 13 Mi'kmaq communities in Nova Scotia, compiled and disseminated the information at a province-wide symposium on moose called *Mawikwamk Wjit Tia'muk* at the cultural centre in the Watmatcook Mi'kmaq community, Cape Breton. Each community sent delegates of Elders, women, hunters and gathers, and youth, who all had some cultural, political, economic, social, and ceremonial interest in moose. The gathering reflected grassroots level representation that holistically expressed community concern for the moose.

The symposium brought diverse community members together to share their experiences and ideas on how best to exercise their rights as Mi'kmaq peoples. This was an important symposium because it identified *netukulimk* as the culturally appropriate mechanism to regulate Mi'kmaq moose harvests and marked a critical rejuvenation of *netukulimk* practice within Mi'kmaq institutions, communities, and homes. *Netukulimk* was central to developing a sustainable hunt that maximized community benefits while simultaneously maintaining a healthy moose population. The debate about harvesting moose for profit has been particularly contentious within communities. Because of the high rates of poverty and few job opportunities in Mi'kmaq communities, the sale of moose was perceived as a potential solution to dire socio-economic conditions. On the other side, moose was understood as a customary food source and an integral aspect of culture whose sanctity is marred by commodification.

Many hunters struggled to align the concept of *netukulimk* within the discourses of collective and individual rights. Resource commodification is complicated by the moral and ethical underpinnings of living right together as espoused by the concept. Collective commodificiation challenges the individualistic tendencies of capitalism and requires an effective economic redistribution model that will prevent contest and conflict. A strategy to legitimize commodification of wild meat and fish within Mi'kmaq communities may rest the necessity to address the serious and declining health conditions of the Mi'kmaq. According to Health Canada (2011), the incidence of diabetes and heart disease within most of the First Nations communities in Canada is very high. Type 2 diabetes is three to five times higher on reserve than for other Canadians (Health

Canada, 2011). The Mi'kmaq articulated that their health and well-being were dependent upon a healthy and sustainable moose population, as is framed in the concept of *netukulimk*.

During the symposium, a well-respected leader of the Mi'kmaq Rights Initiative gave a presentation on the history of Mi'kmaq rights, from the creation of the treaties to their abuse by the colonizers, through to the events surrounding the court proceedings and the Supreme Court of Canada decision that led them to the day where they were sitting down to manage the treaty rights. Part of the presentation included storytelling, a typical Mi'kmaq knowledge-mobilization practice. In this case the presenter recounted a story that he heard from his grandmother, who was from Potlotek Mi'kmaq community. The story revealed that the grand council members were sitting together discussing and allocating the hunting and fishing areas to family districts, a practice that went on for hundreds of years prior to colonization. The historical practices of Indigenous sustainable management are evident in the distant and recent past. Our research documents the patterns and explores how they are revisited today under the concept *netukulimk* as negotiated within Mi'kmaq communities through these processes.

Four central themes emerged from the resource-management strategy consultations and instructed the next steps needed for institution building:

1. hunter safety,
2. selling moose meat and products,
3. establishing a no-hunting period during the year and involvement of non-Natives in Aboriginal moose-hunting activities, and
4. establishing advisory committees.

Deep concerns were raised regarding the environmental health of moose and the continued availability of this resource for future generations. The topics of sustainability, access, and treaty entitlement to non-Native spouses and offspring and seasons were vigorously debated and revealed important power dynamics that need to be comprehended in order to make effective, lasting change. The commodification of moose and reintroduction of commercialization of moose meat in an unsustainable manner was a major worry. Non-Native involvement in the trade of and access to markets was particularly contentious as Mi'kmaq struggle to protect their rights from co-optation but also need regulations to reflect the reality of their daily lives. Prior to the Mi'kmaq hunting guidelines, some Mi'kmaq hunters would exceed vaguely agreed-upon catch limits and sell the moose to non-Aboriginal people for self-profit. Various regulatory strategies were put in place by the Department of Natural Resources to reduce this practice, but the creation and enforcement of regulatory procedures needs to be in the control of the Mi'kmaq in order to fulfill their rights to self-determination.

The Moose Management Initiative is indicative of the process Mi'kmaq use to work through some very contentious issues with their membership about access to and the extent of individual and communal rights. Sustainable access to food and sustenance was prioritized against the competition and conflicts created by commodification and recreational utilization of moose. Sustaining the herd for non-Aboriginal sport hunting was not the definition of sustainability that interested the Mi'kmaq. Furthermore, shifting definitions of sustainability, representing non-Native access to moose through intermarriage or recreational hunting, and those representing the food requirements of the Mi'kmaq, were juxtaposed by the potential of the commercial activities ending cycles of dependency of oppressed peoples. The practice and reimplementation of the concept *netukulimk* is seen as a way to define and legitimize the future sustainable uses of moose by the Mi'kmaq and those who interact with the Mi'kmaq using methods that are more culturally palatable and practicable than the rules imposed by outsiders.

The complexity of addressing inequality in uneven playing fields of power became apparent through the consultations. Mi'kmaq saw many innovative ways by which they could command control of the moose resource for economic development, emphasizing the health benefits of customary foods and producing value-added products for commercial sale that reified Mi'kmaq identity. Distribution of the proceeds of collective-right procurements is a considerable challenge. Trust issues exist at every level of interaction, from the reliability of the Department of Natural Resources management of the herds to the accuracy of population counts, from the bureaucracy in food safety and inspection to the ability of Mi'kmaq government to answer accusations of malfeasance.

Additionally, concerns raised about the possibility of offending the moose clan people through the killing and selling of moose were coupled with fears that commodification might interrupt important cultural practices of sharing meat that are integral to the food, social and ceremonial purposes of the customary hunt, according the *netukulimk* principles. Multiple accountability concerns emerged as tensions between the interpretation of treaty rights as individual and as collective rights. People favouring the exercise of individual rights did not agree that their abilities should be bound by restrictions that may abrogate their treaty rights. The imposition of tags and bag limits troubled hunters who interpreted the R. v. Marshall (1999) and Simon v. The Queen (1985) decisions as unfettered access to hunting and fishing. After centuries of discriminatory regulations, any attempts to regulate the moose hunt through the Nova Scotia chiefs and the tripartite forum involving the federal and provincial governments were viewed with distrust. The hunters were worried about the restriction of their rights through agreements that may be signed by the chiefs without their involvement and notice, as happened problematically in the post-Marshall era with fishing rights, licenses, and their distribution.

Consensus was reached in regard to prioritizing conservation of the herds. *Netukulimk* principles inform a philosophy of "never going without" and respectful use of resources requires that nothing goes to waste (Barsh, 2002). In order to avoid spoilage and sustain *netukulimk* teachings that require the entire resource to be used, it was suggested that meat-processing sites close to Hunters Mountain be provided. Having seasonal closures that reflect Mi'kmaq environmental knowledge were integrated into the sustainability plan. To further enhance the possibility of compliance and equitable enforcement of Mi'kmaq management schemes, an agreement was reached to establish community advisory groups to help manage the moose hunt. Included in the advisory committee are Elders, women, the customary leadership of the grand council, and hunters who could represent the interests of the moose and the Mi'kmaq to governments and provide counsel on ethical hunting. Members of the advisory council are seen as knowledge holders and conduits to the exchange of information from the hunters to the management committee and the representatives sitting at the government table, as well as the Mi'kmaq nation at large.

This approach was used to generate guidelines that were created and agreed upon by Mi'kmaq community members for community members, rather than imposed by some remote authority. Multiple discussions, workshops, and drafts were created by the MMI and resulted in the creation of the community-based consensus-building mechanism that ensures that the guidelines reflect the Mi'kmaq conceptualizations of their relationship with the resource and each other. The strength of this approach lies in the deep and thorough consultation process and the foregrounding of culturally relevant principles of resource management. By creating multiple drafts of the hunting guidelines and involving hunters, youth, Elders, and non-Mi'kmaq hunters in the consultation process, the UINR and the MMI is ensuring that all parties have a say in the final guidelines. This type of consensus building resulted in comprehensive guidelines that promise to ensure the sustainability of the hunt for many generations.

The program is deeply rooted in traditional and contemporary cultural beliefs and practices of the Mi'kmaq people. The concept of *netukulimk* is particularly important in the MMI, as well as other contemporary rights movements in Mi'kmaq territory, and has been a central unifying principle for the MMI. In the wake of the Simon v. The Queen (1985) and R. v. Marshall (1999) decisions, the present is best characterized as a period of restoration due to the reintroduction to the hunt and the re-emergence of *netukulimk* in many communities (Moffitt, 2010).

Mi'kmaq communities are very diverse, yet, through the MMI, communities have reached a general consensus on how to define and conduct what they have determined as responsible hunting practices, to develop alternative strategies for development, such as the potential for ecotourism, to increase the sustainability of cultural and economic well-being in a manner that is more aligned with cultural beliefs and supports the maintenance of the moose population (Moffitt, 2010). The MMI's inclusive, consensus-building model assures that the final guidelines created through the MMI reflect Mi'kmaq conceptualizations of their relationship with the moose and sustainable resource management. The MMI is a process of cultural production encompassed within a larger nation-building strategy (Moffitt, 2010). Mi'kmaq peoples are coming together to discuss what it means to be a Mi'kmaq hunter in the 21st century and what aspects of their customary philosophies should be incorporated into hunting guidelines, and they are generating cultural values that will eventually become recognized as Mi'kmaq law.

Other sustainability-planning strategies involve the mobilization of Mi'kmaq knowledge across generations. Mi'kmaq youth leadership forums and Elder hunters along with Mi'kmaq enforcement agencies are strategically passing on their combined knowledge of hunting and safety to the youth. The Mi'kmaq communities of Indian Brook and Millbrook actively mentor the youth hunters of their communities. RCMP officers and community hunters collaborate to provide the resources for hunting trips to Hunters Mountain. Youth are instructed on ethical hunting traditions and *netukulimk* protocols. Young hunters have the opportunity to spend several nights on the mountain each year, learning to exercise their treaty rights through sustainable hunting practices and community feasting (Mi'kmaq Maliseet Nation News, 2006).

The participation and cooperation between the youth and the RCMP officers carries on the traditions of cultural transfer of knowledge as well as breaking down prejudices and stereotypes that prohibited such exchange from taking place in the past. The mentoring program has become an integral component of the MMI, teaching hunter safety, survival skills, and responsible, respectful utilization of the benefits of Mi'kmaq treaty rights. The young hunters hunt for their community feasts and are taught to take just what they need in the culturally aligned manner. The concept of *netukulimk* is teaching youth how to provide for themselves, their families and communities, and their futures. The bonds formed between the youth and the RCMP officers and community hunters informs respectful relationships with the moose.

Thus, the MMI is a symbol of contemporary cultural beliefs and community values incorporated within larger jurisdiction-building strategies, as the guidelines are formed within Mi'kmaq communities and must be agreed upon at the community level before their implementation (Moffitt, 2010). The Mi'kmaq are identifying the values and beliefs that are integral to their identity as a cultural group and are applying these values to the moose harvest and the management of this traditional subsistence resource.

The guidelines developed through the MMI process are symbols of Mi'kmaq cultural identity and the development of the guidelines is a process of identity formation. Consensus on issues such as safety, community authority, and hunting-advisory groups is symbolically sustainable because it represents how Mi'kmaq peoples believe the moose harvest should be managed (Moffitt, 2010). This is an identity-building process because the Mi'kmaq are developing ideas of what it means to be Mi'kmaq and simultaneously rejecting the aspects of non-Mi'kmaq models that they believe are incompatible with their cultural belief system (Moffitt, 2010). The result of this process is a unique system of resource management that is based on specific community-outlined values, which is likely to foster a successful and long-term relationships between peoples and resources.

Overcoming state obstacles to cultural sustainability

The Unama'ki Moose Harvesting According to Netukulimk or Tia'muwe'l Netuklimkewe'l guidelines were published and distributed in 2009. The guidelines emphasize hunting safety, community authority and hunting-advisory groups, the no-hunting time, identification and non-Mi'kmaq helpers, and hunter reporting for herd management. Initially, voluntary compliance from Mi'kmaq community members was requested from the UINR for a period of two years, during which time revisions, community feedback, and another round of consultations took place (Moffitt, 2010). In conjunction with the UINR initiative, the KMK and the Mi'kmaq Legal Support Network (MLSN) developed alternative justice models that can be used to adjudicate resource-extraction offenses related to moose and will allow for hunting offences to be heard within community justice circles (Moffitt, 2010). At the end of the two-year period, the guidelines were instituted as Mi'kmaq law. The lengthy process was exacerbated by jurisdictional disputes between and federal and provincial governments over regulatory control, fiduciary responsibility, and a lack of willingness on either side to give up power to the Mi'kmaq. These are familiar obstacles in Mi'kmaq rights negotiations and treaty implementation. A focal point of our research partnership is to reveal these impediments and develop nation-rebuilding strategies to overcome the jurisdictional barriers (Jorgenson, 2007).

In October 2011, through the Made-in-Nova Scotia Process, the Mi'kmaq and the Province of Nova Scotia agreed to undertake a customary law pilot project for the regulatory offences related to the moose hunt in Cape Breton. Established under the authority of the Attorney General of Nova Scotia and the province in partnership with the MLSN, the pilot project will see MLSN manage referrals and conduct Mi'kmaq customary justice circles for eligible offences. Mi'kmaq peoples are hopeful about the future of Mi'kmaq governance; however, organizations like the MLSN and its Customary Law Program are chronically underfunded and do not have the resources to autonomously enforce the new regulations (McMillan, 2011).

The three parties to the agreement could not determine the appropriate strategies for Mi'kmaq commodification of the resource and so commercial regulations were left out of the guidelines. As such, the processes of community rejuvenation and the renewal of relationships with resources and territory are not without difficulties. For example, the moose guidelines are subject to the approval of the provincial and federal governments, which also determine how, and to what extent, they can be implemented. In addition, while the Province of Nova Scotia has been relatively supportive of the moose project and the implementation of Mi'kmaq law, participants all noted that it is highly unlikely that the Government of Canada would ever allow similar sets of Mi'kmaq laws in the fisheries industry (Moffitt, 2010). Constant lobbying by the recreational interests to the resources that the Mi'kmaq depend upon for food creates another set of obstacles to sustainable rights mobilization. Sport hunting and catch-and-release salmon fisheries displace the Mi'kmaq food fishery and distance them even further from opportunities to earn moderate livelihoods. It is evident that there is hesitancy within the negotiation process to truly relinquish state power and control to the Mi'kmaq peoples despite the obligation outlined in the R. v. Marshall (1999) decision to acknowledge Mi'kmaq jurisdiction. However, the customary law pilot project is an important first step in collaborative approaches for wildlife and moose management and may lead to wider application of culturally relevant principles and practices of sustainability across the province.

Conclusion

Critical to sustainable rights mobilization is the understanding that the cultural health of the Mi'kmaq Nation requires recognition of Mi'kmaq rights and title, meaningful consultation, and fulfillment of the fiduciary obligations of the Crown. Without rights education and the implementation of Mi'kmaq treaties, systemic discrimination and poverty will continue to contribute to, rather than limit, culture loss and with it Indigenous ecological and environmental knowledge. Such recognition will enhance nation-rebuilding strategies and afford opportunities for reconciliation between Mi'kmaq, federal and provincial governments and their constituents. This is a necessary project of decolonization and cultural realignment. Without proper resources, Mi'kmaq communities and the organizations and institutions within them will struggle to survive and have difficulty thriving.

It is through exploration and explication of these processes that our research partnership with Mi'kmaq communities operates. We cannot begin to understand the present without engaging the past. The colonial injuries are raw wounds informing legal and cultural consciousness. The impacts of policies of assimilation—from the Indian Act to residential schools, to Department of Fisheries and Oceans licenses schemes that removed Mi'kmaq from their customary territories and resources and led to criminalization of Mi'kmaq customary practices as substantiated by the charges that led to the Simon v. The Queen (1985) and R. v. Marshall (1999) decisions—and their attending ontological structures that have created an adversarial atmosphere, collectively have wrought undue harm as evidenced by the impoverished state of many Mi'kmaq communities today. The court decisions demonstrate the recognition of Mi'kmaq nationhood, and the challenges of capacity building, public engagement, and education are being met with coordinated, collaborative, integrated planning for cultural and environmental sustainability. Our projects seek to not only amass and secure Indigenous knowledge of the natural environment and its natural resources but also to build the capacity and ability of Aboriginal communities to participate as equal partners and stakeholders with industry for the sustainable management of those natural resources. Enormous commercial opportunities lie in the full participation of Aboriginal communities with natural resource development, and there is an increasing responsibility on industry to fully and meaningfully consult with Aboriginal communities when industry wishes to extract natural resources or impact the natural landscape.

Under federal and, increasingly, provincial and territorial government legislation, industry has a responsibility to consult and engage Aboriginal communities in major natural resource developments. An area of frustration for industry is the uncertainty in defining and complying with meaningful and lawful consultation. Community members are also concerned that consultation respects and protects sacred knowledge. Competing concerns of unintended consequences in divulging protected and unprotected knowledge, without prejudice to treaty and land-claims negotiations, often represent delays to resource-development interests. All parties would be better served where Indigenous knowledge of the land is comprehensive and centrally located, where processes to access this information are transparent, and where industry can have greater assurance that they can more effectively and efficiently fulfill their duty to consult with Indigenous communities in order to adequately engage, incorporate, and compensate Indigenous knowledge in their industries and governance.

The Supreme Court of Canada R. v. Marshall (1999) decision instigated a redistribution of access to natural resources, allowing for increased opportunities for economic development and autonomy. The potential to remedy patterns of dependency and subjugation for Mi'kmaq communities and other Indigenous peoples across the country, in favour of sustainable community advancement through the affirmation of treaty and Aboriginal rights and through the substantiation of traditional knowledge, marks an unprecedented turn in colonial relations. Our ethnographic and interdisciplinary research investigates Mi'kmaq strategies of treaty implementation, rights negotiation, social-capital expansion, and how they are translated into legitimate actions within Mi'kmaq ecological knowledge, governance, jurisprudence, and socio-cultural perceptions and practices. The Mi'kmaq have entered an intensified period of institution building that has far-reaching economic, political, and cultural consequences for community sustainability. The Mi'kmaq are determining value systems and codes of conduct to help regenerate distinctive cultural identities in neoteric contexts to increase social cohesion in a period of rapid change and to assist in the management of their new relations with each other, their resources, and the larger society. The negotiation processes and the management of new relations are integral to the sustainable success of self-governance, economic independence, and social justice. The empowerment of Mi'kmaq communities is imperative for the creation of negotiated settlements that are in the best interests of the cultural health of the communities and finally break the cycles of negative colonial relations that have plagued developments in these vital areas. These are processes that will be repeated across the country as treaty and land claims are settled in other Indigenous communities.

The program's processes and goals are critical to a variety of immediate needs, including research-capacity development, research-linked dialogues through research inputs for treaty negotiation, and entitlements respecting access to and governance of natural resource use, documentation of cultural history and languages, customary understandings, and practices of core importance to cultural identity, affirmation, and learning. This and future research will contribute to building stand-alone research expertise within the Mi'kmaq Nation in the Atlantic region. This approach enhances the independence and confidence of Mi'kmaq research capacity, thereby empowering Mi'kmaq capacity to define and direct research issues, agendas, and partnerships. The evidence intersects critically with treaty processes, dialogue with governments, public education, and public policy.

Netukulimk narratives work to destabilize epitomizing narratives of "us versus them" and "traditional versus contemporary." They push issues of authenticity, challenging hegemonic ideas of Indigenous peoples as romanticized environmentalists, harmonious peacekeepers, or damaged relics of assimilative policies. The fixed meanings imposed by structural violence are unhinged. Meaning is not fixed; it emerges in practice. *Netukulimk* narratives provide a framework for experiencing the material world and how local stories intersect with larger social, historical, and political processes. The stories make meaningful connections and provide order and continuity in a rapidly changing world. They often subvert official orthodoxies and challenge conventional ways of thinking (e.g., bureaucracies, Indian Act governments, and Supreme Court decisions) that limit the expression and practice of Indigenous rights. *Netukulimk* is resistance to oppression, its practice is the exercise of Mi'kmaq rights, and its translation is cultural mobilization.

References

Asch, M. (Ed.). (1997). *Aboriginal and treaty rights in Canada: Essays on law, equality, and respect for difference.* Vancouver, BC: University of British Columbia Press.

Barsh, R. (2002). Netukulimk past and present: Mi'kmaw ethics and the Atlantic fishery. *Journal of Canadian Studies, 37*(1), 15–42.

Blaser, M., Feit, H., & McRae, G. (Eds.). (2004). *In the way of development: Indigenous peoples, life projects, and globalization*. Ottawa, ON: International Development Research Centre; and New York: Zed Books.

Boldt, M. (1993). *Surviving as Indians: The challenge of self-government*. Toronto: University of Toronto Press.

Borrows, J. (2010). *Canada's Indigenous constitution*. Toronto: University of Toronto Press.

Coates, K. (2000). *The Marshall decision and Native rights*. Montreal and Kingston: McGill-Queen's University Press.

Cornell, S. (1988). *The return of the Native: American Indian political resurgence*. New York: Oxford University Press.

Davis, A., & Jentoft, S. (2001). The challenge and the promise of Indigenous peoples' fishing rights: From dependency to agency. *Marine Policy, 25*, 223–237.

Health Canada. (2011). First Nations, Inuit and Aboriginal health: Diabetes. Retrieved December 2, 2011, from http://www.hc-sc.gc.ca/fniah-spnia/diseases-maladies/diabete/index-eng.php.

Isaac, T. (2004). *Aboriginal law: Commentary, cases and materials* (3rd ed.). Saskatoon: Purich Press.

Jorgensen, M. (Ed.). (2007). *Rebuilding Native nations: Strategies for governance and development*. Tucson: University of Arizona Press.

McMillan, L. (2011). Colonial traditions, cooptations, and Mi'kmaq legal consciousness. *Law and Social Inquiry Journal of the American Bar Foundation, 36*(1), 171–200.

———. (2012). "*Mu Kisi Maqumawkik Pasik Kataq*—we can't only eat eels": Mi'kmaq contested histories and uncontested silences. *The Canadian Journal of Native Studies, 33*(1), 119–142.

McMillan, L., & Davis, A. (2010). "What does this tell about us?" Social research and Indigenous peoples: The case of the Paq'tnkek Mi'kmaq. *Traditional Marine Resource Management and Knowledge Information Bulletin, 27*, 3–16.

Mi'kmaq Maliseet Nation News. (2006). *Mi'kmaq Maliseet Nation news, 17*(3), 1.

The Mi'kmaq Treaty Handbook. (1987). Sydney: Native Communications Society of Nova Scotia.

Moffitt, M. (2010). *Nova Scotia Mi'kmaq: Restorative justice and resource management. Alternative methods for managing fish and moose*. Honours thesis. Antigonish, NS: St. Francis Xavier University, Deptarment of Anthropology.

Niezen, R. (2003). *The origins of indigenism, human rights, and the politics of identity*. Berkeley: University of California Press.

Prosper, K. (2009). Netukulimk: *A circular relationship in shifting ideologies. An investigation into the altered and realigned spiritual and cultural connection shared by moose and Mi'kmaq*. Honours thesis. Antigonish, NS: St. Francis Xavier University, Deptarment of Anthropology.

Prosper, K., McMillan, L. J., Davis, A. A., & Moffitt, M. (2011). Returning to *netukulimk*: Mi'kmaq cultural and spiritual connections with resource stewardship and self-governance. *The International Indigenous Policy Journal, 2*(4). Retrieved from http://ir.lib.uwo.ca/ iipj/vol2/iss4/7.

Pulsifer, M., & Nette, S. (1995). History, status and present distribution of moose in Nova Scotia. *Alces, 31*, 209–219.

Richardson, B., & Erasmus, G. (Eds.). (1989). *Drumbeat: Anger and renewal in Indian country*. Toronto, ON: Summerhill Press and The Assembly of First Nations.

Royal Commission on Aboriginal Peoples (RCAP). (1996). *Report of the Royal Commission on Aboriginal Peoples*. Ottawa: Canada Communications Group.

Royal Commission on the Donald Marshall, Jr., Prosecution. (1989). *Digest of findings and recommendations*. Halifax, NS: Canadian Cataloguing in Publication Data.

R. v. Marshall, 3 Supreme Court of Canada. (1999). Retrieved from http://scc.lexum.org/en/1999/1999scr3-533/1999scr3-533.html.

R. v. Sparrow, 1 Supreme Court of Canada. (1990). Retrieved from http://scc.lexum.org/en/1990/1990scr1-1075/1990scr1-1075.html.

Simon v. The Queen, 2 Supreme Court of Canada. (1985). Retrieved from http://scc.lexum.org/en/1985/1985scr2-387/1985scr2-387.html.

Smith, L. (1999). *Decolonizing methodologies: Research and Indigenous peoples*. London, UK: Zed Books.

Stiegman, M., Prosper, K., & McMillan, L. J. (2013) *Seeking* netukulimk: *Mi'kmaq knowledge, culture, capacity and empowerment*. Film. Canada. Retrieved from http://sites.stfx.ca/anthropology/crc-jane-mcmillan.

United Nations Rio Declaration on Environment and Development (UNDRIP). (1992). A/CONF.151/26(Vol.I). Retrieved January 2, 2011, from http://www.un.org/documents/ga/conf151/aconf15126-1annex1.htm.

United Nations Permanent Forum on Indigenous Issues (UNPFII). (2007). *United Nations declaration on the rights of Indigenous peoples*. New York: Secretariat of the Permanent Forum on Indigenous Issues. Retrieved January 2, 2011, from http://www.un.org/esa/socdev/unpfii/en/declaration.html.

Warry, W. (2007). *Ending denial: Understanding Aboriginal issues*. Peterborough, ON: Broadview Press.

Wicken, W. C. (2004). *Mi'kmaq treaties on trial: History, land and Donald Marshall Junior*. Toronto: University of Toronto Press.

TWELVE

You Are Where You Eat

Developing an Online Tool for Community Food Mapping

Jon Corbett, Casey Hamilton, and Shayne Wright

Introduction

This chapter describes on an ongoing community–university research project that seeks to engage the Central Okanagan community in local food security dialogue using a web-based mapping tool. This project represents a collaborative undertaking between researchers at the University of British Columbia Okanagan (UBCO), the Central Okanagan Food Policy Council (referred to in this chapter as the Council), and the British Columbia Interior Health Authority, as well as a number of local, food-related organizations, farms, markets, and outreach groups. The Central Okanagan represents an interface community, where the rural (producer) and urban (consumer) population exists side by side. Increasingly people want to better understand how and where their food is grown, processed, and sold in order to improve access to, and make informed decisions about, local food. This collaborative project seeks to support these processes by providing a web-based mapping tool that displays information, discussion, and media about local food through a Google Maps interface. "Experts" in the field do not populate the information provided through the map; rather a framework has been developed to enable community members themselves to share their own knowledge and experiences about local food and its availability.

The intent of the project is to stimulate conversation by asking members of the public probing questions related to their food system: Where is our food available? How is it produced? Is our food healthy? Is our food affordable? What influences our choice of foods? Through the map interface, community members can share their own views and begin a dialogue on relevant issues. At the outset of this project, we envisioned the information gained through the mapping to possibly play a role in supplementing traditional government and corporate sources. As well, we thought the dialogue between different community members would help them engage in food-related social action through obtaining a better understanding their food system.

The project began with the Council recognizing the pressing need to support and develop local food security dialogue in the region using web-based tools. It approached the Centre for Social, Spatial and Economic Justice (referred to in this chapter as the Centre) at UBCO for technical support. Together they identified that online mapping tools would be an innovative approach to addressing this issue. Both groups crafted a project proposal and were awarded a Research Interest Group grant through the Institute for Healthy Living and Chronic Disease Prevention (IHLCDP). The IHLCDP funds seek to "support research that links communities with the university with a focus on building research capacity and creating and using new knowledge in ways that benefit individuals, families and communities" (IHLCDP, 2011). The objectives of the IHLCDP grants were aligned with some of the goals of the Council. The Council was a relatively new group and was seeking opportunities for collaboration for a number of reasons. Partnering with UBCO enabled the Council to contribute directly to addressing the issue of local food security. Local data and research is an important tool for food-policy councils, allowing them to demonstrate the level of food insecurity and the current state of the local food system. This information helps to direct the work that a food-policy council does. It may determine what policies/services/systems are missing, which may be acting as barriers, and which support local, sustainable food systems and food access for everyone. This information also supports public education and helps the public understand through relevant, local examples the issues of concern regarding the food system. This public education may lead to specific and concrete areas of improvement in a community.

The Community Food Mapping Project was launched in spring of 2010 and persists at this writing. The specific focus of the project is twofold. First, it includes an "action" component, for which an intuitive and interactive web-based tool has been designed, developed, and deployed to support community engagement in local food issues. This has involved an evaluation phase that was designed to improve the usability of the tool. The project also includes a second, more theoretical, research component that explores key questions surrounding the social implications of engaging citizens using the Geospatial Web (the academic term used to describe the range of new web-based mapping tools including Google Maps, Google Earth, Bing Maps, etc.). This includes examining the implications, opportunities, and impacts of combining online mapping with the efforts of the Central Okanagan Food Policy Council, as well as asking how community mapping supports the Council in its ultimate goal of engaging the public in food issues, and what this engagement actually looks like: is it meaningful engagement, is it long term, and does it influence and shape people's views, beliefs, and ultimate behaviour?

This paper will present on both aspects of the project, in other words both the action and the theoretical components. It will further describe the process of project partners negotiating the project agenda, methods, and evaluation, and finding common ground in the collaborative research process.

Background

Local food and the Geoweb

Local food movements are swiftly gaining traction in the imagination of people throughout North America (Kingsolver, Kingsolver, & Hopp, 2007; Mackinnon & Smith, 2007; Nabhan, 2002). They can be referred to as "movements" because they involve the planned political, cultural, and social organization of individuals, groups, and increasingly whole communities. They are often regional in focus and incorporate both rural and urban spaces (Feenstra, 2002). The roots of local food are in neighbourhood community gardens, farmers' markets, family farms, and roadside stands (Pollan, 2006). The overall movement aims to distinguish between the benefits of locally sourced food versus the industrial food system that operates on an international scale and is dominated by multinational companies (Pollan, 2006). Micheal Pollan (2006) in *The Omnivore's Dilemma* potently describes the implications of North America's move away from local food, illustrating the impact on the health of both the environment and ourselves. Large-scale agriculture or agribusiness has been associated with impoverishing farmers, contributing to climate change, contaminating food with toxins, and reducing both the diversity of food types and cuisine (Halweil, 2004; Nabhan, 2002). Advocates of local food suggest that eating closer to home is redefining our spaces, relationships, and seasonal senses (Halweil, 2004). In all these respects, food movements further promise to rethink our relationships with fellow community members, the local ecosystem, and, above all, eating. An essential component of the emergent local-food movement is the need to communicate its significance to the general public, to support a dialogue related to local-food issues, as well as to improve access to and make informed decisions about locally produced and processed food.

Our project seeks to support these processes by providing an interactive and community-developed web-based mapping tool that displays information, discussion, and media about local food. To understand the significance of maps as a tool to engage communities in social issues, we must first understand the broader field and development of community mapping and participatory geographic information systems (PGIS).

Community mapping

Community mapping can be viewed as a critical movement within the field of cartography. Academics in the field examine how maps most often reflect the views, biases, and perspectives of more powerful groups within society. Despite forces that have served to exclude non-experts from map making—including the requirements for a knowledge of the science of cartography, a high level of numeracy, and access to printing—a growing number of local communities and community organizations have begun to harness the potential power associated with maps for their own gain. This popular evolution of community mapping has occurred alongside the academic discourse about mainstream mapping and cartography's tendency to reflect the interests of the powerful groups in society and maintain existing power structures (Corbett, 2009; Elwood, 2002; Harley, 1988; Harley, 1989; Wood, 1992).

Community maps represent a socially or culturally distinct understanding of landscape and include information that is excluded from mainstream maps, which usually represent the views of the dominant sectors of society. This style of map can therefore pose alternatives to the languages and images of the existing power structures. Community maps often differ considerably from mainstream maps in content, appearance, and methodology.

There are numerous reasons for a community to initiate a community-mapping project; this paper draws on three: to increase the capacity within communities, to help communities draw attention to and communicate important matters internally and with external agencies, and to enable communities to apply pressure for change. These three points are discussed briefly below.

To increase capacity

Perhaps one of the greatest strengths of community mapping is the ability of the mapping process itself to help build community cohesion (Alcorn, 2001; Corbett & Keller, 2005) through providing a forum that brings together and unifies a community. This in turn can help a community sustain a sense of place and a connection to the land (Aberley, 1993; Chapin, 1998; Johnson, 1997; Stone, 1998).

To draw attention to and communicate important matters

The map-making process can also act as a focus for discussions that will assist participants in recognizing concerns and issues within the community. Discussions might raise community awareness about local and regional environmental issues (Flavelle, 1996) or amplify community capacity to manage and protect lands (Poole, 1995). During the course of these discussions, a community can formulate a common vision, which in turn may help participants develop an effective community-based plan for future development (Harrington, 1995). Community mapping is not about being an expert cartographer but about community building. Once a community has a clear understanding of its own identity and a vision for the future, it will be in a stronger position to effectively communicate and deal with external agencies, and it will be more likely to be involved in planning for its own future (Victoria International Development Education Association [VIDEA], 1998).

To apply pressure for change

Community maps have become a tool with which communities can seek recognition and inclusion in governance and decision-making processes, particularly in reference to land and natural resource management (Aberley, 1994; Fox, 1994; Sirait, Prasodjo, Podger, Flavelle, & Fox, 1994). At times they have also succeeded in empowering grassroots efforts to hold governments accountable. In this sense, map making is a form of political action (Alcorn, 2001) that has the capacity to initiate social change.

Participatory geographic information systems

Digital computing and geographic information systems (GIS) rose to prominence in cartography during the early 1990s. A number of academics questioned the potential for these technologies to support community issues (Rundstrom, 1991; Taylor, 1997). Others were optimistic. Brian Harley (1990), one of the world's leading academics at the time, wrote that digital mapping technology delivered, "an unprecedented opportunity to create alternative maps of the world we live in but also the opportunity of reintegrating cartography through linking of all stages of information gathering and processing. No longer need the product be divorced from the world that it is mapping" (p. 13). This reunion of map users with intimate local knowledge of real-world subjects suggests links to community mapping. The PGIS movement grew with a distinct vision of a locally based cartography woven together with modern mapping and communication technologies, which today forms the basis for many current community-mapping projects.

Early adopters of PGIS included a diverse range of community groups advocating a variety of local issues including local revitalization of rental housing and planning collaboratively for neighbourhood redevelopment and local service provision (Craig & Elwood, 1998). These cases made use of maps to gather, organize, and analyze local information. Some groups, representing economically depressed or ethnically segregated areas, produced maps that emphasized aspects of their community either ignored or misrepresented by existing maps, such as parks, libraries, community gardens, and other resources (Dunn, 2007; Elwood, 2006). Other work challenged government information by tracking and mapping statistics at the community level that are not otherwise reflected in municipal- or regional-level information. (Craig, Harris, & Weiner, 2002).

In the last ten years, the increase in Internet capability continues to change the shape and direction of community mapping, in particular the development of what is increasingly referred to as the Geospatial Web, or Geoweb. The Geoweb is the geographic platform for Web 2.0 digital social-networking applications; it includes applications such as Google Earth, Google Maps, Microsoft's Bing Maps, and other location-based Internet technologies (Cisler, 2007; Scharl & Tochterman, 2007). Previous dependency on GIS expertise is challenged in the Geoweb model, where everyone is potentially a contributor, producer, and consumer of geographic content (Haklay, Singleton, & Parker, 2008; Sui, 2008). Geoweb-based technologies are considered more democratic due to their ability to enhance citizen access and participation (Crampton, 2009; Dunn, 2007; Tulloch, 2008). The Geoweb has achieved broad acceptance thanks to its widespread availability on the Internet, its platform independence, and because it is superficially "free" to use, although there are associated costs. For example, some services claim ownership over data collected through their systems, such as Google My Maps, and preserve the right to reuse it (Klinkenberg, 2007; Zook & Graham, 2007). Another reason for the Geoweb's popularity is its ability to aggregate and present user-generated digital content—referred to as crowdsourcing (Hudson-Smith, Crooks, Gibin, Milton, & Batty, 2009) and specifically in the field of geography as volunteered geographic information (VGI) (Goodchild, 2007). This allows for a range of community voices and opinions to be shared, potentially reflecting the inherent heterogeneity within communities and supporting many-to-many communication (Ruesch & Bateson, 1987).

The extent to which this work embodies a people's cartography, where the local citizen and community become empowered to act, remains a key research question. As noted, each project incorporates its own politics, players, and process (Elwood, 2006, 2010), and individual findings can vary widely (Kyem, 2002, 2004), often with contradictory outcomes.

It has been argued that community mapping, sometimes in partnership with organizations, is a way for local communities to express their understanding of home spaces and lands, and thus for these views and understandings to be shared with others. What is interesting is that maps can effectively represent complex spatial relationships that may be understood by audiences in varying ways given their backgrounds, contexts, and personal situations. The situated reading of maps by viewers can be seen as another example where location matters, reinforcing the ideas underlying volunteered geographic information and participatory Geoweb. What is unclear is the extent to which this mapping constitutes effective public participation in informed decision making rather than simply reflecting the position of the mappers.

Substantial research has not yet addressed the societal implications of online map making by the public. The goal of this partnership in research is to engage the Central Okanagan community in a dialogue about their local-food system and to establish an exchange of information between researchers and the wider community on the topic of community food security. By developing a participatory Internet-mapping website with our researchers at UBCO, this research study seeks to contribute to an understanding of both effective development of Geoweb mapping tools as well as effective citizen participation using these tools. The remainder of this chapter focuses on a community-based research project that took place in the Central Okanagan, British Columbia.

Central Okanagan case study

A key ideology guiding the project is that of improving community food security in the region. Food security can be understood to exist "when all citizens obtain a safe, personally acceptable, nutritious diet through a sustainable food system that maximizes healthy choices, community self-reliance and equal access for everyone" (Hamm & Bellows, 2003). Generally, food systems have followed the model of globalization such that local production is quickly becoming less viable. At the same time, the increasing focus on food as a commodity has meant that more people cannot afford to buy enough food. Using a community food-security lens, we follow the food system to understand how many of the issues and problems are in fact socially produced. Weaknesses in the system may not be immediately apparent in the Central Okanagan, which is generally associated with themes of affluence and fine living.

Over the past 80 years, the Central Okanagan has become well-known in Canada for its tree fruit and wine industries. For the past ten years, the tree-fruit industry has been in dramatic decline; between 1991 and 2006, the land devoted to growing apples decreased from 3501 to 1806 hectares (Weicker, 2007). This trend is similar for all other fruit-tree crops including pear, peach, cherry, plum, and apricot. In contrast, the amount of land devoted to growing grapes has dramatically increased; over the same period the area used to grow grapes increased from 249 to 1110 hectares (Regional District of Central Okanagan [RDCO], 2009). These grapes are primarily produced to supply boutique wineries. This move to grapes is substantially more profitable for the farmer; furthermore it reduces the requirement for the Okanagan orchardists to compete with the much larger agribusiness-style fruit industries in Washington and other fruit-producing states in the US (Weicker, 2007). However, it also means that the Central Okanagan is beginning to move away from staple food-crop production to that of luxury, high-cost items.

Local illustrations can help us to contextualize the issue of community food security here in the Central Okanagan using the food-security continuum. As a first line of defence when problems emerge locally, most communities will implement community food banks and soup kitchens for emergency food provision, and here in the Central Okanagan, a number of communities have done so with determination. To move beyond the need for increasing short-term relief, the next phase in developing improved community food security is capacity building. Community food sources may include community kitchens where large amounts of food can be gathered and processed communally, as well as community gardens where public land is assigned to responsible local resident gardeners. The final phase of the food-security continuum is food-system redesign. Existing research shows direct links between our "built environment" and community food security through factors like access to transportation and transit or low-income neighbourhoods where fewer stores exist, areas that are increasingly referred to as "food deserts" (British Columbia Provincial Health Services Authority [BCPHSA], 2011). These issues are particularly relevant in the local region where outlying rural communities lack transportation options and an economic base to support the viability of local retailers.

Community mapping has been proposed as a way to gather and record local knowledge and to focus discussions on a topic, as well as to strengthen community cohesion. Community food mapping is a tool that organizations like the Council may use to move forward their work in food-system redesign. Community mapping can be used as a tool to visually demonstrate the existing local food system and promote awareness of alternatives like local and urban agriculture and the integration of food into new community designs. In Western societies, the issue of hunger and food banks has often dominated food-security dialogue; however, increasingly the debate has expanded to include nutrition, sustainability, and social justice. At the outset of this project, we envisioned the information gained through this mapping to possibly play a role in supplementing traditional government and corporate sources, as well as helping engage citizens in food-related social action through obtaining a better understanding of their food system.

Research

This portion of the project is focused on two compenents: *action research* and *theoretical research.*

Action research

The action component of this research project involves the design, development, and deployment of an intuitive and interactive web-based mapping tool, called Geolive. Geolive is a web-based participatory mapping tool developed at University of British Columbia Okanagan; it combines Google Maps and Joomla!—an open-source content-management system. The application allows users to create and share their own spatial information using a dynamic map-based interface. Geolive enables registered users to drop information markers onto a map, turn different data layers on and off, as well as take part in "instant messenger" type discussions (see Figure 12.1 below). The main focus of the action research agenda is design-centric. In other words how, from a usability perspective, can an online mapping tool be designed and developed to best support the active participation of users in the contribution of location-based content.

Theoretical research

The theoretical component of this research project explores questions relating to the validity and usability of the Geoweb for engaging citizens in local food issues, and it explores how a group of undergraduate

Figure 12.1: Geolive user interface. The left side of the image shows the layer tab, discussion tab, and discussion marker pin that can be dropped directly onto the map.

students uses the online mapping tool to deepen their understanding of food-security issues. This analysis also speculates about the longer-term implications, opportunities, and impacts of combining online mapping with the efforts of the Central Okanagan Food Policy Council.

Methods

This project has used a series of interdisciplinary research methods closely associated with participatory-action research. We have specifically employed community-friendly research methods wherever possible, including during the choice of research questions and subsequent analysis. We have used a series of mixed research methods to analyze the collaborative mapping process through the deployment of surveys, follow-up interviews, participant observation of mapping sessions, and analysis of the mapping participation to better understand the usability and the impact of the project. Each of these methods has been used to gather data that describes participant experiences in community mapping on the Geoweb, and to assess impacts from this participation (Parker, 2006; Schuurman, 2000). This research provides a significant opportunity to better understand and characterize the nature of participation using the Geoweb.

Project process

In addition to the three-member research team representing the main project partners, six community members were invited to join an advisory committee. This group represented local food-security leaders from the Central Okanagan region (i.e., Kelowna, Peachland, West Kelowna, and Lake Country) as well as varying community interests such as municipal government, academia, public health advocacy, local-food production, and non-governmental organizations. The committee convened twice and provided specific direction for the project.

To assess the usability of the Geolive tool and to contribute local food-related information to the map, a second group of participants was invited to collaborate in the research. Sixty-five first-year geography students participated during an agriculture and food security lecture (see Figure 12.2 below). They attended an optional in-class focus session in which they discussed the local food system and during which they were introduced to the Community Food Mapping Geolive website. The online map contained map data layers that displayed components of the local food system; these layers were derived from data provided by the BC Interior Health Authority.

Student participants were guided through a collaborative mapping and discussion exercise that resulted in them directly contributing to discussions about maps. Afterward, they were asked to complete a survey questionnaire. The survey questions sought to establish the technical literacy of the students with respect to interactive media and online mapping. Other questions asked them to describe and evaluate their experience using the Geolive mapping tool and to explain their perceptions of the issues and the information presented. Map themes, including Agricultural Land Reserve and Food Access, were created to provide

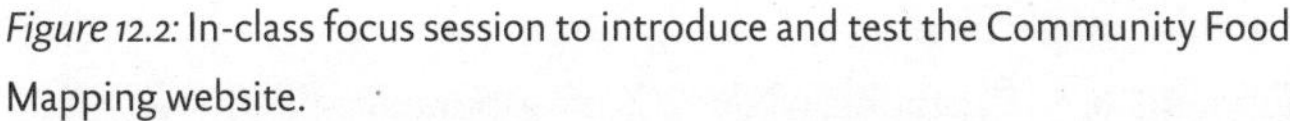

Figure 12.2: In-class focus session to introduce and test the Community Food Mapping website.

cultural, social, and economic context, as well as geographic location, to the issues. The material contributed to the map-based discussion, as well as survey information gathered through the in-class survey, comprises the key data set that informs this paper.

Initial findings

As identified earlier, at the time of this writing, the research project is still ongoing. Therefore the results presented in this paper are only initial findings.

Action research

Geolive was designed to support and encourage volunteered geographic information from the public in the form of geolocated "arguments" or dialogue. The "action" component of this research project seeks to examine the design, development, and usability of the project's Geolive tool. The results of this section are drawn from the in-class survey detailed above.

The survey analyzed the baseline computer-use capacity of students involved in the in-class evaluation. Survey results showed that participants were overwhelmingly comfortable using Internet technologies: 62 out of 65 respondents used Facebook; while 70% of respondents identified that the Internet was their principle tool for accessing information. However, there was an apparent disconnect between the participants' use of the Internet to access information and their willingness to contribute their own views: 73% of respondents did not contribute to online discussions, while 94% never contributed their views using online mapping tools.

Despite the participants' lack of experience adding information to a map, they quickly became comfortable with the Geolive interface. Within the first few minutes of using the tool, students could complete basic tasks. For example, 86% of participants using the map and associated layers could locate the closest food store to where they lived on the map. Using a Likert scale of 5, over 80% of survey responses also identified that the Geolive interface, login function, ease of use, visual quality, and user instructions were either extremely good (5) or very good (4). Qualitative responses identifying specific strengths of the map ranged from expressions of the user interface ("Simple to use") and Geolive functionality ("The interface is very interactive"), through to the potential uses for the map ("Easy access to big amount of information in the same place" and "Identifying where food is available and where it isn't").

During the mapping exercise, we observed that several of the students were able to find an existing discussion marker on the website and begin posting replies before even receiving instructions from the investigators. These replies appeared in "real time" on the projector screen before the entire class. This irreverent introduction did confirm the possibility for the tool to function at a basic level without substantial instruction. We were able to build upon the participants' familiarity with the functionality of Google Maps, and many students were able to start using the tool before hearing any real explanation of how to do so. Without directions on the "topic of conversation" and time to select an appropriate map location, these initial contributions lacked substance and relevance, yet they confirmed that the tool was relatively easy to use for this group of participants, as designers had hoped. The nature of the contributions became more focused and serious as students were asked to sign in and participate in a set of mapping exercises designed to provide a context for the discussions and teach students how to the use the mapping tool.

When asked to identify specific weaknesses of the Community Food Mapping Geolive website, participants identified usability bugs, for example, with "Editing markers, sometimes the user interface freezes when you drop markers." These bugs were indicative of the level of the Geolive development at the time of the initial testing. However, a large number of responses also identified that a lot of the data (provided by the Interior Health Authority) was incomplete or wrongly situated. For example, the "Save on Foods and other health food market in orchard park are missing."

The survey went on to ask the participants what would encourage them to continue to use the site in the future. Interestingly a large number of responses identified that if the site contained up-to-date information regarding available produce, they would be far more likely to revisit the site. As one respondent noted, "if it was more popular and had things such as sale produce or any information on deals at grocery stores or restaurants, this could be very helpful." In other words they identified the tool not as a mechanism to engage with other community members and discuss local food-security issues, but rather a simple directory to access information about cheap food. More than likely this is reflective of student priorities related to accessing affordable food.

When asked to comment on what would prevent them using the tool in the future, a number of respondents felt that it had little attraction for them at this juncture. One respondent captures this view: "There is no real purpose right now—I can use the city business guide and get the same thing with more description." However, this is because they are focused more on what the website can provide them directly rather than on whether the tool has a broader potential to help them engage in local food-related issues. Other responses to the question focused on more technical issues, for example "not iPhone accessible, glitches, spammers, needs moderators, people aren't that interested in this stuff, better integration with Google Maps."

Examining the responses to the "action" component of the research, and specifically the usability of Geolive, we feel that a large number of participants shaped their responses around how they currently interact with and understand the Internet. Many respondents' expectations are that the Community Food Mapping website is shaped around their immediate needs, as well as around the purposes for which they most commonly use the Internet. In many cases, they would like to see the site be designed to make cheap food more easily accessible and so would use the site as a tool to passively access information. They often did not see the mapping website as a tool that would enable them to contribute to discussion and, on a much broader level, consciously attempt to bring about social change. However, when we examined the latter half of the survey that explores the more theoretical agenda of the research, as well as examined the discussions that were posted on the map, a different picture emerges.

Theoretical research

The "theoretical" component of this research project explores questions relating to the validity and usability of the Geoweb for engaging citizens in local-food issues. In particular, it is interested in exploring the potential of the Geoweb to support the critical participation of a group of undergraduate students using the online mapping tool and assessing how this involvement can deepen their understanding of food-security issues. Participation is one of the key aspects of analysis across different parts of this research process. This approach is recognized in specific development practices such as Participatory Learning and Action that places community members at the centre of the decision-making process (Corbett & Keller, 2005). "A participatory mapping project that is well designed and thoughtfully carried out can combine activism, local knowledge and community conceptions of place to define, depict, justify, and... claim space and counter the power of outsiders" (Dana, 2010).

The survey directly asked students to comment on what they learned from the exercise about agricultural and food access issues in the Central Okanagan. A number of respondents commented on the lack of available food options on campus. Responses included identifying the composition of food sources available to students ("There are many more fast food options close to the university than grocery stores") as well as the poor food selection ("There are not a lot of options for students"). In one response this was presented almost as a revelation ("I have realized how there is 0 access to healthy food for students living on residence at UBCO"). When we examine the actual discussion that occurred on the map during the in-class session, it is to possible see an active discussion emerging around the "food on campus" issue (see Figure 12.3 below).

The conversation openly discusses radical, as well as politically charged, issues. One student notes, "We need more food places on

Figure 12.3: Map discussion related to campus food posted during the in-class session.

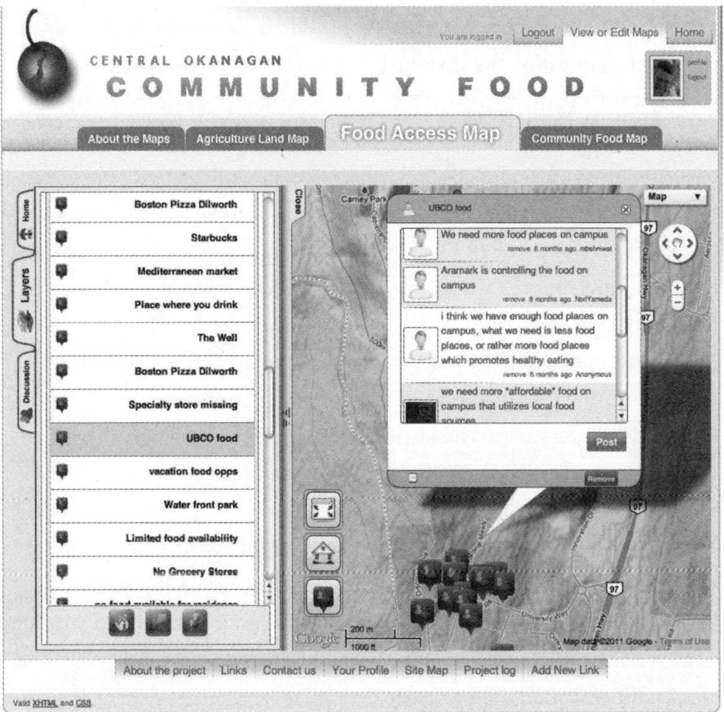

campus." Another immediately responds that the campus-services provider too tightly controls the food on campus. The discussion then moves to where another student states, "I think we have enough food places on campus, what we need is less food places, or rather more food places which promotes healthy eating." This response in turn brings up the point of affordable food with a lament being made that the only reasonably priced food is from a fast-food outlet. The final comment is "point taken." This is a recognition of the truth of the discussion that food is expensive, poor quality, and limited in choice, and possibly the changing of that student's opinion of the need to buy healthier and more local food. This conversation is indicative that, as Dana (2010) notes, the Geoweb perhaps does have the potential to live up to other community-mapping initiatives and "combine activism, local knowledge and community conceptions of place to define, depict, justify, and control territory in a way that can effectively claim space and counter the power of outsiders" (p. 2125). Through online dialogue, supported by the Geolive tool, users are beginning to discuss, then question, and finally openly express views that directly question the sustainability and fairness of the hyper-local food system. In other words, it lays the foundation for critical reflection and engagement in dialogue about these issues, which in turn are a requisite for social action. Because the project is still relatively new, and because social change is a long-term process, it remains unclear how long-term these changes might be, or if they may lead to influence and shape people's views, beliefs, and ultimately behaviour. However, the results from the survey do suggest that this may be the case.

As with the findings in the "action" component of the research, we can see that the dialogue is motivated by the fact that these issues in particular are relevant to the respondents. Furthermore, even if they were not considered relevant before the students came into class that day, after engaging in a map-based discussion related to food on campus, when they left the class, the issue had become relevant to them. This is likely because this issue in particular has an influence on their daily lives. Indeed, we cannot expect people with any interest in the issue to critically engage in discussion. So, in response to our opening question asking how community mapping supports the Council in its ultimate goal of engaging the public in food issues, we can definitively answer that the mapping tool clearly raises awareness of local-food issues even as it provides an online space where people can interact and share their views on the issues. However, from the research results, we cannot speculate whether or not the views and opinions expressed on the site by these undergraduate students are long term, or judge whether or not these views have the ability to influence and shape other map users' views, beliefs, and ultimate behaviour. Furthermore, these results lead us to ask whether or not other groups (i.e., respondents that are not students, youth, Internet users, etc.) might engage with local-food system issues using these Geoweb tools in a way that reflects a different set of priorities and experiences and thus participate in a different set of discussions related to widely different themes—perhaps the nature and content of the dialogue is consistent across the groups. This research area will become a focus in the next stages of the project.

Linking the "action" and "theoretical" components of this research gives some insight into how the Geolive tool might be used in the future by the Council. As previously stated, the tool is relatively easy to use; however, many student participants noted that they did not see any immediate practical purpose for contributing their food-related information on the map. Nevertheless, with some guidance from the facilitators, the users did engage in meaningful online dialogue about their views of the food system and important local food-related issues. This has important implications for the Council, as it indicates that the Geolive tool has potential to be used for strategic purposes. The Council has acknowledged that the tool may prove useful for consultations when purposefully engaging the community for their feedback about specific food system–related topics. Through this consultation process, the public would be participating in a meaningful way, and would, through that process, become more aware and involved in local food-related issues. The Council would then use the information collected to inform any future actions by the Council. In conclusion, the Council sees the Geolive map playing a role in the future engagement of the public on local food-related issues, and this pilot project helped significantly in the creation and crafting of the tool in a way that supported the Council's needs.

Conclusions and next steps

This research project is ongoing. With respect to the collaboration between university staff and a community group, the partnership was a success. The Council was able to build on its ability to conduct meaningful work in the Central Okanagan with its community constituents through the partnership with UBCO. At the same time, the university researchers have been able to provide a resource to a local organization—thus making the university more relevant in the eyes of the community—and at the same time perform graduate research. This project has helped raise the profile of the Council and has given them a useful tool with which to engage the public in local food-security issues and improve the local-food system. The Council will learn the skills required to do basic maintenance of the Community Food Mapping website, and succession planning will occur toward the end of the research project. The Council will continue to use the Community Food Mapping website in order to engage the public on other local-food issues. Through this collaboration, a positive relationship has formed, and there is an appetite for further collaboration.

The future research direction will focus on wider participant engagement in the project and include an assessment of the impact from this participation using a mixed-methods approach and a modified survey. The project will include participants from the public recruited through a media launch and public promotional campaign. The collaborators plan to have members of the public use the website then ask them to complete an online questionnaire based loosely on the survey that was used with the student participants discussed above. We also plan to follow up with the community advisory committee members during semi-structured interviews toward the conclusion of the research project. Presenting to the advisory committee the project website in its final form to elicit feedback will serve to provide insights into the research questions and, at the same time, provide an opportunity to explore the advisory group's perceptions of the mapping website that they first helped to conceptualize. This cyclical research design again draws on participatory-action methodologies: having helped to plan the project, the advisory participants can now observe the mapping project "action" and reflect upon what they have seen, feeding their insight back into the next round of mapping and research.

Authors' note

This paper could not have been written without the financial support of the Institute for Healthy Living and Chronic Disease Prevention, the Work Studies program at UBCO, and the Geomatics for Informed Decision Making (GEOIDE) network Project 41. Furthermore, we would like to take the opportunity to thank the British Columbia Interior Health Authority for providing us with spatial data of the food services in the Central Okanagan, our steering committee for advice and direction, and the first-year students in Geography 129 (Human Geography: Resources, Development, and Society) for testing the site.

References

Aberley, D. (1993). *Boundaries of home: Mapping for local empowerment.* Gabriola Island, BC: New Society Publishers.

———. (1994). *Futures by Design.* Gabriola Island, BC: New Society Publishers.

Alcorn, J. B. (2001). *Borders, rules & and governance: Mapping to catalyse changes in policy and management.* London, UK: International Institute for Environment and Development.

British Columbia Provincial Health Services Authority (BCPHSA). (2011). Planting seeds for solutions: Building communities with food in mind. Retrieved May 29, 2015, from http://www.phsa.ca/HealthProfessionals/Population-Public-Health/Food-Security/default.htm.

Chapin, M. (1998). Mapping and the ownership of information. *The Common Property Resource Digest, 45*, 6–7.

Cisler, S. (2007). *Open geography: New tools and new initiatives.* Santa Clara, CA: Center for Science Technology and Society, Santa Clara University.

Corbett, J. M. (2009). *Good practices in participatory mapping.* Rome, IT: The International Fund for Agricultural Development.

Corbett, J. M., & Keller, C. P. (2005). An analytical framework to examine empowerment associated with participatory geographic information systems (PGIS). *Cartographica: The International Journal for Geographic Information and Geovisualization, 40*(4), 91–102.

Craig, W. J., & Elwood, S. A. (1998). How and why community groups use maps and geographic information. *Cartography and Geographic Information Systems, 25*(2), 95–104.

Craig, W. J., Harris, T. M., & Weiner, D. (2002). *Community participation and geographic information systems.* London and New York: Taylor & Francis.

Crampton, J. (2009). Cartography maps 2.0. *Progress in Human Geography, 3*(1), 91–100.

Dana, P. H. (2010). Participatory mapping. In *Encyclopedia of Geography* (pp. 2125–2126). London, UK: Sage Publications.

Dunn, C. (2007). Participatory GIS: A people's GIS? *Progress in Human Geography, 31*(5), 617–638.

Elwood, S. (2002). GIS use in community planning: A multidimensional analysis of empowerment. *Environment and Planning A, 34*, 905–922.

———. (2006). Critical issues in participatory GIS: Deconstructions, reconstructions, and new research directions. *Transactions in GIS, 10*, 693–708.

———. (2010). Geographic information science: Emerging research on the societal implications of the geospatial web. *Progress in Human Geography, 34*(3), 349–357.

Feenstra, G. (2002). Creating space for sustainable food systems: Lessons from the field. *Agriculture and Human Values, 19*, 99–106.

Flavelle, A. (1996). *Community mapping handbook.* Vancouver, BC: Lone Pine Foundation.

Fox, J. (1994). Spatial information and ethnoecology: Case studies from Indonesia, Nepal, and Thailand. *East-West Center Environment Series, 38*, 38.

Goodchild, M. F. (2007). Citizens as sensors: The world of volunteered geography. *GeoJournal, 69*(4), 211–221.

Haklay, M., Singleton, A., & Parker, C. (2008). Web mapping 2.0: The neogeography of the GeoWeb. *Geography Compass, 2*(6), 2011–2039.

Halweil, B. (2004). *Eat here: Reclaiming homegrown pleasures in a global supermarket.* Washington, DC: Worldwatch Institute.

Hamm, M. W., & Bellows, A. C. (2003). Community food security: Background and future directions. *Journal of Nutrition Education and Behavior, 35*(1), 37–43.

Harley, J. B. (1988). Maps, knowledge and power. In D. Cosgrove (Ed.), *The iconography of landscape* (pp. 277–312). Cambridge, MA: Cambridge University Press.

———. (1989). Deconstructing the map. *Cartographica, 26*(2), 1–20.

———. (1990). Cartography, ethics and social theory. *Cartographica, 27*(2), 1–23.

Harrington, S. (1995). *Giving the land a voice: Mapping our home places.* Vancouver, BC: School of Community and Regional Planning, University of British Columbia.

Hudson-Smith, A., Crooks, A., Gibin, M., Milton, R., & Batty, M. (2009). Neo-Geography and Web 2.0: Concepts, tools and applications. *Journal of Location Based Services, 3*(2), 118–145.

The Institute for Healthy Living and Chronic Disease Prevention. (2011). Research interest group (RIG) grants. Retrieved May 29, 2015, from http://ihlcdp.ok.ubc.ca/opportunities/funding/rig.html.

Johnson, B. D. (1997). *The use of geographic information systems (GIS) by First Nations.* Vancouver, BC: School of Community and Regional Planning, University of British Columbia.

Kindon, S., Pain, R., & Kesby, M. (2008). Participatory action research. In *International Encyclopaedia of Human* Geography (pp. 90–95). New York: Elsevier.

Kingsolver, B., Kingsolver, C., & Hopp, S. (2007). *Animal, vegetable, miracle: A year of food for life.* New York: Harper Collins.

Klinkenberg, B. (2007). Geospatial technologies and the geographies of hope and fear. *Annals of the Association of American Geographers, 97*, 350–360.

Kyem, P. A. K. (2002). Examining the community empowerment process in public participation GIS applications. In *Public Participation GIS (PPGIS).* New Brunswick, NJ: Rutgers University.

———. (2004). Power, participation, and inflexible institutions: An examination of the challenges to community empowerment in participatory GIS applications. *Cartographica, 38*, 5–18.

Mackinnon, J., & Smith, B. (2007). *The 100 mile diet.* Toronto: Vintage.

Nabhan, G. P. (2002). *Coming home to eat: The pleasures and politics of local foods.* New York: W. W. Norton & Company.

Parker, B. (2006). Constructing community through maps? Power and praxis in community mapping. *Professional Geographer, 58*(4), 470–484.

Pollan, M. (2006). *The omnivore's dilemma: A natural history of four meals.* New York: Penguin Press.

Poole, P. (1995). Land-based communities, geomatics and biodiversity conservation. *Cultural Survival Quarterly, 18*(4), 74–76.

Regional District of Central Okanagan (RDCO). (2009). Regional District of Central Okanagan agricultural overview. Retrieved December 3, 2011, from http://www.investkelowna.com/documents/RDCentralOkAgOv.pdf.

Ruesch, J., & Bateson, G. (1987). *Communication: The social matrix of psychiatry.* New York: W. W. Norton and Company.

Rundstrom, R. A. (1991). Mapping, postmodernism, Indigenous people and the changing direction of North American cartography. *Cartographica: The International Journal for Geographic Information and Geovisualization, 28*(2), 1–12.

Scharl, A., & Tochterman, K. (2007). *The geospatial web: How geobrowsers, social software and the Web 2.0 are shaping the network society.* London, UK: Springer.

Schuurman, N. (2000). Trouble in the heartland: GIS and its critics in the 1990s. *Progress in Human Geography, 24*(4), 569.

Sirait, M. S., Prasodjo, S., Podger, N., Flavelle, A., & Fox, J. (1994). Mapping customary land in East Kalimantan, Indonesia: A tool for forest management. In J. Fox (Ed.), *Spatial information and ethnoecology: Case studies from Indonesia, Nepal, and Thailand* (pp. 1–14). Honolulu: East-West Center.

Stone, S. C. (1998). Information technologies, advocacy, and development: Resistance and backlash to industrial shrimp farming. *Cartography and Geographic Information Systems, 25*(2), 113–122.

Sui, D. (2008). The wikification of GIS and its consequences: Or Angelina Jolie's new tattoo and the future of GIS. *Computers, Environment and Urban Systems, 32*, 1–5.

Taylor, J. (1997) The emerging geographies of virtual worlds. *The Geographical Review, 87*, 172–92.

Tulloch, D. (2008). Is volunteered geographic information participation? *GeoJournal, 72*(3&4), 161–171.

Victoria International Development Education Association (VIDEA). (1998). On common ground. *Common Ground Mapping Newsletter, 1*, 1–2.

Weicker, F. (2007). *Developing the tree fruit industry in British Columbia report.* Prepared for the British Columbia Fruit Growers Association by Ference Weicker & Company Ltd, January 2007. Retrieved December 2011 from http://www.bcfga.com/files/file/tree%20fruit%20strategy.pdf.

Wood, D. (1992). *The power of maps.* New York: The Guildford Press.

Zook, M., & Graham, M. (2007). The creative reconstruction of the Internet: Google and the privatization of cyberspace and DigiPlace. *GeoForum, 38*, 1322–1343.

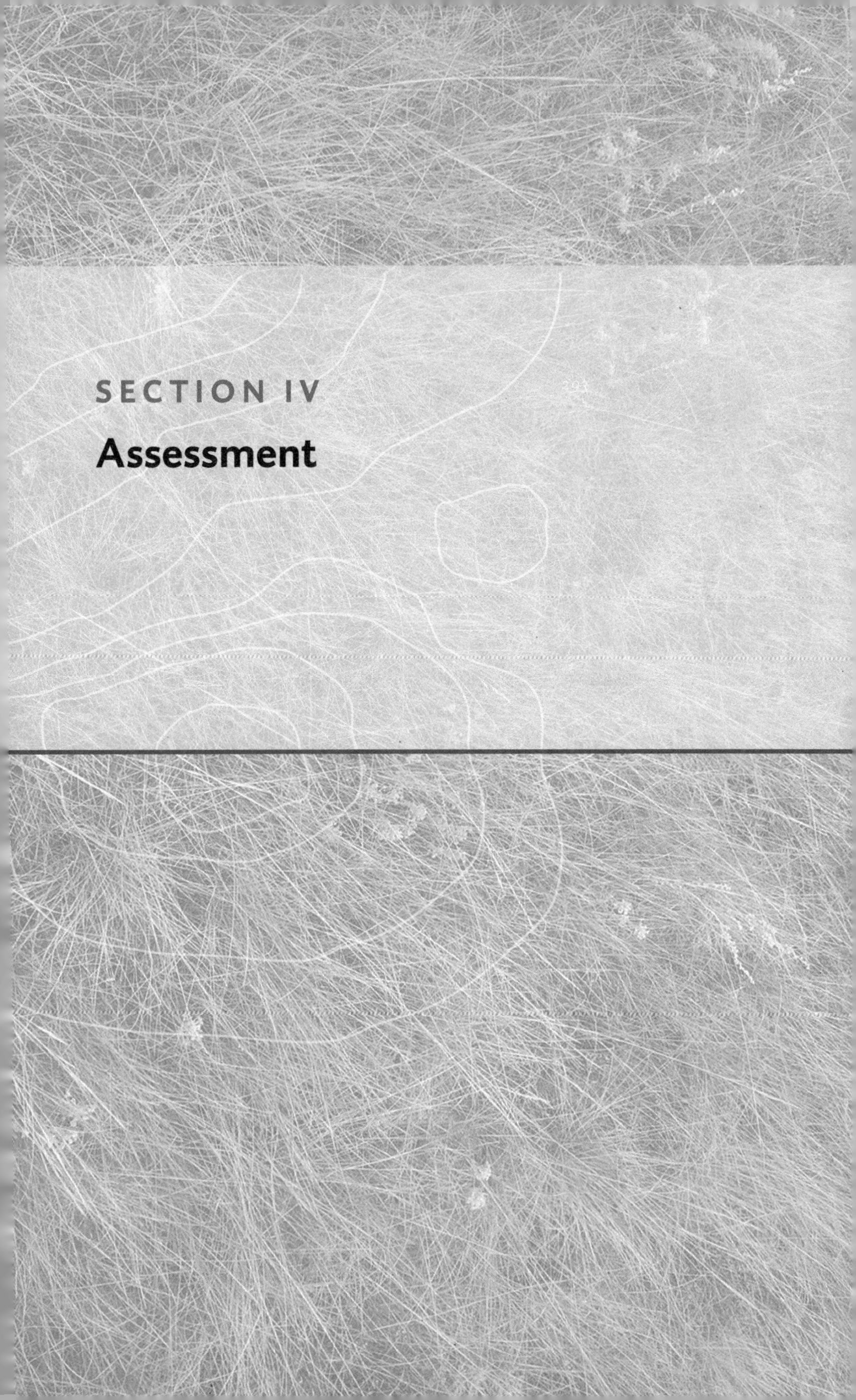

SECTION IV

Assessment

THIRTEEN

An Ecohealth Framework for Evaluating Source-Water Protection, Health, and Well-Being in the Otonabee River Basin

Karen Morrison, Karen Houle, and Meredith Carter

Introduction

Sustainability planning on a watershed basis poses a significant challenge due to the wide variety of competing issues, agendas, natural and political boundaries, and other concerns that require attention. In addition, it highlights the need to think critically about the relationship between human health and ecosystem dynamics in the long and short term, particularly if we are to accept McMichael's (2006) idea of population health as the "bottom line" of sustainability (p. 579). For this, we need ecosystems capable of supporting human health and well-being over the long term. An emerging philosophical framework for ecosystem approaches to health (ESAH, or ecohealth) currently being developed at the University of Guelph and elsewhere, provides a structured approach for evaluating programs that seek to integrate considerations of ecological change and human health and well-being.

In this paper, the Conceptual Resemblances in Ecosystem Approaches to Health framework (CR-ESAH) is applied to source-water protection planning in the Otonabee–Peterborough Source Protection Area (O–P SPA), which covers an area of approximately 3,365 square kilometres and includes the jurisdiction of the Otonabee Region Conservation Authority (ORCA), as well as portions of Haliburton County and northern Peterborough County. The O–P SPA provides the context for this community–university exploration of the ecohealth approach. It connects directly to sustainability and integrated planning through its underlying principles of collaboration and transdisciplinarity. It addresses a key issue for rural community sustainability: the need for inclusive multiscale dialogue and systemic thinking. The ESAH approach can engage the socio-cultural, economic, and ecological dimensions of rural sustainability that operate on multiple spatio-temporal scales.

That watersheds are settings for health and well-being is an idea that is currently being developed in the literature as a means of synthesizing our thinking about ecological systems with human ones (Bunch, Morrison, Parkes, & Venema, 2011; Millennium Ecosystem Assessment [MA], 2003; Parkes et al., 2010). It expands on the notion of "healthy settings" (e.g., healthy cities, healthy community) that has been developed in public health (Dooris, 2005). The watershed can be seen as the best unit for watershed management and source protection planning at a variety of spatio-temporal scales. Watersheds also provide an integrative forum for place-based activities that transcend the hydrological context, such as protection of migratory species and larger biomes (e.g., boreal forests).

Source-water protection in Ontario was adopted as part of the province's multi-barrier response to drinking-water protection following the Walkerton tragedy (O'Connor, 2002). It is fundamentally a program to protect municipal drinking-water supplies for human health implemented by the Ontario Ministry of the Environment, in partnership with municipalities and the province's conservation authorities on a watershed basis. Engaging municipal water users and watershed communities should be linked to Integrated Community Sustainability Planning (ICSP) processes where they exist. This paper presents the results of a community–university initiative that evaluates a regional source-water protection planning process using an ecohealth framework in order to both ground truth the ecohealth framework and to identify how real-world planning processes fit with a holistic academic concept focused on social-ecological systems and human health and well-being. The exchange of information and insight between researchers and practitioners is a key element of this work that will ultimately improve the quality of work in both areas.

Background

ORCA is one of 36 Ontario conservation authorities—local watershed-management agencies that deliver services and programs to protect and manage water and other natural resources in partnership with government, landowners, and other organizations. Conservation authorities promote an integrated watershed approach, balancing human, environmental, and economic needs. Conservation authorities are organized on a watershed basis (Conservation Ontario, 2001). ORCA, established in 1959, has a watershed jurisdiction of 1951 square kilometres, including the watersheds of three rivers and portions of several of the Kawartha Lakes, but it does not include the headwaters of these lakes, which form part of the larger Trent River Watershed. ORCA's vision is to provide leadership to achieve healthy watersheds, where human activity respects the need to conserve, restore, develop, and manage the natural environment for current and future generations of all users of the watershed (ORCA, 2011). Programs currently delivered by conservation authorities include watershed-based monitoring programs, education and outreach, flood warning and flood forecasting, land-use planning and development services, and, more recently, the drinking water–source protection program.

In 2006 the Clean Water Act was passed by the Ontario government to establish a framework for drinking water–source protection across the province. Source-protection planning is the first line of defence in a multi-barrier approach to the provision of safe drinking water that aims to prevent the contamination and overuse of lakes, rivers, and groundwater. This is achieved by evaluating threats to these water sources and establishing policies to prevent, minimize, or eliminate them. The act mandates existing conservation authorities to perform the powers of SPAs for the purpose of source protection planning in a source protection area.

Source protection authorities are administrative bodies mandated to satisfy the requirements of the act in a source-protection area. They are generally composed of the conservation authority boards of directors that are made up of representatives appointed by councils of the municipalities in the conservation authority. Where the jurisdiction of a source protection authority has been expanded to include areas outside of the jurisdiction of a conservation authority, the source protection authority includes additional representation from the municipalities included by the boundary expansion.

Source-protection areas are the area of focus for a source protection authority and are defined in O. Reg. 284/07 of the act. In most cases, a source-protection area is the same as the conservation authority jurisdiction as defined in the Conservation Authorities Act. However, where desirable for the purpose of source protection, watersheds located outside of conservation authority jurisdiction have been included in adjacent source-protection areas or established as independent source-protection areas. In some parts of the province, several adjacent source-protection areas have been consolidated into source-protection regions. The Otonabee–Peterborough Source Protection Area is one of five source-protection areas in the Trent Conservation Coalition Source Protection Region.

The assembly of this case study was driven by ORCA's participation, since 2008, in a dialogue on the theme of Watersheds as Settings for Human Health and Well-Being, undertaken by the Network for Ecosystem Sustainability and Health (Bunch et al., 2011; Parkes et al., 2010).[1] It is also an outcome of the work of the Canadian Community of Practice in Ecohealth, which led to the development of a framework for the education, review, and evaluation of projects and programs.[2] The importance of ground truthing academic constructs in partnership with community partners directly engaged in resource-management initiatives is a critical principle. The sharing of ideas and experiences and the fit, or lack thereof, of ideas and experiences is particularly valuable. In addition to refining our philosophical framework for ecohealth, ORCA, through its participation in this project, is exploring linkages with public health to identify synergies and areas of further collaboration.

Ecohealth approaches are participatory, systems-based approaches to understanding and promoting health and well-being in the context of social and ecological interactions (Waltner-Toews & Kay, 2005). As indicated in Table 13.1, ecohealth is different from other fields in that it explicitly adopts a postmodern idea of "truth": the kind of "truths" emerging from complexity and systems sciences and from the reality of multiple, competing, and non-equivalent perspectives. Ecohealth is different than, but consistent with, recent redefinitions of ecology. Scoones (1999), for example, defines the "new" ecology as having a strong people–place focus, while Vitousek, Mooney, Lubcheno, and Melillo (1997) observe that we are living in a human-dominated ecosphere (also

Table 13.1: A comparison of ecohealth and selected other fields.

Other Fields	*Emphasis/Approach*	*Ecohealth*
Ecology	"Natural" systems, focus on understanding ecosystem dynamics	Anthropocentric, focus on social-ecological systems
Epidemiology	Highlights changes in population health, evidence of trends, outbreaks, vectors and agents of disease, and risk assessment	Addresses "why" and "how" subclinical and clinical concerns are occurring—root causes across animal, human, and environmental systems
Medicine	Focus on individuals, treating exposure; institutional settings; clinical trials generalizable to populations; ideal is to be objective	Systems thinking, draws on diverse knowledge and expertise (traditional ecological knowledge, allopathic, populations and communities in situ); reality is that practitioner is embedded
Environmental Health	Direct and quasi-direct methods; risk assessment	Relationships, patterns, processes, and context
Health Promotion	Planned change of health-related lifestyles and conditions	Engagement of key stakeholders, multiple perspectives to design, and evaluate interventions

Sanderson et al., 2002). Urry (2005) considers the division between the physical and social worlds to be a product of history that is slowly disappearing, providing additional incentive for studying eco-social systems in a more holistic way. As indicated in the Millennium Ecosystem Assessment (2003), systems thinking connects human health and well-being with the direct and indirect drivers of ecological change.

Theoretical approach

ESAH represents an evolving field of practice that seeks to better understand complex social-ecological system interactions as they relate to human, animal, and environmental health. An overarching feature of the ESAH is that it works at all levels against compartmentalization, including: the separation of animal from human health; the local from the global; the objective from the subjective; the facts from the values (Charron, 2011). The ESAH framework put forward in this paper fills a gap in current work by highlighting the critical tensions that are part of such a holistic approach. In the following sections, six commonly discernable features of the ESAH family are briefly described, in what we refer to as the Conceptual Resemblances in Ecosystem Approaches to Health (CR-ESAH) framework. The resemblances include: contextuality, empirically grounded science, complexity, normativity, transdisciplinarity, and the fundamentally contested nature of the field. These features are summarized in Figure 13.1.

The Canadian International Development Research Centre (IDRC) has been a leader in this field. Early definitions of the term focused on three pillars of ecohealth, namely transdisciplinarity, participation, and equity (Lebel, 2003). More recent work from IDRC emphasizes six principles: systems thinking, transdisiplinary research, participation, sustainability, gender and social equity, and knowledge to action (Charron, 2011). Waltner-Toews and Kay (2005) also put forward a well-received definition of ESAH: ecohealth approaches are systemic and participatory approaches to understanding and promoting human health and well-being in the context of complex social and ecological interactions. In Canada, this thinking was informed by the work on ecosystem approaches by the Science Advisory Board of the International Joint Commission for the Great Lakes (1978), as well as the Brundtland Report, *Our Common Future* (Brundtland, 1987). Nonetheless, there is no final or fixed definition for an ESAH. This chapter argues that there are some identifiable features that, taken together, form a distinct, qualitative cluster that has not yet been well-articulated by existing definitions. The features can be considered to have a "family resemblance," a term coined by Wittgenstein (2001). This family resemblance expresses itself as an approach:

> [An] approach...refers not to a framework or methodology but rather to a mindset that orients a process of inquiry that is meant to lead to some action or change in the condition of these same people and their environment. The process of inquiry is unconventional because it is investigating the reasons for the situation while also being a part of the change process.... (Charron, 2011, p. 15)

ESAH's inherent tension—what we are calling its fundamentally contested nature—among these concepts provides it with its compelling and

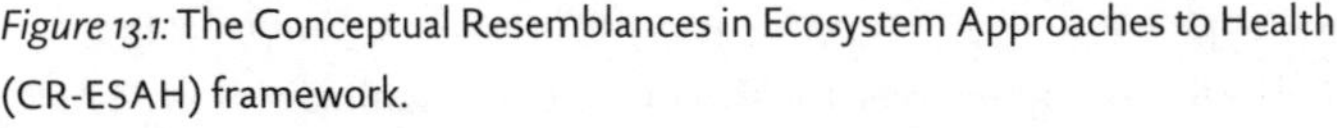

Figure 13.1: The Conceptual Resemblances in Ecosystem Approaches to Health (CR-ESAH) framework.

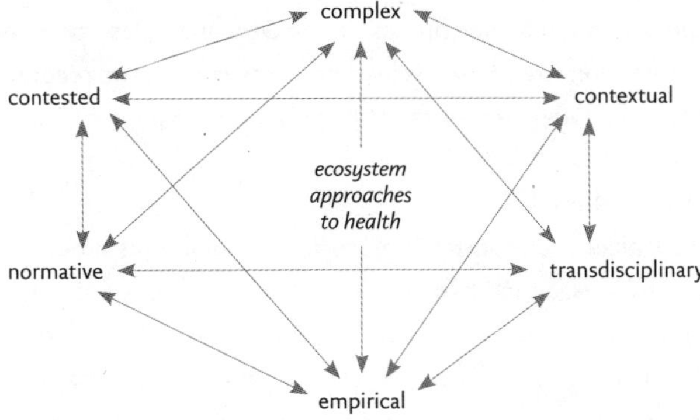

challenging vision for change in social-ecological systems. This tension is fundamental to creating a dynamic process of investigation and action, and it respects the full range of academic tradition and critical inquiry. ESAH are not precriptive, and robust investigations of complex issues that engage with the intersection between ecology and health require that each factor be taken into account, including the contextual nature of the study of each social-ecological system, the need for transdisicplinary inquiry that allows for different knowledge systems (including lived experience and Indigenous knowledge) to be heard, and the need to ground the work done in well-crafted and robust methdologies to create defendable findings. The framework also explicitly acknowledges that the concepts of health and well-being as applied to humans, animals, and ecosystems are value-laden and that this normative aspect of the work affects how studies are designed and interpreted.

There may be many different, legitimate perspectives on the issues at hand, as well as the relationships involved and the value of the information presented, thus, both the process and the findings may be contested. Despite these challenges, ESAH creates robust ground for new avenues of integrative and holistic inquiry based on systems thinking and our emerging understanding of complexity and nonlinearity. They challenge researchers to go beyond the limitations of reductionist inquiry to ask difficult, real-world questions and to keep a critical lens on both the methodologies and the processes of investigation throughout the process. In the following sections, the six conceptual resemblances in ESAH are discussed and then applied to the experience of participating in the source protection–planning process in the Otonabee–Peterborough Source Protection Area. Lessons learned are discussed, and recommendations for improving rural sustainability planning are put forward.

Contextual factors

ESAH recognizes the importance of spatio-temporal context because of its grounding in place and its typical, ongoing commitment to particular communities on the part of its practitioners. Knowing the history of the system in question is fundamental to understanding its trajectory in space and time. ESAH researchers confirm the need to understand the environmental, social, and cultural history of the particular system in question—where the study is taking place (the Otonabee River basin versus the Danube), when the study is being conducted (during spring floods or frozen winters, once a year or hourly, peacetime or wartime?), how and why the current governance/planning regime developed, and what questions are relevant to that place, or those places, at that time. Since findings are precise and specific to the system under investigation, this approach admits and embraces, rather than obscures and laments, the fact that the findings simply may not be generalizable (Kay, Boyle, Regier, & Francis, 1999; Waltner-Toews, Kay, Neudoerffer, & Gitau, 2003). The findings may be generalizable, but the first impulse is to respect the specificity and uniqueness of the context being studied.

Empirical methods

ESAH is not a metaphysical abstraction. It is a form of science. Its scientists—whether natural or social—use mixed methods, from hard numbers to anecdotal evidence. They will have been trained in the norms of sound empirical scientific practice: hypothesis formation, internal and external validity, replicability, and generalizability (Patton, 2002; Yin, 2003). While doing actual research with an ecohealth mindset, one might see intelligent adaption of, and improvisation with, these norms, according to the actual problem in question and the context in which a project is being carried out, although its findings always involve some standard form of data collection and analysis. A commitment to the local and contextual is certainly a challenge given a parallel commitment to standard empirical methods of data collection and analysis. One way that researchers have tried to balance this tension is to spend a long time with, and, in a given research area, find creative ways to sustain the research and support of a community or locale beyond typical funding cycles. Ecohealth researchers also commonly triangulate data from different sources. It is normal to find these scientists working with experts, data sets, scholarly literature, and wisdoms outside of their disciplinary homes in academia and beyond. In the field of ecohealth, the term "ecosystem" itself highlights the importance of studying connections and interactions that go beyond single data points or studies (Odum, 1982). The triangulation of data from diverse sources—especially where animal, human, and environmental data can be put into conversation—and a focus on longitudinal trends over time start to get at these connections and interactions.

Complexity

ESAH is informed by the new sciences and studies of complexity (Gunderson & Holling, 2002; Holling, 2001; Urry, 2005) and systems thinking (Boulding, 1956; von Bertalanffy, 1968; Checkland, 2000; Patton, 2002), including complex adaptive systems (Bryne, 2005; Carpenter & Turner, 2001; Levin, 1998). It pays particular attention to the patterns, processes, relationships, and context (Capra, 2005) that shape the interactions between people, places, and institutions, as well as between biotic and abiotic systems, more generally.

Complexity and one of its corollaries, uncertainty, are fundamental components of how we have to understand ecosystem change. The concepts of social-ecological resilience and ecological phase shifts, based on the nonlinear behaviour of ecosystems, highlight both the systems approach and the fundamental uncertainties we have over how, when, and why sudden and dramatic changes in ecosystem states can occur. In addition, some systems may exhibit emergent properties. A perfect example of this is water, which is an emergent property of hydrogen and oxygen. There is nothing about the properties of either hydrogen or oxygen in isolation that would lead a researcher to believe that their combination would create water. And then, at a higher scale, there are the phase shifts between the solid, liquid, and gas forms of water. Those who study and manage water-based systems, at whatever scale, cannot forget how this nonlinear behaviour is part of the deep nature of the very thing in question.

Other systems may be "nested hierarchies," which react differently to stimuli (e.g., a precipitation event) when defined at different scales. Watersheds are great examples of this. Creating mechanisms for inclusive cross-scale action in complex watershed systems is a significant challenge (Swallow, Johnson, Meinzen-Dick, & Knox, 2006).

Thinking about complexity focuses attention on the role of the scientist upon the system in conducting research. We are increasingly aware that even the act of observation, whether of the data, in the field, or at a stakeholder meeting, changes the system. Koestler (1979) sums up this idea with the metaphor of Janus, the two-headed god of doors and windows, which is another comment on the role and place of the observer in the system. There is an unresolvable tension between insider ("emic") and outsider ("etic") perspectives (Harris, 1976). Waltner-Toews et al. (2003) capture this idea in their article "Perspective changes everything: managing ecosystems from the inside out." ESAH does not make a token nod to this fundamental truth—scientists recognize their influence on study and try to take it up as a component of the study, for better or worse.

Normativity

Ecohealth science is normative. It is not objective or neutral, nor does it pretend to be. Its values influence every part of science: the framing of the questions, the funding directives, and the interpretation of results. On top of this, it is driven by a deep commitment to social and ecological change leading to greater health and wellness of human and non-human systems, in short, to justice.

One clear indication of the normative nature of ecohealth science is indicated by the contested nature of what health actually is, not only in the ecological context but also in terms of how to best operationalize definitions of human health, such as the famous 1947 definition of the World Health Organization (WHO, 1948): "Health is a state of complete physical, mental and social well-being and not merely the absence of diseases or infirmity" (p. 100). Among the three pillars of the IDRC's ecohealth approach are gender equity and community engagement, principles that express and have tremendous normative implications for how to conduct and interpret ecohealth research. Social justice is an emerging theme in the ecohealth field (Houle, 2009; Pimentel, Westra, & Noss, 2000; Soskolne, 2008; Westra, 2007).

The ideals of health, equity (Marmot, 2007), justice (Lee, 2002), sustainable development (Brundtland, 1987), integration—for example, the One Health concept refers to the interconnectedness between human, animal, wildlife, and environmental health (Zinsstag, Schelling, Wyss, & Mahamat, 2005)—and other such normative concepts further shape research questions and the methods used to examine them. It is important to be explicit about this element of ESAH. An explicit normative frame does not automatically compromise ESAH as an empirical science. Philosophers of science have argued that there is a kind of valuable objectivity emerging from, rather than despite, a complete and explicit commitment to justice. Harding (1991) names it "strong objectivity" and argues that from strong objectivity you get better science, in terms of truer depictions of reality and its patterns. In "Whose Science? Whose Knowledge?" Harding develops the case that strong objectivity "can direct the production of less partial and less distorted beliefs" (p. 138) about the world and simultaneously provide a model of "intellectual participatory democracy" (p. 151).

The ethical dimensions of ecohealth research and practice are especially brought to the forefront through the careful and thoughtful inclusion of stakeholders and their perspectives (Charron, 2011) and also in its particular emphasis on process and methodology, including a commitment to social learning (Pahl-Wostl, 2006; Pahl-Wostl et al., 2007). These gestures, in addition to the institutionally articulated ethical concerns related to safe storage or destruction of data, informed consent, handling of animal subjects, and respect for archeological sites and artifacts, often find themselves on a list of institutional protocol for "ethical research." However, even though respect for, and sensitivity toward, persons, process, animal lives, and sacred objects is laudable, these gestures can fall short of the thick sense of normativity (Walzer, 1994), or achieve the strong objectivity espoused by the average ESAH researcher who intends without apology not just to protect his or herself or institution from litigation but "to make positive changes in the world" (Charron, 2011 p. 14). ESAH practitioners see themselves as having a capacity to enact justice as both a quality and an emergent phenomenon that influences and is influenced by their practices. A commitment to working with others, including vulnerable and marginalized populations, decision makers, and other stakeholders, is valuable not first and foremost for its alignment with current good practice but for how this commitment builds and fosters healthy relationships and communities, including epistemic communities. The normative nature of the field may well be one of the main attractions, bringing a very eclectic array of researchers to this field, rather than to another.

Transdisciplinarity

Transdisciplinarity brings with it some specific methodological entailments that shape every step of ecosystem health work: hypothesis formation, study design, data collection, analysis, interpretation, and sharing of results. Transdisciplinarity requires collaborating with peoples from very different cultural, disciplinary, and epistemological backgrounds. In IDRC's original definition, this meant community, researchers, and policy-makers (Forget & Lebel, 2001; Lebel, 2003). It now explicitly includes other ways of knowing, such as traditional, Indigenous, community, and local knowledges and expertise (Charron, 2011; Parkes et al., 2005). Transdisciplinarity goes beyond the term "interdisciplinarity," which is additive and parallel, often only begrudgingly or tokenistically including the social sciences and humanities, the visual and creative arts, and Indigenous peoples. In an interdisciplinary framework, while different perspectives may be invited and expressed, they may not all be heard, synthesized, or in the end treated as if synthesizable. Transdisciplinarity brackets an imperious confidence in a single disciplinary "gold standard" for truth (e.g., a double-blind randomized control study, peer review in select journals) or, in any single standard as the "true" measure of success of a project.

Transdisciplinarity is certainly a much more difficult and courageous approach. Though it may ask us to let go of our grip on the outcomes being committed to, it is fuelled by the profound experiences of emergent properties among the participants (e.g., surprise alliances, the "Aha" moment) along the way. Such emergence occurs when people are willing work hard to hear what the other is really saying, on their own terms, across radically unfamiliar dialects and institutional idioms (Zinsstag et al., 2005) rather than constantly reducing the dissonance to consensus and the strangeness to what is familiar (e.g., myth to statistics, unusual customs to pragmatics, intuition to logic). Keeping such fractal difficulty in play actually means that all parties, not just the ones doing the token consulting, can start to see a new question, or new topic or new observation. A genuinely new, genuinely shared perspective on the issue can emerge that belongs to no one, or no one institutional home: it is collective and it retains the quality of contestedness, which brings us to our last feature of resemblance.

Contested

A mark of working well with, and across, true difference is that we can come to accept that what we find through our investigation is not always something that we can understand or translate into our own terms: into a data-collection practice, into English, into numbers, into reason. There exists real heterogeneity of practices, worldviews, insights, perspectives, and truths, not just variations on a single way of living and seeing. This is true from the level of how we see and think about science all the way to how we think about and see the cosmos. Not understanding something, or not being able to use information or insight (such as Indigenous knowledge) to do any "real" work (e.g., falsifying a hypothesis, furthering an argument, or filling in a table) does not mean it has no place in our work and should be left out, discarded, or kept apart from the heart of the truths we are grappling with. Often the most valuable thing proves to have been the very one we could not appreciate as valuable at the time, but nevertheless kept in our heads or in our notes out of respect for whatever it was being offered to us, by a stranger, by an episode, or by a story. This humility shapes the internal compass of the researcher. Being open to, living and working with, a multiplicity of world views can move us beyond mere tolerance with pluralism and impatience with what we do not understand. We can come to value dissonance, discover wonder, and maintain a renewed capacity to commit to contested, provisional, and even contradictory truths.

Application of principles of approach to source-water protection in the O–P SPA

The unique history and geography of the watersheds that comprise the ORCA watershed and the Otonabee–Peterborough Source Protection Area (O–P SPA) are very important to any study of the basin as a social-ecological system. The SPA covers an area of 3365 square kilometres and includes several of the Kawartha Lakes, along with the Otonabee, Indian, and Ouse River watersheds. Land use is predominantly rural, with some significant areas of agriculture and other areas of seasonal, lake-based tourism. The median income is below the provincial median, and approximately 72% of residents are at least third-generation residents, with only 2% self-identifying as visible minorities. The population of the SPA is 129,299, with 58% of that population residing in the City of Peterborough, which is the largest population centre in the region.

There are 12 municipal drinking-water systems comprised of three surface water intakes, eight existing groundwater systems, and one planned groundwater system within the SPA (Figure 13.2). The O–P SPA includes portions of 12 municipalities, eight of which fall within the current conservation authority jurisdiction, and the remaining four have been added for the purpose of source-protection planning. There are three First Nations within the Trent Conservation Coalition Source Protection Region, two of which are in the O–P SPA, but these lands are under federal jurisdiction and are not subject to provincial legislation including the Clean Water Act and the Conservation Authorities Act. Representatives from First Nations in the O–P SPA are involved in the Source Protection Planning Process, and many local environmental events and initiatives.

Complexity

Given the region's reliance on both surface and groundwater, understanding and monitoring the complex interactions among climate, precipitation, land, and water poses a challenge for all water managers (Falkenmark & Folke, 2002). Flood control is a significant part of the conservation authorities' mandate and has particular local relevance as highlighted by flooding in Peterborough in both 2002 and 2004. The complexity of water-resource management is intensified by the number of water users, which include Hydro One, Peterborough Utilities, and the Trent–Severn Waterway. Each of these users requires different water levels and flows, which can vary significantly by season. For many years, residents and stakeholder groups, such as the Coalition for Water Equity, have raised concerns regarding the fluctuation of water levels along the Trent–Severn Waterway, as water levels are lowered in the fall after the close of the navigation season in many of the Kawartha Lakes. Future population

Figure 13.2: Drinking water systems and municipal boundaries in the Otonobee–Peterborough Source Protection Area.

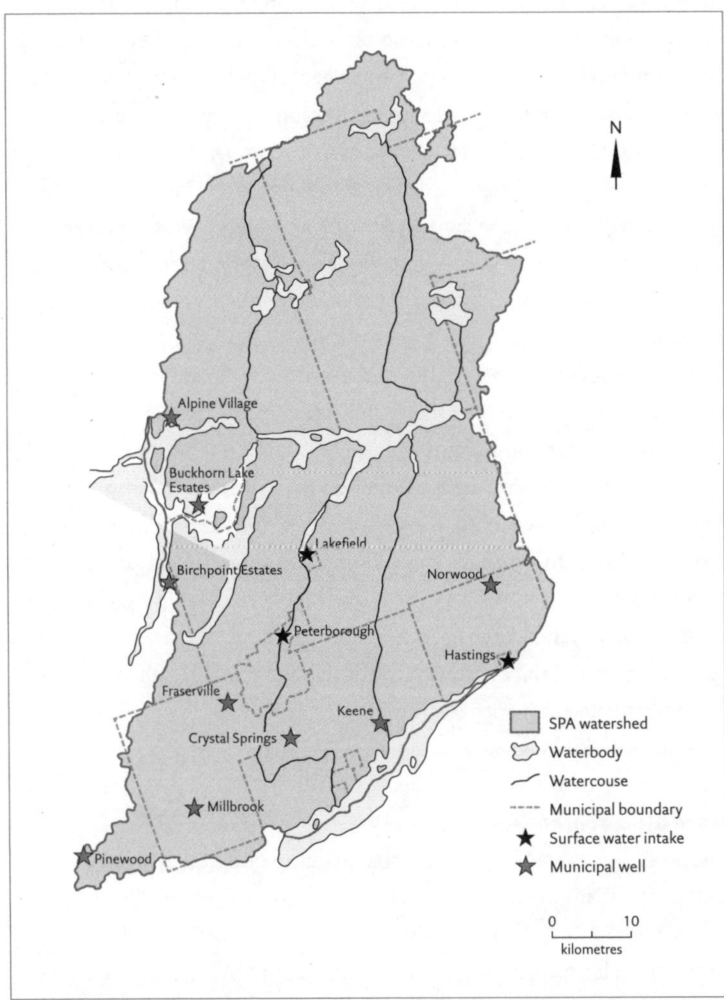

increases are expected in the region as transportation links to the Greater Toronto Area are expanded (major highway extension, passenger rail) and will intensify pressure on natural resources including water and add to the complexity of governing watersheds in the area. While no water-quantity stressors have been identified in the O–P SPA, wise use of water resources is always encouraged.

Empirical understandings

Conservation authorities, including Otonabee Region Conservation Authority, are mandated to undertake watershed-based studies that include monitoring programs to better understand watershed health and environmental changes. Potential impacts of climate change, land/water interactions, and opportunities for restoration and stewardship are other areas of study undertaken by most conservation authorities. Empirical work also focuses on interjurisdictional challenges and integrated watershed management. In the context of drinking water–source protection, detailed studies to determine water budgets, water-quantity stress assessments, surface- and groundwater-system water-quality assessments, a landscape-scale analysis, and potential climate-change implications have been undertaken. As part of the source-protection planning process, consultants were hired to gather information related to the scale and scope of significant drinking-water threats, based on the 21 threats to drinking water identified by the Ontario Ministry of the Environment that can be addressed under the Clean Water Act. Investigations were also undertaken to delineate intake protection zones, wellhead protection areas, significant recharge areas, and highly vulnerable aquifers. This information has then been used to identify potential and existing threats to drinking water, and assisted in the development of measures that can be implemented to manage or mitigate the risks posed by these activities to municipal drinking-water supplies.

Normative approaches

ORCA managers face significant challenges in integrating diverse perspectives among the area's residents on how to define a "healthy" watershed. For many landowners, any infringement of their rights on private land is unwelcome. For others, manicured lawns and full-service amenities reflect the new ideal for rural cottages, while others are promoting organic, re-naturalized landscapes. As in many managed watersheds, ORCA's 2013 Watershed Report Card is one of the ways that the organization synthesizes and conveys normative information to the public about what constitutes a "healthy" social-ecological system. The report card is a tool for decision making as well as public information and education. It is used to target environmental improvement activities with the goal of improving watershed health, which in turn benefits people and the environment. The challenge of implementing social-learning processes that bring together both scientific and lived understandings of the watershed system is ongoing.

Transdisciplinarity in action

Transdiciplinarity is one of the more difficult features with which the ESAH for ORCA engages. The organization takes full advantage of the opportunities it has for stakeholder engagement in decision making and includes, if possible, additional voices and perspectives, such as those from rural and urban residents, and a variety of other stakeholders. There are two First Nations territories within the ORCA watershed, and while First Nations lands fall outside the scope of provincial legislation, efforts are made to involve First Nations in local events and discussions. For example, local First Nations are often involved in water-related events in the area such as World Water Day (March 22) and Earth Day (April 21) by introducing and reflecting on the spiritual dimension of water through the performance of water songs and blessings. Among the challenges of full integration of a transdisciplinary approach is the sheer number of very different scientific approaches utilized by ORCA, including both natural and social sciences. The incorporation of Indigenous knowledge, perspectives, and issues is an ongoing challenge, as is the inclusion of other perspectives, such as those of landowners, long-time residents, and newcomers to the area. Bureaucratic, budgetary, and resource constraints (including staff time and expertise), as well as the default positioning of stakeholder discourse, creates challenges for new understandings and shared visions of the system to emerge. This is an area that requires additional attention.

Contested processes and outcomes

Related to the challenge of transdisciplinarity is the real tension that exists between different perspectives and ways of understanding. This impacts not only what people believe the issues are but also their perspectives on what the boundaries of the system should be. The aforementioned Coalition for Water Equity has a very different perspective on watershed management in the region than the Council of Canadians. One is operating at the local scale and is focused on water-quantity / lake-level issues, and the other is focused on macro-level policy issues related to water quantity and quality. Tensions are also apparent between different water users (e.g., municipal, recreational, industrial, agricultural), different values for different water uses (e.g., irrigation, navigation, recreation, drinking, ambient/ecological), the priority placed on different sources of water (i.e., surface, groundwater), and between government agencies at different scales and their roles in the watershed area. These contested notions of the issues, actors, and values at play in the O–P SPA are part of the ongoing challenge of watershed management, the development and implementation of source-water protection plans, and defining what constitutes healthy watersheds.

Lessons learned

This initiative was successful in both operationalizing the abstract philosophical principles guiding the ecohealth approach and in providing a mechanism to engage this community–university partnership in discussions about the link between ecology and human health and well-being, how such links can be investigated, and how they might serve to enhance rural sustainability and social-ecological resilience. It is part of a longer-term collaboration between ORCA and Network for Ecosystem Sustainability and Health (NESH) that is focused on watersheds as settings for health. The process has included a series of face-to-face meetings across Canada, telephone discussions, and other correspondence, and it has led to collaboration on a series of presentations, proposals, and papers (Houle & Morrison, 2010; Morrison & Carter, 2010; Morrison et al., 2012). Lessons learned from this experience include a reinforced sense that such conversations and constructs have local and academic value, and that taking the time to reflect on the design and implementation of community-level initiatives is important for both those directly engaged in this work and those who seek to understand and evaluate it.

Specifically, the analysis identified many lessons related to rural sustainability planning. Context is important. The history and geography of the watershed area, including prior events and established groups and structures, affect current and future governance possibilities. A thorough knowledge of the history of the local context for governance is needed to design appropriate processes and interventions. It is important to consider whose issues are driving the agenda for change. Government-led initiatives will inspire different interactions and patterns of behaviour in a watershed than those led by non-government or quasi-governmental agencies (such as conservation authorities). In addition, considering who is affected by new control measures or initiatives and whose voices are being heard is key to achieving the social-equity goals of the ecohealth approach. Simply being around the table may not be enough; opportunities to be heard may have to be structured differently to capture the voices of some participants and groups.

There are multiple system descriptions available to watershed managers, including those related to surface and groundwater dynamics, jurisdictional boundaries, and socio-economic groupings. The system description plays a key role in determining what the issues are and who needs to be involved in discussions about water and land use. Competing, conflicting, and contested stakeholder priorities and understandings of the "system" can significantly shape the discussions and opportunities for action. Flexible, multi-level governance arrangements are needed in order for leadership to emerge and be supported in the watershed area (Armitage, Berkes, & Doubleday, 2007; Habron, 2003). This includes mechanisms for resource sharing in order to take advantage of opportunities to leverage programs that address multiple drivers of change in the area. An example of this would be conservation authorities working with local health officers to create public-awareness campaigns that promote both fitness and natural area–based recreation.

Watershed-based meetings and discussions may create fora for discussions about issues that are not solvable, due to either resource and knowledge constraints or, more important, competing and incommensurable worldviews among participants. Thus, achieving consensus may be impossible. Nonetheless, the divergent visions and worldviews add valuable information to, and expand discussions about, the issues and proposed solutions. In the long run, it is better to keep all interested parties in the process than to exclude difficult or unwanted perspectives. There is also a need for many different kinds of scientific studies. Ecological and economic studies need to be complemented by research in the social sciences and humanities in order to capture a more robust understanding of the dynamics of the watershed as a social-ecological system.

Building sustainable and resilient rural communities requires more than just an understanding of water quality or land-use practices. It is important to achieve social and political support for a vision of the future state of the system. Watershed report cards are a good step in that direction, provided there is some overall direction for the end (or desired) state of the system being signalled to the community. Scenario-based planning is another effective tool for communicating the possibility of system change to watershed citizens. Scenarios may in fact allow for a robust conversation about what is needed to build adaptive capacity in watersheds in the face of climate change. These normative discussions about the goal of watershed-governance activities extend as well to discussions about key indicators. For example, what is "safe" ambient water quality? For whom/what? What constitutes a healthy Otonabee River watershed? For whom? When?

The ecohealth framework ground truthed in this study provided a useful way to clarify the elements of the program that either fit or impeded an ecohealth approach. The struggle to apply the concept of transdisciplinarity is significant and can be interpreted as meaning either that the concept is not applicable to the study topic or highlights a challenge in the current planning approach. If the former, one wonders how the synthesis of the multiple perspectives highlighted in the section on multiplicity are understood and interpreted. If the latter, this study highlights the need to think critically about the structure of decision-making processes and the opportunities they provide for the emergence of new understandings of the systems in question, for example through discussion, sharing, and reflection. In a predominantly bureaucratic environment, such as that represented by the source-water planning process, achieving a transdisciplinary understanding may be extremely difficult. Whether or not it is worth the effort is a research question that requires additional attention.

Conclusions

From an ecohealth perspective, the role of watersheds as settings for health seems clear. Current efforts to implement watershed-based planning are impeded by a number of structural and philosophical concerns, including jurisdiction and resources, but also vision, inclusion, and opportunities for new understandings of the system to emerge. This paper applied an ecohealth framework to a regional source-water protection planning process. Through the application of such a framework, the need for inclusive, place-based policies is clear. This paper identified several interesting challenges, including the potential difficulty practitioners experienced in creating integrated sustainability plans that can transcend institutional mandates. Transdisciplinary understanding is the new mantra in the academic literature that seeks to unleash new and emergent understandings of the relationship between humans and the ecosystems that support them. The true test of the concept will ultimately be in its ability to inspire new and different action on the ground. Challenges remain in finding institutional structures and modes of governance that are able to inspire, capture, and hold on to such contested and transdisciplinary understandings. The impact of the current constrictions on planning dialogue and process may not be best suited to facing new and emerging challenges. The exchange of information and insight among researchers, teachers, and practitioners is necessary to improving the quality of academic musings about human/environment relationships, especially in highly theoretical disciplines. Working with local case studies grounds the theory, making it more context sensitive. If the ecohealth framework put forward in this paper is to be useful, additional thinking is needed about how to operationalize the concepts espoused. Learning how to implement, and investing in the development of, such planning systems is of particular importance, given the anticipated impacts on hydrological systems as a result of anthropogenic climate change.

Notes

1. See www.nesh.ca.
2. See www.copeh-canada.org.

References

Armitage, D., Berkes, F., & Doubleday, N. (2007). *Adaptive co-management: Collaboration, learning, and multi-level governance.* Vancouver, BC: University of British Columbia Press.

Boulding, K. E. (1956). General systems theory: The skeleton of a science. *Management Science, 2*(3), 197–208.

Brundtland, G. (Ed.) (1987). *Our common future: Report of the World Commission on Environment and Development.* Oxford, UK: Oxford University Press.

Bryne, D. (2005). Complexity, configuration and cases. *Theory, Culture & Society, 22*(5), 95–111.

Bunch, M. J., Morrison, K., Parkes, M., and Venema, H. (2011). Promoting health and well-being by managing for social-ecological resilience: The potential of integrating ecohealth and water resources management approaches. *Ecology and Society, 16*(1), 6. Retrieved from http://www.ecologyandsociety.org/vol16/iss1/art6/.

Capra, F. (2005). Complexity and life. *Theory, Culture & Society, 22*(5), 33–44.

Carpenter, S. R., & Turner, M. G. (2001). Hares and tortoises: Interactions of fast and slow variables in ecosystems. *Ecosystems, 3*, 495–497.

Charron, D. (Ed.). (2011). *Ecohealth research in practice.* New York: Springer-Verlag, Inc.

Checkland, P. (2000). Soft systems methodology: A thirty-year retrospective. *Systems Research and Behavioral Science, 17*, S11-S58.

Conservation Ontario. (2001). *The importance of watershed management in protecting Ontario's drinking water supplies.* Submission to the Walkerton Inquiry. Newmarket, ON: Conservation Ontario.

Dooris, M. (2005). Healthy settings: Challenges to generating evidence of effectiveness. *Health Promotion International, 21*, 55–65.

Falkenmark, M., & Folke, C. (2002). The ethics of socio-ecohydrological catchment management: Towards hydrosolidarity. *Hydrology and Earth System Sciences, 6*, 1–9.

Forget, G., & Lebel, J. (2001). An ecosystem approach to human health. *International Journal of Occupational and Environmental Health, 7*, S1–S36.

Gunderson, L., & Holling, C. S. (Eds.). (2002). *Panarchy: Understanding transformations in human and natural systems.* Washington, DC: Island Press.

Habron, G. (2003). Role of adaptive management for watershed councils. *Environmental Management, 31*, 29–41.

Harding S. (1991). *Whose science? Whose knowledge? Thinking from women's lives.* Ithaca, NY: Cornell University Press.

Harris, M. (1976). History and significance of the emic/etic distinction. *Annual Review of Anthropology, 5*, 329–350.

Holling, C. S. (2001). Understanding the complexity of economic, ecological, and social systems. *Ecosystems, 4*, 390–405.

Houle, K. (2009). Making strange: Deconstruction and feminist standpoint theory. *Frontiers: A Journal of Women's Studies Special Issue: Knowledge that Matters, 29*(1), 172–193.

Houle, K., & Morrison, K. (2010). *Ecohealth and the philosophy of science.* Paper presented at the Ecohealth 2010 International Conference, London, UK.

Kay, J. J., Boyle, M., Regier, H. A., & Francis, G. (1999). An ecosystem approach for sustainability: Addressing the challenge of complexity. *Futures, 31*, 721–742.

Koestler, A. (1979). *Janus: Summing up.* New York: Vintage Publishers.

Lebel, J. (2003). *Health: An ecosystem approach.* Ottawa, ON: International Development Research Centre.

Lee, C. (2002). Environmental justice: Building a unified vision of health and the environment. *Environmental Health Perspectives, 110*, 141–144.

Levin, S. A. (1998). Ecosystems and the biosphere as complex adaptive systems. *Ecosystems, 1*(5), 431–436.

Marmot, M. (2007). Achieving health equity: From root causes to fair outcomes. *The Lancet, 370*, 1153–1163.

McMichael, A. (2006). Population health as the 'bottom line' of sustainability: A contemporary challenge for public health researchers. *The European Journal of Public Health, 16*, 579–581.

Millennium Ecosystem Assessment (MA). (2003). *Ecosystems and human well-being: A framework for assessment.* Washington, DC: Island Press. Retrieved from http://www.millenniumassessment.org/.

Morrison, K., & Carter, M. (2010). *An ecohealth approach to watershed governance in the Otonabee River basin, Ontario.* Paper presented at the Taking the Next Steps Conference, Alberta Centre for Sustainable Rural Communities, Camrose, Alberta.

Morrison, K. E., Parkes, M. W., Hallstrom, L. H., Neudoerffer, C. V., Bunch, M. J., & Venema, H. D. (2012). *Ecohealth and watersheds: Watersheds as settings for health and well-being in Canada.* Winnipeg, MB: Network for Ecosystem Sustainability and Health (Publication Series No. 3) and the International Institute for Sustainable Development. Retrieved from http://www.iisd.org/pdf/2012/ecohealth_watersheds_canada.pdf.

O'Connor D. R. (2002). *Report of the Walkerton Inquiry part two: A strategy for safe drinking water.* Toronto, ON: Queen's Printer for Ontario.

Odum, W. E. (1982). Environmental degradation and the tyranny of small decisions. *BioScience, 32*(9), 728–729.

Otonabee Region Conservation Authority (ORCA). (2011). About us. Retrieved June 29, 2011, from http://www.otonabee.com/orca/about.

Pahl-Wostl, C. (2006). The importance of social learning in restoring the multifunctionality of rivers and floodplains. *Ecology and Society, 11*(1), 10. Retrieved from http://www.ecologyandsociety.org/vol11/iss1/art10/.

Pahl-Wostl, C., Crops, M., Dewulf, A., Mostert, E., Tabara, D., & Taillieu, T. (2007). Social learning and water resources management. *Ecology and Society, 12*(2), 5. Retrieved from http://www.ecologyandsociety.org/vol12/iss2/art5/.

Parkes, M. W., Bienen, L., Breilh, J., Hsu, L. N., McDonald, M., Patz, J. A....Yassi, A. (2005). All hands on deck: Transdisciplinary approaches to emerging infectious disease. *EcoHealth, 2*, 258–272.

Parkes, M. W., Morrison, K. E., Bunch, M. J., Venema, H. D., Hallstrom, L. K., Neudoerffer, R. C., & Waltner-Toews, D. (2010). Towards integrated governance for water, health and social-ecological systems: The watershed governance prism. *Global Environmental Change, 20*(4), 693–704. doi: 10.1016/j.gloenvcha.2010.1006.1001.

Patton, M. Q. (2002). *Qualitative evaluation and research methods.* Thousand Oaks, CA: Sage Publications.

Pimental, D., Westra, L., & Noss, R. (Eds). (2000). *Ecological integrity: Integrating environment, conservation and health.* Washington, DC: Island Press.

Sanderson, E. W., Jaiteh, M., Levy, M. A., Redford, H., Wannebo, A. V., & Woolmer, G. (2002). The human footprint and the last of the the wild. *BioScience, 52*(10), 453–466.

Scoones, I. (1999). New ecology and the social sciences: What prospects for a fruitful engagement? *Annual Review of Anthropology, 28,* 479–507.

Soskolne C. (Ed.). (2008). *Sustaining life on Earth: Environmental and human health through global governance.* Plymouth, UK: Lexington Books.

Swallow, B., Johnson, N., Meinzen-Dick, R., & Knox, A. (2006). The challenges of inclusive cross-scale collective action in watersheds. *Water International, 31,* 361–375.

Urry, J. (2005). The complexity turn. *Theory, Culture & Society, 22*(5), 1–14.

Vitousek, P., Mooney, H., Lubchenco, J., and Melillo, J. (1997). Human domination of Earth's ecosystems. *Science, 277,* 494–499.

von Bertalanffy, L. (1968). *General system theory: Foundations, developments, applications.* New York: Braziller.

Waltner-Toews, D., Kay, J., Neudoerffer, C., & Gitau, T. (2003) Perspective changes everything: Managing ecosystems from the inside out. *Frontiers in Ecology and the Environment, 1,* 23–30.

Waltner-Toews, D., & Kay, J. J. (2005). The evolution of an ecosystem approach: The diamond schematic and an adaptive methodology for ecosystem sustainability and health. *Ecology and Society, 10*(1), 38. Retrieved from http://www.ecologyandsociety.org/vol10/iss1/art38/.

Walzer, M. (1994). *Thick and thin: Moral argument at home and abroad.* Notre Dame, IN: University of Notre Dame Press.

Westra, L. (2007). *Environmental justice and the rights of Indigenous peoples: International and domestic law perspectives.* London, UK: Earthscan Publishers.

World Health Organization (WHO). (1948). "Preamble to the Constitution of the World Health Organization as adopted by the International Health Conference, New York, 19–22 June, 1946; signed on 22 July 1946 by the representatives of 61 States (Official records of the World Health Organization, no. 2, p. 100) and entered into force on 7 April 1948." Retrieved June 29, 2011, from http://www.who.int/about/definition/en/print.html.

Wittgenstein, L. (2001). *Philosophical investigation: The German text, with a revised English translation.* Malden, MA: Blackwell Publishing.

Yin, R. K. (2003). *Case study research: Design and methods* (3rd ed.). Thousand Oaks, CA: Sage Publications.

Zinsstag, J., Schelling, E., Wyss, K.,& Mahamat, M. B. (2005). Potential of cooperation between human and animal health to strengthen health systems. *The Lancet, 366,* 2142–2145.

FOURTEEN

Seeking Sustainability through Self-Assessment and Regional Cooperation in Newfoundland and Labrador

Kelly Vodden, Ryan Lane, and Craig Pollett

Introduction

Municipalities in rural and small-town Canada face a host of challenges as they strive to fulfill a growing suite of responsibilities and cope with profound demographic, economic, and ecological changes in their communities. These challenges include financial pressures, human-resource shortages, and increasing standards and expectations related to municipal infrastructure, services, and governance (Connelly, Markey, & Roseland, 2009; Douglas, 2010; Nelson, 2003). Particularly since the 1992 Rio Earth Summit and Agenda 21 action plan, one of these expectations is that local governments play a central role in the sustainable-development process (Brugmann, 1996; Evans, Joas, Sundback, & Theobald, 2006; Roseland, 2005; United Nations Conference on Environment and Development [UNCED], 1992). With an "urban bias of sustainability" (Jepson, 2001, p. 506; Parkinson & Roseland, 2002), cities dominate sustainability literature, policies, and programs, but rural municipalities also play important roles in natural-resource governance and ecosystem stewardship, contributing to the social, cultural, and economic well-being of Canadian provinces. However, in much of rural and small-town Newfoundland and

Labrador (NL) and elsewhere in rural Canada, community survival, and thus the ability of rural and small-town settlements and their residents to play these roles within their Canadian and provincial contexts, is a principal sustainability concern.

As in other jurisdictions in Canada and internationally, governments at all levels in NL have looked to regionalism and multicommunity collaboration as a way of coping with rural restructuring and its consequences (Haughton & Counsell, 2004; Markey, Halseth, & Manson, 2008). Regionalization efforts in the province have included: a late 1980s, provincially driven attempt to consolidate communities through amalgamation; the mid-1990s Task Force on Municipal Sustainability; and, after the political failure of the amalgamation agenda, efforts throughout the 1990s and 2000s to encourage municipal regionalization by providing support and incentives. The results have included an array of service-sharing arrangements, restructuring initiatives, and the creation of the Community Cooperation Office (CCO) by the provincial municipal association, Municipalities Newfoundland and Labrador (MNL).

MNL and the CCO have worked with provincial and federal agencies, Memorial University, and other partners to help their members plan and adapt to their changing circumstances. The following chapter describes the development of the Municipal Self-Assessment Tool Kit and associated assessment process by MNL and partnering organizations from 2005 to 2008. The role of self-assessment in the development of Integrated Community Sustainability Plans (ICSPs), and in supporting and encouraging cooperation among neighbouring municipalities, is also discussed. We begin with an explanation of the changing municipal context and then outline how the self-assessment process was initiated, implemented, and linked directly to ICSPs. Finally, we reflect on lessons learned from the self-assessment and ICSP process that have applicability not only for NL but for small municipalities elsewhere in Canada and beyond, and for agencies and researchers that seek to support and collaborate with them. In doing so, we draw from and contribute to a growing literature on monitoring and assessment within the sustainability movement (Kates, Parris, & Leiserowitz, 2005; Smith, 1998) and in local government (Ferrarini, Bodini, & Becchi, 2001; Licon & Balarezo, 2009; Plant, Agocs, Brunet-Jailley, & Douglas, 2005).

Context: Municipal sustainability and the introduction of ICSPs in NL

Municipalities in NL have existed as legal entities for many decades, but there were very few incorporated towns until the years following Confederation with Canada in 1949. Following union with the rest of Canada, new monies flowed into the province and into rural communities, creating the need for locally incorporated government entities to manage these investments. Increasing numbers of settlements became incorporated during the 1970s and 1980s, decades of relative economic stability. Beginning in the late 1980s, however, a decline in the fisheries led to moratoria on the harvesting of northern cod in 1992 and significant population out-migration. Between 1991 and 2001, rural and small-town NL lost approximately 18% of its population (Higgins, 2008). For many communities, out-migration coupled with low birth rates and an aging population resulted in a loss of 20–40% of their population from 1991 to 2006 (Community Accounts, 2006).

As the new millennium began, municipalities were experiencing significant difficulty maintaining their basic operations. There were over 280 municipalities across the province, and more than 75% had less than one thousand residents; over half had less than five hundred (Statistics Canada, 2007). Small-town revenues have often been based on property tax, or even simply a poll tax (also called a head tax). Out-migration therefore meant that municipal revenues were shrinking. Over the same period, financial transfers from the provincial government were also steadily decreasing while health and safety, and financial regulations, among others, were increasing. As a result many municipalities found themselves without enough revenue to provide basic services or maintain appropriate staff levels. A 2007 municipal census indicated that small municipalities, representing 72% of survey respondents, had on average only one full-time permanent staff person (Vodden, Lane, & Beck, 2007). This staff member was/is typically a clerk-manager who works with a part-term public-works employee; although in some cases one person is responsible for tasks ranging from tax collection to water testing.

In addition to these operational and financial issues, small rural communities were facing significant governance challenges. Only (approximately) 50% of towns held contested elections in the 2000s.[1]

Many towns struggled with attracting enough candidates to sit on council and were/are forced to operate with empty seats until a by-election is held. One of the most significant governance gaps has been with regard to community planning. In 2007 less than half of municipalities had an emergency-preparedness or capital-works plan, less than one third had a land-use plan, and very few had economic or sustainability plans. The lack of human and financial resources have been important constraints as only six out of more than 280 municipalities had a planner on staff (Vodden et al., 2007).

In 2003 MNL created the Community Cooperation Resource Centre, or CCRC, now the CCO, to help address growing concerns about community capacity and sustainability. The CCO was designed to act as a catalyst for developing viable and sustainable communities by actively supporting regional cooperation through the provision of information, research, training and education, facilitation, and advisory services (CCO, 2011). One of the centre's first initiatives was to conduct the province's first municipal census in 2003 (with the second to follow in 2007). From the moment the CCO was created, the demand from member municipalities was swift and significant. Municipalities recognized the opportunity to take advantage of an office dedicated to sustainability and cooperation. Unfortunately, the CCO was initially not well-resourced, and it took time to respond to the significant number of inquiries.

In yet another attempt to identify and deal with the mounting sustainability issues for municipalities, in 2004 MNL constituted the President's Task Force on Municipal Sustainability in Newfoundland and Labrador. This task force compiled information from towns regarding the major sustainability issues they had been facing. MNL released the report of the task force in 2005. It identified challenges municipalities were being forced to address as well as specific options available to them. The report identified the need for the Government of NL to make legislative amendments for expanded municipal revenue-generating options and for a greater emphasis on regional cooperation. The task force also recommended that communities conduct sustainability self-assessments and that the MNL's CCO develop and assist member municipalities to deliver their self-assessments as part of an expanded role for the CCO in providing support services for regional efforts.

The CCO initially began with an advisory committee only, which included representatives from municipal, provincial, federal, and academic sectors. Subsequent to the task force on sustainability, MNL hired a staff person to coordinate the efforts of the CCO, with funding support from the Canada–NL Gas Tax Agreement (GTA).[2] Along with the GTA came the requirement for all municipalities to develop an Integrated Community Sustainability Plan (ICSP), and it was recognized that the CCO could play a role in encouraging municipalities to consider regional cooperation as part of their plans for the future.

When the 2006 GTA was signed and released to municipalities, the availability of much-needed municipal funding was the focus of attention. There was little detail available regarding the required development of an ICSP, but there was an assumption that there would be direction provided by senior levels of government to assist in meeting the requirement. Information regarding the development of ICSPs was not provided until 2009, leaving communities ill-prepared to meet the March 2010 deadline for ICSP completion.

MNL, through the CCO, had already begun development of the sustainability self-sssessment concept when the GTA was signed, and when the ICSP requirement came along, it was recognized that self-assessment could serve as a useful initial step in the ICSP process. While the Self-Assessment Tool Kit was in the final stages of development, and continuing into its delivery, the CCO also compiled available resources on ICSP development from across Canada in support of municipal ICSP efforts. The federal government had released scoping documents that provided a general overview of ICSPs as strategic plans with four pillars: economic, environmental, social, and cultural. It was also suggested that through this process municipalities should identify opportunities for collaboration with other municipalities (see, for example, Planning for Sustainable Canadian Communities Roundtable, 2005), but there were few details provided as to how these plans should be prepared. There were also some examples from other provinces of related processes and plans that provided some guidance as self-assessment and ICSP guidelines and support tools were being developed in NL.

Based on the research conducted by MNL, the Department of Municipal Affairs formed a committee with members from MNL, the department, and the Professional Municipal Administrators (PMA). The committee commissioned a firm to consolidate all the available information, including the preliminary self-assessment results, and to make general recommendations regarding the direction of ICSP development in NL. The Department of Municipal Affairs used the results of this work to develop resources for the ICSP process. Two key resources—the ICSP Framework and the ICSP Guide—were released in April 2009 to assist municipalities in meeting their ICSP requirements. The framework also outlined ten suggested steps for developing an ICSP:

1. Complete a sustainability self-assessment questionnaire
2. Review sustainability self-assessment
3. Attend regional ICSP workshop
4. Review ICSP options
5. Identify collaborative ICSP partners (where applicable)
6. Identify ICSP lead
7. Finalize ICSP Framework option
8. Begin ICSP development
9. ICSP review and final council approval
10. Final ICSP submission to Department of Municipal Affairs

The framework acknowledged the sustainability self-assessment as "an integral component and a starting point for the ICSP process," providing a basis for establishing objectives and setting targets (Department of Muncipal Affairs Newfoundland and Labrador [MA], 2009, p. 10).

The Municipal Sustainability Self-Assessment Project

Initiating municipal self-assessment

Years of mounting concern about issues of capacity, funding, and out-migration led MNL's President's Task Force on Sustainability to recommend that all municipalities complete a sustainability self-assessment and consider options for the future of their municipal organization based on the results of this assessment (MNL, 2005). This recommendation, together with a GTA requirement to develop ICSPs, would later develop into the Municipal Sustainability Self-Assessment Project. Through this project, municipalities evaluated the status of their community as well as their financial and operational positions and determined for themselves their ability to effectively and efficiently deliver municipal services. Funded through the GTA, MNL's goal in initiating the Municipal Sustainability Self-Assessment Project was "to be a catalyst for establishing a self-sustaining local government administration that is an essential component of, and proactively supports, the development of viable and sustainable communities throughout the province of Newfoundland and Labrador" (MNL, 2008, p. 1).

CCO advisory committee members began by looking for examples of municipal assessment processes that had been undertaken elsewhere, such as Nova Scotia's municipal indicators program, BC's annual progress reports, which were implemented in association with the 2004 Community Charter, and the Municipal Performance Measurement Program put in place in 2000 under Ontario's Municipal Act (Gergley, 2004; Ontario Ministry of Municipal Affairs and Housing, 2007). Given the municipal context described above, it was determined that MNL's municipal members would benefit from a step-by-step guide that provided suggestions for how to go about assessing their sustainability and could be combined with hands-on support to help communities work through the guide.

Because municipal evaluation was new to the province, and neither local capacity nor the legislative framework were in place to undertake a formal review process, a self-assessment approach was considered the most appropriate. The self-assessment was viewed as both a pilot project and a capacity-building exercise. The CCO committee and its newly hired project officer began to develop the Municipal Self-Assessment Tool Kit. Tool kits are compilations of resource materials such as checklists, questionnaires, guidelines, instructions and/or examples of "best practices." Given the limited planning experience and resources of most of the province's municipalities (including low literacy levels, in some cases) it was clear that the tool kit should be comprehensive, easy to understand, and offer step-by-step guidance through the self-assessment process.

Recognizing that there are many definitions of the term "sustainability" and that the concept was poorly understood within the municipal sector, the group began by clarifying what was meant by municipal sustainability within the NL context. Given the ambiguity of the term, Saha and Paterson (2008) suggest that it is especially important that sustainability is conceptualized from the bottom up. The CCO determined that a sustainable municipality is able to:

1. Govern and democratically represent the interests of its community with significant community support and involvement;
2. Satisfy the responsibilities for municipal administration, services and infrastructure in accord with legislation, including the Municipalities Act and acts governing services such as waste management and water supply;
3. Provide the necessary services and infrastructure at a cost residents are willing and able to pay;
4. Fund services from local financial resources or through partnerships with other agencies;
5. Actively contribute to the demographic, social, cultural, environmental, and economic well-being of its community. (MNL, 2008, p. 2)

The Self-Assessment Tool Kit was designed as a booklet that included: an introduction; answers to questions members were likely to ask, such as time and resources required; an outline of the steps involved; a form for recording meetings and attendance; a self-assessment questionnaire and form for listing supporting documentation; additional questions related to community assets and sustainability; and finally, suggestions for how to interpret and create a plan of action based on assessment results.[3] Three potential options for communities deemed unsustainable were presented, as recommended by the President's Task Force on Municipal Sustainability. The first alternative was to increase efforts to share services with one or more adjacent communities. The second was to enter into a formal merger/amalgamation with another municipality, and the third was to disincorporate and administer services through a regional municipal entity. A fourth option, suggested for all communities as a measure that could be taken in the short term, was to incorporate the self-assessment findings into an ICSP.

The first suggested step was for councils to formally decide to proceed with the self-assessment and to discuss this with their senior staff, whose involvement would be critical to the process. It was then recommended that one or more individuals be assigned the responsibility to prepare background information to assist in working through the self-assessment questionnaire, the core component of the process. Examples of the types of available background information were provided for each relevant question. Examples included the town's policy and procedures manual, budget documents, existing plans, and statistical profiles from Statistics Canada and/or the provincial Community Accounts system.

Next, it was recommended that a workshop (or series of meetings), including members of council and senior staff (a self-assessment group) be held to work through the questionnaire and discussion questions collectively. Ideally, answers to each question were to be reached by consensus after discussion about areas of debate. Towns were encouraged to consider inviting an outside facilitator, provided by the CCO, to help mediate the discussion, clarify questions, and assist in developing future options and next steps. Final answers were to be recorded in the tool kit by an appointed recorder.

The questionnaire consisted of 140 questions in seven categories (see Table 14.1) related to the definition of municipal sustainability provided above. The questions were intended to address the major roles and responsibilities of incorporated municipalities as well as indicators of community sustainability more broadly, including the state of, and opportunities for, regional cooperation. Each section of the questionnaire was developed in consultation with appropriate experts, including representatives of both small and large municipalities, and municipal-sector specialists (e.g., Department of Environment and Conservation water and waste-management officials, the Fire Commissioners Office, and academic advisors specializing in community development). Where accepted minimum levels of service or good governance practice exist they were utilized, such as a debt-servicing level within the provincial benchmark of less than 30%. In other cases there was general agreement among the CCO staff and advisory committee members on guidelines that could be provided, such as 50% or greater being a satisfactory voter turnout in municipal elections. For other indicators, however, such as what constitutes qualified municipal staff or acceptable distance to health-care facilities, it was decided that councils should form their own assessments of what they consider to be acceptable. Rather than imposing a scoring system that may not be understood or appropriate for differing community circumstances, a simple choice of responding No, To Some Degree, or Yes was given for each question (0, 1, and 2 respectively for scoring purposes). Each question was weighted equally. A No or To Some Degree answer was intended to lead to discussion about why the municipality was weak in this area and how these indicators might be improved in the future.

In addition to the self-assessment indicator questions, two additional types of questions were added. Given the growing emphasis on regional approaches to municipal sustainability in the province, two questions were added to the end of the questionnaire to determine if municipalities were willing to move from the more informal and ad hoc existing model of regional cooperation through information and service sharing to more formal, structural arrangements such as amalgamation or forming a regional government. Second, in recognition that each community may have unique challenges and strengths that are not recognized within the questionnaire, the tool kit included a short series of discussion questions about additional aspects of their communities that responding representatives felt had been, or could be, drawn upon to enhance sustainability. This final set of questions drew from the asset-based development approach popularized by Kretzmann and McKnight (1993, 1996). According to these authors, local development is most effective when it is based upon the strengths and resources of communities, rather than on their deficiencies. This section also provided an opportunity for municipal leaders to have input into the indicators being used in the assessment. This section of the tool kit helped to offset concerns about standardized approaches to sustainability indicator development and use that are devoid of local context (Smith, 1998). Since the majority of the questions were standardized, allowing for some comparability between communities, the process and tool kit represented what Brugmann (1996) describes as the "middle course" in the standardized versus localized indicators debate.

Finally, the tool kit stressed that time must be allotted to tally and then discuss the assessment results and implications. This important final step could be continued as part of the ICSP process, but it was considered important for those present at the assessment workshop to reflect immediately after completing the questions about: whether or not the overall assessment seemed appropriate, what actions could be taken to make required improvements or capitalize on local strengths, and what could be the potential role of regional cooperation. Integration of results into the ICSP process and next steps to be taken were also to be discussed. After the completion of the workshop, results were submitted to the CCO.

CCO staff then prepared a summary report with recommendations that were to be tabled and passed at a subsequent council meeting.

The draft tool kit was developed in late 2007 after much discussion and more than three years of effort, but before it could be rolled out across the province the CCO had two important remaining tasks: first, to pilot the process, and second, to secure the necessary financial and human resources to support full implementation. The tool kit was piloted in five communities of varying sizes and apparent level of municipal sustainability (based on the expertise and experience of the advisory committee). Question revisions were made based on the pilot results and, with funding in place by this time from the Federal–Provincial Gas Tax Secretariat, roll-out across the province began.

Implementing the tool kit

Working within the budgetary constraints and being realistic regarding time requirements and the geography of rural NL, MNL hired five full-time staff to deliver the tool kit. A project coordinator supervised the four field staff who facilitated the delivery around the province over a four-month period. The tool kit was offered to every municipality regardless of size, capacity, or geographic location. Schedules were designed around the ability of councils and staff to meet, and assessments often took place at evening meetings. When the project was complete, 249, or 89% of municipalities, had participated. The tool kit was delivered and advertised as the first step in the ICSP process, which is likely to have had a positive effect on the final participation numbers. Other factors at play included the flexibility of the schedule, the availability of facilitators to visit each town office, and therefore that the entire process was at no financial cost to councils aside from staff time. Each participant was provided with a copy of the tool kit to fill in at the session, with each town instructed to have one official copy.

The process was designed as a facilitated session involving all elected councillors and senior staff. The tool kit suggested that members of the public and/or key community groups could also be invited to attend if deemed appropriate, but this was not an option pursued by participating municipalities, who instead opted to keep the process internal at this initial stage. Some towns were able to ensure all required municipal representatives were present while in others participation was less than

Table 14.1: Summary of self-assessment results.

Category	*Avg. % of Municipalities Responding "yes" in this Category*	*% of Municipalities Responding "yes" to Specific Questions*
Governance (27 questions)	57%	> 50%: had council standing committees (63%); council regularly updates their knowledge of municipal government through training (58%); had a contested municipal election (54%)
		< 50%: had an emergency preparedness (42%) or sustainability plan (14%); policy and procedures manual (39%); process to monitor community sustainability and plan implementation (33%)
Administration (17 questions)	82%	> 50%: take minutes at each council meeting (100%); employ qualified staff (97%) with related post-secondary education (71%); reports are submitted on time (90%); computerized office (90%) with Internet (84%)
		< 50%: n/a (all questions answered positively by over 50%)
Finance and Financial Management (16 questions)	73%	> 50%: adopt an annual budget (100%); annual audit completed on time (71%); have the fiscal capacity to take on additional debt (52%)
		< 50%: have less than 10% of taxes in arrears at year-end (41%); local revenue sources stable or increasing (41%); able to maintain a capital works fund (38%)
Service Delivery (26 questions)	58%	> 50%: provide weekly waste collection (100%); inform residents about council decisions and priorities (86%); fire protection response time 14 minutes or less throughout community (84%); recreation program (57%)
		< 50%: have qualified back-up water system operator (34%); non-deposit recycling (26%); 3Rs education (11%); trained recreation personnel (33%)
Equipment and Infrastructure (11 questions)	63%	> 50%: have greenspace, parks, or walking trails (85%); adequately equipped fire protection service (82%); adequate town hall facilities (85%)
		< 50%: water (19%) or sewer systems (16%) less than 20 years of age; operations and preventative maintenance plans for water (24%) and sewage (22%) systems; secondary sewage treatment (13%)

Table 14.1 cont'd

Category	*Avg. % of Municipalities Responding "yes" in this Category**	*% of Municipalities Responding "yes" to Specific Questions*
Community Well-Being (35 questions)	57%	> 50%: volunteer organizations (92%); strong sense of community pride (84%); residents able to participate locally in subsistence activities (98%); stable or growing residential (91%) and business (82%) tax base
		< 50%: stable or growing population (24%); stable or growing school-age population (16%); municipal programs to support arts, culture, and heritage (39%), or local environmental stewardship efforts (37%), reduce energy use (17%) or greenhouse-gas emissions (5%)
Regional Cooperation (8 questions)	66%	> 50%: in a position (80%) and willing (81%) to share services; have service-sharing arrangements (78%), including shared infrastructure (53%); meet regionally to discuss common issues (66%)
		< 50%: share equipment with another municipality (38%)

ideal. Because the tool kit covered many important aspects of community sustainability, those who did attend the sessions were often passionate regarding the answers they provided. The process was intended as a self-assessment, but a facilitator was made available by the CCO to ensure the process and the questions were well understood. While some sessions were brief with very little discussion, other councils debated at great length over some of the questions regarding "adequate" levels of service.

The tool kit was designed to engage participants and open them up to new possibilities of what could be done with limited resources, while offering an opportunity to review and assess their own operations. In addition to the basic sections there was also an opportunity to identify assets that were specific to each community. Many self-assessment groups had little to add in this section. Because this process was new to the vast number of councils, they experienced some difficulty in comprehending both the importance of the assessment overall, and the local assets that they have available. This underlined the importance of facilitation and support tools for planning processes in small communities.

Once the sessions were completed, all the responses were collected and analyzed by the CCO office in an attempt to provide meaningful interpretation to municipalities. Each town retained a copy of its responses, but MNL wanted to provide an interpretation to ensure that its members had some understanding of what the responses meant. Each municipality's unique assets, circumstances, and situations were considered and the results were compiled in individual municipal sustainability self-assessment reports. Each report contained a commentary on the level of participation in the process as well as an analysis of the questionnaire results by section, and general recommendations, particularly when glaring issues arose. Each report also included a table of regional cooperation options and discussed the importance of regional approaches. Depending on the circumstances and apparent capacity of the municipality, a recommendation was made to either attempt a solo ICSP or take part in a regional approach.

Key findings

The final report, developed by the CCO, summarized provincial self-assessment results, confirming that serious weaknesses exist in the municipal planning system. Just 45% of municipalities had a capital works plan in place, 42% an emergency preparedness plan, 30% a land-use / zoning plan less than 10 years old, 15% an economic-development plan, and only 3% (8 municipalities) had a sustainability plan prior to creating the ICSPs. Where plans did exist, only 65% of municipalities stated that their council members were familiar with them (and 82% of senior staff). Results within the governance category portray two different worlds in the municipal sector. Some communities exhibited strong governance capabilities, but for many indicators, including contested elections, committee structure, and council participation in training, only 40–65% fared well. This suggests that many communities are being left behind as expectations of local governance grow. With only 55–66% of municipalities responding positively to questions in five of seven categories of sustainability, this divide applies across most aspects of municipal sustainability.

The most encouraging results were in the administration category. Over 80% of municipalities confirmed that they were able to meet basic administrative requirements such as taking minutes, using e-mail and the Internet, hiring staff they consider to be qualified, and supporting their ongoing professional development (Table 14.1). Municipalities also scored highly overall on financial management, but many faced financial challenges, including inability to take on additional debt or maintain a capital works fund, and more than 10% of the previous year's taxes were still in arrears in most towns. Both human resource and financial capacity were in especially short supply in small towns. The self-assessment results suggested that staff levels and funding in many small municipalities were already stretched beyond their limits. Any additional responsibilities would require additional resources, and those involved in ICSP development would need to be cognizant of those limitations when developing the planning process. In a study of US local government efforts to promote sustainable development, Saha and Paterson (2008) found that lack of adequate funding and lack of knowledgeable staff were top barriers to sustainability initiatives for medium to large urban centres in the United States. These barriers are particularly evident in rural and small town NL, and in many small, rural municipalities across the country (Caldwell, 2010).

These financial and governance challenges have translated into weaknesses in service delivery and infrastructure. As in other provinces, towns in Canada's easternmost province are faced with aging infrastructure. Over 80% of towns have water and sewer systems that are over 20 years old. What is perhaps even more telling is that vast majority (more than 75%) do not have preventative maintenance plans in place, which could help extend the life of these systems and reduce operating costs. Most towns struggle to offer basic municipal services. Just over half have a recreation program, and only 33% feel their recreation volunteers are adequately trained (e.g., First Aid). Only 58% have a water operator trained to the provincially recommended level. Environmental efforts are particularly limited, with few examples of non-deposit recycling (26%), hazardous waste collection (23%), or education programs to encourage waste reduction and diversion (11%). Only 12 municipalities (5%) are taking steps to reduce greenhouse-gas emissions.

On the positive side, 86% keep residents informed of council's decisions and priorities. This suggests an openness that is a basis for increased resident participation in planning efforts such as ICSPs. Question responses also suggest, as have other sources (e.g. Hall, Lasby, Gumulka, & Tryon, 2006; Snowadzky, 2005; Statistics Canada, 2005) that there is a wealth of social capital in NL to draw from in planning and service provision. Leaders report that there is a strong sense of community pride (84%), which is actively fostered by 82% of municipal governments through community celebrations, for example. Demographics are also a serious concern, particularly declines in school-aged children. Nevertheless, results from the majority of towns suggest that volunteerism is stable or growing. Overall, municipal leaders also feel that health and education services and cultural facilities are located within an acceptable distance for their residents. Unemployment levels are higher than the provincial average for most towns, and the number of businesses are declining in approximately half of participating municipalities, yet most towns expressed optimism that local businesses will create more jobs in the future. Growing numbers of building permits and an increasing tax assessment base were also indicators of the province's overall prosperity having a positive impact.

Finally, regional cooperation is a clear trend in the province, in part as a response to the challenges outlined above. Small towns were focused on regional or multi-community municipal cooperation as a way to maintain services, while large towns/cities focus on improvement and relationships (Vodden et al., 2007). Most communities are already sharing services with a neighbouring municipality but are willing and see opportunities to expand this cooperation. Low numbers of towns sharing equipment with others (38%) suggest this may be one area where more can be done.

Integration with the ICSP process

During the developmental stages of the ICSP process, the Department of Municipal Affairs considered the results of the self-assessment project and some of the issues the process had identified. Regarding the issues of capacity and the need for regional approaches, Municipal Affairs offered a financial subsidy for municipalities that completed collaborative ICSPs involving three or more communities. The subsidy was intended to help offset some of the barriers in developing planning partnerships and to encourage regional approaches. As of August 2010, 83 communities had worked together to create 24 collaborative ICSPs.

Municipal Affairs also followed through with another recommendation coming out of the self-assessment process regarding the pillars of sustainability. The tool-kit process had identified issues regarding decision-making capacity and lack of governance structures in many communities. As a result, the final project report suggested that in addition to the four basic ICSP pillars (social, cultural, economic, and environment), communities in NL also required a fifth pillar: governance. This fifth pillar was included in the ICSP structure to force councils to consider improvements to their planning processes, decision-making structures, and compliance with provincial legislation (MA, 2009).

As the ICSP process was developed, the Department of Municipal Affairs provided suggestions and tools such as the ICSP Framework and Guide. These tools explicitly linked the self-assessment process to the development of ICSPs. The ICSP tools included suggestions to use the self-assessment responses and the report provided by MNL as the first step during the community assessment stage of the planning process. Some but not all municipalities followed through on this suggestion. In a sample of 16 ICSPs prepared by 27 towns (four each from small to less than 1000, medium [1000–3999], and large/urban communities [4000+ population]) and four collaborative plans, for example, ten of these 16 plans referenced the self-assessment. All four small towns and three of four medium-sized towns made use of the self-assessment in their planning documents, compared to only one of four large communities. This suggests that the self-assessment process may have been particularly valuable as a starting point for smaller communities with limited planning experience.

For some communities, such as Norris Point (pop. 700) the assessment confirmed areas of concern that had already been identified (CBCL Limited, 2009). For others, such as the Town of Twillingate (pop. 2440), the exercise helped to identify issues that should be examined as they moved forward with the development and implementation of their plan for community sustainability (Whey Consulting, 2010).

Reflections: Outcomes and lessons learned for future sustainability planning in NL

To follow up on the experience of municipalities with the self-assessment process, a short questionnaire was developed by CCO staff and distributed to all participants. The questionnaire included questions regarding the process, the booklet, and the facilitation, and it gave the opportunity to make suggestions for any similar process in the future. The results were very positive. In total, 196 of the 249 municipalities that had participated in the process completed the survey. Over 96% of these respondents found the project to be of value (Lane & Quinton, 2009).

One particular outcome was that community leaders had been encouraged to consider regional cooperation as an option for addressing areas of concern, contributing to the development of collaborative ICSPs that brought more than one-quarter of NL municipalities together with neighbouring communities to plan for their collective futures. This result demonstrates that a combination of incentives and support can encourage regional collaboration. Yet without any particular guidelines provided for a collaborative process or plan, several of these collaborative ICSPs were little more than single municipality plans attached to one another and did little to further intermunicipal relationships. Most communities continue to plan largely on their own, or do not plan at all. This suggests a need for ongoing support of collaborative efforts after the self-assessment and ICSP-development process. Self-assessment results further suggest that communities are divided on regionalization of local government: 45% were opposed to amalgamation, 31% opposed to regional government, but the rest were willing to at least consider these options for addressing their sustainability challenges (Lane & Quinton, 2009). This experience suggested the need to re-open a dialogue in the province on formal approaches to both planning and regionalization.

Through the Municipal Sustainability Self-Assessment Project, participants gained a better appreciation for issues affecting the sustainability of their own municipalities and the surrounding region. The self-assessment helped guide municipal leaders through the first step of what was for many their first community planning process. In many cases the results were incorporated into the ICSP, therefore grounding the plan in local realities. Municipal staff and council members gained familiarity with assessment processes, a potential stepping stone for future municipal monitoring and evaluation efforts.

With a growing global consensus that planning and governance are critical for sustainable development (Evans et al., 2006; Jepson, 2001), and the demonstrated governance challenges faced by NL communities, support tools and hands-on facilitation assistance have the potential to significantly enhance rural community planning and governance capacity, and thus sustainability. Given the importance and potential of partnerships between government and non-government actors in local governance (Agranoff & McGuire, 2003; Caldwell, 2010) support is needed not only for collaboration among municipalities but also for building relationships between local governments and citizens and civil-society organizations. In many NL communities, existing weaknesses in local governance offset concerns raised elsewhere that regionalization efforts jeopardize the political and representative role of local government (Caldwell, 2010). In cases where these roles are not being effectively fulfilled despite small populations, appropriate regional approaches offer the potential to increase participation and engagement in local government affairs.

Neither the assessment tool nor the process were without flaws. The tool kit and the questions within it could be further refined and, in particular, more specific measures and standards agreed upon. Without these measures for many of the selected indicators or a process for checking responses against background documentation, the process relied heavily on the opinions of participants as to what is "acceptable." It was clear that not all participants were being honest or sufficiently critical in some areas. For example, self-assessment results indicate that 90% of municipalities submit required reports to the Department of Municipal Affairs on time. This finding is inconsistent with the experience of the provincial staff members who receive these reports. Consistent with authors in the sustainability-assessment literature who caution against standardization, project team members were concerned that any system of assessing municipalities must recognize the differing circumstances faced by small vs. large, or prosperous vs. declining communities, for example. Yet the component of the tool kit reflecting on communities' unique assets was not taken seriously in many cases, suggesting a preference for an indicators-based approach. There is, therefore, a need to develop a system of municipal benchmarks and an ongoing assessment and monitoring program in NL to build on the self-assessment experience. In doing so, it will be critical to keep in mind lessons learned elsewhere in Canada that emphasize the importance of coupling assessment with continuous learning and actions for improvement (Plant et al., 2005).

The project was a learning process for MNL and its university and provincial government partners. This learning came from both the preparation of the tool kit and its implementation. In preparing for the self-assessment project, we drew from the work of researchers, municipal associations, and local government departments across the country. In turn, others in Saskatchewan, Alberta, and Prince Edward Island have examined the NL experience in advancing their own municipal-sustainability initiatives (CBCL Limited, 2011; Municipal Sustainability Strategy Working Group, 2010; Saskatchewan Ministry of Municipal Affairs, 2010). The project has, therefore, demonstrated the benefits and importance of cross-province information sharing and knowledge networks in addressing issues of concern within the municipal sector and in sustainable community development more generally.

Building on the self-assessment project experience, MNL has subsequently developed a series of projects that combined tool kit and guidebook resources, workshops, and hands-on assistance to support the municipal sector in topics ranging from economic crisis response to climate-change adaptation. The project has demonstrated the value of hands-on support to accompany support materials and of providing this support within the community. While participants indicated in the follow-up survey that the self-assessment process had been useful, only 19% said they would have taken part if they had been required to travel to participate. This demonstrates the critical importance of support delivered at the local level, as well as limits to the willingness and capacity of small communities to invest in planning processes and sustainability initiatives.

The provision of local-level support, however, also requires a commitment of time and financial resources. Project staff members communicated with municipalities by whatever means necessary to increase participation, including e-mail, phone, fax, and mail. This combined with the challenge of attempting to coordinate the field staff facilitators' appointments by region to optimize travel time and resources in a large and sparsely populated province proved difficult and time-consuming, particularly within the allocated budget for the project (Lane & Quinton, 2009). The commitment of resources for the project from the partners involved combined with a strong recommendation from the province that self-assessment was to be the first step in developing an ICSP were critical factors in ensuring municipal participation and project outcomes.

Next steps: Looking to the future

In response to the lessons learned through the self-assessment and ICSP processes, the CCO and its partners have pursued a three-part agenda that includes: (a) assistance with implementing ICSPs, (b) development of benchmarks for municipal performance, and (c) engagement of municipal leaders in a dialogue about the potential for a regional government system.

In 2010 MNL released a series of three discussion papers on regional government[4] that launched the Regional Government Initiative, an MNL-led effort to build on an existing momentum for municipal reform and regional collaboration. The goal is to encourage and support MNL's member municipalities in considering alternatives to the current municipal system that will strengthen local government and better reflect current and changing conditions. In particular, municipal leaders are being asked to consider regional government as a possibility. Through the initiative, different regional-government options are being explored. Discussion about the merits and limitations of each option is taking place within individual councils, in provincial meetings, and in a series of regional workshops that were facilitated by MNL across the province in early 2011. While the outcome of the initiative is uncertain, it has moved the sector forward from the willingness to discuss options identified in the self-assessment process into a facilitated process of dialogue to establish whether or not there is support for reform and, if so, in what form(s).

A second round of regional workshops, led by MNL with advisory support from CCO partners and financial assistance from the Gas Tax Secretariat, were held in 2012. The focus was on ICSPs and community sustainability planning. As small communities of NL, most with less than five hundred people, continue to struggle to provide basic municipal services, many of them have limited capacity to realize the ideas contained in their ICSPs. The few communities that were able to develop plans in the past complain that too often these documents gather dust on shelves, their visions and goals remaining unfulfilled (Daniels, Peckham, Vodden, & Woodford, 2009). If this is the fate of ICSPs in the province, the will to engage in future assessment and/or planning efforts will be dealt a damaging blow. Towns have established visions, goals, and specific project ideas to lead toward these goals. The challenge now is to put these plans into action. This will require a continuation of the commitment, partnerships, resources, and support that made the self-assessment project possible carried forward into ICSP implementation and follow-up.

With this in mind, future regional workshops will create a forum for dialogue between municipalities to assist with the development of partnerships and facilitate joint actions to realize the ideas contained in ICSPs. Provincial government involvement has played a key role in self-assessment and ICSP development. Whether or not the commitment exists to ensure ICSPs are implemented is questionable. The GTA required that the province support local governments in preparing ICSPs but it did not refer to implementation. Requirements for annual reporting on ICSP-implementation progress and linking provincial-funding decisions to ICSPs are just two examples of how credibility can be added to the process. A new GTA signed in 2014 requires that towns continue to use their ICSPs without specifying mechanisms to ensure this occurs (Canada, 2014). Continued support in terms of training and information will also be important. Finally, and most important, communities must see their self-assessments and ICSPs as living documents that can help them in their work and should be revisited and updated over time. Many municipalities are capitalizing on the opportunity provided by, and their investment in, the planning process and moving forward with implementation with the help of partnerships and support from both within and outside their communities.

Finally, at the time of writing, MNL is in the process of revisiting the Municipal Self-Assessment Tool Kit and questionnaire and developing a revised municipal "stress test" to assist in assessing and supporting the need for municipal reform and potentially in delineation of boundaries for regional government. Aside from the self-assessment, municipalities in the province currently have no means of measuring whether or not they operate effectively and efficiently. While the self-assessment identified areas of concern, the next iteration of the process will establish a set of benchmarks but also seek to ask "why?" after every question to better understand how municipalities function and provide an opportunity for discussion and learning. Continued development of assessment methods will assist with future planning and prioritization of investments and, while again supported by senior government and university partners, the initiative will be led by municipal leaders and administrators (Button, Pollett, & Keenan, 2010).

The success of the efforts described in this chapter will depend on overcoming numerous impediments, including limited financial and human resources, disincentives, lack of political will to enter into heated and potentially divisive debates, and the requirement for both policy and legislative change. These are difficult hurdles, but they are hurdles that must be overcome to ensure the sustainability of rural and small-town NL. Partnerships and sharing ideas, knowledge, and experiences in a respectful, deliberate manner provide important forward momentum.

Notes

1. Self-assessment data indicates that 54% of municipalities held a contested election during the 2005 municipal general election (Lane & Quinton, 2009); this fell to 52% in the 2009 election (Government of Newfoundland and Labrador [NL], 2009).
2. Canada–Newfoundland and Labrador Agreement on the Transfer of Federal Gas Tax Revenues 2006–2015 (http://www.ma.gov.nl.ca/ma/publications/gta/agreement.pdf).
3. The tool kit can be viewed at www.municipalitiesnl.com/userfiles/files/SATK%20low%20res.pdf/.
4. See http://www.municipalitiesnl.com/?Content=CCRC/The_Regional_Government Initiative/.

References

Agranoff, R., & McGuire, M. (2003). *Collaborative public management: New strategies for local governments.* Washington, DC: Georgetown University Press.

Brugmann, J. (1996). Planning for sustainability at the local government level. *Environmental Impact Assessment Review, 16,* 363–379.

Button, B., Pollett, C., & Keenan, R. (2010). *Reforming municipal government: Regional government as the protector of municipal autonomy.* Presented to the 2010 MNL Municipal Symposium, April 29, 2010, Gander, NL.

Caldwell, W. (2010). Planning and management for rural development: The role of local government. In D. Douglas (Ed). *Rural planning and development in Canada.* Toronto: Nelson.

Canada. (2014). Administrative Agreement on the Federal Gas Tax Fund. Retrieved from http://www.infrastructure.gc.ca/prog/agreements-ententes/gtf-fte/2014-nl-eng.html.

CBCL Limited. (2009). *Town of Norris Point integrated community sustainability plan 2009.* Norris Point, NL: Town of Norris Point.

———. (2011). *Municipal viability self-assessment toolkit.* Report prepared for The Federation of Prince Edward Island Municipalities (FPEIM). Charlottetown, PEI.

Community Accounts. (2006). Retrieved from www.communityaccounts.ca

Community Cooperation Office (CCO). (2011). Retrieved from http://www.municipalitiesnl.com/?Content=CCRC/About_CCRC-01.

Connelly, S., Markey, S., & Roseland, M. (2009). Strategic sustainability: Addressing the community infrastructure deficit. *Canadian Planning and Policy, 18*(1), 1–23.

Daniels, J., Peckham, J., Vodden, K., & Woodford, B. (2009). *Beyond the document: Economic and socio-economic planning processes.* Report prepared for Gander-New-Wes-Valley Community-based Research Project Steering Committee. St. John's, NL: Memorial University of Newfoundland. Retrieved from http://www.kittiwake.nf.ca/documents/community-research/CBR-Beyond-the-Document.pdf.

Department of Municipal Affairs Newfoundland and Labrador (MA). (2009). *Integrated community sustainability plan framework.* St. John's, NL: Government of Newfoundland and Labrador.

Douglas, D. (Ed.). (2010). *Rural planning and development in Canada.* Toronto: Nelson.

Evans, B., Joas, M., Sundback, S., & Theobald, K. (2006). Governing local sustainability. *Journal of Environmental Planning and Management, 49*(6), 849–867.

Ferrarini, A., Bodini, A., & Becchi, M. (2001). Environmental quality and sustainability in the province of Reggio Emilia (Italy): Using multi-criteria analysis to assess and compare municipal performance. *Journal of Environmental Management, 63*, 117–131.

Gergley, M. (2004). *Project for the implementation of municipal annual reporting final report.* Prepared for British Columbia Ministry of Community, Aboriginal and Women's Services. Victoria, BC: University of Victoria.

Government of Newfoundland and Labrador (NL). (2009). News release, "Municipal nomination results stronger than anticipated," September 16, 2009. Retrieved from http://www.releases.gov.nl.ca/releases/2009/ma/0916n09.htm.

Hall, M., Lasby, D., Gumulka, G., & Tryon, C. (2006). *Caring Canadians, involved Canadians: Highlights from the 2004 Canada survey of giving, volunteering and participating.* Ottawa, ON: Statistics Canada.

Haughton, G., & Counsell, D. (2004). Regions and sustainable development: Regional planning matters. *The Geographical Journal, 170*(2), 135–145.

Higgins, J. (2008). Rural depopulation. Retrieved June 1, 2011, from http://www.heritage.nf.ca/society/depopulation.html.

Jepson, E. (2001). Sustainability and planning: Diverse concepts and close associations. *Journal of Planning Literature, 15*(4), 499–510.

Kates R., Parris, T., & Leiserowitz, A. (2005). What is sustainable development? *Environment: Science and Policy for Sustainable Development, 47*(3), 9–21.

Kretzmann, J., & McKnight, J. (1993). *Building communities from the inside out: A path toward finding and mobilizing a community's assets.* Chicago, IL: ACTA Publications.

———. (1996). *A community building workbook.* Retrieved November 16, 2011, from http://www.abcdinstitute.org/docs/MappingBusinessAssets.pdf.

Lane, R., & Quinton, S. (2009). *Municipal sustainability self-assessment project—Final report.* Report prepared for MNL and the Federal–Provincial Gas Tax Secretariat. St. John's, NL: Municipalities Newfoundland and Labrador.

Licon, C., & Balarezo, T. (2009). Municipal sustainable development possibilities along the US–Mexico border: An interdisciplinary evaluation effort. *International Journal of Sustainability, Technology and Humanism (Revista Internacional de Sostenibilidad Tecnología y Humanismo), 4,* 97–113.

Markey, S., Halseth, G., & Manson, D. (2008). Challenging the inevitability of rural decline: Advancing the policy of place in northern British Columbia. *Journal of Rural Studies, 24*(4), 409–421.

Municipal Newfoundland and Labrador (MNL). (2005). *Strengthening our communities: President's Task Force on Municipal Sustainability discussion paper.* St. John's, NL: Municipalities Newfoundland and Labrador.

———. (2008). *Municipal sustainability self-assessment tool kit.* St. John's, NL: Municipalities Newfoundland and Labrador.

Municipal Sustainability Strategy Working Group. (2010). *Building on strength: A proposal for municipal sustainability.* Report to Alberta Municipal Affairs. Edmonton: Government of Alberta.

Nelson, J. (2003). Rural sustainability in Canada and elsewhere: A historic and civics perspective. *Environments, 31*(2), 73–98.

Ontario Ministry of Municipal Affairs and Housing. (2007). *Municipal performance measurement program handbook.* Toronto: Government of Ontario.

Parkinson, S., & Roseland, M. (2002). Leaders of the pack: An analysis of the Canadian 'sustainable communities' 2000 municipal competition. *Local Environment, 7*(4), 411–429.

Planning for Sustainable Canadian Communities Roundtable. (2005). *Integrated community sustainability planning: A background paper.* Report to the Prime Minister's External Advisory on Cities and Communities. Ottawa, ON: Planning for Sustainable Canadian Communities Roundtable.

Plant, T., Agocs, C., Brunet-Jailley, E., & Douglas, J. (2005). *From measuring to managing performance: Recent trends in the development of municipal public sector accountability. New directions, No. 16.* Toronto: The Institute of Public Administration of Canada (IPAC).

Roseland, M. (2005). *Toward sustainable communities: Resources for citizens and their governments.* Gabriola Island, BC: New Society Publishers.

Saha, D., & Paterson, R. (2008). Local government efforts to promote the "three es" of sustainable development: Survey in medium to large cities in the United States. *Journal of Planning Education and Research, 28*, 21–37.

Saskatchewan Ministry of Municipal Affairs. (2010). *Municipal government sustainability self-assessment tool project concept paper*. Regina: Government of Saskatchewan.

Smith, G. (1998). Are we leaving the community out of rural community sustainability? An examination of approaches to development and implementation of indicators of rural community sustainability and related public participation. *International Journal of Sustainable Development & World Ecology*, 5(2), 82–98.

Snowadzky, B. (2005). *Coming together or going it alone: How resource-dependent communities survive in Newfoundland and Labrador*. Ph.D. dissertation, Department of Sociology, University of New Hampshire, Durham, NH.

Statistics Canada. (2007). 2006 census of population. *Statistics Canada Catalogue no. 97-550-XWE2006002*. Ottawa: Statistics Canada. Retrieved December 29, 2011, from http://stats.gov.nl.ca/Statistics/Census2006/PDF/POP_CSD_Alphabetical_2006.pdf.

———. (2005). General social survey: Criminal victimization 2005. Retrieved June 1, 2011, from http://www.statcan.ca/Daily/English/051124/d051124b.htm.

United Nations Conference on Environment and Development (UNCED). (1992). *Agenda 21*. New York: United Nations.

Vodden, K., Lane, R., & Beck, M. (2007). *The 2007 municipal census of Newfoundland and Labrador*. St. John's, NL: Community Cooperation Resource Centre, MNL.

Whey Consulting. (2010). *Town of Twillingate integrated community sustainability plan 2010–2014*. Twillingate, NL: Town of Twillingate.

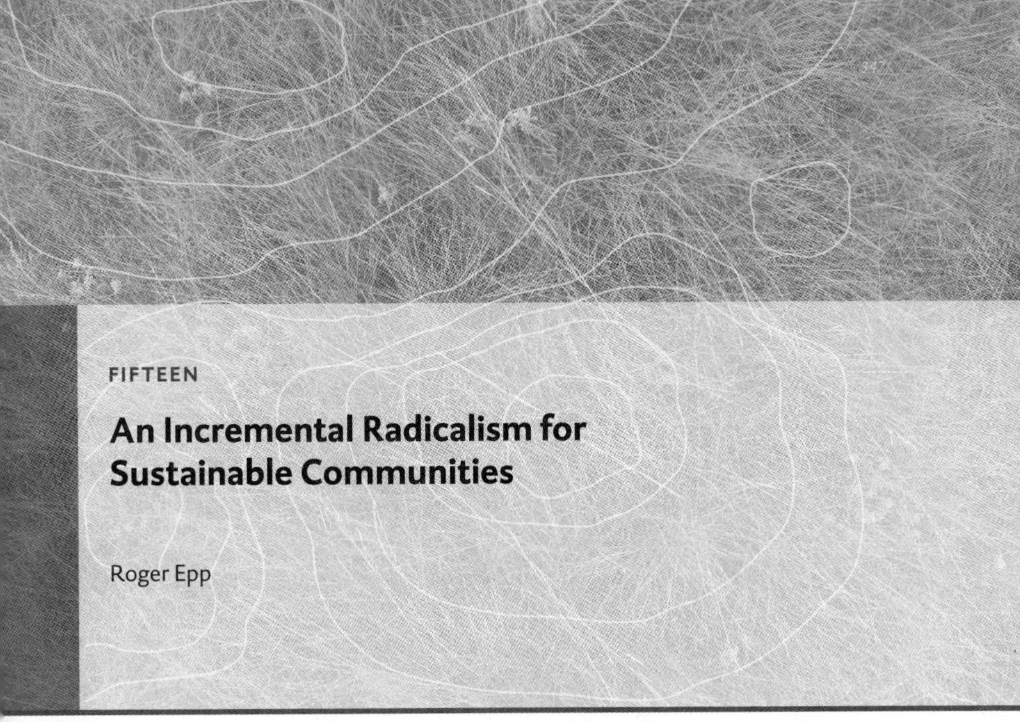

FIFTEEN

An Incremental Radicalism for Sustainable Communities

Roger Epp

> ...the really great contributions to knowledge are likely to take place on the margins of civilization where people are still wrestling with real problems of livelihood.
>
> —Alexander John Watson, *Marginal Man: The Dark Vision of Harold Innis*

> Among all forms of mistake, prophecy is the most gratuitous.
>
> —George Eliot, *Middlemarch*

Beyond playgrounds and dumping grounds

A little more than a decade ago, I co-edited a book, *Writing Off the Rural West*, that was framed by two premises. The first was that rural spaces were being reimagined and remade either as playgrounds or as dumping grounds—out of sight, out of mind—for an increasingly urban society. If they were pretty enough, with marketable glimpses of mountain, ocean, or lake, and preferably within range of a major airport or a metropolitan population, they could be sites for upscale residential and tourist developments, golf courses, ski resorts, or gentrified Main Streets. If not, they were fair game for messy, large-scale, industrial projects—the kind that crowd out room for postcard images of bucolic countryside: garbage and toxic-waste dumps, feedlots and hog-barns, utility corridors, low-wage manufacturing (recycled tires, strawboard, meat), pump-jacks, flare-stacks, open-pit mines (Epp & Whitson, 2001; also Whitson & Epp, 2004; Epp, 2006; Epp, 2008a). Our claim of a much sharper spatial bifurcation was scarcely exaggerated. Nor was it specific to rural Canada (Falk, Schulman, & Tickamyer, 2003; Thomas, Lowe, Fulkerson, & Smith, 2011). At both ends of the continuum, community futures in a global economy were understood to hang on the locational decisions made by outside investors.

The second premise was that the social and economic fabric of rural communities was increasingly strained as a result of this remaking of rural space. Trade liberalization had put commodity-price pressures on those whose livelihoods were based on traditional resource sectors. Deficit-cutting provincial governments had consolidated services in larger, more distant centres, closing small schools and hospitals, regionalizing responsibilities. They had also amalgamated and downloaded new expectations on municipalities even as they diminished their fiscal, legislative, and land-use planning powers, sometimes in order to facilitate the kinds of investment mentioned above. The state's "neo-liberal" face was often most visible in rural places. Rather than balance opportunities across societies and economic sectors, much less encourage people to settle, in the form of the 19th-century National Policy, the role of government now was merely to position jurisdictions competitively to attract mobile capital and the jobs it might create. There were no other meaningful choices. Perversely, for some, rural depopulation became an opportunity, both a cleaner slate for development and leverage against the naysayers. From Alberta to New Brunswick, governments of all political stripes pinned their policy hopes on a rapid expansion of industrial hog production and the low-wage jobs it might generate—locally divisive as that might be. Those rural municipalities that were not likely to be playgrounds faced the challenges of shrinking tax bases and aging, more transient populations. Often their councils succumbed earlier than their residents did to what seemed the realism of imperfect choices, playing the role of desperate suitor with whatever assets they could offer. If not this development, what then?

That was the state of rural Canada not so long ago. In the rough awakening of the mid-1990s, it discovered that its electoral clout was fading in all parts of the country. There was no longer anything special about rural communities or those traditional livelihoods—farming, forestry, fishing—that had come to be regarded as "subsidy industries" or parasites on the public purse. The tough-minded advice from the economists was to move to where the jobs were. Not surprisingly, rural Canada echoed with more than its share of anger, bewilderment, and fatalism.

From that vantage point, this book and the national workshop around which it took shape make a number of significant, positive statements about the ways in which the ground has shifted again for rural communities and rural-related research in this country. First, they suggest that there is a good deal of creativity, stubbornness, and political vitality in rural Canada. If the analysis of the previous decade was weighted, for good reason, toward the large, structural, political-economic forces that buffeted rural communities, subjecting them to decisions made elsewhere, the pendulum rightly has begun to swing back (Parkins & Reed, 2012; Barney, 2011). Enough rural communities have demonstrated that they are not simply the passive recipients of the futures or non-futures that have been projected onto them. In some cases, they have experimented with new forms of activism, not always polished, and not always successful, to save schools or demand environmental monitoring or resist a proposed industrial development that seemed more of a threat than a blessing (Epp, 2012). In other cases, they have reimagined identities and livelihoods in the face of sudden environmental changes as dramatic as the collapse of a four-hundred-year-old fishery or the damage done to British Columbia's forests by the mountain pine beetle. They have lost faith, and sometimes money, in the promise that major investors with global linkages would rescue communities. They have begun to see that resilience—a more appropriate rural word than development—requires local roots, local assets, local leadership, plus the capacity to collaborate and welcome newcomers. Sometimes they have taken significant risks; the sustainability project in Craik, Saskatchewan, is only one of them.

Second, the language of sustainability has enlarged the scope for rethinking rural futures. National and provincial governments have backed away from the singular focus on competitiveness that marked political discourse and policy in the late 1990s. Whatever its limits, the integrated community-level sustainability-planning process that is at the centre of this volume is evidence of such a shift. So is the reintroduction of planning at regional and watershed levels in provinces once as ideologically hostile to it as Alberta in the Ralph Klein era. Concerns about climate change, energy consumption and costs, urban sprawl, and food and wildlife corridors are now a starting point for long-range sustainability planning even in rural places (e.g., Caldwell, 2011). However much the idea of sustainability can be co-opted or stretched, as critics have pointed out, it is not reducible to competitiveness; for one thing, it has fostered a different kind of conversation and set of choices. It has invited communities to say for themselves what it might mean. In rural Canada, the idea of sustainability inevitably evokes real and elemental questions about community survival, as several chapters have noted, but at the same time it has proven robust enough to lead away from the simple logic of survival at any cost. People now talk about healthy communities.

The retreat from a simple competitiveness agenda, however, is not merely a matter of language. On rural policy in particular, provincial governments generally have grown less certain and one-dimensional than they were, say, at the height of the national industrial hog-barn mania (Thu & Durrenberger, 1997; Ervin, Holtslander, Qualman, & Sawa, 2003; Stull & Broadway, 2004). They have had to confront effective pockets of rural resistance. They have been willing to concede urban–rural disparities and even, in exceptional cases, the harm done to rural communities by their own spending cuts.[1] In the short term, the positive result of government perplexity about rural development has been to allow a greater measure of open-ended exploration of aspirations and alternatives. This point, of course, should not be overstated. Global wealth-extracting structural forces have not disappeared; conflicting rural land-use pressures have intensified; and governments, if anything, have tightened the scope of environmental review to fast-track large resource projects and limit community interventions. Moreover, they have been reluctant to relinquish legislative or fiscal powers to municipal authorities to implement unconventional ideas that may emerge from sustainability planning. Still, the cracks have opened.

Third, rural Canada includes Aboriginal communities, which are themselves as diverse and complex as their neighbours. This recognition is a recent one in rural research. It may not have registered fully on the ground, in places where side-by-side settler and Aboriginal communities historically have been divided against each other, their relations marked by mutual isolation, racism, and rivalry for land and diminishing natural resources. The reality, however, is that in almost every part of Canada there are rural communities that will retain schools, hospitals, and retail stores, as well as a capacity for sustainable self-definition, only if they develop patterns of cooperation and interdependence that include Aboriginal communities. In recent years each has proven susceptible to the dubious development schemes that seem to answer the desperate need for jobs and economic spinoffs.[2] In that sense they can be each other's weakest links. But, often, what they also share, though it is seldom observed, is a multigenerational rootedness in a place, a landscape, and therefore, increasingly, a physical and cultural distance from those who would make decisions for them in distant metropolitan capitals. For non-Aboriginal rural communities, the idea that they have things to learn from neighbours who have a much longer history in place may be the most surprising, challenging, and important realization of the present rural generation (Kaye, 2011; Epp, 2008b).

Finally, rural Canada is the site of some of the most innovative, emerging models of university–community collaboration. The workshop's distinctive insistence on co-presentations by researchers and community partners resulted in a sharing of knowledge that moved tentatively—perhaps not enough for all participants—beyond the comfortable rituals of the academic conference. Not surprisingly, the workshop reproduced small echoes of the same discomfort, risk, misperception, language barriers, and mismatched motivations as could be imagined the first time the university researchers came to Pelee Island, Lake Helen, or Chauvin. The chapter in this book resulting from the University of Northern British Columbia's work with the community of McBride (Chapter 8) is particularly thoughtful about the challenges of collaboration. Universities for their part possess a power to validate ideas, identify problems, focus thinking, and serve as honest brokers. When their scholars and students work with communities, they are free of many of the constraints of paid consultancies. But tenure processes, academic timelines, granting cycles, the historic presumption of a near-monopoly on knowledge, and the companion instinct, however well-motivated, to think *for* rather than *with* people—those are real internal roadblocks for universities to work through in making a commitment to community-based research. In that light, the resource-management project with Paqtnkek First Nation in Nova Scotia (Chapter 11) is especially remarkable for its community-guided research design, its training program, its incorporation of Indigenous knowledge, and its dissemination of findings. Likewise, the model of participatory food-systems mapping in the Central Okanagan region (Chapter 12) has the potential to build rural–urban bridges and advance community knowledge through accessible technology—without the need for the university to control the outcomes.[3]

The fair-minded reader will observe that the chapters in this book represent a range of relationships and that they are not equally explicit or self-reflective about reciprocal learning. At the same time, it has proven robust enough to lead away from the simple logic of survival at any cost. The fact that participants in these projects and others from unfamiliar map points across Canada gathered to share outcomes was a powerful first step beyond the limits of local experience and the sense of isolation often felt by rural community pathfinders. They met on a small campus in a small prairie city; and the academic researchers in the room tended to represent universities located outside of major metropolitan centres. Those characteristics are also notable insofar as this book, taken as a whole, points in the direction of a different kind of public accountability and a refreshing openness to multiple ways of knowing that can be at least as rigorous as the conventional standards of the academy. In short, it points toward a future quite unlike the classic ivory tower or town-gown solitudes. The requisite shifts of accountability and openness appear to be embedded, often enough, in face-to-face relationships where universities have taken seriously their obligations to their home regions, and where researchers have found it possible to live integrated scholarly lives among their neighbours.

Lessons learned

This book is not a showcase of model communities—not a collection of "Canada's best." Instead, its chapters describe real places with real histories, real tensions, real geographies, and real challenges. They are works in progress. Their relative successes are unfinished and fragile. What sets them apart from some other communities in rural Canada is simply that they have generated enough good reason and enough of the right leadership, formal or informal, to resist the fatalistic scripts often written for them. They have been willing to take risks, including the risks of honest self-assessment, inviting outside partners, imagining futures, and trying new things.

This book joins a series of rich, close-up case studies to a larger interest in situating the work of community-based public policy in the heterogeneous spaces of rural Canada. To that end, it sorts chapters into a four-fold frame that mirrors an imagined linear progression from problem identification to planning to implementation to assessment—while recognizing at the outset that there are no such neat textbook progressions on the ground. This may be a first general lesson, a useful reminder, if not a surprise.

The communities described here have arrived at the problem of sustainability out of diverse local circumstances. It may have been the collapse of a traditional resource economy, chronic out-migration, conflict over some proposed industrial (or residential) development, or the opportunity presented by lands fortuitously preserved and revalued as wilderness, as ecosystem, as parkland. As is clear, however, from the chapters that put problem identification in the foreground, rural communities do not necessarily coalesce easily, or all at once or, indeed, at all, around a shared definition of sustainability challenge and opportunity. Public champions are crucial. Problem identification, in other words, requires leadership that can frame a question ("why?" or "why not?"), mobilize interest, build partnerships, and, not least, renew itself in the face of delays, doubts, and individual burnout. In some places it might also require the skill to find enough common ground—or a "common lens"—among neighbouring settler and Aboriginal communities whose cultural orientations may seem very different and whose historical relationship has not been close. If the leadership to initiate all this comes from outside of formal political structures, as it often does, nonetheless at some point local governments must share in the same sense of problem—since their engagement not only puts bylaws and funding on the table; it also signals community priority and resolve to provincial and federal authorities.

The concern with capacity turns out to matter at every stage described in this volume. At the planning stage, as the chapters in the second section demonstrate, it is possible to build a process that includes meaningful citizen participation and collaboration with external partners, government, and university; but in each case good practice is deliberate and tailored to place. The process may take the form of formal consultative models and planning tool kits. Doubtless, it relies again on the communication skills and commitments of local leadership. But the key lessons learned in the chapters that highlight the planning process are about collaborative relationships. Rural communities and municipal governments, on their own, will not contain all of the expertise they might need to anticipate the effects of climate change or the opportunities in the emerging creative economy; they may overlook their own best assets. But it is still no easy thing at several levels to engage outsiders in planning rural community futures—at the most practical, which door of which university? For that matter, it is no small thing for credentialled researchers, public servants, or technical experts to appreciate local knowledge and cultural nuances without condescension. Historically, this challenge has been magnified in Aboriginal communities. One key lesson here, and one worth restating, though it may seem trite, is that the relationships required to build planning models and to design community-based research projects can only be built over time, that mistakes will be made, and that only a healthy measure of sensitivity, reciprocity, goodwill, and awareness of the other's institutional imperatives, interests, and limits can generate learning from those mistakes. The stakes are high. The risk in failure is a reversion to patterns of rural dependency and a corrosive fatalism.

One of the instructive things about the essays in the implementation and assessment sections is how attentive they are to the need to align action with critical planning goals. They do not describe linear processes on a think-act-evaluate continuum. They do not separate means from ends. Instead they ask: What is sustainability for this place and how will we know we are becoming more or less sustainable? How can a rare island ecology, for example, be protected in the context of farming and tourism? What cultural dimensions are at the core of sustainability in a Mi'kmaq community? How do those dimensions shape the management of moose populations for food and conservation? What kind of mentorship do they require of the next generation of hunters? What kind of relationship with non-Aboriginal neighbours? There are several implicit lessons in this section. One is that it is possible to advance distinctive, locally directed sustainability initiatives, based on serious collective purposes, around ecology, livelihood, food, and culture. A second is that communities, with time and tools, can make sensible decisions about how much to accommodate conflicting interests, how to mediate between customary and legal-bureaucratic regimes, and how to reach across regional rural–urban divides. A third lesson, not least, is that one outcome of such careful activity is a reskilling of the countryside.

Limits and complexities

In its introduction, this book identifies two knowledge gaps that have been left in the wake of the sustainability-planning process. One, for which it is intended as partial remedy, concerns the exchange of community-level learning. The other concerns the bundle of questions that are still to emerge from the experience of converting plans, with their preferred futures, into actions. What difference will the plans make to the viability of rural communities? How will rural contexts, cultures, and complexities in themselves shape outcomes? How much substitutionary benefit can ecotourism provide, in how many places, without reducing the skilled diversity of a working countryside to a mere playground? If the interplay of broader social, cultural, economic, political, and ecological dynamics framed a window for sustainability planning for municipalities, large and small, in the middle of the previous decade, what course will they take in future? What will they enable or preclude?

In reformulating these questions, I am enlarging the gap without any intention of filling it—and not only for the cautionary reason given by the narrator in George Eliot's 19th-century novel *Middlemarch*, set in the English countryside in another time of social and political upheaval. Some of the chapters here have registered their own tentative observations about complexity and limits. Most often they begin with communication. Even in face-to-face rural places, or especially so, for reasons of size, familiarity, and shared histories, there is nothing simple about informing and engaging citizens. Likely they are unaccustomed to being asked to think out loud about community futures—much less disagree in public with neighbours they cannot avoid in everyday life. They will not easily consider the merits of a new idea apart from what they know of its proponents, their reputations, their family backgrounds. Those are among the sociological realities of rural communities.

At another level, complexity and limits are revealed in the local challenges of reconciling employment and environmental imperatives, individual landowner and community interests, emerging and traditional economies, and newcomer and older cultures. The immediate issue, as the chapters in this book illustrate, might be an oak meadow, an eco-village, organic farming and artisanal foods, water, or the moose harvest. The point is not that rural communities are incapable of making collective decisions or doing surprising new things. Rather, it is that the decisions themselves tell so little of the story. In that respect, it should be said that planning and implementation are not wholly distinct, sequential stages, especially where consultation has been meaningful and inclusive; for an engaged citizenry is both a means and a mark of sustainable communities.

There is a third layer of complexity and limit that features more or less prominently in these chapters: the capacity of local governments. Conventionally, though not universally,[4] municipalities are understood as creatures of the provinces; they derive their authority from legislation they cannot amend. At the extreme, they were created relatively recently for administrative convenience in the delivery of provincial services in Newfoundland and Labrador. Across Canada they generally lack the political ambition, technical expertise, and resources to set an independent course for sustainability that is able to look ahead with imagination, to take on much more than the expected obligations to maintain road and utilities infrastructure, to enforce environmental standards, or to speak in policy terms to the implications of developments that will have a direct impact on their communities. First Nations governments have a dash of constitutional authority, but they face the same practical challenges in exercising it. The reality of limited capacity does not make sustainability planning a cynical exercise; and university partnerships in select places can compensate for some of the technical limits. But defining what future, what kind of countryside, a community might imagine is only one small, significant step on a much longer pathway. In the work of sustainability, the local is not sufficient. It is "nested" within larger ecosystems and divisions of labour (Gismondi, 2006).

What lies beyond it are protracted efforts to build coalitions, manage cooperation within regions and watersheds, negotiate with provincial and federal authorities to remove roadblocks, and make the case against one-size-fits-all policy—all before the next election, when voter backlash or indifference might reset the work. The complexity and limit of scale can appear daunting. While cities and their advocates (e.g., Broadbent, 2008) have succeeded at least in putting an urban agenda on the national political table, rural municipalities have been too scattered to do the same. They do not have a history of visionary thinking about rural Canada as a whole. A decade ago, some of them still saw no better, more responsible future on the horizon than to outbid each other with tax breaks and cheap land in the scramble for any development at all. They tended to resent the criticism of citizen groups rather than harness their energy in positive ways. Rural municipal governments may have warmed recently to the idea of sustainability planning, with the prodding of federal dollars. But it is not clear how much they can lead locally, with or without an active citizenry, or set an enabling agenda at the provincial and national levels.

This partial account of complexity and limit is sobering enough. Indeed, a decade from now, the recent window for sustainability planning might well be regarded as a curious interlude, an interruption in the longer trends toward a "managed democracy" (Wolin, 2008, pp. 239–240) and a global-industrial competition for food, energy, minerals, and water—in which rural places from North America to Africa are subject to intense development pressures. Higher commodity prices already have put a premium on land and resources. Legitimate worries about food security are being leveraged to support land assembly, industrial production, and further enclosure of the genetic commons (Coleman, 2011). The appetite for refined hydrocarbons is voracious as ever. Hydraulic fracturing methods promise to spread the energy windfall to new parts of North America. Appalachian mountaintops are levelled unrelentingly with dynamite for cheap coal while watersheds and rural people living below suffer the consequences. Asian and American refiners are ready to take Canadian oil-sands bitumen as soon as the pipelines can be approved and built through sensitive terrain. Not far north of the workshop location in Camrose, Alberta, meanwhile, multigeneration farm families live with the prospect that, if "market conditions" improve, they will again face displacement over time by a massive 340-square-kilometre coal mine and gasification project they have organized to oppose. Under such pressures it is not impossible to imagine that the spatial reconfiguration of the rural as resource plantation and utility corridor—not a place of community and livelihood—will only accelerate. In that case, some rural communities will be sacrificed in the public interest. The holistic hopes once expressed in the best municipal plans will be overwhelmed.

This may be a dark way to conclude, but at the same time I want to distinguish my position from that taken by David Douglas in his important, contrarian contribution to this book (Chapter 1). For Douglas the sustainability planning exercise is already too little, too late. The environmental crisis is a matter of urgency; the stakes are as high as human liveability; and nothing less than a rapid, radical transformation in our governance, values, economy, and the organization of rural society is required for survival. I do not know how other workshop participants responded to his argument. When his chapter is read against the accounts of fragile, piecemeal successes in a handful of communities in rural Canada, mostly still in the planning stages, it is hard not to regard it as a counsel of despair. He is, I suspect, more right than wrong about the limits of conventional planning as problem solving, especially in the context of a nomadic, extractive global economy. It is not enough for a few, forward-thinking rural enclaves to achieve "sustainability." But it is an exaggeration to imply that the future of the planet will be decided in rural Canada and therefore that those who continue to live there have a particular burden to effect radical change, as if they represented the locus of global wealth, consumption, and/or population. The problem with Douglas's inverted logic model—thinking back, that is, from the future we do *not* want—is that it too becomes problem solving, but on an elusive, super-human scale. Nothing else will save us. From that logic, consultative processes and local steps seem a waste of time. The Chinese government may be a much better bet, whatever its environmental track record to date.

The courage to begin

My preference is to engage rural communities differently. In doing so, I suggest, it is important to affirm both the *local*, as the place where it is possible for people to exercise a hands-on responsibility for the world, to experience a commons, and the act of *beginning*. Political theorist Hannah Arendt calls the latter a "miracle"—a surprise, made with others, that interrupts the ordinary and, though it may not succeed or endure, shows a capacity for freedom (Arendt, 2005, pp. 112–113). By definition, there are no formulas. This book documents a number of acts of beginning in rural Canada, some as seemingly non-political as a purple martin festival. Together, they might be respected as small declarations, courageous assertions, or tangible, placed stakes in the world from which to start to think about what sustains or threatens or can co-exist alongside it. Doubtless those declarations are incomplete, incremental, more sure of what they want to avoid than what they can imagine, but still radical in possibility. Incremental radicalism, indeed, might be a close synonym for rural community sustainability. It is grounded in place, communal, adaptive, *and* continuously self-appraising. It affirms the possibility of "beneficent spirals" (Jacobs, 2004, p. 175)—not just downward spirals. But it offers no grand plan and none of the satisfaction that comes with completion or permanence. Rural communities live instead with visible historic markers of their precarious existence.

No turn of phrase, of course, can make the next steps easier in the face of the pressures described above. Rural Canada, most of it, will scarcely be a place of retreat. It never has been. Rural people who earn a living outdoors will not have the luxury of deciding, like talk-show skeptics, whether or not to "believe" in climate change. Those who must negotiate geographic distance in the course of everyday life will confront first the end of the age of cheap oil and its implications. Sustainable rural communities will need to make alternative provisions and early adaptations part of their own planning. Those who live in closest proximity to watersheds, forests, grasslands, and oceans, to the consequences of decisions made out-of-sight, out-of-mind, do have responsibilities to their own backyards and the world beyond. But they can only cultivate them if the rest of us in this urban country are prepared to respect their vigilance, their knowledge, and their aspirations to remain in place. One more thing—those of us who have grown dependent on complex, long-distance and therefore vulnerable systems to provide us with food, energy, and shelter would do well to respect the rural livelihoods of those whose residual skills should not be taken for granted as we make provision for the sustainability of our own communities. We may need to rely on them.

Notes

1. I am most familiar with the Alberta context. See the strategy document *A Place to Grow* (Government of Alberta, 2005) and an earlier report, meant for internal circulation, on regional disparities (Government of Alberta, 2002). See also Chan and Dixon's "The Creative Economy: An Opportunity for Rural Community Sustainability," in this volume. At the federal level, the Senate's

Standing Committee on Agriculture and Forestry report, *Beyond Freefall: Halting Rural Poverty* (2008), is a remarkable study.

2. The introduction to *Writing Off the Rural West* began with a controversial proposal by the Taiwan Sugar Corporation, with the Alberta government's active encouragement, to build a massive hog-barn complex to produce pork for Asian markets. The proposal was rebuffed in two counties. Several years later, it resurfaced at Beardy's & Okemasis First Nation in central Saskatchewan as a joint venture with the band. Several First Nations and Metis communities in northern Saskatchewan, meanwhile, have been identified as possible sites for a nuclear-waste storage facility. The willingness of band leadership to entertain such proposals reflects not only the urgency of poverty and unemployment but also the desire to exercise the independent powers of self-government after more than a century of paternalism and colonial oversight.
3. On various dimensions of community-engaged scholarship, see the special issue of the *Journal of Higher Education Outreach and Engagement* (2012). One need only imagine the dilemmas faced, first, by the culturally sensitive, community-engaged scholar, approaching the tenure decision, who respects the decision of a partner Aboriginal community that certain findings should not be published, or not published yet, and, secondarily, by the committee that reviews her research dossier.
4. I do want to note the powerful alternative reading of local self-government given by Magnusson (2005) as more akin conceptually and historically to Aboriginal self-government, based in each case on practices that predate the contemporary emphases on state sovereignty and constitutional recognition.

References

Arendt, H. (2005). Introduction into politics. In J. Kohn (Ed.), *The promise of politics* (pp. 93–200). New York: Schocken.

Barney, D. (2011). To hear the whistle blow: Technology and politics on the Battle River branchline. *Topia: Canadian Journal of Cultural Studies, 25*(Spring), pp. 5–27.

Broadbent, A. (2008). *Urban nation: Why we need to give power back to the cities to make Canada strong*. Toronto: Harper Collins.

Caldwell, W. (Ed.). (2011). *Rediscovering Thomas Adams: Rural planning and development in Canada*. Vancouver: University of British Columbia Press.

Coleman, W. (Ed.). (2011). *Property, territory, globalization: Struggles over autonomy*. Vancouver: University of British Columbia Press.

Epp, R. (2006). Two Albertas: Rural and urban trajectories. In M. Payne, D. Wetherell, and C. Cavanaugh (Eds.), *Alberta formed, Alberta transformed* (pp. 726–746). Edmonton: University of Alberta Press; Calgary: University of Calgary Press.

———. (2008a). A prairie future—for people: Conservation as livelihood, knowledge and community. In R. Warnock, et al. (Eds.), *Homes on the range: Conservation in working prairie landscapes.* Proceedings of the 8th Prairie Conservation and Endangered Species Conference (pp. 23–31). Regina: University of Regina, Canadian Plains Research Center.

———. (2008b). *We are all treaty people: Prairie essays.* Edmonton: University of Alberta Press.

———. (2012). Off-road democracy: The politics of land, water and community in Alberta. In D. Taras & C. Waddell (Eds.), *How Canadians communicate IV: Media and politics* (pp. 259–279). Edmonton: Athabasca University Press.

Epp, R., & Whitson, D. (Eds.). (2001). *Writing off the rural west: Globalization, governments, and the transformation of rural communities.* Edmonton: University of Alberta Press.

Ervin, A., Holtslander, C., Qualman, D., & Sawa, R. (Eds.). (2003). *Beyond factory farming.* Saskatoon: Canadian Centre for Policy Alternatives, Saskatchewan.

Falk, W., Schulman M., & Tickamyer, A. (Eds.). (2003). *Communities of work: Rural restructuring in local and global contexts.* Athens: Ohio University Press.

Gismondi, M. (2006). The nature of local reach. In J. Johnston, M. Gismondi, and J. Goodman (Eds.), *Nature's revenge: Reclaiming sustainability in an age of corporate globalization* (pp. 137–153). Peterborough, ON: Broadview Press.

Government of Alberta. (2002). *Regional disparities in Alberta.* Edmonton: Department of Economic Development.

Government of Alberta. (2005). *A place to grow: Alberta's rural development strategy.* Retrieved from http://www.assembly.ab.ca/lao/library/egovdocs/2005/alrdi/147677.pdf.

Jacobs, J. (2004). *Dark age ahead.* New York: Random House.

Journal of Higher Education Outreach and Engagement. (2012). *Special Issue: Community-Engaged Scholarship. 16*(1).

Kaye, F. (2011). *Goodlands: A meditation and history on the Great Plains.* Edmonton: Athabasca University Press.

Magnusson, W. (2005). Are municipalities creatures of provinces? *Journal of Canadian Studies, 39*(2), pp. 5–29.

Parkins, J., & Reed, M. (Eds.). (2012). *The social transformation of rural Canada: New insights into community, culture, and citizenship.* Vancouver: University of British Columbia Press.

The Senate Standing Committee on Agriculture and Forestry. (2008). *Beyond freefall: Halting rural poverty.* Ottawa: The Senate. Retrieved from http://www.parl.gc.ca/Content/SEN/Committee/392/agri/rep/rep09jun08-e.pdf.

Stull, D., & Broadway, M. (2004). *Slaughterhouse blues: The meat and poultry industry in North America.* Belmont, CA: Thomson Wadsworth.

Thu, K., & Durrenberger, E. (Eds.). (1997). *Pigs, profits and rural communities.* Albany: State University of New York Press.

Thomas, A., Lowe, B., Fulkerson, G., & Smith, P. (Eds.). (2011). *Critical rural theory: Structure, space, culture.* Lanham, MD: Lexington Books.

Whitson, D., & Epp, R. (2004). *The Canadian clearances.* Canadian Broadcasting Corporation, Radio One, *Ideas.*

Wolin, S. (2008). *Democracy Inc.: Managed democracy and the specter of inverted totalitarianism.* Princeton, NJ: Princeton University Press.

Contributors

Don Alexander (Ph.D., MCIP) is a professor in the Department of Geography at Vancouver Island University, and his work focuses on urban sustainability and place-making. He is particularly concerned with what he perceives as a failure in land-use planning vis-à-vis these objectives.

Kirstine Baccar is a policy advisor in the Economic & Resource Development Unit (EDRU) for Nishnawbe Aski Nation (NAN). She is responsible for the development of the EDRU and management of the Energy, Housing and Infrastructure, Winter/All-Weather Roads, Mining and Lands, and Resources Units. Kirstine advises NAN on legislative and government directives.

Michael Barr is coordinator of the Alberta North American Waterfowl Management Plan (NAWMP). The Alberta NAWMP was created with the goal of protecting and restoring waterfowl habitats in order to sustain waterfowl populations.

Mary A. Beckie is an associate professor in the Faculty of Extension at the University of Alberta. Her work focuses on sustainable community development and community-based resource management, particularly as they relate to the roles of local government, civil society, and the social economy.

Moira J. Calder is an editorial assistant and indexer at the Legislative Assembly of Alberta. She has a master's degree in communications and technology from the University of Alberta.

Meredith Carter is the manager of Environmental and Technical Services at the Otonabee Region Conservation Authority in Peterborough, Ontario. She is involved in a variety of programs including drinking-water source protection, watershed health monitoring, and environmental education and stewardship. Her work involves collaboration with a variety of community and government partners with a focus on enhancing local watershed conditions and promoting integrated watershed management.

Yolande E. Chan is associate vice-principal (research) and E. Marie Shantz Professor of MIS at Queen's University. Her research is largely concerned with knowledge management, information-technology management, and innovation. She previously directed The Monieson Centre, Queen's School of Business. While there, she focused on community economic development and revitalization.

Sean Connelly is a lecturer in the Department of Geography at the University of Otago. He teaches courses in environmental management and sustainable community development, and his research explores the challenges and opportunities of scaling up sustainable community development and local food–system initiatives.

Jon Corbett is an associate professor in Community, Culture and Global Studies at University of British Columbia's Okanagan campus. Jon's community-based research investigates participatory mapping processes and tools that are used by communities to help express their relationship to, and knowledge of, their territories and resources.

Anthony Davis is a professor in the Department of Sociology and Anthropology at Mount Saint Vincent University, where his research examines the relations between culture, social power, and systems of domination through the lens of local ecological knowledge and resource management.

Jeff A. Dixon (B.Comm. Hon., M.Div.) is the associate director of The Monieson Centre. He works to connect leading research with real-world business and community needs. Jeff has spoken internationally on rural economic development issues, including the emergence of the creative economy as a rural-development strategy.

David J. A. Douglas, Professor Emeritus, Rural Planning and Development, University of Guelph, is a long-term researcher, teacher, consultant, policy adviser, and rural-development practitioner in all Canadian regions, and numerous international settings (e.g., EU, Japan, Indonesia, Ukraine). His most recent publication is "Rural Planning and Development in Canada" (2010).

Roger Epp is a professor of Political Science at the University of Alberta. His work has focused on the politics of rural communities in the prairie West, including new forms of local activism, land-use conflict, agricultural/food futures, traditions of agrarian thought, and Aboriginal–settler relations.

Kelly Green is currently a transit operator with the City of Edmonton. While in Craik, Kelly was involved in the local sustainability movement. This included a retro-fit, straw bale–wrapped house, organic gardening, off-grid living, media production and promotion, and volunteering with many community-organized projects and activities.

Lars K. Hallström is a political scientist at the University of Alberta, and director of the Alberta Centre for Sustainable Rural Communities. His work is largely concerned with issues of environment, sustainability, and governance, and in particular with questions of citizen engagement, expert knowledge, public policy, and social, health, economic, and environmental inequities.

Greg Halseth is a professor in the Geography Program at the University of Northern British Columbia, where he is also the Canada Research Chair in Rural and Small Town Studies and director of UNBC's Community Development Institute. His research examines rural and small-town community development, and community strategies for coping with social and economic change, all with a focus on northern BC's resource-based towns.

Casey Hamilton is a registered dietitian with a strong interest in food systems. She is currently completing her master's of science in the area of urban agriculture policy development in Kelowna. She is extremely involved with the work of the Central Okanagan Food Policy Council and is playing a lead role with the Fruit Tree Project, a local gleaning and skill-building program.

Karen Houle is an associate professor of Philosophy at the University of Guelph. Her areas of expertise are Ethics and Political Philosophy. She is the author of numerous articles on Deleuze, Derrida, Foucault, and other philosophers, and the co-editor of *Hegel and Deleuze: Together Again for the First Time* (Northwestern, 2013). She is also author of *Responsibility, Complexity and Abortion: Toward a New Image of Ethical Thought* (Lexington, 2013).

Glen T. Hvenegaard is a professor of Geography and Environmental Studies at the University of Alberta Augustana Campus. His work focuses primarily on the conservation aspects of ecotourism, biogeography, environmental education, and rural sustainability.

Melanie Irvine is a project geologist with the Geological Survey with the Department of Natural Resources, Government of Newfoundland and Labrador. Melanie leads a climate change–related project developing a monitoring program for vulnerable coastal areas in Newfoundland and Labrador. Melanie's M.Sc. research in Geography (Memorial University) concerned climate change adaptation in Nunavut.

Bernie Jones is a retired planning and community-development professor and consultant. His work in BC and Colorado covered homelessness, housing, food security, cultural planning, and community planning, among other issues involving social justice and community participation. He chairs the Chemainus Residents Association and the North Cowichan Chemainus Advisory Committee.

Robert Keenan works on intermunicipal cooperation with Municipalities Newfoundland and Labrador. He is focused primarily on issues of rural municipal sustainability, particularly with respect to service and infrastructure management.

Rhonda Koster is the director of the School of Outdoor Recreation, Parks and Tourism at Lakehead University. Her work is focused on rural tourism, with questions regarding tourism as a regional development strategy, capacity for tourism within rural and First Nations communities, and evaluation of tourism within a community economic-development framework.

Ryan Lane is a community and municipal development consultant. His work is focused on municipal development and community strategic planning, with a special interest in regional and innovative local solutions to local problems.

Sean Markey is an associate professor with the Resource and Environmental Management program and an associate with the Centre for Sustainable Community Development at Simon Fraser University. Sean's research concerns issues of local and regional economic development, rural and small-town development, and community sustainability.

Shelly McMann is the CAO for the Village of Chauvin. Her work is largely related to administering the operations of the village to ensure a comfortable, safe, and economical place in which residents live, work, and play.

L. Jane McMillan is the Canada Research Chair in Indigenous Peoples and Sustainable Communities and an associate professor in the Department of Anthropology at St. Francis Xavier University. As a legal anthropologist, Jane's primary research interests focus on collaborative critical policy analysis, decolonizing justice strategies, and implementing and sustaining Indigenous treaty rights and cultural capacity building.

Morgan E. Moffitt is a Ph.D. candidate at the University of Alberta specializing in environmental and legal anthropology.

Karen Morrison is an assistant professor in the Population Medicine Department of the Ontario Veterinary College, University of Guelph. Her work is largely concerned with issues related to environmental change and human health and well-being, and in particular with questions related to water governance, transdisciplinary research, and public policy. She is currently vice-president of the International Association for Ecology and Health.

Karsten Mündel is an Associate Professor of Global and Development Studies as well as the Associate Dean, Academic at the Augustana Campus of the University of Alberta. Much of his research involves understanding how students can learn from and with rural communities in and around Camrose, Mexico and Cuba. He has also collaborated with the City of Camrose to develop the community's Municipal Sustainability Plan.

Craig Pollett is CEO of Municipalities Newfoundland and Labrador (MNL). Craig plays a leadership role in lobbying and advocacy, membership development and services, and policy research and development. Prior to his work with MNL, Craig worked in economic development and policy analysis with Memorial University and the Government of Newfoundland and Labrador.

Kerry Prosper is a band councillor for Paqtnkek Mi'kmaw Nation. He is an avid hunter, knowledge translator, and spiritual guide. His research interests include exercising Indigenous rights through customary practices.

Mark Roseland is director of the Centre for Sustainable Community Development and a professor of Resource and Environmental Management at Simon Fraser University. Mark lectures internationally and advises communities and governments on sustainable-development policy and planning; he is also the founder of Pando Sustainable Communities, a new network for sustainable communities researchers and practitioners.

Laura Ryser is the research manager of the Rural and Small Town Studies Program at the University of Northern British Columbia. Her research has examined rural and small-town restructuring, labour mobility, institutional barriers to change, rural poverty, social-learning mechanisms, and building capacity within the voluntary sector.

Claire Sanders recently completed her M.Sc. in Biology at the University of Windsor and is currently completing her B.Ed. Her career includes extensive environmental research and outreach experience in both the applied sector and educational sector.

Jennifer Sumner is a lecturer in the Adult Education and Community Development Program at OISE / University of Toronto. Her research interests focus on sustainability, food, rural communities, and organic agriculture. She is the author of *Sustainability and the Civil Commons: Rural Communities in the Age of Globalization*, and co-editor of *Critical Perspectives in Food Studies*.

Kelly Vodden is an associate professor (research) at the Environmental Policy Institute, Grenfell Campus and Department of Geography, Memorial University. Her research focuses on collaborative governance and sustainable community and regional development, particularly in Canada's rural and small-town communities and coastal regions.

Marc von der Gonna (RPF) is the general manager of the McBride Community Forest Corporation (MCFC). MCFC has the exclusive timber rights to 60,000 hectares surrounding the Village of McBride,

British Columbia, which it manages for the maximum social, environmental, and economic return to the community.

Shayne Wright completed his master's degree at University of British Columbia's Okanagan campus. His research involved developing geographic information technologies for the geospatial internet (GeoWeb). He was involved in a number of community mapping projects providing user interface design, GIS mapping support, and training. His current research interests include technology and maps for engagement, participation, and learning, and societal implications of the GeoWeb.

Index

Figures and tables indicated by page numbers in italics

Other Titles from The University of Alberta Press

Unsustainable Oil
Facts, Counterfacts and Fictions
Jon Gordon

288 pages | 10 B&W photographs, 2 maps, bibliography, notes, index
978-1-77212-036-3 | $45.00 paper
978-1-77212-098-1 | $36.99 EPUB
978-1-77212-099-8 | $36.99 Amazon Kindle
978-1-77212-100-1 | $36.99 PDF
Petroculture | Energy Humanities

The Peace-Athabasca Delta
Portrait of a Dynamic Ecosystem
Kevin P. Timoney

608 pages | Wall map plus over 450 figures: maps, illustrations, graphs, charts, photographs, aerial photographs, notes, bibliography, appendices, index; colour throughout
978-0-88864-603-3 | $160.00 cloth
978-0-88864-730-6 | $90.00 paper
978-0-88864-802-0 | $72.00 PDF
Nature | Ecology | Rivers | Petroleum Industry

Writing Off the Rural West
Globalization, Governments and the Transformation of Rural Communities
Roger Epp and Dave Whitson, Editors

368 pages | Notes, references
Copublished with Parkland Institute
978-0-88864-378-0 | $34.95 paper
Sociology | Rural Studies | Political Science